Bureaucratic Politics
and Foreign Policy

SECOND EDITION

Bureaucratic Politics
and Foreign Policy

Morton H. Halperin

Priscilla A. Clapp

with

Arnold Kanter

BROOKINGS INSTITUTION PRESS
Washington, D.C.

Copyright © 2006

THE BROOKINGS INSTITUTION

1775 Massachusetts Avenue, N.W., Washington, D.C. 20036
www.brookings.edu

Library of Congress Cataloging-in-Publication data

Halperin, Morton H.
    Bureaucratic politics and foreign policy / Morton H. Halperin, Priscilla A. Clapp.
        p.   cm.
    Includes bibliographical references and index.
    ISBN-13: 978-0-8157-3409-3 (pbk.: alk. paper)
    ISBN-10: 0-8157-3409-3 (pbk.: alk. paper)
    1. United States—Foreign relations administration. I. Clapp, Priscilla. II. Title.

    JZ1480.H35 2006
    327.73—dc22   2006026348

            2 4 6 8 9 7 5 3 1

The paper used in this publication meets minimum requirements of the American National Standard for Information Sciences—Permanence of Paper for Printed Library Materials: ANSI Z39.48-1992.

Typeset in Minion

Composition by OSP, Inc.
Arlington, Virginia

Printed by R. R. Donnelley
Harrisonburg, Virginia

Contents

Preface

The purpose of this book is to help readers understand the process by which decisions are made and actions are taken by the U.S. government in the field of national security and foreign policy. The views of its authors have been inspired and influenced by a variety of experiences in the executive branch—in the Defense Department, in the State Department, and on the National Security Council—over a period of nearly forty years. Morton Halperin also has spent many years working with Congress. However, the book is decidedly not autobiographical. Rather, it is based predominantly on the published works of other participants in and observers of the national security bureaucracy. An extensive bibliography of these books and manuscripts is included at the end of the book.

The reader will find a number of long quotations. They are meant to be read. In many cases they are illuminating descriptions of events by a participant; in a few cases they are analyses of key issues, stated clearly and succinctly. They are essential to the book's central themes. Read them.

When this book was first published by the Brookings Institution more than thirty years ago, it was set firmly in the context of the cold war. The world has changed dramatically since then, not only through the realignment of power, alliances, and ideology, but also in how technological advances have transformed the way we communicate and conduct business, both nationally and internationally. It is not surprising that those evolutions have affected some of the structures of national security and foreign policy decisionmaking in the U.S. government and therefore some of the propositions advanced in the original book. Amazingly, however, the original book's thesis remains essentially valid today as a tool for explaining how bureaucracy affects policy decisions and their implementation.

This version of *Bureaucratic Politics and Foreign Policy* is thus largely a reaffirmation of its predecessor, incorporating new materials drawn from the events of the intervening thirty years. We have revised the sections of the book dealing with those government structures and processes that have evolved, and we discuss other significant players that have emerged with the changing policy environment. Most important, a new section has been added to reflect the expanding role of Congress in the decision process and the complex nature of bureaucratic structures and rules on Capitol Hill.

In addition to the expanding role of Congress, several historical developments warrant special mention here. First is the degree to which humanitarian values have assumed greater prominence and weight in the foreign policy process, affecting policy structures, players, and arguments. Second is the impact of the Goldwater-Nichols Act of 1986 (the Defense Reorganization Act) on the role of the Joint Chiefs of Staff in national security decisions. Third is the expansion of the size and role of the White House executive offices—the National Security Council, the new Office of Homeland Security, and the Office of the Vice President—and the impact of that expansion on the president's role in the policy process. Fourth is the number of additional significant actors in the foreign policy process, including essentially domestic agencies and departments that have developed international concerns, new agencies like Homeland Security, and new bureaus in the State Department and Defense Department and nongovernmental organizations. And finally, we must acknowledge the degree to which new technology has transformed communications within the bureaucracy; communications between Washington and overseas missions; communications between governments; the influence, nature, and role of the press; and the sheer volume of real-time information available to the U.S. government and general public.

We remain grateful to those who provided assistance to us in preparing the first edition, as explained by Morton H. Halperin in the original preface:

> More of this book than I care to acknowledge was taught to me by two of my professors: Warner Schilling (under whom I studied at Columbia College in 1956–57) and H. Bradford Westerfield (Yale University, 1958–59). My interest in the subject was rekindled by the formation at Harvard in 1966 of the "May Group," which met from time to time to discuss the role of bureaucracy in the making of national security policy.

I learned much from the members of that group, which included Graham T. Allison, Joseph L. Bower, Fred C. Ikle, William W. Kaufman, Andrew W. Marshall, Ernest R. May, Richard E. Neustadt, Don K. Price, and Henry S. Rowen.

In July 1966 I went to work in the government, intending to stay for one year as a "participant-observer"; I stayed for nearly three, but quickly lost my status as "observer." I did, however, learn much about how the bureaucracy functions and about the obligations and responsibilities of a middle-level in-and-outer. My greatest debt is to the late John T. McNaughton, in memory of whom this book is dedicated. McNaughton was killed tragically in an airplane disaster in August 1967 just as he was preparing to move from his post as Assistant Secretary of Defense for International Security Affairs to become Secretary of the Navy. From McNaughton I learned much about how to operate effectively while maintaining one's integrity and concentrating on important issues.

I learned also from the two men who served as Secretary of Defense while I was in the Pentagon—Robert S. McNamara and Clark Clifford— from my two other bosses, Paul C. Warnke and Henry A. Kissinger, and from numerous colleagues in the federal government, among them Philip Farley, Leslie C. Gelb, Haakon Lindjord, Winston Lord, Richard C. Steadman, Frederick C. Wyle, and Adam Yarmolinsky.

In the years since we collaborated at Brookings on the book's first edition, we have both accumulated much more experience inside government. While the intellectual structure of the book is still essentially academic, its propositions are now even more informed by firsthand experience. We are grateful to the many dedicated public officials with whom we practiced the art of policymaking in the bureaucracy. We also would like to thank Denis McDonough and Scott Lilly for their help reviewing the chapter on Congress. Finally, we offer special thanks to Michael Fuchs for research assistance on this edition and to Arnold Kanter for his important contributions to the first edition and for carefully reviewing portions of the revised text.

ON THE NOTES IN OUR BOOK

The footnotes pinpoint for the reader where the passages that we quote are located and the episodes that we cite are described. For that purpose, an author's last name, the title or short title of a source, and a page number or similar designation suffice. The sources in full are identified in the references and bibliography, which begin on p. 365.

The bibliography includes three sections, each alphabetized separately. Section A is a comprehensive list of the memoirs of individuals involved in the making of U.S. foreign policy during the period from the end of World War II until the mid–1970s. Some memoirs from the post–cold war period also are included, but the list is far from comprehensive. Section B, likewise focused on participants in the policy process, lists a number of interviews conducted, recorded, and transcribed by the John F. Kennedy Library. Section C—for "non-memoirs"—includes all other sources that we consulted, whether quoted or not. Since the source referred to in the first note to chapter 1 ("The Dynamics of Nuclear Strategy") is an address rather than a memoir or an interview, it is entered under the author's name (Robert S. McNamara) in section C. In that entry the title of the periodical that printed the complete address is given (*Department of State Bulletin*), along with the date of issue (October 9, 1967).

More than one citation may come from one author, and an author's writings may be included in more than one section. McNamara, for example, is also listed in section A, as the author of *The Essence of Security*.

Bureaucratic Politics
and Foreign Policy

CHAPTER ONE

The ABM Puzzle:
An Introduction to
Politics inside
Government

On September 18, 1967, Secretary of Defense Robert S. McNamara rose to deliver an address entitled "The Dynamics of Nuclear Strategy" to a meeting of United Press International editors and publishers in San Francisco. He stressed that neither the United States nor the Soviet Union had increased their security in any way by deploying strategic nuclear weapons, and he suggested that the United States had bought many more weapons than it needed only because of a groundless fear that the Russians would step up their arms production. Having sketched this general background, McNamara turned to a subject that was then in the headlines—namely, the possibility of American deployment of an antiballistic missile (ABM) system.

He pointed out that the United States had substantially improved its technological capability. But he emphasized that even an advanced ABM system could easily be defeated if the Soviet Union simply fired more offensive warheads or dummy warheads than there were defensive missiles capable of dealing with them. Proceeding with that line of argument, he asserted:

> Were we to deploy a heavy ABM system throughout the United States, the Soviets would clearly be strongly motivated to increase their offensive capability so as to cancel out our defensive advantage.
>
> It is futile for each of us to spend $4 billion, $40 billion, or $400 billion—and at the end of all the spending, and at the end of all the

deployment, and at the end of all the effort, to be relatively at the same point of balance on the security scale that we are now.[1]

Until then the Johnson administration had been resisting substantial pressure to deploy an ABM. The secretary of defense, however, did not conclude his statement there; rather, he took another tack. He argued that it was important to distinguish between an anti-Russian ABM and an ABM system designed to defend the United States against emerging Chinese nuclear capability. Reviewing the arguments in favor of a deployment against China, he announced, "We have decided to go forward with this Chinese-oriented ABM deployment; and we will begin actual production of such a system at the end of this year."[2] Before concluding, McNamara returned to his earlier theme:

> There is a kind of mad momentum intrinsic to the development of all new nuclear weaponry. If a weapon system works—and works well— there is strong pressure from many directions to procure and deploy the weapon out of all proportion to the prudent level required.
>
> The danger of deploying this relatively light and reliable Chinese-oriented ABM system is going to be that pressures will develop to expand it into a heavy Soviet-oriented ABM system.
>
> We must resist that temptation firmly, not because we can for a moment afford to relax our vigilance against a possible Soviet first strike, but precisely because our greatest deterrent against such a strike is not a massive, costly, but highly penetrable ABM shield, but rather a fully credible offensive assured destruction capability.
>
> The so-called heavy ABM shield—at the present state of technology— would in effect be no adequate shield at all against a Soviet attack but rather a strong inducement for the Soviets to vastly increase their own offensive forces. That, as I have pointed out, would make it necessary for us to respond in turn; and so the arms race would rush hopelessly on to no sensible purpose on either side.[3]

Why had Robert McNamara used a speech that was largely anti-ABM in tone and substance to announce an ABM deployment? Some Washington reporters speculated that he had been overruled at the last minute; what he meant to be an anti-ABM speech had been converted by others in the administration into a vehicle for announcing an ABM deployment. Others argued that the speech should be taken at face value: the administration had come to

1. McNamara, "The Dynamics of Nuclear Strategy," p. 448.
2. Ibid., p. 450.
3. Ibid.

the conclusion that an ABM against Russia was not desirable but that one against China was necessary.

Those in the audience and the country who had followed the issue wondered how the secretary's speech related to the annual budget message delivered by President Lyndon Johnson in January 1967. The president had asked for funds to deploy an ABM system but had stated that he would defer a decision to start construction pending an effort to begin strategic arms limitation talks with the Russians. At that time the president was vague about the purpose of the ballistic missile defense but stated that the funds might be used to deploy an ABM "for such purposes as defense of our offensive weapons systems."[4] McNamara, in his speech, had briefly mentioned the defense of Minuteman missiles only as a possible add-on to the ABM deployment against China.

The purpose for which the administration was deploying its ABM system was further clouded in the coming weeks. The Joint Chiefs of Staff and leading senators, including Richard Russell, chairman of the Senate Armed Services Committee, described the ABM deployment as the beginning of a large anti-Russian system, even though McNamara had warned against attempting one. McNamara himself continued to describe the system as a defense against China; the president said nothing. As the first steps toward deployment were made, it appeared that the initial construction was no different from what it would have been if the purpose were to protect American cities against a large Russian attack.

These puzzles have usually prompted an all-inclusive question that is assumed to have a single answer: why did the United States decide to deploy an anti-Chinese ABM system in the fall of 1967? In trying to explain foreign policy decisions, most observers assume that decisionmakers are motivated by a single set of national security images and foreign policy goals. Supposedly, decisions reflect those goals alone, and actions are presumed to flow directly from the decisions. Thus, "explanation" consists of identifying the interests of the nation as seen by its leaders and showing how they determine the decisions and actions of the government.

With this approach, the explanation offered for the American decision to deploy an ABM against China would be that the American government decided that its interests in the Far East required a Chinese-oriented ABM system but that a system against the Soviet Union made no sense because of the technological difficulty of building a system against a militarily sophisticated opponent. Sometimes such explanations are sufficient; they provide

4. Johnson, *Public Papers of the Presidents of the United States, 1967*, bk. 1, p. 48.

all that anyone needs to know or wants to know when his interest in an issue is limited. Often such explanations are the best that can be constructed, given the data available. This is true not only of the decisions and actions of foreign governments, particularly ones with a closed decision system, but also, unfortunately, of many contemporary American decisions. In cases where someone seeks more detailed and satisfactory answers, such explanations are highly inadequate. They often require positing a very unusual set of interests to explain decisions and actions. In the case of the ABM, one would have to conjure up a set of interests that explain why different officials of the American government made conflicting statements about whether or not a large ABM system against the Soviet Union was a good idea and whether or not the system to be deployed would be a first step toward an anti-Russian system.

There is no question that the reality is different. The actions of the American government related to foreign policy result from the interests and behavior of many different groups and individuals in American society. Domestic politics in the United States, public attitudes, and the international environment all help to shape decisions and actions. Senators, representatives, and interest groups are involved to varying degrees, depending on the issue. The relevant departments of the federal bureaucracy are involved, as is the president, at least on major issues. The participants, while sharing some images of the international scene, see the world in very different ways. Each wants the government to do different things, and each struggles to secure the decisions and actions that he or she thinks best.

Here we focus predominantly on part of this process—that involving the bureaucracy and the president as he deals with the bureaucracy. *Bureaucracy*, as the term is used here, refers to civilian career officials and political appointees, as well as to military officers. For some issues, distinctions between these groups need to be made and will be made, but most of what we have to say about the interests and maneuvers of the bureaucracy applies to career officials, political appointees, and military officers alike. Our attention is directed primarily to political and military rather than economic issues.

Since our goal is to describe the national security decision process, particularly that part of it where organizational or personal interests are brought to bear on the issue at hand, we begin with a discussion of participants. Who is involved? What interests do they have? How do those interests affect their stands on particular issues?

Part 1 deals with these questions, concentrating on those parts of the bureaucracy concerned with political-military affairs: the White House (including the National Security Council), the State Department, and the CIA and the Defense Department. The discussion of the role of shared images about what the national security requires is followed by a discussion of organizational and presidential interests. We then explore the factors that determine how a participant develops a stand on an issue.

Part 2 considers the process by which participants and organizations struggle to bring about the decisions that they want. It considers how issues arise and are shaped by the rules of the game. The degree to which participants plan their maneuvers is considered, and that discussion is followed by a discussion of information and arguments and the process by which presidential decisions are made. Finally, Part 2 explores sources of power in the bureaucracy and the kinds of decisions that emerge. The focus is on issues that work their way up through the bureaucracy, ultimately requiring a decision by the president.

Part 3 turns to the generally ignored question of what happens after the government makes a decision. Here we trace the process by which presidential decisions become government actions. The reader will have to keep in mind that the events described in each section often occur simultaneously or in quick succession.

Part 4 explores how Congress views foreign policy issues, and it attempts to apply the same bureaucratic approach used in the rest of the book to Congress. At the end of the book, in Part 5, we return to the ABM case to show how the approach used throughout provides a framework for considering four puzzles that arose with regard to the ABM decisions:

—Why, in January 1967, did President Johnson ask Congress to appropriate the funds to deploy an ABM system but state that he would defer a decision to initiate the deployment pending an effort to get the Soviets to engage in talks on limiting the arms race?

—Why was the decision to deploy an ABM announced at the end of a speech whose main purpose was to explain why an ABM defense against the Soviet Union was impossible and undesirable?

—Why did Secretary of Defense McNamara describe the system as one directed against China, while the Joint Chiefs of Staff and senior senators described it as a first step toward a full-scale defense against the Soviet Union?

—Why was the system authorized for deployment designed and deployed as if its intent were to protect American cities against a large Russian attack?

The purpose of this analysis—and of the book as a whole—is to help the reader understand how decisions are made and to predict likely courses of behavior. The book provides only part of the answer, however, since it focuses only on that part of the decisionmaking process that involves the bureaucracy and the relation between the bureaucracy and the president. Since Congress became increasingly involved in the executive branch policymaking process after the Vietnam experience, we have included a chapter that explores Congress through the same bureaucratic prism used to understand the executive branch. However, the role of public opinion is not treated in depth. Furthermore, not every national security decision becomes subject to the pulling and hauling described in the following chapters. The book seeks to explain elements of the foreign policy decision process that, for one reason or another, are often overlooked or at least not taken into account systematically. The concluding chapter suggests that the analysis has important implications for U.S. foreign policy. In the end, readers will have to judge for themselves the utility of the approach.

PART I

Interests and Participants

CHAPTER TWO

National Security
Interests

All participants in the national security decisionmaking process profess to be pursuing the national interest and much of the time they believe that they are. Nonetheless, they often have differing notions about what the national security interest is. In forming their definitions, participants look to common conceptions of the national interest, but they also seek other clues.

SHARED IMAGES

When participants share a set of global images, those images will decisively shape the stand they take on particular issues. During the cold war period, a majority of American officials (as well as the American public) held a set of widely shared images. At the end of the cold war, however, there was a period in which there was not a single set of images held by most participants. Then, after the terrorist attacks on the World Trade Center and the Pentagon on September 11, 2001, a new set of shared images began to emerge.

The shared images of the cold war period may be summarized as follows, in the language employed at the time.

—The preeminent feature of international politics is the conflict between communism and the free world.

—Every nation that falls to communism increases the power of the communist bloc in its struggle with the free world.

—The surest simple guide to U.S. interests in foreign policy is opposition to communism.

—Russian intentions toward Western Europe are essentially expansionist. So, too, are Chinese intentions in Asia.

—The main source of unrest, disorder, subversion, and civil war in under-developed areas is communist influence and support.

—The United States—and only the United States—has the power, ability, responsibility, and right to defend the free world and maintain international order. The rest of the free world must contribute as much as possible to the U.S. effort to defend against aggression.

—The United States has an obligation to aid any people resisting communism at home or abroad.

—Peace is indivisible. Therefore collective defense is necessary. The new international order is based primarily on U.S. assumption of responsibility for other states' security, in support of which the United States must show itself ready to resist aggression. Thus any expansion of communist influence must be resisted.

—Concessions made under pressure constitute appeasement, which only whets the appetite of aggressors.

—Coalition governments are inevitably taken over by the communists.

—The third world really matters because, first, it is the battleground between communism and the free world; second, Western capital will generate economic development and political stability with a minimum of violence; and third, instability is the great threat to progress in the third world.

—The United States can play an important role in inducing European integration, which will solve the German problem.

—Military strength is the primary route to national security.

—The United States must maintain military superiority over the Soviet Union, including the ability to destroy the Soviet Union after a Soviet first strike.

—Nuclear war would be a great disaster and must be avoided.

—U.S. prosperity depends on the economic health of other developed nations, a favorable U.S. balance of payments, and the preservation of the American gold supply.[1]

The new set of shared images that began to emerge after the terrorist attacks of September 11 might be characterized as follows:

---

1. This list draws heavily on Allison, "Cool It: The Foreign Policy of Young America," pp. 144–60. In particular it relies on his chart of what he calls "Axioms of the Postwar Era." See also May, "The Nature of Foreign Policy: The Calculated versus the Axiomatic," pp. 666–67.

—The collapse of the Soviet Union unleashed centrifugal forces that gave rise to new security threats in the form of rogue states and international terrorism.

—The preeminent feature of international politics today has become the conflict between international terrorists and rogue states and the democratic world.

—The surest simple guide to U.S. interests in foreign policy is opposition to rogue states and international terrorism.

—The United States—and only the United States—has the power, ability, responsibility, and right to defend democracy and maintain international order. Other nations must contribute as much as possible to the U.S. effort to defeat international terrorism.

—The United States has an obligation to aid any nation fighting international terrorism.

—Other nations must contribute as much as possible to the U.S. effort to defeat international terrorism.

—At the same time, the post–cold war liberalization of trade in advanced technologies has facilitated the access of poor nations and forces of evil to some of the most destructive military power available, including nuclear, chemical, and biological materials.

—These universally available technologies can be used to create "asymmetric" threats by small or medium-sized states to conventional military power, thereby challenging U.S. ability to apply military force.

—Peace is indivisible. The new international order is based primarily on U.S. assumption of responsibility for confronting rogue states and international terrorism, in support of which the United States must show itself ready to use force—if necessary, in a preemptive manner.

—Concessions made under pressure constitute appeasement, which only whets the appetite of aggressors.[2]

These lists are admittedly oversimplified and are not intended to imply that all perceptions of national security are naïve. They are meant to illustrate the sort of common denominator from which more refined perceptions of national security derive. Naturally, not every participant in the U.S. government supported the cold war images, nor does everyone support the post-9/11 set of beliefs.

---

2. This list is drawn in part from Suskind, *The Price of Loyalty*, pp. 76–77, quoting assumptions articulated by Defense Secretary Rumsfeld in 2001.

SHIFTING IMAGES

The examples provided above bring us to a discussion of the ways in which images may shift, in some cases because of something as routine as a change in personnel. In other cases, events in the outside world may bring about fundamental changes in the way American society looks at the world. With the dissolution of the Soviet Union and the end of the cold war in the early 1990s, the traditional set of shared images quickly became irrelevant, except perhaps to a small group of conservatives who still saw Russia and China as strategic threats. The 1990s came to be characterized more by competing images, which did not provide the broad framework for national security decisionmaking that had previously guided the process. Concerns about the developing world came to be based more on human rights, governance, and trade issues, with groups disagreeing on where to place the emphasis. In the absence of a clear strategic threat besides the possibility of an accidental nuclear launch, decisions about the use of U.S. military force became a matter of restoring regional stability or policing gross injustice, as, for example, in Somalia, the first Gulf War, and NATO's spring 1999 attack on Yugoslavia. U.S. international power came to be identified with economic as much as military strength. Not until September 11—with the sudden emergence of a clear threat to U.S. security from international terrorism and weapons of mass destruction in the hands of rogue states or terrorists—did a new set of shared images begin to coalesce into consensus.

Changes in personnel also can affect shared images, but the effects usually are limited more to images of American policy toward particular regions. In such cases, the set of shared images guiding policy is likely to be held by a relatively small number of individuals whose concerns society as a whole is hardly aware of. As the Soviet Union fell apart in 1990, a small but very senior group in the first Bush Administration successfully challenged the prevailing notion among most Europeans and the European Bureau of the State Department that a united Germany would destabilize the region.[3] The group of "neoconservatives" who came in with the second Bush administration succeeded in promoting the notion that active U.S. military intervention in Iraq was the key to regional stability in the Middle East and to the war against terrorism.

It sometimes happens that images are shared widely within the bureaucracy and among those currently in senior government positions but not within American society as a whole. In this situation, the introduction of new participants from outside government (and outside the usual channels of

---

3. This process is amplified in Zelikow and Rice, *Germany Unified and Europe Transformed*.

recruitment) might bring about changes in shared images. It could be argued, for example, that the shared images of the "neocons" who drove foreign policy during the first term of the second President Bush did not reflect those of American society as a whole. When many of them were replaced in the second term by appointees whose images of national interest were more reflective of popular norms, the Bush administration's approach to foreign policy became more accommodating.

President Carter, on the other hand, wanted his administration to reflect popular U.S. concerns about the promotion of human rights, so he brought a cadre of officials into his administration, particularly in the State Department and National Security Council, who made promotion of human rights, including the effects of U.S. foreign arms sales, a central tenet of U.S. foreign policy. The human rights position in the State Department was elevated to the assistant secretary level, and the office was given authority to clear on many national security decisions. Subsequently, human rights and humanitarian issues became increasingly embedded in the decisionmaking process with the demise of the Soviet era.

However, it is rare for the images shared within the government to diverge radically from those in society as a whole, and the appointment of individuals who cannot accept the broader images shared within the bureaucracy is probably equally rare. Moreover, the socialization process within the government is such that individuals who come in with doubts about or in ignorance of particular aspects of the set of shared images prevalent in the bureaucracy frequently find themselves quickly coming to support them.

Dramatic changes in the outside world, either at home or abroad, may be so sharp that they intrude upon the perceptions of even those with fixed ideas of foreign policy, leading to changes in shared images. At the same time, the changes in reality that occur at home can affect beliefs about what the public will stand for or what the public will demand, an important part of the set of shared images shaping policy in the United States. Arguments about public mood play a role in internal debate about foreign policy proposals and shift with reality as that reality becomes manifest. In addition, images of the outside world held by government officials bear some relation to the set of shared images held by the larger foreign policy community and by the electorate at large. If the gap becomes too large, the political cost of maintaining a policy dependent on these images will come to appear excessive. Thus, as changes in national mood lead to changes in the images of the world held by the population at large, these changes come to be reflected within the bureaucracy. The causes of such changes in national mood are complex and varied and lie beyond the scope of this book. However, it is important to recognize that changes in national mood do affect changes in the images shared by the bureaucracy. This may well be the most important way in which general public attitudes affect foreign policy in the United States, although the time that it takes the bureaucracy to respond can be substantial.

On some occasions, events in the outside world force changes in images. For example, the proposition that ideology would prevent the Soviet Union and communist China from ever thinking of each other as potential military opponents was widely accepted within the American government throughout much of the postwar period, but it had become an untenable proposition by the mid-1960s. With the exception perhaps of the September 11th terrorist attacks, changes in the world usually do not produce unambiguous evidence of the need to alter images immediately. Most events can be interpreted various ways, and their effect on U.S. interests and the way in which the world operates is difficult to assess. Gradually, changes in international reality do bring about changes in the set of shared images within the American government, but the effect is rarely direct and immediate. In some cases, images may change even though reality does not, or reality may change substantially without bringing about any change in the beliefs of officials. It took years for the bureaucracy to grasp the transformational impact of the political changes that President Mikhail Gorbachev was developing in the Soviet Union and Eastern Europe in the late 1980s.

A proposed course of action that can be shown to be unambiguously necessary to preserve a shared objective will be agreed to by all. However, such agreement is a very rare event. Widely shared images often do lead to agreement on basic objectives and therefore to the exclusion of certain conceivable courses of action. Thus, confronted with a developing Russian intercontinental ballistic missile (ICBM) capability and the initial deployment of a Soviet ABM system, no one suggested that the United States need not be concerned at all and could sit back and permit the Soviet Union to gain strategic superiority. Nor did anyone openly argue that the United States needed to build a large ABM system so that it would be in a position to carry out, at a time of its own choosing, a strategic nuclear attack against the Soviet Union. In the early and mid-1960s, the debate within the government about ABMs was carried out in the context of a shared belief that American strategic superiority was necessary as "insurance" and that it could and would be maintained. Some, including Secretary of Defense Robert McNamara, no longer accepted the value of superiority, but they had to argue as if they did.

CLUES TO NATIONAL SECURITY INTERESTS

There is always great uncertainty about what is going on in the world and what the effects of alternative courses of action will be. The way that individuals cope with that uncertainty is affected by their background—the personal experiences, intellectual baggage, and psychological needs that they bring with them—as well as by their position in the bureaucracy.

All participants, depending on where they sit, see a somewhat different face of an issue because their perception of the issue is heavily shaded by their particular concerns. What is primarily a budget issue to one participant is an issue of foreign relations to a second and of congressional relations to a third. Those in the Defense Department and the Budget Bureau concerned with limiting military spending tended to view ABM deployment as a budget issue. Scientists in the Pentagon and in the so-called defense industry felt ABM deployment would maintain the technological superiority of the United States. Officials in the Arms Control and Disarmament Agency viewed the issue in terms of possible arms control agreements with the Soviet Union. Foreign Service officers in the Western Europe division of the State Department were concerned with the effect of ABM deployment on U.S. relations with European allies and on the cohesion of NATO. Participants sensitive to the president's relations with senior congressional leaders who supported the ABM program saw the issue in terms of future dealings with Congress. Secretary McNamara assessed ABM deployment in terms of decreasing spending for strategic forces and increasing the prospects for arms control arrangements with the Soviet Union. Army officials saw the issue in terms of the size of the army budget and maintaining an army role in strategic nuclear deterrence. The president, sitting at the top, saw the issue in terms of his own sense of what national security required, his relations with McNamara and with military and congressional leaders, his own desires to keep spending down and to reach agreement with the Soviet Union, and his desire not to give his political opponents an election issue.

Thus each participant may focus on a different face of the issue and sense different dangers and opportunities. For budget officials, preventing large expenditures was most important, and the rationale given for any system and the way that decisions were communicated to foreign governments were matters of relative indifference. For State Department officials, the cost of the ABM program was not important, for the funds did not come from the State Department budget, but the way that the issue was communicated to U.S. allies and to the Soviet Union was a matter of great concern. Where individuals sit in the process determines in large part the faces of the issue that they see and helps to determine the stakes that they see involved and hence the stand that they take. We thus need to identify briefly who the main participants are before considering the effects of their personal experience, background, and official position on the decisions that they make.

Participants

The president stands at the center of the foreign policy process in the United States. His role in and influence on decisionmaking are qualitatively different from those of any other participant. In any foreign policy decision widely believed at the time to be important, the president will almost always be the principal figure determining the *general* direction of actions. Thus it was President Lyndon Johnson who made the final decision that the United States should deploy an ABM system. It was the first President Bush who made the final decision to launch the Gulf War in January 1991 and the second President Bush who made the decision to attack Iraq in March 2003.

Furthermore, the president serves as the surrogate for the national interest. Many senior participants look to the president as a blueprint for clues to the national security. His perception and judgment of what is in the national interest are dominant in the system. A strong president—with a clear sense of direction and leadership—can have a very strong influence on the images shared by bureaucrats, Congress, and the public.

Although the president is the principal decisionmaker on important foreign policy matters, he does not act alone. He is surrounded by a large number of participants with whom he consults, partly at his pleasure and partly by obligation. Other participants are arrayed around the president at varying distances determined by the probability that he will need to consult them. For convenience, participants whom he regularly consults are called "senior" participants and those who have access to the president only very infrequently or only through a senior participant are called "junior" participants. It is important to note that whether a particular participant is senior or junior is only imperfectly related to his or her position in the formal hierarchy.

Whom the president consults depends in large part on the nature of the issue. Regardless of who is president, Cabinet officers and heads of relevant agencies will be consulted from time to time because of their formal responsibilities and access to information. Law and custom dictate that the Cabinet officers involved in foreign policy issues almost always include the secretary of state, the secretary of defense, and the national security adviser and those involved in economic matters include the secretary of the treasury as well as White House economic advisers and sometimes the U.S. trade representative. The Joint Chiefs of Staff are consulted particularly on military budget issues and matters concerning the possible use of military force. The director of national intelligence will be consulted when information about foreign governments or groups, particularly hostile ones, is viewed as critical.

These officials are routinely influenced by their subordinates, with whom they in turn consult. The secretary of state usually depends most heavily on the deputy secretary, the under secretary for political affairs, and the regional assistant secretary most directly concerned. Bureaus with specialized responsibilities such as policy planning, political-military affairs, arms control, economic affairs, counterterrorism, human rights, and congressional relations also are involved, as are the secretary's principal assistants, counselors, and the under secretaries.

On national security issues related to foreign policy, the secretary of defense is likely to consult with the military services, with his deputy, and with the under secretary for policy and the assistant secretaries in that office. Particularly on budget matters, he also consults with the comptroller, under secretary for procurement, and others responsible for systems analysis and research and development. The chairman of the Joint Chiefs of Staff and his colleagues, the service chiefs of staff, are supported by their respective staff. The director of national intelligence joins with his colleagues from the State Department and Defense Department to produce formal national intelligence estimates. The director also consults with his current intelligence and scientific intelligence staffs and, when covert operations are involved, with Central Intelligence Agency operations staff. In many cases, military commanders in the field (known as CINCs) and American ambassadors and their staff are involved. Officials from agencies such as the U.S. Agency for International Development, the Department of Agriculture, the U.S. Trade Representative, the Department of Commerce, and the Department of the Treasury may become involved in economic decisions.

Others who may be consulted, depending on the particular president and his preferences, include members of the White House staff and specialists on national security or foreign policy as well as political advisers, speechwriters, and managers of the president's legislative program. President Kennedy brought more advisers into the process after the Bay of Pigs incident. All presidents since Nixon have relied heavily on the staff of the national security adviser. The second President Bush involved his political adviser Karl Rove in major decisions across the board, thus ensuring that domestic political considerations were brought strongly to bear on foreign policy and national security decisions.

The second President Bush also added another significant entity to his panoply of sources of advice on national security issues. In response to congressional pressure after 9/11, he created the Department of Homeland Security (headed by a secretary with full cabinet status) by combining a number of existing offices from several departments with overlapping domestic and international responsibilities. It was the first time in U.S. history that the Defense Department and related agencies were unable to deal with a primary security threat on their own. Homeland security staff was added to the White House Executive Office to incorporate the responsibilities for terrorism that originally were invested in the National Security Council. Although the Department of Homeland Security initially had serious problems integrating its highly disparate parts into an effective single entity, it nonetheless became a player in the national security policy framework almost immediately because the terrorist threat, unlike traditional threats to U.S. security, involved not only external defense but also domestic defense and police agencies.

Some of these participants are career officials; others are "in-and-outers" who come from careers outside the government for limited periods of government service. Often they are lawyers, bankers, businessmen, or experts from universities or think tanks. Although not formally members of the national security bureaucracy, individuals outside the executive branch are frequently consulted by the president and have significant influence on decisionmaking. Some senators and representatives are senior participants in the sense that they are routinely contacted by the president for advice and support. They tend to be the chairperson or a high-ranking member of a congressional committee with direct responsibility for national security affairs (for example, the Armed Services, Foreign Relations, Appropriations, and Intelligence Committees), and they have discretionary power over the federal budget. During the cold war influential members of Congress were important participants regardless of their direct legislative responsibilities for national security policy, but as Congress legislated a more formal policy role for itself as a body, presidents have turned less and less to individual members outside the formal process.

Since the end of the cold war, Congress increasingly has taken the initiative to direct foreign policy decisions within the bureaucracy, especially with regard to foreign economic and military assistance and humanitarian issues. Because the legislative branch enjoys certain rights to control the operations and budgets of the executive branch, from time to time the exercise of those rights has a very direct effect on either the outcome of a particular decision or the decisionmaking process itself.

Finally, Congress serves as an important forum for the discussion of national interests and the shared images that define those interests. On both the ABM program and issues involving the use of military force in Vietnam, Iraq, and elsewhere, Congress has played a major role in weighing the arguments and making vital funding decisions. In 1967, members of Congress applied heavy pressure for an ABM deployment, whereas in 1969 Congress came within one vote of denying deployment—contrary to the wishes and beliefs of the president—and at least the broader national security debate over the ABM program was aired in committee hearings. During the remaining years of the cold war and for long afterward, key members of Congress continued to keep an ABM development program alive by including funds in the defense budget, whether the administration requested them or not, and by keeping pressure on successive administrations to pursue an ABM program.

Sometimes individuals outside government are participants in the national security policy process. Private citizens who are close personal confidants of the president are included in this category. Private interest groups, such as defense contractors affected by foreign policy decisions and nongovernmental organizations (NGOs) with foreign policy agendas, often seek influence; they may be consulted by the president from time to time, and they are routinely involved through their contacts with Congress. Other outsiders may be formally invited to participate in the process, usually for limited periods of time and with narrowly defined responsibilities. The various presidential commissions and study groups are examples.[4]

Determining the Stand Taken on an Issue

With this brief listing of participants, we come back to the question of how each participant determines which positions are in the national interest. Given the intellectual difficulty of dealing with uncertainty, it is surprising that participants do have strongly held positions on particular issues. In part, that may be the result of what has been called the "51-49 principle." That is, participants who judge an issue to be very close and who only with some difficulty come down on one side or the other by a very narrow margin nevertheless feel obliged to advocate their position as if they believed it 100

4. Readers unfamiliar with the formal structure of the foreign policy process may wish to consult a standard work in the subject, such as Nathan and Oliver, *Foreign Policy Making and the American Political System*.

percent. They recognize that if they show great uncertainty, their views will not be taken seriously.

However, participants usually do not see issues as arbitrary, and they tend to find strong grounds to favor one position. Participants often employ two different techniques to simplify the problem of determining what is in the national interest: first, they employ techniques for choosing among options less rigorous than those required by an analytic model, and second, they equate a desirable state of the world beyond the borders of the United States with a desirable state of the world at home. That is, they come to define the national security interests of the United States in terms of the health and well-being of the organization to which they belong, the interests of the president, or their own personal interests, all of which are discussed in the following chapters.

Whether they look directly to events in the outside world or to organizational, presidential, or personal interests as a surrogate for national security interests, participants need a means of monitoring threats and judging how to respond to them. We consider first the use of analytic techniques and then turn to what John Steinbruner calls cognitive processes.

ANALYSIS. A "rational" approach assumes that individuals seeking to determine what is in the national interest of the United States would list a series of objectives and attempt to put them in hierarchical order; next they would examine a series of available alternatives and consider the cost and gains of each alternative in relation to the hierarchy of objectives. They then would search for additional information that would reduce the range of uncertainty and permit them to calculate what position was indeed good for the country. Armed with that analysis, they would take a particular stand on an issue but would be ready to change that position if additional information or better calculations became available.

Such a mode of thinking, applied directly to national security interests, no doubt does seem logical to many of the participants. When an analysis or a set of arguments substantially reduces the range of uncertainty and unambiguously points to the desirability of a particular stand, that position is likely to be adopted by most, if not all, participants. However, making such calculations involves enormous costs in time and intellectual resources. Seldom do participants, in fact, engage in such research to determine what is in the national interest. The problems are too difficult, and time is short. Even if a participant looks to organizational, presidential, or personal interests to make that determination, analytic processes are likely to prove to be too cumbersome. Thus, whatever the source of clues to the national interests, individuals are likely to use shortcuts in place of an analytic model.

COGNITIVE PROCESSES. According to John Steinbruner, in order to avoid time-consuming analysis, participants focus on a few variables and develop a set of programmed responses to changes in any one of those variables.[5] Events in the outside world are screened to filter out variables that would create uncertainty. Moreover, participants tend to respond to changes in each variable separately, producing fragmented responses to each change. Steinbruner finds that individuals deal with uncertainty in the outside world by using several standard techniques:

—*Use of pat images and arguments by analogy.* Individuals frequently attempt to determine which previous event, either in international politics or in their own personal experience, most closely relates to the event at hand, and then they seek to reason by analogy. Thus the impulse to avoid another Munich played a major role in shaping the reaction of many government officials to the Vietnam situation. They did not want to be seen as weak for not standing up to the enemy.

—*Inferences of transformation.* This technique, commonly known as "wishful thinking," involves the assumption that if a problem is recognized, eventually it will somehow be solved, in a manner that one cannot specify. Thus one need not worry about that problem but can focus on others.

—*Inferences of impossibility.* Using this technique, a participant rules out a particular option by arguing that a critical premise on which it depends is, in fact, impossible.

—*Negative images.* Through this technique, a possible option is ruled out by predicting dire consequences if that option is implemented. Opponents of ABM deployment argued that any decision to deploy an ABM system would inevitably lead to a very large system and eliminate the prospects for any negotiations with the Soviet Union.

Using these techniques, individuals can resolve uncertainty in deciding among multiple options and find certainty in support of a particular position. Steinbruner identified three typical patterns of thinking by which participants relate their interests to the stands that they take, and each pattern seems to be typical of a particular set of interests:

—Those who focus directly on national security interests are likely to exhibit *ideological thinking.*

—Those who focus on organizational interests reflect *grooved thinking.*

5. Steinbruner, *The Cybernetic Theory of Decision,* chap. 4.

—The president's interests frequently are reflected in *uncommitted thinking*.

Ideological thinking is characterized by a very abstract and extensive belief pattern that is internally consistent and tends to be extremely stable. Generally, the belief pattern is characterized by emphasis on a single value (say, fighting communism or terrorism, seeking disarmament, or pressing for human rights) that tends to be pursued independently of reality as others may perceive it. Officials who hold to such a pattern are frequently known as "theologians" within the government, and in Anthony Downs's terms are "zealots."[6] Individuals whose position is characterized by ideological thinking use various techniques, such as the selective perception of information, to maintain their views in the face of conflicting information. Because of the consistency of their position, they are able to act quickly and with confidence when others see ambiguity or are uncertain as to how to behave.

Ideological thinking generally characterizes in-and-outers who enter the government with strong commitments in a particular area. For in-and-outers and "regulars" alike, commitments often arise out of the first professional contact with an issue or from a seminal event in their past. For example, President Nixon's view of the Cuban regime seems to have been strongly affected by his long conversation with Fidel Castro during Castro's visit to the United States during the Eisenhower administration.

Ideological thinking also tends to characterize staff members who have had a long period of involvement in a particular area and become committed to a particular doctrine, such as the need for American hegemony. It may be exhibited by military officers or bureau chiefs in small interacting groups who commit themselves to a particular ideology that enhances the importance of the activity in which they are engaged.

Those whose approach is dominated by ideological thinking tend to see all issues in terms of a particular value, to disregard conflicting information and roadblocks, and to press hard for a solution that would support the dominant value.

Participants who exhibit *grooved thinking* tend to focus on a few key variables and to have a programmed response to those particular variables. They are repeatedly confronted by the need to respond to particular events and do so by breaking a complex problem into its parts and responding in a programmed way to each part. Often such individuals see national security in terms of organizational interests. For example, a State Department official responsible for maintaining good relations with an American ally is likely to focus on reports from the foreign office of that country and statements by the

6. Downs, *Inside Bureaucracy,* p. 88.

country's leaders. When signals from those sources suggest that there is a problem, he or she will respond with certain programmed responses, such as sending the ambassador to talk to the prime minister or requesting that Washington issue a statement of reassurance. Such individuals tend to ignore signals for which they have no set response, such as the statements of new opposition leaders or evidence of growing political or economic unrest.

This pattern of thought is typical of career officials, particularly relatively low-level officials, who need to act constantly and become accustomed to regularized patterns of behavior. Many low-ranking Army officials, perhaps even senior officials, responded to the ABM program in this way. They monitored Russian activities and typically responded to a Russian deployment by arguing that the United States needed to match that deployment. They also responded to Russia's increased offensive capability by arguing that the United States needed to add a direct defense specifically to deal with that offensive capability. Grooved thinking tends to produce routine responses to changes perceived one by one, and it ignores larger factors that might render the response inappropriate.

Uncommitted thinking characterizes those officials who must deal with generalized concepts, who are habitually confronted with uncertainty, and who tap a variety of information channels that stress the importance of different problems and advocate different solutions to problems. Exposed to alternative patterns of belief designed to bring order to great uncertainties, individuals exhibiting uncommitted thinking adopt different patterns at different times for the same problem. That may appear to outsiders to be oscillating, because the uncommitted thinker seeks freedom of maneuver by avoiding the integration of problems that appear to others to be closely related.

This pattern of thought often characterizes the president, who in dealing with a particular problem may have little past experience and little firsthand knowledge. Issues tend to come to him and his closest associates in an abstract or generalized form, and pressures come from many sides. The White House tends to relate each theory to its sponsors and to appeal to the allegiance of as many groups as possible.

President Johnson's behavior in dealing with the question of the ABM program suggests the pattern of uncommitted thinking. Secretary of Defense McNamara attempted to get him to see the issue in terms of the danger of stimulating the arms race and of vastly increasing military expenditures. McNamara argued that the program was unnecessary and would increase the risk of nuclear war. Senior military officers and leading congressional figures, in contrast, attempted to persuade Johnson to see the issue in terms of the importance of maintaining American strategic nuclear superiority.

Since each of these views appeared sensible on its own terms, Johnson moved back and forth between supporting and opposing the ABM program. He probably never made a firm judgment of his own as to which of the two views was correct. Rather, he responded to short-run pressures in an effort to keep the participants from breaking out and denouncing his decision. The president's behavior appeared to be a form of oscillation because his decision was characterized by uncommitted thinking in an effort to find a consensus that would satisfy all of those putting pressure on him.

When a persuasive case is made that a certain stand is required or ruled out by the interests of the United States, most participants agree to the decision. Indeed, much of what goes on in the government involves efforts to analyze an issue from the point of view of shared images and to persuade others that the requirements of national security, flowing from those shared images, require that a particular stand be taken. However, despite shared images, determining the national interest is often an elusive goal, and participants frequently find it difficult to develop a stand simply by focusing on national security directly. In such cases they often look to organizational and presidential interests and explore them in light of their personal interests.

CHAPTER THREE

Organizational Interests

To the extent that participants in the national security decisionmaking process come to equate national security with the interests of their organization, what stands do they tend to take and how do their stands relate to their organization's interests? Do organizations always seek to grow larger and do more things? This chapter attempts to specify in detail the organizational interests of the Defense Department, the State Department, and the Central Intelligence Agency and of their components.

MISSIONS, CAPABILITIES, AND INFLUENCE

Most organizations have a mission to perform, either overseas or at home, and some organizations need to maintain expensive capabilities in order to perform their mission effectively. Most important, in order to fulfill their mission, all organizations must seek *influence*.

Organizations are formally charged with specific missions. Some of those missions can be accomplished entirely at home (such as maintaining good relations with Congress); others require actions abroad (such as deterring a Soviet attack on the United States). Participants in making a policy decision examine any proposal to gauge whether it would help their particular organization carry out its missions. For example, in examining the ABM deployment proposal, the Budget Bureau and the Comptroller's Office in the Pentagon were concerned with how it would affect their ability to keep down the military budget. State Department officials were concerned with the impact of deployment on relations with European allies and with the Soviet Union.

The missions of some organizations in the national security field encourage them to maintain substantial and expensive *capabilities* that may be employed abroad. The armed services, for example, are responsible for creating and maintaining very expensive military forces. Organizations with expensive capabilities see the face of an issue that affects their ability to maintain what they view as the capability necessary to take a variety of actions.

Organizations with expensive capabilities are particularly concerned about budget decisions and about the budgeting implications of policy decisions. Organizations with low-cost capabilities are relatively unconcerned about budget implications but highly concerned about the immediate implications of specific policy decisions. That is an important difference, for example, between the armed services and the State Department. The case of the ABM proposal illustrates the point. For the U.S. Army, it meant a bigger budget and a greater role in strategic warfare. State Department officials, on the other hand, cared much less about costs and capabilities than about how the decision would affect U.S. relations with allies and potential adversaries. The fact that an ABM system might cost several billion dollars while an alternative way of reassuring allies of protection from Soviet nuclear attack might cost very little did not affect State Department interests, since State neither paid the costs nor operated the capabilities.

All organizations seek to have greater influence in order to pursue their other objectives. Those that have large operational capabilities seek influence on decisions, in part, to maintain the capability to perform their mission. Some organizations—the office of the under secretary for policy in the Defense Department, for instance, and the policy planning staff in the State Department—have neither large capabilities nor stable, clearly defined missions. Their *organizational* goal tends to be to gain influence in pursuit of ideological concerns. Staff members of those organizations share with their counterparts in other organizations the belief that they can best judge the nation's security interests.

In one way or another, the pursuit of influence itself is felt to be in the national interest. Not only is influence necessary to protect the organization's other objectives, but senior members of the organization are considered by junior members to be especially qualified to advise the president on what the national interest is. Therefore the stand that a participant takes on an issue is affected by the desire to maintain influence, and that desire could lead to support for certain policies that require greater reliance on the organization. Participants prefer courses of action that require information from them or that they will be asked to implement. They recognize that they gain influence if such decisions are made. The desire for influence can also lead organizations to avoid opposing a particular policy in the belief that to do so would reduce their influence on other issues. To develop a reputation for losing a policy debate reduces a group's standing with other groups.

Organizational Essence

Organizations have considerable freedom in defining their missions and the capabilities that they need to pursue those missions. The organization's *essence* is the view held by the dominant group within the organization of what its missions and capabilities should be. Related to essence are convictions about what kinds of people—with what expertise, experience, and knowledge—should be members of the organization.

Career officials generally have a clear notion of what the essence of their organization is or should be. In some organizations the same view of the organization's essence is shared by all those in the same promotion and career structure. In other cases there are differences. The differences may concern the particulars of a broader agreed essence, or they may reflect struggles for dominance. In either case, conflicts often arise among subgroups within a single career structure to define the essence of the organization. Struggles over essence and the results for some of the major national security organizations are discussed below.

Air Force

The dominant view in the Air Force since its inception as a separate service just after World War II has been that its essence is to fly combat air missions. Until the end of the cold war the dominant view was that those missions should focus on the delivery of nuclear weapons against targets in the Soviet Union. With the Soviet threat gone, Air Force officers debated whether to continue to focus on delivering nuclear weapons, to stress the value of conventional strategic bombing, or to provide support for ground combat operations. The debate was won by those emphasizing conventional strategic bombing with precision munitions. The Air Force argued that such bombing played a decisive role in the Kosovo campaign and in the first Gulf War.

The struggle within an organization to determine what organizational role should be stressed is well illustrated by the debate within the Air Force

Tactical Air Command (TAC) during the cold war. TAC officers seeking to enhance the role of their command had a difficult problem. On one hand they were obliged to pay lip service to TAC's formal mission—to provide combat air support for ground forces. On the other hand, they were tempted to seek to develop capabilities for the role seen as the essence of the Air Force—namely, the combat delivery of nuclear weapons against the Soviet Union—by creating what Alain C. Enthoven and K. Wayne Smith described as a "junior SAC."[1] This dilemma shaped the arguments used by the Air Force in an effort to get a new tactical airplane, at first called the TFX and in a later version called the F-111. The officer largely responsible for the design of TAC, General F. F. Everest, argued that the TFX was essential to meet the three missions of his command, which were to maintain air superiority, to disrupt enemy supply lines, and to supply close air support.

However, in a careful study of the TFX decision, the political scientist Robert J. Art reports that General Everest's underlying motives were, in fact, quite different:

> These three missions represented TAC's dogma, to which Everest had to pay lip service. It appears, however, that he was interested primarily in having his new aircraft penetrate enemy defenses at a low level at supersonic speeds while carrying nuclear weapons. The reason Everest wanted such an aircraft is self-evident. In the late 1950s American military doctrine still concentrated primarily on maintaining a strategic nuclear retaliatory capability in order to ensure that deterrence was a credible posture. Under such a doctrine, TAC, as well as the Army, suffered from a relative lack of funds. The Air Force received a large share of the military budget; but within that service, the Strategic Air Command (SAC) received the preponderant portion of those funds. By trying to acquire a nuclear capability for TAC and by thus providing it with an ability to deliver nuclear weapons in a way that SAC'S B-52 bombers could not (by low-level, supersonic interdiction), Everest attempted to protect the present identity of and future role for TAC. (The Army did exactly the same thing when it stressed that the United States lacked an ability to fight limited conventional wars. It too used doctrinal arguments as a means of protecting its service identity and share of defense funds.)[2]

The most successful challenge to the Air Force's definition of its essence arose because of the development of ICBMs. Ironically, however, the impetus

1. Enthoven and Smith, *How Much Is Enough?* p. 9.
2. Art, *The TFX Decision,* p. 16.

for the development of missiles came largely from outside the Air Force and was bitterly resisted at first by Air Force officers who continued to give highest priority to the development of combat aircraft. Herbert F. York, former director of Defense Research and Engineering, reported on the resistance within the Air Force to the decision by the Defense Department to give the highest priority to the development of ballistic missiles following the Soviet Union's successful testing of an ICBM and the launching of Sputnik:

> General Curtis E. LeMay, the man with the cigar, was the commander of the Strategic Air Command (SAC) at the time. As I recall his personal view of the priorities, he placed the B-52H first (it was then called the B-52 Squared) and the B-70 second (it was then called the WS-110). The nuclear airplane (ANP) was somewhere in the middle of his short list, and the long-range missiles were at the bottom. He and other leading Air Force generals managed to make it clear to the contractor that they personally considered the B-70 to be at least as important as the ICBMs, whatever the official priorities might be, and they ordered first flight by the end of 1961.[3]

To LeMay and the Air Force, missiles sitting in silos just could not compare to flying bombers.

In the 1960s, with the growing emphasis on non-nuclear forces and increased recognition of the inhibitions against using nuclear weapons, the Air Force was forced to choose between continued reliance on nuclear delivery and its ability to play the dominant role as the deliverer of other kinds of weapons against enemy targets. After considerable initial resistance the Air Force finally came around to accepting a non-nuclear role, recognizing that that was the way to maintain its dominance in delivery of weapons by air.[4]

The part of the Air Force that was least effective in challenging the dominance of SAC was the Military Airlift Command (MAC), charged with movement of men and materiel, primarily for the Army. In the evaluation of possible alternatives to relieve the blockade of Berlin in 1948, the Air Force bitterly resisted the airlift concept because it would use up all of the planes it believed to be necessary for the combat role of the Air Force.[5] After the successful airlift, the Air Force failed to exploit the success to enhance its prestige, and as explained by Paul Y. Hammond, the reasons for not capitalizing on the episode related to the top officers' view of the essence of the service:

3. York, *Race to Oblivion: A Participant's View of the Arms Race,* p. 53.
4. Sorensen, *Kennedy,* p. 588.
5. Murphy, *Diplomat among Warriors,* p. 318.

Why did the Air Force thus fail fully to exploit the public relations value of the notable achievement of air power in the Berlin airlift? And why did the extraordinary and unexpected experience of the airlift have so little effect upon the developing dispute over roles and missions? Any answers to these questions must be wholly speculative, but some seem possible. The airlift was a freight-carrying operation which served to demonstrate the importance of air transport. But the Air Force has been paring its transport facilities to a minimum in order to maximize its strategic bombing forces. Supporters of strategic air power, the predominant strategic doctrine in the Air Force, might have viewed the airlift as a potential threat to the primary mission of the Air Force, and feared that airlift publicity would only give substance to the charges which had often been voiced in Army circles that the Air Force was neglecting its duty to provide air transport for Army troops. This answer to the first question suggests an answer to the second. Since the airlift was more relevant to Air Force-Army relations than to Air Force-Navy relations, and since the latter were the ones which were currently raising the inter-service issue of roles and missions, the airlift had no direct relationship to the aviation controversy then developing. Moreover, as has been indicated, boasting about the airlift could have been shared by the British and even the Navy. Sharing of aviation responsibilities was not what the Air Force was trying to enlarge.[6]

Years later, in the mid-1960s, the Air Force did accept procurement of a large number of C-5A troop-carrying airplanes, but only because the move was forced on it by civilians. When Air Force officers are given their own way, their priorities have always been clear: to protect the role of the Air Force in the strategic delivery of weapons by air. Its other two missions—of close air support and airlift—are essentially services it provides to the Army. It is the strategic mission that keeps the Air Force independent from the Army.

Navy

Navy officers agree on the general proposition that the essence of the Navy is to maintain combat ships whose primary mission is to control the seas against potential enemies. Unlike the Air Force, where the Strategic Command (SC) and its predecessor SAC have usually dominated the other commands, the Navy has been affected by serious disputes among three groups: Navy flyers

6. Hammond, "Super Carriers and B-36 Bombers," p. 485.

(the brown-shoe Navy), who emphasize carrier-based air units; seapower advocates (the black-shoe Navy), who stress the surface Navy; and submariners, who focus on attack submarines. During the cold war a fourth group came to be identified with the Polaris submarines. No senior Navy officers see the essence of the Navy as involvement in transport, and that function has received relatively little attention.

In the early cold war period, the Navy struggled to maintain its capability despite a tight budget and the rise of the Air Force. Navy aviators were locked in a struggle with the Air Force over the relative role of supercarriers and B-36 bombers and, within the Navy, over the relative roles to be accorded to carriers, submarines, and conventional ships. Although the carrier admirals argued with the Air Force that the carriers could do a better job of firing nuclear weapons against targets in the Soviet Union, their primary interest was in targets connected with naval warfare, such as submarine bases and air bases of planes directed at sea operations. Within the Navy, the struggle was about which kind of force could best dominate the seas. The victory of the carrier admirals was signified by the offer of the Navy to scrap many ships then currently under construction if in return the relatively modest Navy budget in the late 1940s might be used to construct supercarriers for the delivery of nuclear weapons.[7] Such thinking continued to play a large role in Navy calculations, leading to emphasis on aircraft carriers and their mission long after many outside observers concluded that carriers had been rendered obsolete by developments in Soviet naval capabilities.

After the end of the cold war, the Navy kept the aircraft carriers in a central role as versatile platforms for both strategic conventional bombing and close air support in regional conflicts. That posture continued to challenge the role of the Air Force, which was dependent on land bases, while tacitly conceding that no nation was capable of challenging the United States at sea.

The most serious challenge to the dominant role of the aircraft carriers came from proposals first suggested by small groups within the Navy to develop a submarine missile-launching capability. Superficially the two roles were the same, since both carriers and submarines armed with Polaris missiles could deliver nuclear weapons against the Soviet Union.

However, the Polaris missiles, besides being "unpiloted," were directed primarily at the destruction of Soviet cities and played only a very limited role in control of the seas. Thus, in their opposition to Polaris missiles, which would deprive them of aircraft, the carrier advocates had the support of much

7. Ibid., p. 470.

of the rest of the Navy. Senator Henry M. Jackson reported on his frustration in seeking to win support for the Polaris program within the Navy:

> I was interested in this program from the very outset, going back many, many years. I found that in trying to get the Navy to do something about it, I ran headlong into the competition within the Navy for requirements in connection with their day-to-day operational needs, whether it was anti-submarine warfare or limited war requirements; whatever it was. . . . I was told that this strategic system would just eat away and erode their limited funds. . . . The result was that Polaris was not pushed hard until Sputnik came along.[8]

When the program passed from the research and development stage to procurement, the Navy's resistance once again was aroused because of the large amount of funds necessary to procure a substantial number of Polaris submarines. In approaching the problem, the Navy took the stand traditionally taken by the services when civilians seek to force programs on them that they view as contrary to the essence of their activity. As noted by Enthoven and Smith:

> In its budget requests for fiscal years 1961 and 1962, the Navy budgeted for only three Polaris submarines in each year. One of the first things that President Kennedy and Secretary McNamara did when they came into office was to speed up the Polaris program and to authorize the building of ten Polaris submarines in each of these fiscal years. Nobody, to our knowledge, has since questioned the necessity or the wisdom of that action. But at the time, senior Navy officers, when confronted with arguments for increasing the Polaris program based on urgent national need, replied: Polaris is a national program, not a Navy program. By this was meant: the Polaris mission is not a traditional Navy mission and therefore should not be financed out of the Navy's share of the defense budget.[9]

Army

Career Army officers agree that the essence of the Army is ground combat capability. They are less interested in those functions that they view as peripheral, such as advisory roles in Military Assistance Advisory Group (MAAG) missions, air defense, and the special Green Beret, Delta, or counterinsurgency forces.

8. Senator Jackson, quoted in Armacost, *The Politics of Weapons.*
9. Enthoven and Smith, *How Much Is Enough?* pp. 16–17; *Innovation,* pp. 65–66.

In the 1950s, there was considerable dispute among career officers about the degree to which the Army should be organized primarily for nuclear warfare rather than conventional ground combat operations. From the early 1960s, a battle raged concerning the role of Special Forces. Beginning with President John F. Kennedy's efforts to enhance the role of the Green Berets, some officials in the Army, with outside support, struggled to give the role of Special Forces equal weight with that of conventional armored divisions.

President Kennedy came into office believing that American security would be challenged by guerilla forces against whom American power would have to be used in limited and quite special ways. He therefore began an effort to develop such a capability within the Army. That ran contrary to the Army's definition of its essence, which involved ground combat by regular divisions, and by and large the Army was able to resist Kennedy's effort. Special Forces played only a limited role in Vietnam, and the Army disbanded the Green Berets shortly after Kennedy's death.

Congress took up the challenge with the Goldwater-Nichols legislation that created both a Special Forces command with a global reach and an office within the civilian side of the Department of Defense to champion Special Forces. Nevertheless, the Army continued to rely primarily on divisional units in various combat operations, including the first Gulf War and the peacekeeping operations in Haiti and the Balkans. During the second Bush administration, Defense Secretary Donald Rumsfeld pressed hard for greater reliance on Army and other special forces, ensuring that they played a significant role in both Afghanistan in 2001 and the Iraq invasion of 2003.

Advocates of air and missile defense within the Army have not proclaimed that the element of warfare that most interests them should become the dominant form of Army activity. They have merely said that it deserves a partial role, and they have made headway with the argument that the money for air and missile defense would not come from the Army ground combat forces. According to air and missile defense advocates, the funds would otherwise be spent on equivalent programs in the other services. In the 1950s, faced with growing emphasis on strategic delivery systems, some Army officers sought to get the Army involved in the deployment of medium-range ballistic missiles. In the 1960s, such Army efforts focused on ABMs. Although those Army programs failed to elicit the all-out commitment aroused by issues believed to affect the organizational essence of the service, there was some steam behind them. The Army, a more eclectic group with many long and differing historical traditions, does have greater tolerance for diverse groups even though its essence remains the conduct of ground combat.

Central Intelligence Agency

CIA career officials are split into three groups according to their notion of what the essence of the agency ought to be: intelligence gathering, clandestine operations, or intelligence analysis. Each group has looked to senior officials in the agency for support of its own notions.

One group, once headed by Richard Helms, emphasizes intelligence gathering, believing that the primary function of the CIA should be to conduct operations that are designed primarily to get information about potentially hostile governments or terrorists and organized crime. During the cold war period, the group also believed that the CIA should be involved in limited clandestine operations in foreign countries to support movements such as labor unions or political parties friendly to the United States. In the post–cold war environment and especially since 9/11, this group has emphasized clandestine gathering of information from human sources from rogue states and terrorist groups.

In contrast, a second group, once headed by Richard Bissell, Helms's predecessor as head of the Directorate of Plans at the CIA, believes that the CIA should actively intervene in events abroad. This group led the CIA during a period of the cold war when it was involved in relatively large-scale covert operations in Iran and in Guatemala, as well as when it embarked on the U-2 program and the Bay of Pigs invasion. CIA involvement in Laos and in Vietnam also represented the influence of this group's notion of what the agency's function ought to be. Clandestine operations were constrained in the 1970s and 1980s, however, when Congress and the American public became concerned about the agency's motivation and effectiveness. Evolving military doctrine in the post-9/11 period has revived the popularity of clandestine operations, particularly in the war on an elusive and highly unconventional terrorist enemy and in dealing with rogue states. CIA units apparently played an important role in Afghanistan and in the early stages of the war in Iraq in 2003.

A third group, which has considerably less influence, emphasizes intelligence evaluation. It has often been said that the CIA gets 90 percent of its information from public sources, and a large part of its staff is involved in the evaluation of material received from both clandestine and public sources. Members of the third group believe that the conduct of clandestine activities, whether for intelligence gathering or for covert operations, jeopardizes the CIA's claim to impartiality and reduces its involvement in policy issues. At various times some members of this group have supported the separation of the clandestine service, which performs both covert intelligence gathering and covert operations, from the rest of the CIA, believing that intelligence analysis will never capture the attention of the top leadership of the agency as long as the agency is engaged in clandestine operations.

Foreign Service

In contrast to career officials in the military services and in the CIA, Foreign Service officers are agreed on the essence of their profession. The basic function of the State Department and hence of the Foreign Service is seen as reporting on the activities of foreign governments that have relevance to the United States, general representation of American interests abroad, and negotiation of specific issues when directed by the government.[10] Charles W. Thayer, a former Foreign Service officer, approvingly noted the traditional views:

> Secretary Cordell Hull once said he required four things of his ambassadors: to report what was going on; to represent the United States before foreign governments and publics; to negotiate United States government business; and to look after American lives and property.[11]

Career Foreign Service officers view their enterprise as an elite organization composed of generalists, and they resist the introduction into the department of novel functions and of experts who might be needed to perform those functions. In the immediate post–World War II period, Foreign Service officers were appalled to discover that various agencies had been disbanded and their personnel assigned to the State Department. They were particularly concerned about the transfer of propaganda officials and intelligence analysts. Robert Murphy, a senior Foreign Service officer, commented on the situation:

> Meanwhile, in Washington, the weakened Department of State suffered a postwar influx of manpower from unexpected sources, some of it dumped by President Harry S. Truman and Secretary Byrnes from liquidated war agencies such as the Office of War Information, the Office of Strategic Services, and others. The new employees arrived—*certainly not at the request of the Foreign Service*—without qualification examination or security screening, and they created an awkward situation. . . . At the

10. Harr, *The Professional Diplomat*, pp. 35–40, 43–44, 243–44; Smith Simpson, *Anatomy of the State Department*, p. 3; and Andrew M. Scott, "The Department of State: Formal Organization and Informal Culture," p. 3.

11. Thayer, *Diplomat*, p. 81.

same time greatly increased responsibilities were heaped upon the State Department. Foreign Service officers, no longer limited to orthodox consular and diplomatic activities, were allocated to propaganda, intelligence, and military government, and became involved in many of the conflicts arising from Soviet expansion.[12]

Many Foreign Service officers resisted the policy ordained in a letter to ambassadors from President Kennedy (and renewed by every president since then) telling them that they would have operational control over all programs in their bailiwick, including at least some of those of the Central Intelligence Agency.[13] The officers feared that control over such programs might prove to be embarrassing and would prevent them from focusing on the important functions of reporting and negotiation. A retired Foreign Service officer, Ellis Briggs, expressed that point of view with regard to the functions of an ambassador:

> In theory each ambassador is responsible for all government operations conducted within his jurisdiction. That is a good thing, but in practice it would be manifestly impossible for a chief of mission to accomplish, as ambassador, anything in the way of business with the government to which he is accredited, if in addition he tried personally to supervise all the programs operated in the name of the American government within his bailiwick. Liaison with other agencies is customarily delegated to the ambassador's overworked deputy, who in turn must rely on the senior members of the embassy staff, an appreciable part of whose time is devoted to preventing the representatives of other agencies, who invariably regard themselves as diplomats, from damaging the delicate machinery of international relations.[14]

During the postwar and cold war periods, career Foreign Service officers viewed the regional bureaus of the State Department—those dealing with Europe, East Asia, the Near East and South Asia, and Africa and Latin America—as the heart of State Department operations. They believed that the assistant secretaries for those regions should be career officials and should have flexibility in managing relations with the countries included. They resisted the growth of functional bureaus, such as those dealing with economics and political-military affairs, in part because such bureaus were at that time dominated by civil servants or in-and-outers rather than by Foreign Service officers. In the early post–World War II period, State Department officials

12. Murphy, *Diplomat among Warriors*, pp. 451–52 (italics added).
13. Jackson Subcommittee, *Administration of National Security*, pp. 8–10.
14. Briggs, *Farewell to Foggy Bottom: The Recollections of a Career Diplomat*, p. 166.

saw a threat from nonregional bureaus, and the United Nations bureau particularly worried them because of an influx of non-career officers who had been planning for the establishment of the UN during the war. After a brief struggle, Foreign Service officers were able to confirm their dominance of the department and uphold the regional bureaus, particularly the Bureau of European Affairs.[15]

With the end of the cold war, the State Department changed itself substantially to adapt to a much more complex overseas mission and to comply with congressional pressure to absorb its subordinate, but autonomous agencies, the United States Information Agency (USIA) and the Arms Control and Disarmament Agency (ACDA). The Foreign Service no longer cultivates its elitist self-image, and officers overseas are now much more involved in operations and not just in diplomacy and reporting. With the increased emphasis on human rights, narcotics, terrorism, and other concerns, a plethora of new reporting requirements, both public and confidential, has been levied on the State Department and its overseas missions by Congress and the White House. New functional bureaus have been added to the State Department organizational structure, along with a layer of under secretaries, creating complex competing interests at the working level.

As the cold war period drew to a close, the predominance of the regional bureaus also broke down. While still primarily concerned with managing bilateral and regional relations, the regional bureaus no longer dominate the policy process and often are overruled at the under secretary level and above. Regional and functional assistant secretaries are more often non-career political appointees than they are Foreign Service officers. Furthermore, the differences in the priority of various geographic regions that prevailed during the cold war have largely disappeared. In the course of their careers Foreign Service officers tend to become associated with one or two geographic bureaus through the regional expertise they acquire in their overseas assignments, and they may also become associated with a particular functional expertise through their Washington assignments. However, the strong identification with competing regional subgroups, such as "Europeanists" or "Arabists," that prevailed during the cold war period is no longer so significant. Subgroups in the State Department do not tend to rally around particular kinds of missions, as in the case of the CIA or the military services. Rather, they take sides over the relative attention to be given to different issues, such as human rights, democracy, or narcotics, in particular in bilateral or regional relations.

15. Wishnatsky, "Symbolic Politics and the Origins of the Cold War," pp. 3–5.

Congress

After the Vietnam War, Congress began to insert itself more formally into the national security and foreign policy decisionmaking process, partly through legislation and partly through the activity of its swelling committee staff. As it became more involved, it also began to acquire many of the characteristics of the bureaucracy in the way that it related to policy decisions.

It too has players in different positions who see different faces of an issue and compete to affect outcomes. While much of the competition occurs at the staff level, it also can represent the interests of elected officials in their domestic constituency. Thus congressional approaches to national security and foreign policy often are even more likely to be motivated by domestic politics than those of the executive branch. (Part 4 of this volume explores the bureaucratic aspects of Congress's approach to foreign policy.)

ENHANCEMENT OF THE ORGANIZATION'S ESSENCE

An organization's image of its essence shapes its conception of its interests. The concern with essence is manifested in several ways.

—An organization favors policies and strategies that its members believe will make the organization as they define it more important. For example, during the 1950s, the Air Force favored the "new look" strategy, which called for reliance on nuclear weapons, while the Army favored the flexible response strategy, which implied reliance on conventional ground forces. In the early post–World War II period, the State Department resisted efforts to rely on the UN and on economic cooperation if such efforts entailed reliance on experts outside the Foreign Service. It also fought for a policy that would involve direct bilateral diplomatic dealings with the Soviet Union and with the countries of Western Europe.

—An organization struggles hardest for the capabilities that it views as necessary to the essence of the organization. It seeks autonomy and the funds needed to pursue the capabilities necessary to fulfill its missions. Thus, long after most experts had concluded that Skybolt was not technically feasible, the Air Force continued to seek the missile as a means of preserving the manned strategic bomber.

—An organization resists efforts to take away the functions that it views as part of its essence. It seeks to protect those functions by taking on additional functions if it believes that forgoing the added functions may ultimately jeopardize its sole control over the essence of its activities. The Navy and Air Force, for instance, insist on performing the troop transport role for the Army, and the Air Force rejects the Army's efforts to perform the close air support role. If the Army transported its own troops by sea, it might well build ships that would enable Army troops to come ashore firing—the (not previously discussed) essence of the Marine Corps's activity. Dreading such an "infringement," the Navy demanded in the 1960s that the Army's proposed fast-deployment logistics (FDL) ships be constructed in such a way that they could not be used for amphibious operations. To cite another example from the same period, the Air Force, failing to kill the medium-range missile program, fought to take on the program itself because it feared that the Army would use the program as a foot in the door to take on the strategic deterrence mission.

—An organization is often indifferent to functions not seen as part of its essence or as necessary to protect its essence. It tends not to initiate new activities or seek new capabilities even when technology makes them feasible. Thus the Air Force did not press for the adoption of intercontinental ballistic missiles, and the program had to be forced on it from the outside. Similarly, the Navy did not seek the role of delivering nuclear weapons from submarines. If assigned such functions, organizations will devote as few resources to them as they can; for example, the Air Force and the Navy have devoted limited resources to techniques for conducting airlifts and sealifts while insisting on performing the transport function. Ambitious career officers avoid serving in "unessential" activities. U.S. Army officers in Vietnam, for example, preferred leading troops in combat and serving on combat staff to taking advisory assignments.

—Sometimes an organization attempts to push a growing function out of its domain entirely. It begrudges expenditures on anything but its chosen activity. It is chary of new personnel with new skills and interests who may seek to dilute or change the organization's essence. For example, after World War II the Army urged the creation of a separate Air Force in the belief that, if it were not done, flyers would come to dominate the Army, changing the conception of its role.[16] Similarly, Foreign Service officers resisted the assignment of new responsibilities until, during the 1980s and 1990s, Congress created new geographic and functional bureaus and forced the State Department to incorporate USIA and ACDA into its operations, against the advice of career officers.

16. Smith, *The Air Force Plans for Peace*, p. 19.

In short, an organization accepts new functions only if it believes that to refuse to do so would be to jeopardize its position with senior officials or if it believes that the new function will bring in more funds and give the organization greater scope to pursue its "own" activities. The military services describe functions not related to their essence as "national programs" rather than service programs and demand that the funding for them be counted outside their regular service budget. For many years, the Navy took that position in relation to the submarine-launched missile program, and the Army did so in relation to the ABM.

ROLES AND MISSIONS

From what has been said so far, it follows that internal political conflicts over roles and missions arise constantly within the government. Furthermore, fights over roles and missions are particularly acute when they have an impact on the essence of the contending organizations.

Three classic disputes that divided the military services in the 1940s and afterward illustrate this struggle: the dispute between the Navy and Air Force over naval aviation, between the Army and Air Force over combat support, and between the Army and the Marines over Marine participation in ground combat operations. The first has run its course, but the other two have continued into the post-9/11 period. Two conflicts involving the CIA also have persisted: the struggle between the CIA and the armed services over control of covert combat operations and the conflict among CIA, the State Department, and the armed services over the domain of each in intelligence gathering and evaluation. With regard to Congress, there are continuing struggles among committees over questions of jurisdiction and between Congress and the executive branch on the question of prerogatives in the conduct of foreign policy and national security. Because career officials feel so strongly about the essence of their respective organizations, the conflicts have been intense and have affected officials' stands on issues as well as their implementation of decisions. Each of the conflicts is discussed in turn.

Naval Aviation

The depth of feeling in the Navy and the Air Force about the role of naval aviation is reflected in Secretary of Defense James Forrestal's report of a conversation that he had with Air Force General Hoyt Vandenberg in 1948:

I remarked that there were these fundamental psychoses, both revolving around the use of air power:

(1) The Navy belief, very firmly held and deeply rooted, that the Air Force wants to get control of all aviation;

(2) The corresponding psychosis of the Air Force that the Navy is trying to encroach upon the strategic air prerogatives of the Air Force.[17]

The intensity of the disputes comes from the fact that each service sees its essence as threatened by the presumed intentions of the other. The Air Force fears that the Navy will seek to expand its air power until it dominates the strategic offensive mission. On the other hand, the Navy fears that the Air Force seeks to take over the entire air mission—controlling all airplanes, whether based at sea or on land—or, at a minimum, all airplanes based on land, even those involving control of the seas.[18]

Some Navy aviators trace the fight back to 1925, when the Army Air Force group headed by General William A. Mitchell sought to take complete control of all air forces, and the conflict raised its head intermittently throughout the cold war period. In the post–World War II conflict over unification of the air forces, the Air Force sought to get control over all land-based air operations. The struggle was further exacerbated by the fact that naval air enthusiasts, having recently won the struggle for dominance within the Navy, were not prepared to yield anything to the Air Force. In the end, the controversy over naval aviation became the stumbling block to Navy support for unification, which was necessary to get congressional approval. A compromise was finally reached when President Truman allowed the Navy authority over aircraft to be used in conjunction with all matters related to control of the sea.

The controversy was not over, however. In 1948, the Air Force argued for absorption of all naval air functions into its forces, while the Navy went on the attack by criticizing the effectiveness of Air Force strategic bombers and arguing that supercarriers could perform the strategic bombing mission more effectively. That led to the famous revolt of the admirals: when the Navy was denied authority to build supercarriers, several admirals resigned and took their case to the public.

In the 1950s Navy aviation commanders and the Air Force quarreled about the proposed nuclear-powered airplane. The Air Force, originally uninter-

---

17. Millis, *The Forrestal Diaries*, p. 466 (cited hereafter as *Forrestal Diaries*).

18. On the controversy between the Navy and the Air Force over air power, see *Forrestal Diaries*, pp. 222–26, 228–29; Caraley, *The Politics of Military Unification*, pp. 79, 96; and Hammond, "Super Carriers and B–36 Bombers," pp. 488, 538–39.

ested in the project, began to be concerned when the Navy pressed for a nuclear-powered airplane that could fly off aircraft carriers and perform the strategic mission. From then on both services vied for the nuclear-powered airplane despite increasing evidence that such an aircraft simply was not technologically feasible.[19] The dispute arose again in connection with the TFX—a proposed joint fighter. The Air Force sought an airplane that would carry only nuclear weapons and could carry them over long distances. The Navy sought a short-takeoff plane with limited range. Robert Art explained:

> The Navy was so insistent because of its own perspectives. It had no real interest in seeing a plane built with such a long ferry range. If missiles had reduced the strategic and interdiction roles of aircraft, including naval aircraft, a plane that could fly across the Atlantic, nonstop, without refueling, and that could be deployed from semi-prepared fields would be even more injurious to the Navy's interests: such a plane could only downgrade the role of the aircraft carrier. If it could fly over oceans, there would be no need to transport it over them. If it could operate from semi-prepared fields, there would be less need for carriers to stand offshore to service it. On the other hand, the Missileer was the ideal aircraft for the Navy. It would protect the fleet, including the aircraft carriers, from an enemy air attack. It would thereby ensure the safety of aircraft like the F-4H, which were designed to perform tactical missions from aircraft carriers.
>
> Each service thus saw its future threatened by the other's TFX design. The Air Force wanted to extend the life of the airplane. The Navy wanted to do the same for the aircraft carrier. Both knew that the TFX program was going to be costly. Each knew that the supply of defense funds was limited. Neither wanted its future programs jeopardized by those of the other. The result of these opposing perspectives was three months of interminable discussion, delay, and disagreement.[20]

The controversy has also affected combat operations. In Korea and especially in Vietnam, the Navy sought as large a role as possible for carrier-based aircraft in an effort to demonstrate that carriers could operate as effectively, if not more effectively, than land-based air power. The Air Force, on the other hand, sought to restrict the role of the Navy, arguing that it could deliver weapons more effectively and more cheaply. The controversy probably led each service to exaggerate the effectiveness of its bombing in order to outshine

19. Lambright, *Shooting Down the Nuclear Plane*, pp. 9, 13–14.
20. Art, *The TFX Decision*, p. 46.

the other. After Vietnam, neither service feared for the existence of its air capability, but they continued to feud over their relative roles; neither service has any doubt that the other service will always go after a larger share of the air mission. Inasmuch as both Air Force and the Navy aviators see flying combat air missions as their essence, the conflict between them has been inevitable and has shaped a good deal of the overall rivalry between the two services, which has continued through the Gulf War and the war in Iraq.

Combat Air Support

In contrast to the Navy, which opposed unification of the air forces and favored the status quo, the Army was anxious in the late 1940s to divest itself of its air units in order to protect the essence of its ground combat mission. It therefore was in no position to argue very hard about its need to keep some air capability. Thus the Army came to depend on the Air Force not only for transport and interdiction but also for combat support—airplanes that fly in the immediate vicinity of a battle to give support to infantry.

In the 1950s, the Army began to have second thoughts about its decision. It recognized that the Air Force was giving its highest priority to strategic bombardment and therefore was neglecting missions of concern to the Army. The Army considered its autonomy to be at stake, and the Air Force believed a potential threat to its essence was developing. General Matthew B. Ridgway described the situation in the following terms in his memoirs:

> There is an understandable opposition in the Air Force to the development of those types and the procurement of those number of aircraft for which the Army has so vital a need. The helicopter and the convertiplane do not now fit into the pattern of the Air Force's primary missions, or the limitations of its budget. Nor does the young airman want to fly the close-support and assault aircraft—the dive bombers, cargo ships, the transport planes that carry the paratroopers. He wants to fly jets, for that is where the glamour and the glory lies. And I don't find it in my heart to blame him.
>
> But somebody must man these planes and the Army, of course, has considered seeking to relieve the Air Force of its unwanted burden. Plans have been advanced whereby the Army would develop its own specialized assault aircraft, and recruit and train its own pilots to fly them, and to a slight degree this has been done. If neither manpower nor dollars were to be considered, such an idea would be feasible. Since manpower

and dollars both are very much to be considered, the prospect that the Army will be able to develop its own aviation in the near future is highly improbable.

Ridgway concluded:

I think perhaps there is a balance to be found somewhere, a reasonable compromise. Of one thing, though, I am sure. To do its job on the battlefield, to gain its objectives in the least time with the least loss of life, the Army must have the support of combat aircraft that can fly in any kind of weather, under all conditions incident to enemy interference, both in the air and from the ground, and deliver its bomb load, or its rockets, on target with the accuracy of a field gun. If the Air Force should develop such planes, we would be deeply pleased. If they continue to ignore our needs in this respect, we eventually will have to develop them *ourselves*.[21]

Toward the end of the 1950s, the Army was pressing an all-out assault on Air Force control of tactical air. After his retirement as Army Chief of Staff, General Maxwell D. Taylor made public the Army position:

Since 1947, the Army has been dependent upon the Air Force for tactical air support, tactical air lift, and for long-range air transport. Throughout this period, the Army has been a dissatisfied customer, feeling that the Air Force has not fully discharged its obligations undertaken at the time of unification. The Air Force, having something which the Army wanted, has been in a position to put a price upon cooperation and to insist upon acquiescence in Air Force views on such controversial issues as air-ground support procedures, air re-supply, and control of air space over the battlefield. As technical improvements in weapons and equipment offered the Army the possibility of escaping from dependence upon the Air Force, the latter has vigorously resisted these efforts and has succeeded in obtaining the support of the Secretary of Defense in imposing limitations on the size and weight of aircraft procured by the Army, on the ranges of Army missiles, and on the radius of Army activities in advance of the front line of combat.

As a result of the controversies arising from the dependence of the Army on the Air Force, the two services have been constantly at loggerheads. They have been unable to agree on a doctrine for cooperation in battle. They are at odds as to the adequacy of levels of Air Force support for the Army, and as to the suitability of types of Air Force equipment to

21. Ridgway, *Soldier*, pp. 314–15.

furnish this support. Because of the very high performance of their air-planes, designed primarily to meet the needs of the air battle today, the Air Force is not equipped to discharge its responsibilities to the Army in ground combat. Having witnessed this unhappy state of affairs for over a decade, I am convinced that the Army must be freed from this tutelage and receive all the organic means habitually necessary for prompt and sustained combat on the ground. It should have its own organic tactical air support and tactical air lift, or rather the new weapons and equipment which will perform the functions presently comprehended under those two headings.

Special restrictions of size, weight, and in the case of weapons, of range should be abolished forever and the Army encouraged to exploit technology to the maximum to improve its weapons and equipment habitually necessary for prompt and sustained ground combat. It is essential to end the present fragmentation of the land force function, particularly at a time when the role of land forces should assume increased importance under the strategy of Flexible Responses.[22]

In return, Taylor proposed that the Army cede the continental air defense mission to the Air Force. Since that was a mission that neither considered part of its essence, Taylor was not giving up very much, nor would the Air Force see it as much of a compromise.

The Air Force was nevertheless in a bind. Unwilling to devote substantial resources to development of tactical air power and unwilling to adapt itself to the Army's requirements for tactical air support, the Air Force found itself without a convincing rebuttal from the national viewpoint.

By the time of Vietnam, the Army was persuading others that it needed to develop its own combat air support. Secretary of Defense Robert McNamara had been pushing air mobility, thereby getting the Army into helicopters to carry troops. Improvements in helicopter technology enabled the Army to begin using support helicopters for combat missions as well as troop transport and so to reduce its dependence on the Air Force. Despite the increased attention that the Air Force gave to tactical combat operations in response to the Army's encroachment, the Army emerged from the Vietnam War with more pilots than the Air Force and with even greater determination to develop its own organic air capability. It has continued to do so, developing major helicopter group support capabilities, but it has failed to wrest the fixed-wing combat role from the Air Force.

22. Taylor, *The Uncertain Trumpet*, pp. 168–70.

The Role of the Marines

The Marine Corps sees itself as an elite combat unit primarily designed for amphibious operations—that is, landing shiploads of armed men under combat conditions. Some Marine Corps officers would like to see their service also take on specialized ground combat operations not involving amphibious operations. The conflict between the Marine Corps and the Army, like that between the Navy and the Air Force, goes to the essence of each service. The controversy about the definition of the functions of the Marines and the size of the Corps was a major issue in the unification battle of the late 1940s.

Some Marine Corps officers feared that the Army wanted to integrate the Marines into the Army as a specialized unit. If nothing else, the Army sought to limit the Marine Corps to the role of auxiliary to the naval fleet. That would limit the job of the Marine Corps to accompanying landing parties to protect Americans in wartime and during disturbances in foreign countries and to providing expeditionary forces to attack bases that were of exclusive interest to the Navy and that could be overcome by small combat units.[23] The principal area of contention then was large amphibious operations. The Marines argued that such operations were more clearly within their scope of activity, while the Army suggested that such operations should come under Army control.

In the mid-1950s, the Army, struggling for control over the limited-war strategy, feared that the Navy and the Marine Corps together would seek to take over that mission. The Marines could argue that they were the only integrated force containing its own sea transport and air combat capability and therefore that they were the most effective unit for limited-war operations. General Taylor spoke out:

> As for the Marines, the Army acknowledges their potential contribution to limited-war situations occurring on or near the coast but resists vigorously any suggestion that the Marines should become a second Army and take over any part of the Army's role of prompt and sustained ground combat.[24]

During the Vietnam War, the Marines were assigned to general combat responsibilities and occupied a critical area close to the demilitarized zone. In conducting operations in this area, the Marines sought to demonstrate that they could carry out counterinsurgency operations more effectively than the Army. The Army, on the other hand, sought to show that Marines, because of

23. Caraley, *The Politics of Military Unification*, p. 67. See also *Forrestal Diaries*, pp. 224–25, and Hammond, "Super Carriers and B–36 Bombers," pp. 529–30.

24. Taylor, *The Uncertain Trumpet*, p. 100.

their independence, could not be effectively fitted into an Army chain of command. That debate probably affected the Army unwillingness to adopt the strategy of combined action patrols pioneered by the Marine Corps and may also have affected the decision by General William Westmoreland to assign the Marines the highly difficult task of defending the Khe Sanh base, close to the demilitarized zone.[25] The Marines have participated in major combat operations, including the Gulf War and the war in Iraq, but they have sought to resist being assigned to peacekeeping missions, including the U.S. occupation of Iraq.

The Question of the CIA

The CIA frequently collides with the military services over the conduct of relatively large-scale covert operations and intelligence gathering programs. Those operations lie at the heart of the CIA mission as conceived by many of its career personnel, and yet they arouse the misgivings of the Pentagon about creating an alternative military capability. The debate is largely carried on behind closed doors, but it came into the open in the controversies surrounding the Bay of Pigs invasion, the Cuban missile crisis, U.S. actions in Indochina, and the war in Iraq in 2003.

The CIA had responsibility for training the Cuban forces to be used in the Bay of Pigs invasion and for planning the military operations. The Joint Chiefs of Staff gave only cursory review to the plans and later were in a position to argue that the operations had been botched by the CIA. As a result, President Kennedy turned responsibility for such operations over to the Pentagon.[26]

In the opening days of the Cuban missile crisis, the military services, particularly the Air Force, challenged the CIA's control of U-2 flights over Cuba. As long as U-2s were used in relatively peaceful situations in which the likelihood of combat was small, the Air Force was more or less content to have the CIA manage the program. However, as the possibility of conflict heated up in the Caribbean, the U-2 forays began to look more and more to the Air Force like a separate air capability, and a campaign was mounted that ultimately succeeded in taking that function away from the CIA.

The dispute over U.S. operations in Indochina centered on CIA influence over the Montagnards and other irregular forces in Laos and South Vietnam. Early in the 1960s, the military apparently succeeded in having the Special Forces take over arrangements with the Montagnards, but the CIA seems to

25. Corson, *The Betrayal,* pp. 77–80.
26. Sorensen, *Kennedy,* p. 630.

have counteracted by gaining substantial influence over the Special Forces themselves.[27]

This struggle has factored into U.S. strategy in Afghanistan and Iraq, with the CIA and the military competing for the lead in the covert combat operations that preceded large-scale operations in both wars and fighting over operational control of the Predator unmanned aircraft, especially when it is outfitted to fire munitions.

Other Conflicts

From time to time, new technological developments have produced other role and mission conflicts among the armed services, often overlapping with the ongoing disputes described above. In the early post–World War II period, the development of nuclear weapons produced a fight over which branch would be assigned the weapons. The Air Force originally had a virtual monopoly on nuclear weapons. That control was first challenged successfully by the Navy on the grounds that its carriers could effectively deliver such weapons; later the Army introduced tactical nuclear weapons that would be supplied to ground forces.

The development of strategic missiles also produced controversy over roles and missions, although it lacked the intensity of the other fights because it did not threaten the essence of any of the services. The Air Force, however, did see some infringement on its strategic primacy. It tried for a while, without success, to prevent the development of the Polaris submarine force, a program pushed by civilian analysts and scientists rather than by the Navy itself. The Air Force was more successful in resisting the Army's effort to enter into the strategic offensive realm through the development of medium-range missiles. For a time, both services had medium-range missile programs, but the Air Force was able to secure authority over the development of such weapons.[28]

All three services competed for a role in space exploration, with the Air Force first getting the upper hand and then losing status to the newly created National Aeronautics and Space Administration (NASA) in 1957. It sought to recoup that loss by infiltrating NASA with active duty Air Force officers.

27. Hilsman, *To Move a Nation: The Politics of Foreign Policy in the Administration of John F. Kennedy*, p. 455.
28. Armacost, *The Politics of Weapons Innovation*, p. 63.

IMPLICATIONS OF ROLES AND MISSIONS

The conflict over roles and missions, particularly as it relates to the essence of each agency's activity, produces several characteristic forms of behavior in the pursuit of organizational interests.

—*Disputes over roles and missions affect the information reported to senior officials.* For example, according to a former Air Force intelligence officer, both the Air Force and the Navy exaggerated the effectiveness of their bombing of North Vietnam. Both recognized that the postwar dispute over the Navy's bombing role would be affected by evaluation of their bombing operations in Vietnam. Each service, believing (or fearing) that the other would exaggerate, decided to emphasize the positive in order to protect its position.[29]

—*In implementing missions that they know to be coveted by another organization, organizations may bend over backward to avoid giving any reason to increase their bureaucratic competitor's share of the mission.* Townsend Hoopes, who was then under secretary of the Air Force, reports that he saw this process at work in the Air Force request for an additional seventeen tactical fighter squadrons as part of a proposed increase in American forces in Vietnam in March 1968 following the Tet offensive:

> Moreover it was a matter of some delicacy in Army-Air Force relations because it touched the boundary line between the assigned roles and missions of the two Services. If the Air Force did not provide close air support in a ratio satisfactory to the Army, that would strengthen the Army's argument for developing its own means of close support. Already, through the development of helicopter gunships of increasing power, speed, and sophistication, the Army had pressed against that boundary.[30]

—*In periods of crisis, career officials calculate how alternative policies and patterns of action will affect future definitions of roles and missions.* Participants have learned over time that changes in roles and missions frequently occur during crises. Thus an organization concerned about its mission and desiring either to expand it or prevent others from expanding theirs at its expense will be particularly alert to both challenges and opportunities during a crisis. Because this phenomenon is widely understood, organizations must be on guard: they cannot trust other organizations not to take advantage of a crisis. Frequently, an organization whose functions were expanded during a

29. Blachman, "The Stupidity of Intelligence," pp. 271–79.
30. Hoopes, *The Limits of Intervention,* pp. 161–62.

crisis tries to argue that it has now established a precedent and should continue to perform the new function. Thus organizations seldom put forward options that might lead to changes in roles and missions that are perceived to be detrimental to their essence. If such options are suggested by other participants, they may argue that those options are infeasible. Participants may also feel obliged to distort information reported to senior officials in order to guard against the danger that it will affect roles and missions in the future. Disputes over roles and missions also affect policy stands and the way policy decisions are implemented.

During the Cuban missile crisis, for example, both the CIA and the military services were concerned with how intelligence operations during the crisis would affect future definitions of roles and missions. A key episode was described by Graham Allison:

> The ten-day delay between decision [to direct a special flight over western Cuba] and flight is another organizational story. At the October 4 meeting, where the decision to dispatch the flight over western Cuba was made, the State Department spelled out the consequences of the loss of a U-2 over Cuba in the strongest terms. The Defense Department took this opportunity to raise an issue important to its concerns. Given the increased danger that a U-2 would be downed, the pilots should be officers in uniform rather than CIA agents, so the Air Force should assume responsibility for U-2 flights over Cuba. To the contrary, the CIA argued that this was an intelligence operation and thus within the CIA's jurisdiction. Besides, CIA U-2s had been modified in certain ways that gave them advantages over Air Force U-2s in avoiding Soviet SAMs. Five days passed while the State Department pressed for less risky alternatives, and the Air Force (in Department of Defense guise) and the CIA engaged in territorial disputes. On October 9, COMOR [the Committee on Overhead Reconnaissance] approved a flight plan over San Cristobal, but, to the CIA's dismay, the Air Force rather than the CIA would take charge of the mission. At this point details become sketchy, but several members of the intelligence community have speculated that an Air Force pilot in an Air Force U-2 attempted a high altitude over-flight on October 9 that "flamed out," i.e., lost power, and thus had to descend in order to restart its engine. A second round between Air Force and CIA followed, as a result of which Air Force pilots were trained to fly CIA U-2s. A successful over-flight did not take place until October 14.[31]

31. Allison, *Essence of Decision*, pp. 122–23.

Autonomy

Career officials of an organization believe that they are in a better position than others to determine what capabilities they should have and how they should fulfill their mission. They attach very high priority to controlling their own resources so that they can use those resources to support the essence of the organization. They want to spend the money allocated to them as they choose, to station their manpower as they choose, and to implement policy in their own fashion. They resist efforts by senior officials to control their activities.

In particular, priority is attached to maintaining control over budgets. Organizations are often prepared to accept less money with greater control rather than more money with less control. Even with fewer funds, they are able to protect the essence of their activities. The priority attached to autonomy is shown by the experiences of various secretaries of defense. Robert McNamara caused great consternation in the Pentagon in 1961 by instituting new decision procedures that reduced the autonomy of the armed services, despite the fact that he increased defense spending by $6 billion and did not directly seek to alter their roles and missions. Melvin P. Laird, in contrast, improved Pentagon morale in 1969 by increasing service autonomy in budget matters while reducing the defense budget by more than $4 billion. At the start of the Clinton administration, Secretary Les Aspin caused great concern by suggesting that he would reduce both autonomy and spending. During the early days of the administration of the second President Bush, the military reacted with caution to Secretary Rumsfeld because he threatened both the autonomy and the roles of the services, even as he increased spending.

Organizations also seek total operational control over the forces required to carry out a mission and are reluctant to undertake shared operations involving forces of other organizations. To avoid encroachment by other agencies, they seek to report directly to the president, in hopes that that will mean infrequent interference in their affairs. For example, the Office of Strategic Services pressed hard at the end of World War II for the creation of the Central Intelligence Agency, which would no longer be subordinate to the Joint Chiefs of Staff but would report directly to the president. The quest for autonomy also means that organizations resist undertaking operations in which control is shared with foreign governments; the military services therefore seek bases under U.S. control and resist integrating forces.

We have already mentioned that the quest for autonomy on the part of the military services affected the unification struggle in the late 1940s. The drive to establish the Air Force as a separate service was fundamentally a quest for autonomy, and Air Force doctrine and strategy were stated in terms that would justify autonomy.[32] The Navy resisted the unification plan precisely because it saw the plan as a threat to its autonomy. Fearing that the Air Force would use the integrated structure in an effort to dominate the other services, the Navy argued that the secretary of defense should be coordinator of the services but not have operational control over them. The Army was in a dilemma: it had to choose between autonomy for its operations by maintaining an integrated air combat arm or give that up in order to prevent Air Force officers from coming to dominate the Army. It chose to "let the Air Force go" in order to maintain autonomy over its favored field of action, ground combat operations. It has been struggling since then to regain some air capability.

The State Department's quest for autonomy has led it to reject White House interference in its ongoing operations and to resist non-career ambassadors as well as special presidential envoys.

The quest for autonomy has a significant impact on the stands and actions of organizations in general. The following patterns show up repeatedly.

—In negotiations among organizations about desirable actions, each prefers an agreement that leaves it free to pursue its own interests even if that appears to an outside observer to lead to an uncoordinated and hence inefficient policy. Thus both the Air Force and the Navy preferred the situation in which Polaris missiles were controlled independently of Air Force missiles and strategic bombers because it allowed each service to develop its own strategic doctrine and its own targeting objectives. Both services, but especially the Navy, resisted efforts to create an integrated command, and only with great reluctance did the Navy acquiesce in a joint strategic targeting organization set up under intense civilian pressure in the early 1960s. In Vietnam, the services conducted largely independent combat operations, with each service getting a share of the target areas. Each preferred that to an overall plan that would limit its autonomy. While the military services have had to yield to intense congressional pressure to conduct joint operations, they continue to support strategies that permit them as much autonomy as possible.

The State Department has frequently maintained its autonomy in the conduct of diplomatic negotiations and political relations with foreign governments by leaving the Treasury Department and the foreign aid agencies free to conduct their own bilateral negotiations and arrangements on trade and aid matters. That tendency is reinforced by the preference of other agencies to conduct their own foreign relations without interference from the State

32. Smith, *The Air Force Plans for Peace*, pp. 14, 27, 28.

Department. In recent years, the proliferation of overseas activities by a wide variety of Washington agencies has created an expanding management challenge for the State Department as it tries to house these agencies in embassies and ensure at least a modicum of policy coordination of their activities.

After 9/11, when many stressed the need for a central office to coordinate counterterrorism activities, the CIA and the FBI resisted efforts to integrate the counterterrorism effort as they struggled to expand their roles.

—In devising options for senior officials, organizations tend to agree on proposals that exclude any joint operations and that leave each free to go its own way and continue to do what it prefers to do. As one keen student of the Washington bureaucracy observed:

> Over time, each agency has acquired certain "pet projects" which its senior officials promote. These are often carried out by one agency despite concern and even mid-level opposition from others, as part of a tacit trade-off: "We'll let you do your thing, and you let us do ours." Such deals, or "non-aggression treaties," are almost never explicit, but are nonetheless well understood by the participants. The results from such arrangements obviously vary. Sometimes programs are in direct conflict. Waste and duplication are frequent; lack of information about what one's colleagues are doing is common. These are all direct costs of the multi-agency system, which is too large and scattered to come under one driver.[33]

In budgetary negotiations, organizations most often seek a compromise whereby subordinate officials are committed to set limits but are free to spend money however they see fit within that limit.

—In presenting policy proposals to senior officials, organizations typically indicate that the proposed course of action is infeasible unless they are given full freedom to carry it out. During the 1958 Quemoy crisis in the Taiwan Strait, the Joint Chiefs of Staff repeatedly pressed for freedom to use nuclear weapons on their own authority and informed the president that they could guarantee to defend the offshore islands against the Chinese attack only if granted that autonomy.[34] In developing their preferred overseas base structure, the armed forces are especially concerned with ensuring their freedom to conduct operations without the interference of allied governments. That leads them to insist on the need for unambiguous U.S. control over bases, as

33. Holbrooke, "The Machine That Fails," p. 70.
34. Eisenhower, *The White House Years*, vol. 2, *Waging Peace, 1956–1961*, p. 299 (cited hereafter as *Waging Peace*).

they did in the case of the Trust Territories in the Pacific and for many years in the case of Okinawa. Where that is not feasible, the armed services press for bases in countries that they judge to be unlikely to object to any operations that they wish to conduct. That was apparently a major motive for the military's efforts to develop bases in Spain.[35] In the post–cold war period, however, U.S. military autonomy over bases outside the United States has declined. The military nonetheless seek to establish bases in countries such as the Central Asia "Stans," whose governments, they believe, are less likely to seek to impose restrictions on their activities.

—An organization seeks to guard its autonomy by presenting only a single option to the president or to Cabinet officials so that they cannot choose an option that might interfere with the organization's preferred course of action. U. Alexis Johnson, for many years the senior State Department Foreign Service officer, has said that he objected to President Kennedy's introduction of procedures that prevented the Secretary of State and the Secretary of Defense from conferring with each other and arriving at a consensus before meeting with the president. Since then the role of the national security adviser has made it much more difficult if not impossible for the two secretaries to present a single option to the president.[36]

Organizational Morale

An organization functions effectively only if its personnel are highly motivated. They must believe that what they are doing makes a difference and promotes the national interest; that the organization's efforts are appreciated and that its role in the scheme of things is not diminishing (and preferably that it is increasing); and that the organization controls its own resources. Above all, the career official must believe that there is room for advancement in the organization and that the organization is seeking to protect his or her opportunities for advancement. In order to keep the possibility of promotion to top positions open, an organization resists efforts to contract the size of the organization (unless the contraction is necessary to protect the essence of its activities). It also strives to ensure that top jobs are held primarily by its own career officials. Thus the Foreign Service generally opposes the appointment of non-career ambassadors, although it has learned to accept some non-career

35. Lowi, "Bases in Spain," pp. 677–78.

36. U. Alexis Johnson, John F. Kennedy Library Oral History Interview, pp. 14–15. See also Schlesinger, *A Thousand Days: John F. Kennedy in the White House,* p. 557, and Scott, "The Department of State," p. 6.

appointees as inevitable. The military services struggle for the post of chairman of the Joint Chiefs of Staff as well as positions that put their representatives in charge of integrated commands (such as commander in chief in Europe and in the Pacific). They oppose efforts to close out functions if doing so would mean a reduction in the number of senior personnel.

Career personnel are assigned to appear to give everyone a reasonable chance of promotion rather than to put people in the slots where they are likely to do the most good. Military officers compete for roles in what is seen as the essence of a service's activity rather than in other functions where promotion is less likely. Thus the commander of the ill-fated *Pueblo* tells us of his great disappointment at being appointed commander of that ship rather than of a submarine.[37] So, too, Army officers compete for roles in combat organizations rather than advisory missions. Foreign Service officers sought assignments in political sections and on regional desks rather than in economic sections or in specialized bureaus when such assignments were perceived to be the key to advancement.

An organization resists functions that it believes may interfere with career advancement patterns either by bringing in people who would not be eligible for the top spots or people who would, because of their senior rank, fill the top spots and foreclose advancement for others. Both considerations affected the Air Force's decision not to fight for the air defense mission at the time of the separation of the Air Force from the Army.[38]

Organizations also seek to maintain morale by laying down codes of conduct for their staff members that seek to avoid conflict within the group. Andrew M. Scott reports, for example, a series of injunctions about how Foreign Service officers are to deal with each other: "Play the game, don't rock the boat, don't make waves, minimize risk taking."[39]

Organizations may also seek to maintain morale by seeking a homogeneous group of career officials. According to research cited by Harold Seidman, both the military services and the Foreign Service were relatively homogeneous during the cold war, although the two groups differed in terms of the area of the country from which they tended to draw their personnel.[40]

Because they have learned the vital importance of morale in the effective functioning of an organization, bureaucrats give close attention to the likely effects on morale of any change in policy or patterns of action. They shun

37. Bucher, *Bucher: My Story,* pp. 2–3.
38. Smith, *The Air Force Plans for Peace,* pp. 101–2.
39. Scott, "The Department of State," p. 4. See also Argyris, *Some Causes of Organizational Ineffectiveness within the Department of State,* pp. 13.
40. Seidman, *Politics, Position, and Power: The Dynamics of Federal Organization,* p. 113.

changes that they feel will severely damage morale—even changes that would probably improve the organization's effectiveness in carrying out its mission—and they are especially concerned about the effects on promotion patterns. Short-run accomplishment of goals and even increases in budgets take second place to the long-run health of the organization.

For example, almost every observer of U.S. operations in Vietnam concluded that extending the tour of duty of commissioned Army officers from one year to two or three years would substantially improve the U.S. military performance. Yet the Army refused to make the change. That was not because the Army disagreed with the assessment of effectiveness; rather, the Army believed that there would be immediate adverse effects on morale if officers were sent to Vietnam for either an indefinite period or a prolonged period such as three years. In addition, particularly in the early stages of the war, Army leaders felt that there would be long-range morale problems if only a small percentage of career Army officers had combat experience in Vietnam, since those officers who did would have an inside track on promotions. They believed it desirable not only for morale but also for improving the effectiveness of the service over the long run to give as many career officers as possible experience in Vietnam.[41]

Budgets

Career officials examine any proposal for its effect on their organization's budget. All other things being equal, they prefer larger to smaller budgets and support policy changes that they believe will lead to larger budgets.

There is, however, a substantial asymmetry between the Department of Defense and the Department of State in regard to the impact of policy issues on budgets. The State Department budget is relatively small, and few of the foreign policy matters with which the State Department deals have any direct effect on its budget. For the military services, most policy issues are likely to have important budgetary implications. For example, the ABM program had no implications for the State Department budget, but it had very important consequences for the budget of the Army and the Defense Department as a whole.

An organization is usually quick to question whether a proposed change that generates a new function will in fact lead to a budget increase or merely add to its responsibilities without any corresponding increase in its budget.

41. Yarmolinsky, *The Military Establishment*, p. 20; Hersh, *My Lai 4: A Report on the Massacre and Its Aftermath*, p. 6.

The calculation of whether a new function will lead to an increased budget depends in part upon the nature of the budget process. For example, during the 1950s the budgets for the military services were largely determined by allocating fixed percentages of an overall budget established by the president. In general, new responsibilities had to be financed out of existing budgets. By contrast, during the 1960s there was no explicit budget ceiling. The budget was determined by the secretary of defense on the basis of functional categories and responsibilities. Thus the services believed that new functions tended to mean increased budgets.

Whether a new function leads to new funds (and hence should be desirable) or to a reallocation of old funds (and hence may need to be resisted) depends also in part on whether the new function is seen as closely related to existing functions. For example, the Army was interested in acquiring responsibility for the deployment of medium-range ballistic missiles (MRBMs) in the 1950s, in part because doing so would give the Army a strategic nuclear role that it hoped would justify increasing its existing share of the overall defense budget. On the other hand, the Air Force recognized that MRBMs would simply be considered another strategic weapon and that it would be forced to finance missile development and deployment out of the existing Air Force budget. Thus, in terms of budget interests, the Army sought the MRBM role while the Air Force was reluctant to take it on. On the other hand, the Air Force's desire to protect its existing roles and missions meant that if there was to be an MRBM program, the Air Force was determined to have it.

Organizations are vigilant not only about their absolute share of the budget but also about their relative share of a larger budget. That observation applies particularly to each of the military services, although it may also apply to various branches of USAID, the overseas assistance organization. They fear that once established levels change in an adverse direction, the trend may continue, leading to a substantial reduction in the activities of a particular service, which could have substantial effects on morale.

As a precaution, each of the armed services tends to resist proposals that, although they promise more funds, may lead to a relatively smaller increase in its budget than in the budgets of other parts of the defense establishment. The services individually prefer the certainty of a particular share of the budget to an unknown situation in which budgets may increase but shares may change. For example, in 1957, the Gaither Committee appointed by President Dwight Eisenhower recommended substantial increases in the budgets of all three services, arguing the need for secure second-strike retaliatory forces and for larger limited-war capabilities. However, none of the services supported the proposals, in part because none was certain how the expanded budget would be divided.[42]

Organizations' Stands on Issues

Participants who look to organizational interests to define national security interests seldom feel the need to engage in a full-scale analysis of a particular issue. Rather, their reactions reflect "grooved thinking": they respond to a particular stimulus in a set way. That approach leads to the emergence of a typical pattern of responses within an organization. We have already referred to the traditional State Department opposition to negotiations by presidential emissaries or the president himself and its opposition to proposals that would appear to require the State Department to involve itself in direct intervention abroad. State Department officials often propose negotiations as the way to solve a problem and want to keep talks going longer than others might want in hopes that mutual concessions will lead to a diplomatic agreement.

Each military service supports foreign policies that justify maintaining the forces that it believes are necessary to maintain the essence of the service and favors strategies that presume that precisely those forces will be used in the event of hostilities. Each opposes mixed forces or combined service operations. The military usually also support proposals that give them new equipment. They tend to emphasize the procurement of forces and overall force structure even at the cost of combat readiness and real combat capability.[43]

The military services view issues involving American bases overseas in terms of the interests of their own organizations. Each service favors the retention of the bases that it uses and that suit a military strategy that accords with its force structure. Senior officers are particularly sensitive to possible actions that might jeopardize their bases. According to Arthur Schlesinger Jr., Secretary of State Dean Rusk discovered that when he proposed that the Bay of Pigs invasion be transferred to the American naval base at Guantanamo.

> He [Rusk] reverted to a suggestion with which he had startled the Joint Chiefs during one of the meetings. This was that the operation fan out from Guantanamo with the prospect of retreating to the base in case of failure. He remarked, "It is interesting to observe the Pentagon people. They are perfectly willing to put the President's head on the block, but they recoil from the idea of doing anything which might risk Guantanamo."[44]

42. Halperin, "The Gaither Committee and the Policy Process," pp. 360–84.
43. Enthoven and Smith, *How Much Is Enough?* pp. 10–11.
44. Schlesinger, *A Thousand Days*, p. 257.

The attitude of the armed services toward military commitments and the use of force is surprising to observers who expect a bellicose approach. In general, the military oppose new commitments for the United States and have in general been opposed to or neutral on postwar American interventions. (On the other hand, when interventions do occur, the services push for authority to employ the full range of available forces.)

The services are often reluctant to take on new commitments, feeling that their forces are already stretched too thin. The military have learned that the allocations given to them do not necessarily correspond to the number of commitments that the United States undertakes, and therefore they see new commitments as adding new obligations without additional forces. Dean Acheson related a typical example from the era when the French wanted help to hold on to Indochina:

> As the year wore on without much progress and we ourselves became bogged down in the negotiations at Panmunjom, our sense of frustration grew. A review of the situation in late August, before I left for a series of meetings in the autumn of 1951, brought warning from the Joint Chiefs of Staff against any statement that would commit—or seem to the French under future eventualities to commit—United States armed forces to Indochina. We did not waver from this policy.[45]

On the issue of American military intervention, the armed services have been in general quite cautious. At different times they have resisted proposals for intervention, remained neutral, or asked for authority to use all their existing forces to make the gamble of involvement less risky if taken at all. Professionally they prefer a conservative estimate of the readiness of forces, and they are sensitive to the danger of using forces where they might be defeated or where they would be drawn away from the primary theater of operations. This military attitude first manifested itself during the Berlin crisis of 1948. General Lucius Clay, who had direct responsibility for Berlin, favored sending an armed convoy down the road from the American zone of Germany to Berlin. President Harry S. Truman was prepared to support this proposal if it won the endorsement of the Joint Chiefs. The Joint Chiefs, however, refused to recommend such action. Moreover, the Air Force was itself opposed even to the airlift.[46]

---

45. Acheson, *Present at the Creation: My Years in the State Department*, p. 675.

46. Murphy, *Diplomat among Warriors*, p. 316; Truman, *Memoirs*, vol. 2, *Years of Trial and Hope*, pp. 124–26 (cited hereafter as *Years of Trial and Hope*).

At the time of the outbreak of the Korean War in June 1950, the military made no recommendation for intervention. Indeed, the top commanders were known to believe that though Taiwan was vital to the security of the United States, Korea was not. Consequently Truman was forced to agree to defend Taiwan as the price of gaining military acquiescence in the Korean intervention. The military were not the driving force in planning the Bay of Pigs operation, which was largely a CIA endeavor. In the case of the possibility of intervention in Laos in 1961, the military were opposed unless granted full authority to use all forces. They also pressed for an all-out strike if any action were to be taken against Cuba in 1962. The services were not the driving force behind the American involvement in Vietnam.

In the run-up to the Gulf War in 1991, General Colin Powell, the chairman of the Joint Chiefs, requested a meeting with the president to ensure that he was giving equal weight to nonmilitary strategies. Powell later explained his concern, as follows:

> War is a deadly game, and I do not believe in spending the lives of Americans lightly. My responsibility that day was to lay out all options for the nation's civilian leadership. However, in our democracy it is the President, not generals, who make decisions about going to war. I had done my duty. The sanctions clock was ticking down. If the President was right, if he decided it must be war, then my job was to make sure we were ready to go in and win.[47]

However, military reluctance to enter into half-hearted or ill-backed commitments leads to the desire for increased capability to carry out a mission once intervention begins. As soon as the United States committed itself to the defense of South Korea, the Joint Chiefs pressed for a rapid buildup of American forces. Similarly in the case of Vietnam, the Joint Chiefs pressed for a larger, quicker buildup and for attacks on North Vietnam. In the Gulf War, the military brought the full weight of their conventional forces to bear. Key military officers and Colin Powell, the former chairman of the Joint Chiefs and the then current secretary of state, cautioned the second Bush administration against going to war with Iraq. But once it was clear that the president would go forward, against their better judgment, they called for larger forces than Secretary Rumsfeld and his civilian advisers thought necessary.

In the early years of the cold war, the services pressed for the right to use nuclear weapons in any military conflict. The first such effort came during the Berlin blockade, when the military, supported by Secretary of Defense James

47. Colin Powell, *My American Journey*, pp. 466–67.

Forrestal, pressed the president to agree that the atomic bomb would be used if necessary.[48] President Eisenhower did make a generalized decision that the armed forces could plan on the use of nuclear weapons in the event of conflict,[49] but he resisted pressure to delegate authority in any particular crisis. The military nonetheless continued to press him—for example, during the Quemoy crisis of 1958.[50] The Joint Chiefs pushed hard for advance authority to use nuclear weapons when the Kennedy administration was considering intervention in Laos in 1961.[51] Since then, however, the military have come to recognize that presidents are not ready to use nuclear weapons and they have pressed instead for the authority to use overwhelming conventional force.

This chapter is the longest in the book, and the reader may feel somewhat uncertain why so much detail has been provided. Recall that our purpose was to explain organizational interests. Career officials, including those who come to head organizations such as the Joint Chiefs of Staff, often develop their position largely by calculating the national interest in terms of the organizational interests of the career service to which they belong. Even in-and-outers are sometimes "captured" by the organizations that bring them into government. It is necessary to understand the details of those interests if one is to avoid the erroneous notion that organizations simply seek to grow in size. The details of organizational interests, the essence of groups as defined by the members, and the competition of groups over roles and missions are likely to be unfamiliar to readers, and they are important factors in understanding how a large number of participants come to see issues and what motivates them to take the stands that they take. Before discussing specifically which participants come to rely mainly on organizational interests, we need to consider a second major class of interests, those of the president.

48. David E. Lilienthal, *The Journals of David E. Lilienthal*, vol. 2, *The Atomic Energy Years, 1945–1950*, p. 406 (cited hereafter as *Journals*).
49. Snyder, "The 'New Look' of 1953," pp. 427, 433–35.
50. Eisenhower, *Waging Peace*, p. 299.
51. Hilsman, *To Move a Nation*, pp. 129, 133–34; Schlesinger, *A Thousand Days*, pp. 338–39.

CHAPTER FOUR

Domestic Politics
and Presidential
Interests

If some participants in the national security decisionmaking process, particularly career officials, find their clues to what the national interest is in their definition of the interests of their own organization, others, particularly in-and-outers at high levels, detect clues in their conception of presidential interests. Presidents and their close associates frequently come to decide what stand to take largely in relation to the problem of maintaining power or of getting reelected. Presidents and those concerned with domestic problems and the domestic economy also may equate national security with avoiding recession or inflation or promoting specific domestic programs such as welfare reform or highway construction.

It should be noted at the outset that the consideration in this chapter of the domestic political factors entering into the stand that a president takes on foreign policy issues should not be construed as a critical judgment of the legitimacy of such considerations. Foreign policy and national security decisions are multiple-value choices and are rarely reached on the basis of a single, overriding view of any single problem that excludes all other considerations. Domestic political considerations and personal interests are an inescapable part of the decisionmaking process, especially at the White House level. However, they usually are dismissed or not considered at all in formal analyses of decisionmaking in the area of national security. This chapter is meant to bring them into focus.

DOMESTIC POLITICS

There is a very strong and widely held view in the United States that it is immoral to let domestic political considerations influence decisions that may affect war and peace. Supposedly, foreign policy should be bipartisan. This belief is so strongly held that senior officials frequently deny in public—and even apparently to themselves—that they take domestic politics into account in making national security decisions.

Richard E. Neustadt offered a historical explanation of this phenomenon, contrasting the American situation to that of the British:

> I have a strong impression that on his [Prime Minister Harold Macmillan's] side of the water, front-bench politicians of the time could give party-political concerns free play in foreign policy—to say nothing of economic policy—with a straightforward consciousness quite inadmissible, indeed almost unthinkable, for Presidents on our side.
>
> We proceeded then in an inhibiting framework of "bipartisanship" built by FDR and Truman—and maintained by Eisenhower after his own fashion—to afford support for a revolution in our foreign relations, breaching the isolationist tradition. Men who had been bred in that tradition before shifting ground themselves now sought to keep the country with them on the plea that "politics stops at the water's edge." This, for them, could not be a mere slogan. For them it was a virtual imperative of personal conduct. Truman tried to live by it and rarely let his conscious mind admit inevitable lapses. Eisenhower seems to have done the same.[1]

The reluctance to admit that one is taking domestic political interests into account means that they are seldom discussed explicitly within the government. Officials recognize that for the public to know that domestic political factors are being openly considered would be extremely damaging because of the belief that such considerations are immoral. Participants are aware that somebody opposed to a certain policy in the area of foreign affairs that is being justified on domestic grounds will almost certainly leak such information. David Lilienthal, then head of the Atomic Energy Commission, reported on a discussion within the Atomic Energy Commission about a sensitive issue that the military services sought to raise with the president. He noted in his diary that one member of the commission talked about the "election year political atmosphere in which this issue would be dealt with, saying this was

1. Neustadt, *Alliance Politics*, p. 87.

a bad time to raise it." Lilienthal disapproved. "I thought his point was dangerous because there were some who would then assert that a decision against the military would simply be a political decision by the President, which could be quite damaging."[2]

Presidents often instruct officials not to take domestic politics into account in making their recommendations. Thus President Truman is quoted as saying to Secretary of Defense James Forrestal, "Look, Jim, when you take a thing as serious as this to the American public you should forget about political considerations."[3] Truman also instructed the State Department not to take account of domestic politics in making its recommendations, and here he had an additional reason in mind. He believed, as he once said to State Department officials, "You fellas in the Department of State don't know much about domestic politics."[4] Beneath the surface, of course, domestic politics does enter into the making of foreign policy. It is incumbent on political scientists to bring this out even though evidence is relatively hard to come by.

> Ted—Have you considered the very real possibility that if we allow Cuba to complete installation and operational readiness of missile bases, the next House of Representatives is likely to have a Republican majority? This would completely paralyze our ability to react sensibly and coherently to further Soviet advances.[5]

That note, passed by Douglas Dillon to Theodore Sorensen at a meeting of the so-called ExCom of the National Security Council during the height of the Cuban missile crisis, is one of the few instances on the public record of a frank consideration of domestic politics. Nevertheless, there is no doubt that domestic interests do affect the stand that participants take. In commenting almost a decade later on the Cuban missile crisis, John Kenneth Galbraith laid out the choice of conflicting objectives and the rationale for giving consideration to domestic politics:

> In the Cuban missile crisis President Kennedy had to balance the danger of blowing up the planet against the risk of political attack at home for

2. Lilienthal, *Journals*, p. 374.

3. Bush, *Pieces of the Action*, p. 295.

4. Quoted in Clark and Legere, eds., *The President and the Management of National Security*, p. 169. Paige, *The Korean Decision*, p. 141, reports that in response to a request from Under Secretary of State Webb to consider the political aspects of sending the Seventh Fleet into the Straits of Formosa, President Truman "snapped back, 'We're not going to talk about politics. I'll handle the political affairs.' Thus the conference did not consider any questions dealing with domestic politics."

5. Sorensen, *Kennedy*, p. 688.

appeasing the Communists. This was not an irresponsible choice: to ignore the domestic opposition was to risk losing initiative or office to men who wanted an even more dangerous policy.[6]

Lyndon Johnson's concern with domestic politics was acute during his consideration of ABM deployment in 1967. As he considered the military's recommendation to initiate deployment and his secretary of defense's advice to postpone it, Johnson could not and did not ignore domestic politics. There could be little doubt in his mind that the Republican presidential nominee, whether Richard Nixon or Nelson Rockefeller, could well make weaponry a major issue in the campaign. At the urging of the secretary of defense and under intense budget pressures, Johnson had permitted the non-Vietnam portion of the military budget to decline, at least in real terms, and he was regularly rejecting proposals from the Joint Chiefs of Staff to develop and deploy a whole array of new weapons systems. Opposition to his defense program was building, particularly among leaders in the Senate and the House. The ABM program was rapidly becoming a symbol of "preparedness." Johnson had to recognize that, if he did not deploy an ABM, he was open to the political charge of failing to take a step that would save American lives in the event of war. Kennedy had apparently scored effectively against Nixon in 1960 on the missile gap issue, and Johnson was reluctant to run the risk that the "defense gap" issue would be used against him.

Former National Security Council (NSC) assistant Richard Clarke has described the interplay between President Bill Clinton's preoccupation with the domestic political uproar over his personal indiscretions and the decision to launch a military strike on al Qaeda targets in August 1998, after the terrorist attacks on two U.S. embassies in Africa. Although the president had ordered his staff to disregard any domestic political considerations in that decision, the public perception was that it had been an attempt by the president to divert attention from his own problems.[7]

A particularly important reason for searching out domestic political considerations in analyzing the foreign policy process is that many career officials routinely (if somewhat surreptitiously) take them into account.[8] Bureaucrats have learned that presidents will simply not take seriously proposals that are totally out of bounds in domestic politics, and they recognize that presidents

6. Galbraith, "Plain Lessons of a Bad Decade," p. 32.
7. Clarke, *Against All Enemies*, pp. 184–189.
8. Two former officials who attested this point without qualification are Joseph M. Jones, in *The Fifteen Weeks: February 21–June 5, 1947*, p. 149, and Karl Lott Rankin, in *China Assignment*, p. ix.

do, in fact, make such calculations. Although domestic considerations are discussed quietly, they are discussed at all levels of decisionmaking on national security issues. First, the president and his principal advisers are assumed to weigh the possible effect of foreign policy issues on elections. Second, they are assumed to keep the president's overall program in mind in approaching any given decision in the area of foreign affairs.

Presidential Elections

There is much debate among political scientists about the effects of foreign policy issues on presidential elections. Most studies seem to show that foreign policy issues play a relatively minor role, although the image of a candidate as being knowledgeable in foreign policy and a man of peace is of value.[9] Presidents and potential presidents themselves see a closer link than analysts do between the stands that they take on foreign policy issues and the outcome of presidential elections. The range and diversity of issues that presidents believe can affect their domestic political posture and their chances of reelection are reflected in a study of Lyndon Johnson's calculations by Philip L. Geyelin:

> At this point, the Johnson reasoning comes full circle and takes on deep significance in his approach to the major crises of his first two years. For example, the reasoning would begin with his assessment that it would be bad politics at home to cave in quickly to Panamanian rioters (even though he was prepared to be more than generous, by any previous standards, when the appearance of pressure was removed); that it would be unpopular to allow the U.S. position to collapse in Vietnam, even into a "neutralist" solution, because of the "appeasement" stigma this might carry with it; that even slight risk of "another Cuba" in the Dominican Republic would be political suicide; that a full cross-section of Congress was against the MLF [the proposed NATO multilateral nuclear force]; that disarmament proposals or recommendations for easing East-West trade barriers would stir the cold warriors of Congress at a period of maximum tension over Vietnam (but not, let it be noted, at other times); that foreign aid to countries whose citizens burn libraries or whose rulers denounce U.S. policy in Vietnam or elsewhere is political anathema.[10]

Presidential calculations about the impact of foreign policy on elections seem to relate to three goals:

9. See, for example, Campbell, Gurin, and Miller, *The Voter Decides.*
10. Geyelin, *Lyndon B. Johnson and the World,* p. 148.

—generating a popular image of the president among the electorate
—denying a potential opponent a major issue
—appealing to particular interest groups.

GENERATING A POPULAR IMAGE OF THE PRESIDENT. In general, presidential popularity appears to go up—at least in the short run—when the president is seen as acting vigorously on almost any issue, even though the consequences of his actions are not yet known. Presidential initiatives in foreign policy are frequently seen as desirable because they show that the president is in command and seeking solutions to problems.

More specifically, during the cold war presidents and their domestic political advisers often believed that the president's popularity could be increased, with desirable consequences for the next presidential election, by demonstrating that he was a man of peace willing to take whatever steps necessary, short of appeasement, to reduce world tensions. Both James Haggerty, President Eisenhower's press secretary, and Eric Goldman, a sometime speech writer for President Johnson, sought to persuade their respective bosses to undertake a major campaign of speeches and world travel designed to portray them as men of peace, and both advisers expected such a tour to have a favorable influence on the next election. Haggerty was successful in selling the proposal to Eisenhower, which resulted in an extended world trip in 1959 that many believe helped Richard Nixon in the 1960 election; it certainly was urged on Eisenhower for that purpose.[11] In both cases, the State Department objected because of its concern with maintaining its autonomy and keeping the president out of diplomacy. In Eisenhower's case, with the death of John Foster Dulles and with the new secretary of state, Christian Herter, exercising relatively little influence on the president, the State Department's objections were overruled. In Johnson's case, LBJ's initial approval of the proposal was changed when Secretary of State Dean Rusk strenuously objected.[12] Many observers have interpreted various moves by President Nixon, including his visits to Russia and China and the SALT agreement, as aimed in part at creating an image of himself as a man of peace, an image he exploited with great skill in his landslide victory in 1972.

After the terrorist attacks of 9/11, executed by an enemy with whom negotiations were not possible, President Bush wanted to be seen as ready to take

11. Hughes, *The Ordeal of Power: A Political Memoir of the Eisenhower Years*, p. 278; Anderson, *The President's Men*, p. 191.
12. Goldman, *The Tragedy of Lyndon Johnson*, pp. 223–24.

whatever actions were necessary to defeat international terrorism. Former NSC staffer Clarke wrote:

> From within the White House a decision had been made that in the 2002 congressional election and in the 2004 reelection, the Republicans would wrap themselves in the flag, saying a vote for them was a vote against the terrorists. "Run on the war" was the direction in 2002.[13]

Even when the second President Bush's conduct of the war in Iraq came under fire in 2004, both major candidates for president still presented themselves as resolute in the war on terrorism and both believed that the election would turn in large part on whether the president's actions were seen as effective in dealing with the war on terror.

DENYING POTENTIAL OPPONENTS A KEY ISSUE. As has been suggested, President Johnson's ABM decision may have been influenced by the notion that if he failed to deploy an ABM system, his opponent in the 1968 election would use the issue against him. Such considerations affect presidents throughout their first term, for the four-year period between elections looks quite short to them. For example, Theodore Sorensen reports that President Kennedy's decision to proceed with a civil defense program in 1961 stemmed partly from the possibility that a "civil defense gap" would be used against him as he had used the "missile gap" against Richard Nixon.[14] Even in a second term, presidents are concerned about providing an issue to the candidate of the opposition party. That concern affected President Clinton's deferral of a decision about an ABM deployment in 2000.

During the cold war presidents were especially concerned about the effects of permitting a country to "go communist." All of them were mindful of the attacks on President Truman because of his refusal to intervene in the Chinese civil war and prevent the Chinese communists from coming to power. "Do not let a country fall to communism" was balanced by a second injunction, "Do not commit American troops to ground combat." After President Truman's commitment of American troops to battle in the Korean War, the contradiction between the two injunctions created a dilemma for the presidents who followed him. Roger Hilsman described one instance in which contradictory pressures were brought to bear on President Kennedy and his White House advisers in a dramatic and explicit way:

13. Clarke, *Against All Enemies*, p. 242.
14. Sorensen, *Kennedy*, p. 614.

In the midst of the President's nicely balanced political and military moves on Laos, the Republican leadership in Congress chose to make a public statement opposing an agreement in Laos which would lead to a coalition government that included Communists. But when the President consulted the leaders of both parties, he found that they were also united in opposing any commitment of American troops to Laos.[15]

Some interpretations of U.S. policy in Vietnam have argued that Kennedy sought to walk the line between not losing a country to communism and not openly committing ground troops to battle.[16]

Apprehensions about losing a country to communism were often linked with fears of reviving McCarthyism—the search for nonexistent communists or communist sympathizers at the source of American defeats. The most explicit suggestion of the importance of those factors in shaping U.S. Vietnam policy is contained in a report by Kenneth O'Donnell, a special assistant to Kennedy, as corroborated by Senate Majority Leader Mike Mansfield. O'Donnell asserts that Kennedy had decided to withdraw from Vietnam but had put it off until after the 1964 presidential elections because he believed that he could not be reelected if he withdrew from Vietnam and permitted the country to go communist. This is how O'Donnell has told the story:

> In the spring of 1963, Mike Mansfield again criticized our military involvement in Vietnam, this time in front of the congressional leadership at a White House breakfast, much to the President's annoyance and embarrassment. Leaving the breakfast the President seized my arm and said, "Get Mike and have him come into my office." I sat in on part of their discussion. The President told Mansfield that he had been having serious second thoughts about Mansfield's argument and that he now agreed with the senator's thinking on the need for a complete military withdrawal from Vietnam.
>
> "But I can't do it until 1965—after I'm reelected," Kennedy told Mansfield.
>
> President Kennedy felt, and Mansfield agreed with him, that if he announced a total withdrawal of American military personnel from Vietnam before the 1964 election, there would be a wild conservative outcry against returning him to the Presidency for a second term.
>
> After Mansfield left the office, the President told me that he had made up his mind that after his reelection he would take the risk of unpopu-

15. Hilsman, *To Move A Nation*, p. 134.
16. See, for instance, Gelb, "Vietnam: The System Worked," pp. 140–73.

larity and make a complete withdrawal of American forces from Vietnam. "In 1965, I'll be damned everywhere as a Communist appeaser. But I don't care. If I tried to pull out completely now, we would have another Joe McCarthy red scare on our hands, but I can do it after I'm reelected. So we had better make damned sure that I am reelected."[17]

In the wake of the Vietnam experience in the 1970s, Congress and the American public became highly averse to committing U.S. forces to fight communism in the third world. Therefore, when President Ford and his secretary of state, Henry Kissinger, became concerned about Soviet attempts to take over Angola through Cuban surrogate forces and decided to undertake a covert program of support for the anticommunist opposition leader Savimbi, they felt caught in a dilemma. "Washington in July 1975 was in a surreal mood. We were being battered by Aleksandr Solzhenitsyn and the conservatives for not being rough enough on Communism and criticized by the liberals (and the African Bureau of the State Department) for being far too obsessed with Communism. Congressional harassment was guaranteed if we went ahead and might involve a replay of the Vietnam debate concluded only a few months earlier."[18] While the conservatives who brought Ronald Reagan to office in 1980 remained adamant about countering Soviet military power, the American public's aversion to foreign military engagement after the country's experience in Vietnam limited the president's options to act against Soviet encroachment in the third world for the remainder of the cold war years.

APPEALING TO PARTICULAR INTEREST GROUPS. Specific decisions can gain presidents across-the-board support or cost them the support of particular groups that have a special interest in foreign policy issues. The appeal to a particular group may be made directly, by public statements or actions designed to attract them; in other cases, the appeal may be made indirectly. Individuals who have strong influence with a group may be placated by a particular foreign policy action that in turn leads them to urge support from the group at election time.

A celebrated case of the influence of domestic political considerations on a president's position on a foreign policy involves President Truman and his stand on Palestine. One must note that the evidence here is somewhat ambiguous. Both Richard Neustadt and Dean Acheson concluded that Truman's decisions were not influenced by domestic political calculations. Ache-

17. O'Donnell, "LBJ and the Kennedys," pp. 51–52.
18. Kissinger, *Years of Renewal,* p. 806.

son said flatly: "He [Truman] never took or refused to take a step in our foreign relations to benefit his or his party's fortunes. This he would have
regarded as false to the great office that he venerated and held in sacred
trust."[19] Other advisers had a different view. Some were constantly urging
him to take actions that they believed would solidify the Jewish vote and
secure funds for his election campaign. Both his secretary of defense, James
Forrestal, and his secretaries of state, James Byrnes and George Marshall,
were convinced that Truman's decisions regarding Israel were largely influenced by the Jewish vote. At a critical meeting to discuss early recognition of
the state of Israel, Truman had invited Clark Clifford, one of his principal
domestic political advisers who also occasionally involved himself in foreign
policy matters. Marshall interpreted Clifford's attendance as a clear indication that Truman would decide the issue on domestic political grounds and
was reported to have said, "Mr. President, this is not a matter to be determined on the basis of politics. Unless politics were involved, Mr. Clifford
would not even be at this conference. This is a very serious matter of foreign
policy determination."[20]

One study of the origins of the cold war further suggests that Truman's
concern about the growing disaffection for the Democratic Party among ethnic minority groups with Eastern European attachments was one of the reasons that he took a strong stand against Soviet efforts to dominate such
countries as Poland, Czechoslovakia, and Hungary.[21] After the cold war, the
desire to appeal to the same groups influenced President Clinton's decision to
support NATO expansion, with those countries first on the list of new members. The perceived influence of the Cuban exile population on Florida's vote
in national elections, along with intense Cuban lobbying efforts in Washington, have effectively constrained all presidents to a position of increasingly
harsh sanctions against Cuba for the lifetime of Fidel Castro.

In some cases, presidents may appoint particular individuals to public
office of one kind or another in the foreign policy field in the hope of gaining their support in a forthcoming election campaign or gaining the support
of ethnic or other minority groups that look to that individual. In his effort
to secure Senator Strom Thurmond's support within the Republican party for
his presidential election bid, Richard Nixon reportedly promised Thurmond
that if he were elected president, he would negotiate a textile agreement that
would reduce imports of Japanese and other foreign synthetic textiles into the

19. Acheson, *Present at the Creation*, p. 176. See also Neustadt, *Alliance Politics*, pp. 83–84.
20. Anderson, *The President's Men*, pp. 118–19. See also *Forrestal Diaries*, pp. 309–10, 347;
Byrnes, *All in One Lifetime*, p. 373; and Phillips, *The Truman Presidency*, p. 198.
21. Wishnatsky, "Symbolic Politics and the Cold War."

United States and that he would support ABM deployment. Upon election, Nixon apparently felt obligated to meet both of those commitments.[22]

Presidents may also seek to influence elections by awarding defense contracts that gain the support of particular business organizations and perhaps bolster employment in key areas. Herbert York, then a senior Defense Department official, recalled that the contract for a new manned bomber for the Air Force was in serious trouble in the closing days of the Eisenhower administration:

> Then, during the 1960 campaign for the Presidency, the B-70 was given a brief new lease on life. Even before the new fiscal year started, on July 1, 1960, about $60 million had been tacked onto the originally planned $75 million. This extra money was supposed to be used for development work on some of the most critical weapons subsystems; and in combination with other readjustments in the project, it was to make possible the construction of a single prototype aircraft. However, a program leading to only one prototype never made sense, and going through such a step was nothing more than an exercise in salami tactics. Thus, in August, another $20 million was added for a second plane. Then, just days before the Nixon-Kennedy election contest in November, 1960, the Department of Defense announced that it was bringing the total B-70 budget for the then current fiscal year up to $265 million. As a result of these increased funds, the number of airplanes to be built was increased to four for sure, with eight more possible, and the four were to be prototypes of a "usable weapon system." In California, the announcement of this new lease on life was accompanied by a detailed statement by North American Aviation about the recent sad history of declining employment in southern California and how these funds would change all that. Although Nixon did carry California in 1960, Kennedy won nationally, and the B-70's new lease on life ran out almost immediately.[23]

Maintaining Presidential Power

In calculating interests in a foreign policy decision, the president and his advisers consider how the president's stand on a particular issue may affect his ability to accomplish other goals. All presidents learn, as Richard Neustadt has

---

22. Chester, *The American Melodrama: The Presidential Campaign of 1968*, p. 447; Wills, *Nixon Agonistes: The Crisis of the Self-Made Man*, p. 271.
23. York, *Race to Oblivion*, pp. 56–57.

explained, that the presidency is simply a license to seek to persuade. Presidential power must be carefully husbanded and used shrewdly if the president is to go beyond his role as clerk in terms of his ability to influence events.[24] One basic aim is to avoid the appearance of failure. To seek to accomplish something and to fail is to signal to others that one can be beaten. Thus presidents are reluctant to undertake foreign policy programs if they believe that they have only a modest chance of success.

The president proceeds warily on those issues that arouse major passions and interests either in the population as a whole or within a significant group whose support he values on other issues, domestic or foreign. We have already mentioned the fear in the 1950s and 1960s of turning loose torrents of domestic opposition by appearing to be "soft on communism." President Kennedy and his brother Robert, according to the latter's memoirs, discussed impeachment as a possible penalty for failing to get the Russian missiles out of Cuba.[25]

Even when the president is confident of weathering opposition, he dislikes spending his time and energy fighting to regain the initiative. Presidents attempt to be careful in choosing the issues on which they will fight hard against sustained domestic opposition. They easily convince themselves that an action that is necessary to avoid such a fight is in the national interest because it will leave them free to pursue other programs that are vital to national security. Lyndon Johnson justified his decision to involve the United States deeply in Vietnam without making the extent of the commitment obvious largely on the grounds that doing so would leave him with the time and the political support necessary to pursue the Great Society program. When he decided to attack Iraq, the second President Bush was convinced that he could bring domestic public opinion to accept that his action was essential to the war on terrorism.

Sometimes the attitude of small groups or even single individuals is as important to the president as his general popularity. Presidents are particularly concerned about maintaining the support of their predecessors. Ex-presidents are likely to give such support or at least to refrain from overt attack on their successors; however, if they threaten to come out of retirement or if a president feels that his action will bring them out of retirement, he is likely to move slowly. Nothing would do more to legitimize the opposition than the support of an ex-president. One of the most dramatic cases on record of an ex-president (and ex-vice president) seeking to influence the policy of a successor is the strong stand on the China question taken by both Eisen-

24. Neustadt, *Presidential Power*.
25. Kennedy, *Thirteen Days*, p. 67.

hower and Nixon in 1960. Eisenhower apparently informed Kennedy that although he hoped and intended to support the new administration on foreign policy issues, he would consider it necessary to return to public life if communist China threatened to enter the United Nations. In the book he wrote a few years later, Nixon related with satisfaction that he too pressured Kennedy to block China:

> I then brought up an issue which I told him [Kennedy] was one on which I had particularly strong views—the recognition of Red China and its admission to the UN. I did so because just the day before, Senator George Smathers had told me that Chester Bowles and some of Kennedy's other foreign policy advisers were urging him to reappraise our position on that issue. Kennedy said that he was opposed to recognition of Red China. He indicated, however, that strong arguments had been presented to him in favor of the so-called "two Chinas policy." Under this policy, Nationalist China would retain its seat on the Security Council, and Red China would have only a seat in the Assembly. This would mean that Red China would have only one vote out of about a hundred in the Assembly and would not be able to block UN action by veto. Kennedy said that proponents of this policy were contending that Red China could not do any damage in the UN under such circumstances.
>
> In expressing my strong opposition to this policy, I pointed out that the issue wasn't whether Red China had one vote in the Assembly, or even the veto power. What was really at stake was that admitting Red China to the United Nations would be a mockery of the provision of the Charter which limits its membership to "peace-loving nations." And what was most disturbing was that it would give respectability to the Communist regime which would immensely increase its power and prestige in Asia, and probably irreparably weaken the non-Communist governments in that area.[26]

Under those pressures Kennedy backed off and set the China issue aside.

Another group that presidents looked to for support during the cold war and were reluctant to challenge openly, until Nixon felt forced to do so, was what was known as the Eastern Foreign Policy Establishment. Joseph Kraft believed that lack of support from the president's own party as a whole created a need to turn to this group:

26. Nixon, *Six Crises*, pp. 408–9. On Eisenhower, see Schlesinger, *A Thousand Days*, p. 480.

Since they could not count on purely partisan political support, each one of the four Presidents turned, in putting across foreign policy measures, to a grouping of prestigious figures from the worlds of law (John McCloy, Dean Acheson, and John Foster Dulles), finance (Averell Harriman, Eugene Black, and Robert Lovett), the press (Henry Luce, Arthur Hays Sulzberger, and Barry Bingham), and the military (Generals George Marshall, Bedell Smith, and Lucius Clay). Time after time, when Administration foreign policy objectives were in hazard before the Congress, members of this group were wheeled up to cow, cajole, or charm the legislators into submission. Because they were all internationalist in outlook, generally connected with the East and its bigger schools and foundations, and usually members of the Council on Foreign Relations in New York, as the years wore on, the group acquired, from an English counterpart, the name of the Establishment. And to a large extent, it can be said that from 1940 through 1965, the United States followed the Establishment foreign policy.[27]

The desire to have the support of this group probably influenced Kennedy's perception of the Skybolt missile crisis. As his meeting with Prime Minister Harold Macmillan approached, Kennedy received several phone calls from leading members of this Establishment, and he was confronted with a lead editorial in the *Washington Post* warning him not to jeopardize relations with the British. Feeling acutely the need for the support of this group of men in any move to reduce tensions with the Soviet Union, Kennedy felt that he had to reach some compromise. He could not challenge them on an issue close to their hearts—good relations with a Conservative leader of Great Britain.

After Vietnam and particularly in the post–cold war years, the Establishment dissipated into several distinct groups of opinion and became much less influential on the president and Congress. Nongovernmental organizations (both liberal and conservative) and think tanks began to have more influence, particularly in Congress and ultimately on the president. The bipartisan nature of the foreign policy establishment was to a large degree shattered and presidents came to rely on the individuals and organizations associated with their own party. Because the Establishment was no longer monopolistic, its influence declined.

Over the years, the leaders of Congress have been perhaps the single most important group whose support on a range of issues the president has sought. In cases where congressional action is needed to authorize the expenditure of

27. Kraft, *Profiles in Power*, pp. 16–17.

funds or to ratify a treaty, congressional leaders can virtually exercise a veto. In other cases, the president may have the freedom to act without legislative authorization but hesitates to do so if he recognizes that a move he makes will be exceedingly unpopular with Congress and will generate opposition to other policies, perhaps including policies in the domestic sector.

For example, during the cold war congressional leaders, particularly those on the Joint Atomic Energy Committee, were concerned about preventing the sharing of American nuclear information and control of American nuclear weapons with any foreign power. That concern played a major role in shaping presidential attitudes toward the question, especially in light of presidents' desire to get the committee's cooperation in promoting the peaceful uses of atomic energy.

In some cases, presidents go to Congress not because they believe that congressional authorization is required but to strengthen their position internationally. Perhaps the most vivid example is the question of congressional support for the use of military force. In 1973, reacting to the war in Vietnam, Congress passed the War Powers Resolution to assert its constitutional prerogatives with regard to declaring war and to restrict the authority of the president to conduct war without congressional approval. Every president since then—and even some members of Congress—has opposed the resolution on constitutional grounds and scrupulously avoided invoking it when faced with the question of deploying U.S. armed forces abroad. At the same time, presidents have felt the need for a clear statement of congressional support before sending troops into battle. Writing about decisionmaking for the Gulf War in 1991, Brent Scowcroft, national security adviser to the first President Bush, described it thus:

> Although we did explore options for the involvement of Congress, we never seriously contemplated invoking the War Powers Resolution. We were confident that the Constitution was on our side when it came to the president's discretion to use force if necessary: If we sought congressional involvement, it would not be authority we were after, but support.[28]

Ultimately, the House and the Senate passed resolutions authorizing the president to use force against Iraq provided that he had exhausted all efforts to get Saddam Hussein to comply with the UN resolutions. As President Bush recalled:

28. Bush and Scowcroft, *A World Transformed,* p. 398.

I felt the heavy weight that I might be faced with impeachment lifted from my shoulders as I heard the results. In truth, even had Congress not passed the resolutions I would have acted and ordered our troops into combat. I know it would have caused an outcry, but it was the right thing to do. I was comfortable in my own mind that I had the constitutional authority. It had to be done.[29]

As he contemplated another war against Iraq in 2002, the second President Bush calculated that, in the aftermath of 9/11, he would have wider congressional support to attack Iraq than his father had in 1990. Although some of his advisers suggested that he had constitutional authority to go to war without the support of Congress, he decided to seek a congressional resolution authorizing the use of force to strengthen his position with Iraq and with the UN Security Council. (In fact, his domestic political advisers even saw it as a means of strengthening Republican candidates in the 2002 mid-term election.) Administration officials convinced moderates in Congress that strong support for the resolution would oblige the UN Security Council to make Saddam Hussein comply with its earlier mandates, and the resolution passed both the House and Senate with large majorities.[30]

PRESIDENTIAL STANDS

The desire to avoid a major domestic row or to keep the good will of a significant domestic group may lead presidents to alter their stands on national security issues in an effort to build a wide consensus or to maintain the appearance of consistency. Presidents also seek to package their proposals to gain maximum public support and, when necessary, engage in logrolling.

—*Consensus building.* Presidents often are not content to put together merely the minimum coalition necessary to secure adoption of a policy. In addition to getting particular decisions and actions approved, they have their overall influence and long-run relations to think about; therefore they seek to bring as many groups as possible along with a particular decision. Thus they often are willing to modify and change a proposal even though its advocates in the bureaucracy tell them that enough support already exists to have the proposal adopted as it stands. The desire to build a broad consensus is sometimes aimed at bringing a particular group on board that might cause diffi-

29. Ibid, p. 446.
30. Woodward, *Plan of Attack*, pp. 167, 168–69, 203–04.

culty for the president on some other issue. Moreover, wide support at the outset hampers remaining opponents who cannot be won over.

—*Maintaining the appearance of consistency.* Presidents guard against any appearance of inconsistency that would give their opponents an opening to attack them in the political arena. For example, after having successfully resisted strong pressure from the Joint Chiefs of Staff and the Republican leaders of Congress to interpose American forces to defend Taiwan following the defeat of the Chinese Nationalists on the mainland, President Truman decided to defend the island when he made the decision to intervene with American forces in Korea. Truman recognized that to fight against communist expansion in Korea but not in Taiwan would open him to the charge of inconsistency. In order to get the widespread support that he viewed as necessary for his involvement in Korea, Truman felt obliged to reverse the decision and involve the United States in the as yet uncompleted Chinese civil war.[31]

—*Packaging policies for public consumption.* In order to minimize public opposition, presidents frequently explain and justify their decisions in rhetoric that they believe will secure maximum domestic political support for their proposals even if it does not precisely reflect the reasoning that led them to the decisions. They seek an explanation that will draw the widest possible support and make it difficult for opposition groups to challenge them.

A fateful example is the public rationale given for Truman's decision to aid Greece and Turkey in 1947. The British government's decision that it could no longer provide aid to Greece and Turkey was conveyed to the American government in 1947, and the reaction of administration officials was swift and virtually unanimous. Greece and Turkey were seen as states of pivotal importance to checking Soviet military power in the Mediterranean. With the withdrawal of British aid it was clear that the two countries would be under severe pressure unless American aid were given. A task force quickly worked up an aid package; however, the crucial problem was considered to be congressional support.

A group of congressional leaders was called to the White House by the president for a critical meeting on February 27, 1947. Secretary of State George Marshall led off by laying out the administration's case for aid to Greece and Turkey. Marshall evidently presented the argument in the traditional manner in which the issue had been considered within the American government. Greece had been a loyal ally, he asserted, and aid was a matter of humanitari-

31. Paige, *The Korean Decision*, pp. 62–189; Acheson, *Present at the Creation*, pp. 350, 369, 405–06, 422; Rankin, *China Assignment*, pp. 29, 155; Caridi, *The Korean War and American Politics*, pp. 58–60.

anism. Aid to Turkey could be justified in terms of the importance of maintaining the British position in the Middle East and barring the area to Soviet advances. According to the accounts provided by both Joseph M. Jones and Dean Acheson, the presentation did not go down well with congressional leaders preoccupied with the impact of such aid on the budget. Sensing that the discussion was going rather badly, Dean Acheson moved quickly to try to repair the situation. The report in his memoirs is succinct and vivid:

> In desperation I whispered to him a request to speak. This was my crisis. For a week I had nurtured it. These congressmen had no conception of what challenged them; it was my task to bring it home. Both my superiors, equally perturbed, gave me the floor. Never have I spoken under such a pressing sense that the issue was up to me alone. No time was left for measured appraisal. In the past eighteen months, I said, Soviet pressure on the Straits, on Iran, and on northern Greece had brought the Balkans to the point where a highly possible Soviet breakthrough might open three continents to Soviet penetration. Like apples in a barrel infected by one rotten one, the corruption of Greece would infect Iran and all to the east. It would also carry infection to Africa through Asia Minor and Egypt, and to Europe through Italy and France, already threatened by the strongest domestic Communist parties in Western Europe. The Soviet Union was playing one of the greatest gambles in history at minimal cost. It did not need to win all the possibilities. Even one or two offered immense gains. We and we alone were in a position to break up the play. These were the stakes that British withdrawal from the eastern Mediterranean offered to an eager and ruthless opponent.

According to Acheson, the ploy worked:

> A long silence followed. Then Arthur Vandenberg said solemnly, "Mr. President, if you will say that to the Congress and the country, I will support you and I believe that most of its members will do the same." Without much further talk the meeting broke up to convene again, enlarged, in a week to consider a more detailed program of action.[32]

The president's public speech calling for aid to Greece and Turkey thus came to embody the so-called Truman Doctrine, which indicated that the United States would supply aid to any free people resisting communist subversion. As Richard Neustadt has noted, the anti-Russian tone of the case, while somewhat at variance with the internal thinking of the administration,

32. Acheson, *Present at the Creation*, p. 219.

nevertheless helped to crystallize a public and congressional mood that assured a large consensus of support for the policy.[33]

Half a century later, the administration of the second President Bush inflated and slanted intelligence to convince the American public that Iraq was a direct threat to the United States by virtue of its possession of weapons of mass destruction and its support for the al Qaeda terrorist group.

In many cases, a president's appointment of the head of a program is based on his perception of the need to get wide support for the program. That often means appointing an individual who, being less committed to the program than the president, therefore gives skeptics some confidence that the program will not run away with itself. For example, Truman appointed Paul Hoffman to run the Marshall Plan as a way of ensuring congressional support for the program, and he appointed Bernard Baruch to be the American representative to the UN body seeking to negotiate on nuclear disarmament.[34] In other cases, appointments may be made to ensure general support. For example, President Eisenhower apparently felt obliged to consult fully with Senator Robert Taft on his appointment of members to the Joint Chiefs of Staff.[35]

—*Logrolling.* In some cases, a president's interest in a particular issue is dominated by his desire to get a particular decision on another issue. President Truman's tenure provides two striking examples of presidential interest being defined in such terms and leading to decisions of great significance for relations among the People's Republic of China, the United States, and Japan. The first of the examples, to which reference has already been made, was Truman's decision to defend Taiwan, and the second was his decision to force the Japanese to recognize the government of Taiwan as the government of China.

In recalling the latter episode, it is necessary to remember that, because Britain and the United States could not agree whether the government in Peking or the government in Taipei was the legitimate government of China, neither government was represented at the San Francisco Peace Conference of 1951, where the peace treaty with Japan was signed. The absence of a Chinese signature on the peace treaty raised questions in the United States about which "China" Japan would recognize following independence. The position taken by John Foster Dulles (who had been appointed especially to negotiate the peace treaty), Secretary of State Dean Acheson, and President Truman was conditioned by their desire to see the Senate ratify the treaty. Any question

33. Neustadt, *Presidential Power*, pp. 50–51. See also Jones, *The Fifteen Weeks*, pp. 138–43, 154–55; De Rivera, *The Psychological Dimension of Foreign Policy*, pp. 345–48.

34. Acheson, *Sketches from Life of Men I Have Known*, pp. 129–30; Truman, *Years of Trial and Hope*, pp. 7–8; Conant, *My Several Lives*, p. 493.

35. Snyder, "The 'New Look' of 1953," p. 412.

about what stand was necessary to secure ratification was removed when fifty-six members of the Senate sent a letter to the president that read as follows:

> As Members of the United States Senate, we are opposed to the recognition of Communist China by the Government of the United States or its admission to the United Nations.
>
> Prior to the submission of the Japanese Treaty to the Senate, we desire to make it clear that we would consider the recognition of Communist China by Japan or the negotiating of a bilateral treaty with the Communist Chinese regime to be adverse to the best interests of the people of both Japan and the United States.[36]

In an effort to head off a fight over ratification of the treaty, Dulles made a trip to Tokyo along with Senators Margaret Chase Smith and John Sparkman. Following their discussions, Japan's prime minister, Shigeru Yoshida, agreed to write a letter to Dulles stating Japan's intention to recognize the Nationalist Chinese regime. Whatever Yoshida's own intentions might have been and whatever the views of the American government officials on the desirability of the action, this issue was cast in terms of a trade for Senate support of the peace treaty.

An agreement between President Nixon and Representative Mendel Rivers, chairman of the House Armed Services Committee, provides another example of trading. In 1970 Nixon agreed to increase spending on naval shipbuilding in order to get the support of Rivers for the Safeguard ABM system. According to reporters, the agreement stipulated that Rivers would go along with the president's request for the system provided that the administration would agree to spend additional funds that Congress would appropriate for ship modernization.[37]

In other cases, trading may occur over a domestic political issue and a foreign policy issue. The president may change his stand on a foreign policy question in order to get support for a domestic issue, or he may alter his stand on a domestic political question in order to get the support of some other actor, perhaps a congressional leader, on a foreign policy question. An example of the former is provided by the decision of the Eisenhower administration in March 1953 not to cancel development of a nuclear airplane. The president's principal science advisers were united in the belief that such an airplane was, in the words of a National Security Council decision, "not required

36. Cohen, *The Political Process and Foreign Policy: The Making of the Japanese Peace Settlement*, p. 151. See also Acheson, *Present at the Creation*, pp. 603–05; Sebald, *With MacArthur in Japan*, pp. 284–87.

37. *Washington Post*, April 11, 1970.

from the viewpoint of national security." That judgment, however, came up against the view of Representative Carl Hinshaw, who was then chairman of the Joint Committee on Atomic Energy Subcommittee on Research, Development, and Radiation. The Eisenhower administration was hoping to get substantial changes in the Atomic Energy Act in order to allow private industry to enter the atomic power field. Eisenhower thus saw the issue of the nuclear airplane in terms of the needed cooperation of the Joint Atomic Energy Committee on the civilian nuclear power issue, and the nuclear airplane program was reinstated.[38]

The range of presidential interests that affect presidents' stands on national security issues clearly goes far beyond the dictates of domestic politics discussed above. Presidents want to do what the national interest demands. Their perspective of the national interest is, as we have seen, often conditioned by a set of factors that are entirely different from those that condition the bureaucratic perspective. On one hand, a president inevitably becomes conscious of how his leadership will be assessed in retrospect. On the other, he is constantly faced with a myriad of pressing decisions on both domestic and foreign policy, and he must make trade-offs and resolve conflicts among them. No sector of the national security bureaucracy is faced with either situation.

Those who have observed presidents close at hand have frequently warned of the great difficulty of putting themselves in the shoes of the president and determining where he will look for clues to the national security interest. Theodore C. Sorensen, who was extremely close to President Kennedy, expressed this traditional diffidence:

A President knows that his name will be the label for a whole era. Textbooks yet unwritten and schoolchildren yet unborn will hold him responsible for all that happens. His program, his power, his prestige, his place in history, perhaps his reelection, will all be affected by key decisions. His appointees, however distinguished they may be in their own right, will rise or fall as he rises or falls. Even his White House aides, who see him constantly, cannot fully perceive his personal stakes and isolation. And no amount of tinkering with the presidential machinery, or establishment of new executive offices, can give anyone else his perspective.[39]

As Sorensen suggests, a president often becomes preoccupied, particularly in the later stages of his administration, with how he will be portrayed in the history books. Presidents during the cold war often wished to be acclaimed as

38. Lambright, *Shooting Down the Nuclear Plane*, p. 18.
39. Sorensen, *Decision–Making in the White House*, pp. 83–84.

men of peace who, through courage and perseverance, reduced the probability of war. A president also is aware of his responsibility for the future of the country and the need to protect it from its enemies. Thus a president must often simultaneously be a man of peace and a man of strength and courage. Arguing that American strength and determined American action are the way to secure lasting peace is, in many respects, an effort to avoid that dilemma.

Because many issues come at him at once and from different directions and because many pressures are involved, a president's behavior is characterized, perhaps to a surprising extent, by what we have called uncommitted thinking. He often responds at any one time to whichever pressures are momentarily strongest, whether they come from particular elements in the bureaucracy, from foreign governments, or from his own domestic political concerns. In the case of the ABM program, Johnson's position at any one time may have reflected the strongest pressures being brought to bear on him at a given point. At some points he seemed to share the arms control interests of his secretary of defense, at other times the fears of the military, and on other occasions the concerns of his domestic political advisers.

It would be both impossible and irrelevant to describe here the full range of special presidential interests that affect decisionmaking at the White House. We believe that the types of presidential interests outlined in this chapter are those that are most likely to get attention within the national security bureaucracy itself. Not only do they shape the president's own perspective and the way that he reacts to the bureaucracy, but also many within the bureaucracy can be persuaded sometimes to view the national security in terms of these particular presidential interests. Even many of those who are not necessarily sympathetic to the president's perspective on national security, particularly with regard to domestic politics, still take such factors into account in arriving at their own stand on national security issues or in planning strategies for getting the desired decisions. With this in mind, we are ready to consider in full how various participants shape their conception of national security.

CHAPTER FIVE

Interests, Faces, and Stands

The previous chapters have suggested a number of interests that officials are predisposed to protect in developing a position on a matter of national security. Of course efforts are made to determine the nature of threats and sensible responses to them, but the interpretation of events inevitably reflects organizational, presidential, and personal interests. For most participants those interests blur together. Richard Neustadt explained:

> For every player, any move toward action brings an element of personal challenge wrapped in a substantive guise. Of these his stakes are made. The substance is important, never doubt it, for that is what the game is all about. But so is the personal element. It makes no difference whether the move is of his own making or arises from sources outside his control. Either way, involvement of his job in some degree involves himself. Attached to his position are assorted expectations in the minds of his associates, evoked by its requirements and his career. Attached to his position also are his expectations of himself. Both sorts of expectations are reflected in his interests. He is man-in-office, with a record to defend and a future to advance, not least in history. The personal is tightly interwoven with the institutional. It is a rare player who can keep the two distinct, much less view both apart from substance.[1]

In general a person's stand derives from his or her personal experiences, career pattern, and position in the bureaucracy. It is not always profitable to

1. Neustadt, *Alliance Politics*, pp. 76–78.

look at individuals' personal experiences for clues to their stand on an issue. The issue may be one that they have not previously been involved in and that does not trigger any highly charged cognitive, emotional, or psychological reaction. Quite often, however, a particular issue evokes a deep personal response emanating from earlier encounters. An official may have had professional experience with a related set of issues in the past. Alternatively, the issue may invoke strong feelings because it seems analogous to a historical event or a vivid event in his or her private life.

CAREER PATTERN

The career pattern of participants also plays a part in predetermining the sources to which they look for guidance in determining the interests of national security. The guides of career officials are likely to differ from those of in-and-outers with ties in the banking, legal, or think tank communities. The position that individuals occupy in the bureaucracy also helps to determine the clues that they select to guide them to the national interest. Officials with operational responsibilities are likely to be preoccupied with the problems generated by the activities that their bureau or organization must perform. Individuals' perceptions also are affected by whether they receive information from a variety of sources that produce conflicting reports about the outside world or whether, on the contrary, the information comes from a single source that presents a unified and sharply defined picture. Individuals' perspectives are further affected by whether their subordinates pull them in different directions or press them in a single direction. They also are affected by how they perceive pressures from above and from colleagues in different agencies and bureaus. In general a person's position in the bureaucracy determines what face of an issue he or she sees and what seems important.

Career Officials

Within the context of shared images, career officials' views are shaped in substantial part by their desire for promotion. Few career officials expect major opportunities for their own personal advancement to emerge outside the government bureaucracy, and they quite naturally attach significant importance to getting ahead within the government. Military officers are concerned about reaching flag or general officer rank, while State Department officials eye ambassadorships. Members of neither group see any contradiction between their quest for advancement and the quest for national security, believing that the government and the nation will benefit from their services at higher levels.

The desire for promotion leads career officials to support the interests of the organization of which they are a member, since they recognize that in large measure, promotion depends on being seen as advancing the interest of the organization. They may calculate that if the organization grows, there will be more room for promotion. To be seen fighting for the organization is seen as the way to get promoted. President Nixon's Blue Ribbon Panel on the Defense Department reached this conclusion and stated it in strong terms:

> The fact that promotions are within the exclusive authority of an officer's parent Service creates an incentive for an officer, even when serving on assignments with unified organizations, to adhere closely to the official Service position of his parent Service on issues in which he is involved. This circumstance can influence the objectivity of an officer's performance. The extent to which this undesirable incentive motivates officers cannot be precisely measured, but there can be no question that many officers are convinced that any evidence of a deviation by them from their parent Service's official position will seriously jeopardize their chance for further promotion.[2]

In reviewing Foreign Service promotion policies, a Department of State task force found the situation to be similar:

> Under the present system, the key factor in determining whether an officer will be promoted is the efficiency report written by his immediate supervisor. The knowledge that the good opinion of his supervisor is crucial in determining whether an officer advances at a normal rate or falls behind and is eventually selected out can act as a powerful deterrent to his forthright expression of views on policy matters which may be at variance with the views of his supervisor.[3]

Officials learn that it is important to be liked by their superiors, to render them personal services, and to demonstrate their ability to get along not only with superiors but also with colleagues. They conclude that one must behave prudently in internecine conflicts and avoid showing any personality traits that could engender disagreements and difficulty.[4] A former official in the

2. Blue Ribbon Defense Panel, *Report to the President and the Secretary of Defense on the Department of Defense*, p. 140.

3. Macomber, *Diplomacy for the 1970s*, pp. 21–22.

4. See, for example, Davis, "Bureaucratic Patterns in the Navy Officer Corps," pp. 394–95; Harr, *The Professional Diplomat*, pp. 208–9; Simpson, *Anatomy of the State Department*, p. 33.

Defense Intelligence Agency (DIA) described how the taboo against "making waves" affected career military officers assigned to that agency:

> Imagine, if you will, what the prospect of a tour with DIA looks like to a military officer. He knows or soon learns that he will be thrust into a position in which, on occasion, his professional judgment will vary markedly from that of his parent service. He will be expected to defend a position that could enrage his Chief of Staff—but officers who do so more than once get known fast and are accorded an appropriate "reward" at a later date in terms of promotion and assignment. Consider also that a tour at DIA—normally two to three years— is very short when compared to a 20-to-30 year military career. And so most officers assigned to DIA go through a predictable pattern. They come on board as "hard-chargers," ready to set the world on fire. They stick to their principles through one or two scrapes. Then they become a little more circumspect, letting individual issues slide by and rationalizing that it wasn't a crunch question anyway. Finally, they resign themselves to "sweating out" their tours and playing every situation by ear. They avoid committing themselves or making decisions. They refuse to tackle the agency's long-term organizational ills because doing so would make too many waves.[5]

The desire to be promoted can also lead an official to undermine the effectiveness of his or her potential competitors. Such actions must be handled subtly so that the official does not get a reputation for seeking to hurt others or reducing the effectiveness of the organization. Yet ways are found. One observer of the State Department suggested that briefings of one's superiors and inferiors are carried out largely with this motive in view.

> Take the briefing of colleagues prior to their assumption of new assignments. This is of primary importance, yet it is more neglected than performed. Why? Knowledge is power. The mistakes of one's competitors improve one's own chances of advancement. So one is tempted to brief one's colleagues as slightly as possible. This is a subtle means of reducing competition for promotion, and of course it is employed generally against non-members of the fraternity. It obviously can have a disastrous effect on the Department's performance.
>
> The situation is similar for such an elementary technique for coordination and stimulation as the staff meeting. An Assistant Secretary, for

5. McGarvey, "The Culture of Bureaucracy," pp. 73–74.

instance, will indeed meet with his subordinates as often as three mornings a week. This sounds impressive as an operating device until one finds that too generally the Assistant Secretary tends only to pick his colleagues' brains for information and opinions useful to him in his thrice-weekly meetings with the Secretary, neglecting to make himself useful to them—by informing them, stimulating them, pitching their thinking and action to higher, more dynamic levels.

Conversely, most participants in staff meetings are all too often reluctant to bring up matters of real importance. This was pointed out almost twenty years ago as characteristic of the Under Secretary's staff meetings. It is applicable to most meetings today, because few officers wish to appear less than omniscient or wish to invite poaching on their preserves.[6]

The desire to be promoted can likewise lead participants to hold back information that they believe may create domestic political embarrassment for them and for the organization. During the cold war period, for example, the negative consequences for Foreign Service officers who reported the weakness of the Chinese Nationalists and the strength of the Chinese Communists apparently had a substantial impact on perceptions of what was safe to report if one wished to be promoted. James C. Thomson Jr. discussed a similar situation with regard to Foreign Service officers' reports from Vietnam:

> In addition, the shadow of the "loss of China" distorted Vietnam reporting. Career officers in the Department, and especially those in the field, had not forgotten the fate of their World War II colleagues who wrote in frankness from China and were later pilloried by Senate Committees for critical comments on the Chinese Nationalists. Candid reporting on the strengths of the Viet Cong and the weakness of the Diem government was inhibited by the memory. It was also inhibited by some higher officials, notably Ambassador Nolting in Saigon, who refused to sign off on such cables.[7]

Few career officials have any qualms about supporting the interest of the organization to which they are attached. It is quite natural for individuals who spend their life within a career service to come to believe that the functions of that organization are vital to national security.

As James G. March and Herbert A. Simon have pointed out, the activities of a particular organization are much more concrete than the generalized interest of the government as a whole and hence are felt to be the operational

6. Simpson, *Anatomy of the State Department*, pp. 4–41.
7. Thomson, "How Could Vietnam Happen?" p. 200.

way to promote the national interest.[8] Moreover, an individual comes to know his or her organization and to believe that it can do a good job. The individual is likely to be more aware of the shortcomings of rival organizations and hence to believe that they will not do their assigned tasks well.

Thus, for career officials the personal interest in promotion merges with the belief that their organization's welfare is vital to the national security. With a clear conscience, they support the interest of their organization and strive for a privileged position for the subgroup to which they are attached.

In-and-Outers

With less time to work for their goals and with other interests to pursue, in-and-outers hope for quick results and look to a variety of sources for guidance. Their view is shaped in part by the shared images held by various subgroups within society and by the images prevalent in the professional groups with which they have associated before entering government service and to which they may return. Those outside reference groups continue to shape their perception of the national interest, and many "temporary" officials have a personal interest in continuing to be respected by their outside professional peer group. Personal experiences also are likely to play a major role, separating those who have a deep involvement in an issue beyond official policy from others who come to it fresh with only their experiences in the bureaucracy as a guide. Those with extra government involvement may have a strong attachment to a particular position and exhibit ideological behavior. Some in-and-outers hold general views about international politics that distance them somewhat from the preoccupations of any one organization or administration. Still other in-and-outers contemplate elective office after their employment in the bureaucracy.

Desire for Involvement and Effectiveness

In-and-outers may be less patient and cautious, but nearly all participants in the policy process desire to be involved in decisions and actions of major importance. They wish to see themselves as being effective and influential in shaping those decisions. The desire to be involved most acutely affects participants who are not routinely and inevitably part of the decisionmaking process. It is difficult for a president not to involve the secretary of state and the secretary of defense in decisions, and it is difficult in turn for those offi-

8. March and Simon, *Organizations*, p. 156.

cials to exclude their principal operating officers. Other officials who are on staff or in advisory or planning positions need to struggle to remain involved. As both Will Sparks and George E. Reedy, both of whom worked in the White House, have observed, the problem is particularly acute on the White House staff. Reedy put it this way:

> For other White House assistants there is only one fixed goal in life. It is somehow to gain and maintain access to the President. This is a process which resembles nothing else known in the world except possibly the Japanese game of go, a contest in which there are very few fixed rules and the playing consists of laying down alternating counters in patterns that permit flexibility but seek to deny the flexibility to the opponent. The success of the play depends upon the whim of the President. Consequently, the President's psychology is studied minutely, and a working day in the White House is marked by innumerable probes to determine which routes to the Oval Room are open and which end in a blind alley.[9]

During the Clinton administration, Robert Rubin, who served first as head of the National Economic Council in the White House and later as secretary of the treasury, came to office with a clear strategy for maintaining effective access to the president. Rubin had been advised as follows by President Reagan's chief of staff:

> He suggested that I always be in the room whenever the chief of staff spoke to the President about economic policy and also that I shouldn't go to see the President unless I had something substantive to say to him. . . . At the same time, I should make sure to meet with the President regularly.[10]

Closely related to the desire to be involved is the desire to be effective, to have one's views taken seriously and carry weight with the president. James C. Thomson Jr. clearly described the nature of what he called the "effectiveness" trap, as well as two of its consequences—keeping participants from speaking out or from resigning:

> The "effectiveness" trap [is] the trap that keeps men from speaking out, as clearly or often as they might, within the government. And it is the trap that keeps men from resigning in protest and airing their dissent outside the government. The most important asset that a man brings to bureau-

9. Reedy, *The Twilight of the Presidency*, p. 88. See also Sparks, *Who Talked to the President Last?*

10. Rubin, *In an Uncertain World*, p.112.

cratic life is his "effectiveness," a mysterious combination of training, style, and connections. The most ominous complaint that can be whispered of a bureaucrat is: "I'm afraid Charlie's beginning to lose his effectiveness." To preserve your effectiveness, you must decide where and when to fight the mainstream of policy; the opportunities range from pillow talk with your wife, to private drinks with your friends, to meetings with the Secretary of State or the President. The inclination to remain silent or to acquiesce in the presence of the great men—to live to fight another day, to give on this issue so that you can be "effective" on later issues— is overwhelming. Nor is it the tendency of youth alone; some of our most senior officials, men of wealth and fame, whose place in history is secure, have remained silent lest their connection with power be terminated. As for the disinclination to resign in protest; while not necessarily a Washington or even American specialty, it seems more true of a government in which ministers have no parliamentary backbench to which to retreat. In the absence of such a refuge, it is easy to rationalize the decision to stay aboard. By doing so, one may be able to prevent a few bad things from happening and perhaps even make a few good things happen. To exit is to lose even those marginal chances for "effectiveness."[11]

The striving for power and effectiveness predisposes individuals to take stands in favor of actions that involve them in implementing and monitoring what is done, and they favor actions for which they are likely to get the credit. Thus two individuals who agree on objectives may disagree on the means because of their personal stakes in how a decision is carried out.[12] Once an individual is given a mission, he has a strong desire to "do something" in order to demonstrate his effectiveness and increase the likelihood that he will get future assignments. Henry Kissinger has observed that American negotiators, regardless of their previous position, often become advocates for the maximum range of concessions in negotiations that they are conducting. They want to claim success.[13] Arthur Schlesinger Jr. has maintained that Arthur Dean, charged with negotiating arms control arrangements with the Soviet Union by President Kennedy, assumed such a stance, desiring above all to accomplish something.[14]

11. Thomson, "How Could Vietnam Happen?" pp. 201–02. See also *Sorenson, Decision-Making in the White House*, pp. 62–63.

12. Neustadt, *Presidential Power*, pp. 46–47.

13. Kissinger, *American Foreign Policy*, p. 32.

14. Schlesinger, *A Thousand Days*, p. 505; Sorensen, *Decision–Making in the White House*, pp. 62–63.

The desire to remain involved and effective also leads officials whose influence depends largely on the confidence of the president to faithfully execute his decisions and take stands that they believe that he would want them to take. Acheson described in his memoirs the care that he took to maintain the confidence of the president. Neustadt reported that Dulles was equally motivated by the need to have Eisenhower's confidence if he was to be involved and effective:

> Eisenhower first appointed Dulles without knowing much of him except by reputation, and reportedly without much liking him. Dulles took the post intent on gaining presidential confidence. He hungered to be an effective Secretary, and he evidently saw no other way to go. Despite appearances, especially in retrospect, everything I know about their early years suggests that Dulles did not find it easy going. Temperamentally there seem to have been few affinities between them. Operationally, the President had ideas of his own, experience to boot, and an unmatched acquaintance among foreign statesmen, especially in Europe. As Eisenhower took hold of his job he came increasingly to do as other Presidents had done, picking and choosing among numbers of advisers of whom Dulles was but one. Dien Bien Phu affords us an example. There are others. This reached a peak, reportedly, in preparations for the Summit during 1955, where Eisenhower went on Eden's urging to the cheers of aides such as Nelson Rockefeller and Harold Stassen, but not Dulles. There the President assumed the working chairmanship of his own delegation in a burst of personal activity. Six weeks later he was stricken by a heart attack. Only after that attack did Dulles win his way into unrivaled eminence as "Mr. Foreign Policy." He did so by responding scrupulously to his ailing chief's dependence on him.
>
> Thereafter it appears that Dulles kept Eisenhower's confidence in the same way he had won it. During the entire Suez crisis, for example, he apparently cleared every move with Eisenhower in advance, emphatically including cancellation of the Aswan Dam, and also every phase of SCUA [Suez Canal Users Association]. As I read the record, Eisenhower was no "patsy" in this process. Far from it, he was laying down the law: he wanted peace. Dulles strained to keep it. He had every reason to exert himself. For in his circumstances all the gains of presidential confidence, so recently acquired to his satisfaction, would be risked by warfare with his name on it, with blame, in Eisenhower's eyes, attached to him.[15]

15. Neustadt, *Alliance Politics*, pp. 104–05.

The desire to be involved and influential may also lead participants to hold back information that they know their boss would find unpleasant or to avoid issues that they know he or she would rather leave alone.

HOPES FOR FUTURE ELECTIVE OFFICE

One of the things that distinguishes the American system from a parliamentary regime is that most of the president's principal advisers are not themselves competitors for his office or indeed for any elective political office. Whereas senators and representatives take their prospects for reelection into account in arriving at a stand, most members of the executive branch do not, since they have no intention of running for public office.

In certain cases, however, such interests do exist and may affect an adviser's stand on issues. Sorensen pointed out that presidential advisers with political ambitions of their own may place their own reputation and record ahead of that of the president. He noted that such individuals are not necessarily suppressing their conscience or forgetting about the national interest; rather, they come to believe sincerely that their own future is important to the national interest.[16] Harold Stassen did not abandon his own presidential ambitions while serving as an aide and disarmament adviser in the Eisenhower White House. Harry Truman's first secretary of defense, Louis Johnson, was widely reported to have presidential aspirations, and it was believed that that affected his stand on issues.[17]

Although in recent history very few Cabinet officers have aspired to the presidency (the first President Bush, who was director of central intelligence in the Ford administration, and William Cohen, the Republican secretary of defense in the Clinton administration, being exceptions), a larger number have sought election to the Senate, and that may well have influenced their stands on issues. It has been suggested, for example, that in one case Clinton Anderson enhanced his future political prospects while serving as secretary of agriculture in the first Truman administration. Anderson was present at a Cabinet meeting in which the discussion concerned the resignation of Ambassador Patrick J. Hurley as the American representative in China. Hurley had resigned suddenly, with a blast at the administration, and the question at hand was what to do and how to replace him. Anderson suggested that the appointment of George C. Marshall, who had been chief of staff for the Army

16. Sorensen, *Decision–Making in the White House*, p. 75.
17. Paige, *The Korean Decision*, pp. 3–31; Hammond, "NSC-68: Prologue to Rearmament," p. 293.

during World War II, would take the headlines away from Hurley's resignation. Secretary of Defense Forrestal and Secretary of State Byrnes quickly agreed with Anderson's suggestion, and Truman overcame his reluctance to ask Marshall to serve in a difficult post on short notice by asking him to take the post as a temporary assignment rather than to serve as ambassador.

Anderson's intention was indeed to drive Hurley out of the headlines, but a desire to help President Truman was not necessarily his prime motive. Byrnes speculated that Anderson was thinking of his own political future:

> Later it occurred to me that there might be a touch of political strategy in Anderson's suggestion of Marshall. Hurley had been in New Mexico for some time since his return from China, and the press had reported that he was considering becoming a Republican candidate for the United States Senate. It was possible that Anderson, a New Mexico Democrat, had in mind that the news of Marshall's appointment would blanket the report of Hurley's resignation. It did. Later, Clinton Anderson and Hurley became candidates for a senatorial seat. Mr. Anderson was elected and has served with distinction.[18]

OFFICIAL POSITION

Position within the bureaucracy also is bound to affect the stance that officials take—whether they have managerial responsibilities, whether they receive information from conflicting sources, whether they are exposed to conflicting pressures from subordinates. Where participants sit in relation to channels of action strongly biases what kind of issues come to seem important to them and on which they are likely to take a stand and get involved.

A participant's conception of his or her role (which is, for the individual, the equivalent of mission for the organization) further predisposes an official toward a particular view of what constitutes national security. Some *in-and-outers* guide themselves by explicit theories of the national interest. Others define it in terms of loyalty to the president or to a Cabinet officer or another official who is their immediate boss. Others come to see their loyalties in terms of the organization that they serve. With in-and-outers specifically, the answer to the question of what clues they respond to in deciding what serves national security depends on the variety of personal experiences that they bring to their job, the variety of positions that they have held in the bureau-

---

18. Byrnes, *All in One Lifetime*, pp. 328–29. See also *Forrestal Diaries*, p. 113.

cracy, and the differences in their conceptions of their role. Several typical patterns can be identified.

Some senior positions and many junior positions involve primarily the management of programs. Individuals in such positions at high levels include the civilian heads of the three military services, the secretary of energy, and the administrator of the U.S. Agency for International Development (USAID). Such officials, especially if they have had little previous personal involvement in a particular issue, are likely to come to reflect the interests of their organization. Much of their time and attention are taken up in dealing with their subordinates and solving problems put to them by subordinate officials. Much of their information comes from those subordinates, and they soon become keenly aware of the difficulties in operating the program and convinced of its importance to the national security. In several respects in-and-outers adopt the outlook of career officials.

Many in-and-outers occupy staff positions. That is to say, they are not in the direct line of responsibility for the management or operation of programs; rather, they serve either as personal staff assistants to senior officials or in staff organizations, such as the State Department's policy planning staff and the Defense Department's policy offices. These individuals frequently are recruited into such positions because they have had substantial previous professional involvement with the relevant substantive issues. Often they come in with strong views on a particular subject. Such officials are likely to exhibit ideological thinking, particularly on issues that have previously been of major concern to them. They focus on one or two key variables and see many issues in terms of the pursuit of those variables, whether the issue is European integration, arms control, or fighting terrorism. Here the exchange of attitudes between careerists and in-and-outers flows the other way. Some career staff who have spent most of their service in a planning or other staff agency with continuing attachment to a single set of issues may come to reflect the same kind of ideological thinking and often may be indistinguishable from in-and-outers in the same position. Junior officials in staff jobs may worry about being "sidelined." Since they have no regular involvement with issues, they feel that they must fight their way in, and they become conscious of the relationship between the stand that they take and the degree to which they are involved.

White House staff officials and even presidents often express the hope that *Cabinet officers* will take the perspective of the president rather than reflect the organizational interest of the department that they head. McGeorge Bundy, who was assistant for national security affairs to President Kennedy and President Johnson, expressed a typical position when he asserted that "Cabinet officers are special pleaders" and "should run their part of the government for the Administration—not run to the Administration for the interest of their part of the government." But as Harold Seidman observed after quoting McGeorge Bundy, "One might as well echo Professor Henry Higgins' plaint in *My Fair Lady*, 'Why can't a woman be more like a man?' as ask 'Why can't Cabinet members act more like Presidents?'"[19] The pressures on Cabinet officers from their subordinates, as well as from outside groups, is so great that they often come to see themselves as their department's representative to the president. For example, when James Forrestal was secretary of the Navy, he saw his job explicitly as maintaining the autonomy of the Navy.[20]

Although Cabinet officers are under strong pressure to support the interests of their organization, those pressures are by no means the only ones. Many officers feel countervailing pressures from the president and from their Cabinet colleagues. Many of them have not had extensive personal experience with the issues that they are now called upon to confront, and most of their previous experience was not set in the framework of "the national interest." Thus Cabinet officers' behavior is often characterized by what we have called uncommitted thinking. They tend to respond to the immediate pressures on them, whether from the president, their subordinates, or their colleagues, and their reaction to the push-and-pull of those pressures looks to an outside observer like inconsistent behavior.

White House political advisers, particularly those without any regular and routine responsibility for national security matters, often come to see foreign policy issues largely in terms of domestic politics and the possibilities of their own involvement. They are likely to take stands on issues that increase the probability that they will be involved, and they are likely to feel the strongest pressure from the president's own concerns.

Thus far we have presented the cast of characters—the participants in the national security policy process—and attempted to explain where they are likely to look for clues to the national security. Shared images limit the extent of disagreement, but within those parameters different experiences and responsibilities, different modes of thinking, and different reference points lead participants to different stands on issues. We now explore the process by which participants struggle to secure the decisions that they want.

19. Seidman, *Politics, Position, and Power*, p. 75.
20. *Forrestal Diaries*, p. 167.

PART II

Decisions

CHAPTER SIX

Initiative
and Rules

As far as the bureaucratic system is concerned, the main factors that influence the outcome of the process by which issues are raised are the standing of the participants, the rules (formal and informal) that guide an issue through the system, and the information and analysis that participants use to choose among alternative positions and to argue their case. On many issues, the disposition of the president is a further determinant.

Our presentation concentrates on decisions made at the presidential level. That is not meant to imply, however, that decisions made at lower levels are necessarily less important. Much of the work of the bureaucracy is carried out at lower levels, and many of the decisions made below the presidential level actually determine the outcome of decisions that come to the president for approval.

The bureaucratic system is basically inert; it moves only when pushed hard and persistently. The majority of bureaucrats prefer to maintain the status quo, and at any one time only a small group is advocating change. The time and resources of any one person in the bureaucracy are limited, and when a participant does desire change, he or she must choose carefully the issues on which to do battle.

During the cold war period, most policy issues were not new; the same or similar issues arose time and again. Organizations thus developed well-understood and predictable positions. Even most senior participants from "outside" were likely to have encountered the issue in the past and to have a view on it. In the majority of cases, moreover, the choice was between current actions and a single alternative being pushed by participants desiring change. For most participants, most of the time, the effort to determine what stand to take on an issue did not involve a canvass of alternatives. Rather, they examined a particular issue in terms of their own interests and arrived easily at a stand. Even when an issue was new—or new to particular participants—it was likely to be presented to them in a way that reflected their own interests, and they would be able immediately to identify what stand to take. With the end of the cold war and the dramatic series of changes that the world experienced over the following decade, culminating in the September 11 terrorist attacks on the World Trade Center and the Pentagon in 2001, the uncertain environment itself became more of a factor in forcing policy issues to the fore. The bureaucracy simply could not afford to avoid them, and many of the traditional cold war stands were no longer relevant or appropriate. Bureaucrats developed new sets of institutional stands to promote their own interests in the changing environment. By the end of the first term of the second President Bush in 2004, their stands were in the process of becoming as structured as those of bureaucrats during the cold war period.

In general, once an issue has been defined and participants have developed a stand, those desiring change are likely to raise the issue when events, as they perceive them, either provide opportunities for change theretofore absent or increase the cost of continuing to operate without change. During the cold war, it was rare that changes in the environment alone would lead to changes in participants' interests or in their judgments about the desirability of particular decisions. The Army, for example, had been continuously in favor of an ABM deployment since the mid-1950s, when the concept of the ABM was developed. However, it began to press seriously for deployment only in the late 1950s and again in the mid-1960s, when technological innovation, domestic politics, and Soviet action made success seem more likely. When its efforts were overtaken by the conclusion of an ABM Treaty with the Soviet Union, the Army had to wait until the Reagan administration, when the president's fascination with the concept created an opportunity to revive arguments in favor of ABM deployment. Those arguments were pursued intermittently during successive administrations, when the Army believed that technological innovation, continuing support from conservative politicians, and ultimately the rise of the "rogue state" threat made success seem likely.

In some cases, the degree of determination to seek a decision may be related to a particular event that creates more favorable circumstances, as with the breakthroughs in technology in the mid-1960s that made an ABM system seem significantly more attainable. In other cases, ideological thinking might be the motivating factor for a group to seek a particular decision. They watch constantly for an opportunity to present their desired decision as the solution to a president's or a secretary's problem. The neoconservatives in the second Bush administration saw the removal of Saddam Hussein in Iraq as the long-term answer to securing a more benign environment for Israel in the Middle East. They used concerns about the al Qaeda terrorist threat after 9/11 and Saddam's pursuit of weapons of mass destruction to argue the urgency of attacking Iraq.

Pressing for Decisions

We have suggested some of the opportunities that lead participants to seek decisions. Those and other circumstances under which issues enter the decision process can be categorized as follows.

—*Dramatic changes in the actions of other nations or outside actors.* Sometimes the proponents of an issue find in the actions of another nation the rationale for proposing the change that they desire. Events abroad may provide opportunities to initiate a general policy review, for instance, and during that review a particular issue can be introduced. The death of Stalin, the French defeat of the European Defense Community, Castro's takeover in Cuba, the collapse of the Berlin Wall, and the terrorist attacks of 9/11 all allowed officials to argue that the premises for previous decisions had changed and that a reexamination was in order. Often in such cases, participants seek the chance to put forward solutions that they have already developed. When the Soviet Union exploded an atomic bomb, the proponents of a crash H-bomb program in the United States used the occasion to argue that the United States now had to move forward with that program. After 9/11, proponents of invading Iraq used the new sense of fear to renew their proposal.[1]

On the other hand, changes abroad do not guarantee a change in U.S. policy. Participants who fear that review of an issue will lead to decisions that they do not desire resist the argument that new decisions are needed. In early 1989, when pressed by a new administration on the question of German reunification, the European Bureau of the State Department advised that "the issue of German reunification is never far below the surface. However, the Germans themselves do not wish to increase the salience of this issue at this time. Nor do the other Europeans. There is no more inflammatory and divisive issue, and it serves no U.S. interest for us to take the initiative to raise it."[2]

1. Clarke, *Against All Enemies*, p. 32. Woodward, *Plan of Attack*, pp. 1–4.
2. Zelikow and Rice, *Germany Unified and Europe Transformed*, p. 26.

Some events are so unexpected that they force officials to develop views on an issue that simply did not exist before. Thus, following the unexpected fall of the Berlin Wall later in 1989, the State Department was actively pursuing German reunification less than a year later. Even in such unusual cases, however, established interests continue to influence perceptions. It also is quite possible that an issue is foreseen but that no participant has an incentive to seek a decision before the event occurs. High officials in particular are usually reluctant to commit themselves on hypothetical situations or to indulge in serious contingency planning. For example, although the possibility of Russian missiles in Cuba had been the subject of much debate before the autumn of 1962, only when there was indisputable evidence that Russian missiles were in Cuba did senior participants develop their stand on alternative options designed to get the missiles removed. Similarly, nearly forty years later, senior officials were inclined to view international terrorism as a threat to U.S. interests or facilities outside the United States; before September 11, they did not seriously contemplate or plan for the possibility of a major attack on U.S. territory.

Conventional analyses of foreign policy usually assume that the actions of other nations are the major stimulus for U.S. foreign policy decisions. We contend that they are only one stimulus, and not even the more frequent one. Most decisions are responses to domestic pressures, and the actions of other nations often figure merely as devices for argument.

—*New technology.* Changes in technology may open up new possibilities and force officials to make decisions. Changes may be cited to bolster the plausibility of the argument for a particular decision and hence lead to a more intensified effort to secure the desired result. Thus a major change in the debate about the ABM system occurred in 1965, when breakthroughs in antiballistic missile technology led many scientists and engineers to argue that an ABM was now feasible. Before then, the Army's efforts to press for ABM deployment could be checked by the testimony of most civilian scientists, who maintained an ABM system simply could not be designed to intercept a large number of incoming missiles. After 1965, expert testimony went substantially in the other direction, and the Army intensified its efforts to secure a favorable decision.

—*Changes in the shared images of the society or bureaucracy.* Changes in the shared images within the society or within the bureaucracy may be perceived by participants as an opportunity to reopen issues because the changes signify a changing domestic mood. For example, efforts to change the China policy of the United States were intensified in the late 1960s and early 1970s to capitalize on the dramatic change in the public's attitude toward the "Chinese threat"—a shift that greatly reduced the cost to the president of seeking to move into political and economic contact with the People's Republic of China. Similarly, in response to domestic pressures, human rights and democratic values, which were largely a rhetorical issue during the cold war, have become a fundamental and universal tenet of U.S. foreign policy. Presidents often are forced by domestic constituencies to emphasize humanitarian issues at the cost of other interests in U.S. foreign relations. Even if a given policy is not shaped mainly by domestic political constraints, changes in the domestic situation may create an opportunity to argue that there are new constraints that require new decisions. For example, many of those arguing against a continuation of the expansion of the American effort in Vietnam in early 1968 did so on the premise that further American aggression would have very serious domestic political costs that would outweigh foreign policy gains.

Even if a change in shared images is restricted to the bureaucracy it may likewise create an opportunity to present a new set of arguments in favor of a decision. Within the Nixon administration, opponents of a large ABM system were able to take advantage of the new acceptance within the bureaucracy of the impossibility of maintaining American strategic nuclear superiority. They could argue that the system was not necessary for maintaining American deterrence—now conceived of in terms of "sufficiency" rather than "superiority"—and hence should be ruled out.

—*Routine events.* A number of routine events require the American government—and in some cases the president personally—to state in public or to foreign governments a definite position on a particular issue. Such routine events provide at least an opportunity for participants to get an issue to the president and to press for a new decision. Once again, the case of the ABM system is illustrative. After Congress first voted funds for a system in 1966, the president was obliged each year to take a stand on ABM deployment in his annual budget message. Because of the public interest in the issue, there was an annual debate within the bureaucracy about what stand the president should take. International conferences may also force such decisions. If the UN is about to vote on the issue of restrictions on the use of biological weapons, or if the North Atlantic Council is about to take a stand on the desirability of a European security conference, the president must make a decision about what positions his ambassador should take.

In other cases, routine events simply provide an opportunity for raising an issue. Thus if the president of the United States is to make a speech—an annual event such as the State of the Union message or a speech to a convention—"subjects" may be suggested. Visits of foreign leaders to Washington and presidential trips abroad also provide such opportunities.

—*Changes in personnel.* Changes in personnel, particularly shifts among senior participants, are likely to be viewed as opportunities to seek new decisions. Career officers and junior participants may reopen issues on which they had previously lost if they believe that their defeat was related to the position of a departing official. In that spirit, the Joint Chiefs of Staff reopened a number of issues following the departure of Secretary of Defense Robert McNamara, believing that any other secretary of defense—and perhaps the new secretary of defense, Clark Clifford, in particular—was more likely to be sympathetic to their position.

New administrations generally feel obliged to review many of the decisions of the previous administration, and in the process career officials may try to push ahead with programs held up in the past. In the case of the Bay of Pigs invasion of Cuba, CIA planners saw an opportunity with the change of administration to press for a firm decision to proceed with an operation that they had been unable to get approved by the Eisenhower administration. When the second Bush administration came to office, political appointees worked with some career officials to repudiate a number of positions taken during the two Clinton terms on issues such as the Kyoto Protocol, on greenhouse gases; the agreement with North Korea to provide fuel if the government stopped pursuing nuclear weapons; the International Criminal Court; and ultimately, the ABM treaty with Russia.

—*Self-generated efforts.* In some cases, participants may decide to seek a decision even in the absence of dramatic changes in the actions of other nations, breakthroughs in new technology, significant changes in shared images, or important changes in personnel. Combinations of minor changes in several of those categories may create the opportunity to seek a new decision. Alternatively, the cost to an organization of continuing with business as usual may increase to the point that it is prepared to devote more effort to seeking change than it did in the past. A new approach to a problem may also lead participants to believe that they have an opportunity to obtain a new decision. The cumulative weight of closely spaced events is demonstrated in Herbert York's recollection of developments in the fall of 1952. He mentions "the invention and demonstration of the hydrogen bomb, the election of Eisenhower and the concomitant extensive personnel changes throughout the executive branch (the first complete change in twenty years), and the growing accumulation of intelligence reports which first indicated and then confirmed that the Soviet Union had already launched a major program for the development of large long-range rockets."[3] Out of a reconsideration of the missile question at that time came six crash programs to develop nuclear-tipped missiles.

RULES OF THE GAME

Participation in the decisionmaking process does not occur at random. There are numerous written and unwritten rules governing how an issue may enter the system, who can become involved, who must be consulted, and so forth. The rules of the game are devices for ordering how minds are brought to bear on a problem. Some rules derive from constitutional and legislative delegation of power; others are spelled out in executive orders and other executive documents. An unwritten code of ethics determines how a participant must relate to others in the bureaucracy. This code is constantly evolving, through changes in the written rules, personnel, and the general environment.

Perhaps the most visible set of rules in the national security bureaucracy involves the use of the National Security Council (NSC). President Truman, under whom the council was created, used it relatively infrequently and in an ad hoc way. President Eisenhower established a very formal National Security Council system, but it was virtually abolished by the Kennedy administration. President Johnson almost never used the council. The Nixon administration reestablished a formal NSC system with a group of subcommittees. Subsequent administrations have maintained the formal structure, which has evolved over time, to give the assistant to the president for national security affairs and his or her staff a key role in chairing interagency committees. The 9/11 Commission described the NSC in 2004 as follows:

> Since 1989 each administration has organized its top NSC bodies in three layers. At the top is the National Security Council, the formal statutory body whose meetings are chaired by the president. Beneath it is the Principals Committee, with cabinet-level representatives from agencies. The Principals Committee is usually chaired by the national security adviser. Next is the Deputies Committee, where the deputy agency heads meet under the chairmanship of the deputy national security adviser. Lower-ranking officials meet in many other working groups or coordinating committees, reporting to the deputies and, through them, to the principals.[4]

3. York, *Race to Oblivion*, p. 83.
4. National Commission on Terrorist Attacks upon the United States, *Staff Statement No. 8: National Policy Coordination*, March 24, 2004, p. 2 (www.9–11 commission.gov).

However, the attention focused on alternative NSC systems because they are visible tends to obscure the fact that most business is conducted outside of those systems. There always are other procedures for handling routine matters, even those that come before the president, and crises tend to be treated in different ways whether or not a formal system exists. Thus in contrasting administrations it is misleading to focus on the various formal NSC procedures. Rather, one must look at the entire range of established procedures and action channels for moving issues to the president.[5]

Some writers have argued that procedures make no difference—the participants and the setting determine what decisions are made. Procedures indeed are less important than shared images, the interests of the participants, and their power. Nevertheless procedures can make some difference. After playing a part in abolishing a number of formal requirements, including those in the NSC system, McGeorge Bundy later told an interviewer that he was "less impatient with procedures."[6] President Eisenhower, who received much criticism for his formal NSC system, made the following observation in his memoirs:

> Organization cannot make a genius out of an incompetent; even less can it, of itself, make the decisions which are required to trigger necessary action. On the other hand, disorganization can scarcely fail to result in inefficiency and can easily lead to disaster.[7]

Colin Powell, former chairman of the Joint Chiefs of Staff (JCS), blamed staff procedures for making the institution ineffective in the policy process:

> The sixteen-hundred-member joint staff that worked for the JCS spent thousands of man-hours pumping out ponderous, least-common-denominator documents that every chief would accept but few Secretaries of Defense or Presidents found useful. The tortuous routines worked out for processing this paper flow would have done credit to a thirteenth-century papal curia— successive white drafts, buff drafts, green drafts, and finally the sanctified, red-striped decision paper. These failings in the JCS were more than bureaucratic. In my judgment, this amorphous setup explained in part why the Joint Chiefs had never spoken out with a clear voice to prevent the deepening morass in Vietnam.[8]

5. The above reference also describes the small group formed during the Clinton administration to work outside the formal NSC system and restrict participation in sensitive security decisions involving the president. The first Bush administration used a similar device, called the "core group."

6. Graff, *The Tuesday Cabinet*, p. 96.

7. Eisenhower, *The White House Years*, vol. 1: *Mandate for Change, 1953–1956*, p. 114 (cited hereafter as *Mandate for Change*).

8. Powell, *My American Journey*, p. 398.

Powell welcomed the 1986 Goldwater-Nichols Defense Reorganization Act, which gave the chairman the right to voice his own opinion to the secretary and the president, leaving the other chiefs free to disagree. There seems to be little doubt, therefore, that procedures do make a substantial difference in determining who is involved, in what order, and with what control over the process.

Where Do Rules Come From?

The rules of the game derive from a number of sources, ranging from law to tradition. The Constitution itself establishes the basic framework of presidential and congressional responsibilities, as well as limitations on the government's powers. Congress also influences the rules of the game by designing legislation to limit the powers of the executive branch or by demanding information from the executive. Congress has on occasion changed the rules within the executive branch by insisting that certain kinds of determinations be made by particular officials, thereby requiring that they be brought into the game or requiring that certain actions be pushed to the level of that official. Congress's role in altering the rules of the game is discussed further in part 4.

The president can affect the rules of the game by reorganizing the executive branch of the government through formal orders or through informal directives to the Cabinet officials concerned. The first President Bush's national security adviser, Brent Scowcroft, added a "principals committee" to the NSC structure to facilitate NSC meetings without the president. The Cabinet officers may, in turn, alter the rules within their own departments by the directives that they issue on procedures for making decisions.

Many of the rules of the game, however, develop over time without any changes in the constitutional system, legislation, executive orders, or even orders from department chiefs. They arise from the operational habits and traditions that evolve in bureaucratic organizations, as described by a former State Department official:

> Once things have happened [in government], no matter how accidentally, they will be regarded as manifestations of an unchangeable Higher Reason. For every argument inside government that some jerry-built bureaucratic arrangement should be changed, there are usually twenty arguments to show that it rests on God's own Logic, and that tampering with it will bring down the heavens.[9]

9. Frankel, *High on Foggy Bottom: An Outsider's Inside View of the Government*, p. 30.

How Do Rules Affect the Process?

The rules of the game differ according to what kind of issue is involved. For example, budgets, legislation, cables, and commitments of military force all move in different channels under different rules. The rules in each case specify several things:

—*Who has the action?* "Having the action," a term widely used within the bureaucracy and almost unknown outside, refers to the individual or organization responsible for moving an issue through the government and for taking the initiative in drafting whatever papers are to go to the president. Even if a number of agencies must be consulted, one agency normally has the action. Within that agency a particular bureau has the action, and it is in charge of consulting and coordinating with other parts of the same agency. Within the other agencies to be consulted one particular bureau also has the action for that agency and is in charge of consulting with others. In a process that began during the Nixon administration and became more institutionalized in the Clinton and second Bush administrations, the NSC staff often has the action in drafting the memorandum to go to the president for his decision.

—*Who must sign off?* Before a document is addressed by a senior official, either a department head or the president, it must have the concurrence not only of the action bureau but also of a number of other bureaus within the department. In some cases Cabinet officers will not address a memorandum unless it has been cleared by other agencies involved. An example of how extensive the clearance process can become was offered by Richard Holbrooke:

> A new Under Secretary of State discovers that a routine cable—the kind that Under Secretaries are not supposed to see— on the Food for Peace Program has received 27 clearances before being sent out. No one is able to convince him that 27 different people needed to agree to the dispatch of such a message.[10]

In recent years, as bureaus and offices in the State and Defense Departments have proliferated and the speed of computers has brought more efficiency to the production of documents, the clearance process has become even more complex. When an issue moves to the president for his approval, concurrence frequently is required from a number of different agencies as well as from one or more individuals on the White House staff. In other cases the rules permit the national security adviser to take an issue to the president without informing other agencies or without getting formal clearances on

---

10. Holbrooke, "The Machine That Fails," p. 71.

the memorandum. That practice became even more widespread during the second Bush administration.

—*How high up must an issue go?* The rules generally specify the sorts of issues that have to go to the president, which ones must go to Cabinet officers, and which can be signed off at lower levels. Issues brought up in the form of congressional legislation must receive presidential attention. Executive orders delegate some of the president's authority to specific Cabinet officers. More frequently, however, the operating rules are not written down anywhere but are understood intuitively by those involved.

—*Through what channels does an issue move up to the president?* The rules of the game specify what issues should move through formal National Security Council procedures, what issues can move by virtue of a memorandum from a particular secretary or the national security adviser to the president, and what issues come through budgetary or other special channels. In many cases there is some flexibility and leeway at certain points in the process, but generally a standard procedure is designated for moving a particular issue.

—*Can informal channels be used?* In almost all cases there are alternative ways to secure clearances from particular agencies and departments. Clearances occur at varying levels in different departments depending on the informal network of people who know each other and feel solidarity on a particular issue. A president usually has at his disposal information that comes to him informally in what is described in the bureaucracy as "bootleg" copies of memoranda.[11] (Chapter 11 discusses in greater detail the use of informal channels to the president.)

What varies greatly is the willingness of presidents to act on such information. Truman and Kennedy were more prepared to move on the basis of information obtained in informal ways, whereas Eisenhower and to a lesser extent Johnson insisted on more formal channels. Robert Cutler, who served as Eisenhower's assistant for national security affairs, described his first and only effort to move informally to the president:

> And, when I was new on the job, Pete Carroll and I suggested to the President trying to save the tottering regime of Premier Mayer of France by at once telephoning to Churchill to arrange for the announcement of a U.S.-U.K.-France conference in Bermuda. The President looked at us quizzically: "You boys think you are Assistant Secretaries of State? Go talk to Bedell Smith [General Walter Bedell Smith]." We did.[12]

11. Clark and Legere, eds., *The President and the Management of National Security,* p. 125.
12. Cutler, *No Time for Rest,* p. 316.

However, by the turn of the twenty-first century, presidents were much more willing to take the advice of the national security adviser and act without hearing the views of the Cabinet heads.

—*In what form does an issue come to the president?* For issues that do move up to the president, the president himself sets the rules that specify either in general or in relation to the issue at hand whether he is to receive an agreed recommendation of his principal advisers, alternative recommendations from each of his principal advisers, or simply a set of stated options from which he may choose a course of action.

On routine matters all presidents prefer and press for agreed recommendations from their principal advisers. That saves them the trouble of having to get into the issue to make a decision and also avoids putting them in the position of overruling their senior associates. However, presidents differ as to whether they want an agreed recommendation on major issues or their advisers' separate views. President Nixon, in instituting a new National Security Council system at the beginning of his administration, emphasized that he wished to receive from the bureaucracy a series of stated options, regardless of whether they were being recommended by any of his principal advisers. He indicated he would then receive the advice of his principal associates on the various options before making his own decision. President Truman apparently preferred to get alternative recommendations from his principal associates. Presidents Clinton, Eisenhower, and Johnson, in contrast, emphasized the importance of unanimous recommendations from their advisers. Johnson's memoirs are replete with references to his efforts to get his principal advisers to agree with each other and his reluctance to take action unless they did.[13] Eisenhower, even on issues of major concern and personal interest to him, preferred to have agreed recommendations before he acted. Sherman Adams, after reporting President Eisenhower's great interest in disarmament, explained how the issue was handled in the Eisenhower administration:

> The President urged Stassen to keep on searching aggressively for a new way to break the disarmament deadlock at the next United Nations Disarmament Subcommittee meeting in London in 1957. Stassen prepared for presentation in London a long list of proposals. When these ideas were ready to be discussed, the President went over them in a meeting attended by Dulles, Stassen, Wilson, Radford, and William Jackson. Stassen wanted to conduct exploratory talks with the British and needed an agreement about the subjects for negotiation. Dulles wanted to try an agreement that

13. Johnson, *The Vantage Point.*

would test the intentions of the Soviets. Radford was wary of any agreement to reduce our strength that would be based on the good faith of the Soviets. Strauss talked about the difficulty of detecting underground blasts and of devising a reliable inspection system. Nobody completely agreed with anybody else. His patience exhausted, the President interrupted the game of musical chairs. "Something has got to be done," he declared. "We cannot just drift along or give up. This is a question of survival and we must put our minds at it until we can find some way of making progress. Now that's all there is to it." The discussion began again until it reached the point where the President said to Stassen, "Now take these things we've discussed to Lewis Strauss and the Defense people and get up a paper on which they can agree." As everybody arose to leave the room, Stassen collected his notes and went back to work again. That was how it went with disarmament talks most of the time.[14]

Why Are Rules Obeyed?

Incentives to obey the rules of the game derive from law, habit, and organizational pressures. Some rules must be obeyed on penalty of a jail sentence. The Comptroller General of the United States monitors the actions of the executive branch to be sure that they are in conformity with the Constitution and the laws passed by Congress, particularly with regard to the expenditure of government funds. The Office of Management and Budget performs a similar function for the president, in addition to developing the executive branch budget. Even more important than legality is the strong sense on the part of most participants that the rules of the game ought to be obeyed; an individual who joins an organization implicitly agrees to accept the rules under which that organization operates. That does not mean, of course, that individuals do not ignore some of the rules some of the time or seek to change the rules on occasion to further their own interests and objectives. But in general most participants, especially career officials, simply accept the rules of the game as a matter of course and follow them. Even when habits and legal requirements are not compelling, participants obey the rules if they feel that the advantages of disobeying or ignoring them to achieve a particular objective will in the long run be outweighed by the adverse consequences of having once ignored the rules. For example, participants may calculate that if they redefine the rules of the game so as to exclude a particular individual from consideration

14. Adams, *Firsthand Report*, p. 326.

of an issue, he or she may well exclude them from consideration of another issue when he or she has the action.

Compliance with the rules of the game is further enforced by monitoring groups within government organizations and by senior officials themselves who may withhold concurrence or refuse to forward a document. Participants find that if they do not follow the rules of the game their proposals simply do not get cleared. Personal relations and anticipated personal reactions also play a role. The probability that an offender or his or her boss will get an angry phone call as a result of noncompliance with the established rules is, in most cases, a strong incentive to follow the rules of the game.

Why Do Rules Change?

Changes in rules come about because of personal relationships among participants, because particular participants decide to make an effort to change the rules, or because personnel arrive and depart. The most important of these factors is the personal relationship between presidents and senior participants and between senior participants and their key subordinates.

PERSONAL RELATIONS. When the president is known to rely heavily on the judgment of a senior Cabinet official and when that official is prepared to assert him- or herself, the rules may be heavily influenced. Traditionally in foreign policy, the most important personal relationship was that between the president and the secretary of state. Truman's relationship with Acheson and Eisenhower's with Dulles, for example, meant that, regardless of any formal procedures, the secretary of state could make decisions affecting other departments and have them obeyed; it also meant that policy issues tended to funnel through the secretary to the president. When the secretary of state is unwilling to assert him- or herself or is not seen as being the president's principal adviser, access to the president tends to be more diffused. If several senior participants are equally close to the president, none yields to the others' judgment. As the role of the national security adviser grew from the 1970s on, the relationship between the president and secretary of state became somewhat diluted. In the Carter administration the national security adviser, Zbigniew Brzezinski, often influenced the president against the advice of Cyrus Vance, the secretary of state. Vance eventually resigned in protest after President Carter decided to heed Brzezinski's recommendation to launch a military mission to rescue the American hostages being held in Iran and the attempt failed. During the first Bush presidency, the national security adviser,

Brent Scowcroft, and Secretary of State James Baker worked in close partnership with the president. President Clinton encouraged many voices to weigh in on policy decisions and engaged his vice president as a core component of the process. The second Bush presidency continued the tradition of a strong vice president but allowed serious differences between Secretary of State Colin Powell and Secretary of Defense Donald Rumsfeld to surface during the first term and often appeared to play senior cabinet officials against one another.

The determination of who is a senior participant and what rules they observe depends heavily on the inclination of the president. Some participants will be senior, regardless of their formal position, because of their personal standing in the political or intellectual community. Averell Harriman, assistant secretary of state for Far Eastern affairs under Kennedy, was a senior participant, as was Adlai Stevenson when he was ambassador to the United Nations, long before the formal rules made the occupant of the position a senior participant. During the second Bush administration, the position of ambassador to the UN was downgraded again. In other cases, participants carry weight (or indeed figure in the making of foreign policy at all) because of personal relations with the president. That was true not only of Attorneys General Robert Kennedy and John Mitchell but also of Roger Hilsman, who as director of intelligence and research in the State Department had the ear of President Kennedy.

After the cold war period, presidents began to assign increasing responsibility in the policy process to their vice presidents, beginning in the later Reagan administration with Vice President Bush. President Clinton gave Vice President Al Gore specific areas of responsibility within the policy process, including leadership of a multiyear program to build wide-ranging bilateral relations with countries, such as Russia and South Africa, with whom friendly relations had been out of the question earlier. To meet his expanded responsibilities, Vice President Gore maintained a much larger staff than previous vice presidents. That structure continued and even expanded under Vice President Cheney, who was given unprecedented authority and even autonomy in the national security decisionmaking process by the second President Bush. In the words of one former official, "The Office of the Vice President has representatives at the assistant secretary level, deputies level, and principals level. They are there at every meeting, acting as an independent agency with independent views."[15]

15. *The Financial Times,* U.S. edition, February 18–19, 2006, p. 7. Bob Woodward in *Plan of Attack* describes in detail the critical role of Vice President Cheney in shaping President Bush's post–9/11 response to the terrorist threat, especially the attack on Iraq.

The same considerations affect the rules of the game within a department. The secretary's style and personal relations with his subordinates affect the extent to which his deputy's authority is accepted, who will have access to him, and the extent to which the formal rules are followed. The fact that Secretary of Defense McNamara had confidence in the techniques of systems analysis and in the individuals doing systems analysis in the Pentagon meant that they were consulted and involved in a broad range of issues. Secretary of Defense Melvin Laird showed less confidence in both the method and the individuals and tended to rely more heavily on military judgments.[16] By virtue of the trust placed in him by Secretary of Defense Caspar Weinberger, Richard Perle, the assistant secretary for international security policy, was able to insert himself into the highest levels of the policy process, consistently attempting to scuttle arms control negotiations with the Soviets during the first Reagan administration.[17]

ASSERTIVENESS. Another aspect of the influence of personal relations on the rules of the game is the effect of maneuvers by participants who succeed in convincing other participants to involve them in particular actions because it would be costly not to do so. Individuals who assert their right to be heard on an issue—who are known to complain to the Cabinet officer involved if they are not consulted—are likely to be consulted because of the perception that not to notify them means unnecessary fuss and disagreement, while an individual who is passive is less likely to be heard. Thus the rules of the game are shaped so that some State Department "country directors" are always consulted on economic or scientific matters pertaining to "their" country, while others are never consulted.

In that way, the role of any particular individual in a particular job can be influenced by the actions of his predecessors. If previous assistant secretaries of state for European affairs have asserted the right to be consulted on trade issues affecting western Europe, then a new incumbent is likely to be consulted, at least until he or she indicates a lack of interest in such issues. Alternatively, if his or her predecessors have not been involved in a question, the new incumbent may have to assert the right to be consulted.

Sometimes senior officials deliberately use aggressive subordinates to push a reluctant bureaucracy into accepting new policies. Apparently that was the case during the Clinton administration when the NSC was trying to press

16. *New York Times*, September 13, 1969; *Wall Street Journal*, February 10, 1970.
17. Talbott, *The Master of the Game*, p. 163.

agencies to take the terrorism threat more seriously. The 9/11 Commission provided an example of this phenomenon:

> Clarke [then chairman of the NSC's Counterterrorism and Security Group] was a controversial figure. A career civil servant, he drew wide praise as someone who called early and consistent attention to the seriousness of the terrorism danger. A skilled operator of the levers of government, he energetically worked the system to address vulnerabilities and combat terrorists. Some colleagues have described his working style as abrasive. Some officials told us that Clarke had sometimes misled them about presidential decisions or interfered in their chain of command. National Security Adviser Berger told us that several of his colleagues had wanted Clarke fired. But Berger's net assessment was that Clarke fulfilled an important role in pushing the interagency process to fight bin Laden. As Berger put it, 'I wanted a pile driver.'"[18]

MANEUVERING TO CHANGE RULES. Although most participants obey the established rules most of the time, maneuvers to change rules occur fairly frequently. Participants often believe that they can change the rules in ways that will increase their influence or result in particular decisions that they desire. They think carefully about change if the existing rules have resulted in a bad decision or failure to focus proper attention on an issue. President Kennedy made a number of changes in the rules of the game as a result of the Bay of Pigs fiasco. A new president or a new Cabinet officer may seek to change rules because of a preferred style of behavior or because he believes that things were not done properly under his predecessor. Other changes occur as a result of cumulative frustrations. Thus President Eisenhower devoted a substantial amount of time in the last few years of his administration to changing the decisionmaking procedures within the Department of Defense, and he did so expressly because of his belief that the United States was continuing to spend too much money on defense and getting inefficiently designed forces.[19]

There are a number of ways that participants can alter the rules. Presidents frequently readjust the procedures for making major national security policy decisions, including the form in which they receive suggested options and alternatives. That may drastically affect the degree to which the rules require unanimity among the departments. In some cases, rather than seek-

18. National Commission on Terrorist Attacks upon the United States, *Staff Statement No. 8,* March 24, 2004, p. 3 (www.9–11commission.gov).
19. Eisenhower, *Waging Peace,* pp. 217, 222, 484.

ing to change the system in general, key participants establish a unique set of rules for a particular activity. General George Marshall, for example, when sent on a mission to China to seek to negotiate a compromise between the Communists and the Nationalists, arranged with Truman for a unique decisionmaking arrangement that involved sending his reports and recommendations to under secretary of state Acheson, who in turn carried them directly to the president.[20]

When he feels that a particular approach has not been included in analyzing a set of issues, the president may create a new office and install in it an individual whom he expects to bring to bear the desired expertise and approach to policy issues.[21] Secretary of Defense Rumsfeld created a new intelligence office, the Policy Counterterrorism Evaluation Group, in the Pentagon during the second Bush presidency to produce intelligence analysis that would support the president's desire to stage a preventive attack on Saddam Hussein.[22] Instead of creating a new position, however, the president may simply direct that certain individuals be brought in who were not previously involved in a particular range of issues; alternatively, a participant can be told that he or she is no longer to be involved.

Changing the rules may involve the creation of a new channel for moving issues to decision, or it may simply involve moving an issue from one existing channel to another. For example, the ABM question was moved by President Nixon from the channel of direct bilateral relations between the president and the secretary of defense into the National Security Council, where a number of other agencies would be consulted. George F. Kennan reports that the role of the Planning Council in the Department of State was substantially changed when he was told he could no longer present papers to the secretary without the concurrence of the relevant regional assistant secretary.[23]

NEW PARTICIPANTS. Changes in personnel probably account for a substantial part of the changes in the rules of the game, even when that may not be the intention. The replacement of Clark Clifford by Charles Murphy as special counsel to the president in the fall of 1949 altered the involvement of the White House staff on national security matters. Clifford had been especially

---

20. Acheson, *Present at the Creation*, p. 143; Acheson, *Sketches from Life*, pp.150–51.

21. For a discussion of the different ways in which presidents have changed or might change the rules in an effort to get better advice from the military, see Halperin, "The President and the Military."

22. Pillar, "Intelligence, Policy, and the War in Iraq," *Foreign Affairs* 85, no. 2 (March-April 2006), p. 24.

23. Kennan, *Memoirs, 1925–1950*, p. 465.

interested in such matters and had developed a wide range of contacts with officials in various agencies. Murphy, who was not especially interested, had not developed comparable contacts and consequently played a negligible role in such matters, reducing the likelihood that the president would receive information informally.[24]

Similarly, changes in personnel bring about changed conceptions of particular roles in the bureaucracy. That can have a major effect on rules, especially where senior participants are concerned. For example, Secretary of Defense McNamara explicitly saw his role not only as arbitrator among the armed services and manager of the Defense Department but also as innovator in strategy and weapons procurement. Thus the rules of the game on defense budget issues and strategy issues were quite different under McNamara than they had been under his predecessors, particularly Charles Wilson and Neil McElroy. Secretary of Defense Donald Rumsfeld played a similar role in the second Bush presidency.

If the change in personnel consists of promotion of a career official to fill a job previously occupied by another career official, the results are likely to be considerably less dramatic. That is especially frustrating when one hopes to find a career official who will challenge the interests of his organization as defined by that organization. President Eisenhower tried to appoint an Army chief of staff who would accept his strategy of massive retaliation—a strategy that entailed a severe cut in the size of the Army because of its all-out emphasis on nuclear weapons. He was, however, constrained to choose among the senior officers of the Army, and both of the men he appointed to the position, General Matthew Ridgway and General Maxwell Taylor, ultimately resigned and publicly denounced the policy. When the issue turns on debate within a branch of the armed services as to its essence, then promotion of particular individuals can make a difference. Thus both sides in the struggle within the Army over whether heavy emphasis should be given to an Army medium-range missile program sought to put their men into the right positions.[25]

Senior participants, and even some at lower levels, have wide scope within which they can define the nature of their job and their interests. The rules of the game very quickly adjust to the interests of senior participants and the standing of those officials with the president. Each new administration tends to produce its own set of rules. When Arms Control and Disarmament Agency (ACDA) director Eugene Rostow succeeded in getting President Reagan to appoint Paul Nitze chief negotiator for intermediate-range nuclear forces

24. Hammond, "NSC-68," pp. 336–37.
25. Armacost, *The Politics of Weapons Innovation*, pp. 122, 167.

early in the Reagan administration, he set the stage for serious arms control negotiations with the Soviet Union in an administration that appeared otherwise determined to repudiate arms control.[26]

What we have referred to as the rules of the game are often described as the structure of national security decisionmaking or the organizational arrangements of the foreign affairs bureaucracy. Much attention is given to changes in those structures and in particular to the varying ways in which presidents use the National Security Council and its apparatus. The premise of this book is that the rules do not dominate the process, although, to the extent that they structure the game, they do make a difference. That still leaves considerable room for participants to maneuver. We have seen them maneuvering to change the rules in their favor. We turn now to how participants plan their moves within whatever framework of rules exists—plan, that is, to get the decisions that they want.

26. Talbott, *Master of the Game*, pp. 168–69.

CHAPTER SEVEN

Planning a
Decision Strategy

We use the term "planning" here to describe the process of systematically working out a strategy designed to secure a desired government decision and action.[1] Usually planning focuses on the president, because often the decision wanted is one that only the president can make. (Sometimes planning in our sense may involve keeping an issue from getting to the president.) Frequently, the central problem in planning is to determine how one can get the issue to the president, put him in a position where he believes he has to make a decision, and then get him to decide in one's favor. That involves structuring the issue and affecting who participates in the process. Of course, the president himself may initiate or engage in planning.

DEFINING THE ISSUE

Once a participant or coalition of participants reaches the conclusion that the time is right to seek a decision, those parts of the bureaucracy with a direct interest in the issue usually become aware of the move toward a change. Initial efforts to head off the reopening of an issue sometimes succeed. If not, however, most officials with an interest at stake come to accept that an issue

1. Confusion is generated by the common use of the word "planning" to mean a number of things. Here it is used in the sense of laying out a scheme designed to secure a desired government decision and action. In the title of the State Department's Policy Planning Staff or Council, the word means an organization that would mainly write papers estimating the long-run consequences of possible courses of action if undertaken by the government, although members of the staff do from time to time engage in planning in the sense used here.

is being reviewed and that there is, according to their view, either danger of or opportunity for a new presidential decision. That recognition often occurs sequentially. More and more organizations and participants come to recognize that a presidential decision may in fact be made. In some cases, recognition moves from the top of the government downward, particularly if it is the president who is initiating policy review, or it may move upward, from lower levels of the government.

Most issues are not new, having already been defined in terms of the interests involved. However, when an issue is revived or when a novel proposal is being made, some participants analyze the implications for their view of national security and for their own interests. Those who feel the need for such analysis are likely to be those less affected by the outcome than other participants. Often these relatively open-minded participants are the ones whose allegiance is fought over in the struggle to secure the desired presidential decision.

Once participants recognize that an issue is under review, they must determine just what kind of decisions they want and what changes and actions they expect to follow. They also must determine what bad decisions they are most anxious to avoid and, finally, consider what compromises they are prepared to make.

After defining the end goal of their actions, participants must determine in what order to present the elements to be decided. Often they seek a decision in principle or a decision that they believe will lead to the ultimate decision desired. They try to get the president to make what seems like the easier choices before raising more difficult issues on which the president is less likely to decide in their favor. In February 1968, when General Earle Wheeler, chairman of the Joint Chiefs of Staff, and General William Westmoreland, chief of American military forces in Vietnam, concluded that the United States should invade Laos and Cambodia, they also concluded that, in order to do so, they needed a substantial increase in American forces in Vietnam. General Wheeler decided to take the decisions one step at a time. After a meeting with Westmoreland in Saigon, Wheeler returned to Washington and presented his famous request for 205,000 additional troops.[2] He did not tell the president or other participants in Washington that the troops were wanted so that the United States could invade Cambodia and Laos. As he later explained:

> Back in Washington I emphasized how Westy's forces were very badly stretched, that he had no capability to redress threats except by moving

2. See Johnson, *Vantage Point*, pp. 388–415, for the presidential account of this episode.

troops around. I emphasized the threat in the I Corps. More attacks on the cities were, I said, a possibility. I argued that Westy needed flexibility and capability. I talked about going on the offensive and taking offensive operations, but I didn't necessarily spell out the strategic options [that is, that the troops were to be used to invade Cambodia and Laos].[3]

Sometimes decision strategies are designed from the top down. Philip Zelikow and Condoleezza Rice, who were on the NSC staff in the first Bush presidency, described White House planning in the early days of the administration to extract policy decisions from a reluctant bureaucracy to demonstrate American leadership in response to the rapid political evolution then under way in Europe:

> Still lacking, in March 1989, any significant policy initiatives to use in launching such a diplomatic offensive, the White House had decided to create action-forcing events, including presidential trips and speeches that would oblige the government to develop policies.[4]

Having made the calculations about their operational goals and the sequence in which to pursue them, participants must develop a concrete plan of action. They must determine in what form to raise the issue, what kinds of policy analyses are likely to be needed, who should be brought in and how, who should be kept out and how, and how high up to go. Will the president come down on the "right" side, or should the issue be kept out of the presidential purview? The participant developing a plan also needs to determine which argument to use with which other participants, when and how. He or she needs to consider the strategy likely to be adopted by opponents and to develop, at least on a contingency basis, plans for meeting them. Finally, periodically during the process, he or she needs to reassess where the plan is going—whether the strategy should be changed or the effort to get a favorable decision (or to resist an unfavorable one) should be abandoned.

WHO IS INVOLVED?

A participant seeking a decision or seeking to block one is wise to ask him- or herself who else is likely to be involved in the process. Perhaps the key issue is to determine who is likely to be particularly influential with the president on the range of issues involved. Neustadt has said that perhaps the most active

3. Henry, "February 1968," p. 24.
4. Zelikow and Rice, *Germany Unified and Europe Transformed*, p. 25.

game in Washington is seeking to determine who has influence with the president on what issues.

Since officials and advisers often have a choice of whether or not to get involved, the participant planning the strategy needs to consider who, perhaps, could be persuaded to stay out. He or she recognizes that some participants are natural allies who, for their own reasons, are prepared to support the desired decision. Others are potential converts, who might be brought along by either persuasion or bargaining. Still others are probably neutral. Finally, there are those participants whose goals are incompatible and whose opposition will have to be overcome. Perhaps the "balance of forces" can be altered by convincing an individual or faction not to participate.

Opting In or Out

Whether to become actively involved is a critical choice for each potential participant if the rules of the game have not already settled the question. In general, being "in the game" is the more desirable option for most participants, but there are times when some will find it more advantageous to opt out. In some cases the rules of the game make it almost impossible for some officials to remain totally out of a particular struggle, since their views are almost certain to be requested by the president or by a Cabinet officer. Even in such cases, however, they can temporize if they choose. Thus the Joint Chiefs of Staff (JCS) carried out only the most perfunctory evaluation of the CIA plan for the invasion of Cuba in 1961 and made it clear that responsibility rested with the CIA. Dean Rusk, secretary of state in the Kennedy and Johnson administrations, often managed to avoid involvement in key issues. For example, aware that his presence in Nassau at a meeting with U.K. leaders in 1962 might be interpreted by some State Department officers as a form of support for their desire to eliminate the British nuclear force and convinced that the outcome of the Nassau talks would be the opposite (which he himself desired), Rusk chose to honor a long-standing commitment at a diplomatic dinner rather than accompany President Kennedy to Nassau to meet Harold Macmillan.[5] Cabinet officers may find that they must at least appear not to be involved, in order to throw the public off the scent of a crisis issue that has not yet reached decision. Other officials find that their responsibilities do not routinely involve them in an issue but do give them an opportunity to fight to be involved; they then have to weigh the advantages of involvement against the cost of fighting their way in.

5. Letter to Morton H. Halperin from Dean Rusk, January 8, 1973.

Such calculations and others can be summed up in a hypothetical check-list that a prudent official might draw up for himself to judge whether to get involved in an impending decision.

—*Time and energy.* An analysis of a particular decision frequently misses the fact that no matter how important the issue may appear to an observer in retrospect, it was only one of a large number of issues confronting any senior participant at the time. Participants are concerned about a great many things. The importance of particular issues is impressed upon them by their subordinates, and they must pick and choose. They have neither the time nor the energy to fight every issue brought to their attention, no matter how important it may seem to their subordinates or to an outside observer. Henry Kissinger offered this explanation of Secretary of Defense McNamara's failure to get involved in a number of early debates about Vietnam strategy:

> McNamara's profundity in analysis had to give way to a very practical problem: how many times a month could he go to the mat with the JCS? He had to decide very deliberately which issues he could confront them with. If one wants to explain why it is that McNamara's theories about the war in Vietnam were not always matched by implementation, espe-cially toward the end, the primary reason was that he felt that confronted with issues of ABM, troop deployment, force levels, renewal of the strate-gic force, and Vietnam strategy, he could only handle so many of these cases simultaneously. He picked those which he thought were crucial at the moment.[6]

—*Reputation with the president.* Senior participants value their reputation with the president highly, and they carefully assess how involvement in any particular issue may affect their relationship. They want to "win" with the president, they want to impress colleagues, and they want what they recom-mend to work if their advice is taken. Secretary of Defense McNamara, for example, was reluctant to get involved in the issue of how to fight the war in Vietnam, for he did not believe that his competence on that issue was greater than that of the Joint Chiefs of Staff.[7] Secretary of State George C. Marshall refused to endorse JCS efforts to get a substantial increase in the military budget in 1949 because he did not believe that the chiefs would spend the money in a sensible way that would increase American security.[8] Senior par-ticipants are reluctant to come to the president with what they know is unwel-

6. Kissinger, "Bureaucracy and Policy Making," p. 91. On the general question, see Caraley, *The Politics of Military Unification*, pp. 263–64.

7. Brandon, *Anatomy of Error*, p. 29.

8. Schilling, "The Politics of National Defense: Fiscal 1950," pp. 193–95.

come advice and risk an argument or quarrel with him. They recognize that any president will tune out senior participants who frequently come to him with counsel that he finds uncongenial, and therefore they save such attempts for issues on which they feel very strongly. It was such a calculation that kept Joseph Califano from involving himself in Vietnam issues when, during the Johnson administration, he moved from the Pentagon to the White House to become a principal adviser to the president on domestic policy issues.[9] Desiring to protect their reputation with the president, senior participants are reluctant to challenge him on issues where he does not view them as having expertise or competence. That concern heavily influenced what issues Secretary of State John Foster Dulles chose to get involved in:

> Dulles saw himself as Eisenhower's exclusive advisor on foreign policy and went to great lengths to protect this position. But the consequence of this was that the more an issue moved away from the center of foreign policy, the more carefully Dulles would pick his ground before asserting himself with the President. Dulles was very conscious of Ike's military background, and he knew that Ike had a lot of respect for Admiral Radford [Chairman of the Joint Chiefs of Staff]. And on economic matters, he watched what Humphrey would do first. He also thought it was hazardous to guess what Congress wanted.[10]

Senior participants are equally concerned with what their colleagues will think if their advice is rejected by the president. They recognize that their ability to operate effectively in the bureaucracy on issues of paramount concern to them depends on being known by other participants for effectiveness with the president. Dean Acheson and John Foster Dulles both guarded their reputations carefully, and that is part of the explanation for Dulles's unwillingness to get involved in military budget issues and economic issues. If he lost on those issues, people would begin to wonder whether he would indeed always win on diplomatic issues.

In 1948, Secretary of Defense James Forrestal had to decide whether to get involved in what was shaping up as a major confrontation between the Joint Chiefs of Staff and the chairman of the Atomic Energy Commission, David Lilienthal. At that time, the Atomic Energy Commission had complete custody and control of all nuclear weapons; contingency plans called for them to be turned over to the military only after the president had authorized their use.

9. Anderson, *The Presidents' Men*, p. 368.
10. Interview with Robert Bowie, October 22, 1964, as quoted in Edgerton, *Sub-Cabinet Politics and Policy Commitment*, p. 8.

The Joint Chiefs, unhappy about the situation because it denied them complete autonomy over the weapons, pressed for a change that would have the weapons turned over to military custody as soon as they were operational. Lilienthal, with the support of members of the White House staff, vigorously resisted such a move. Forrestal openly succumbed to pressure from the military and weighed in on their side, after he had rejected the advice of Lewis L. Strauss, who was then a member of the Atomic Energy Commission and later became its chairman. As the latter related it:

> "Don't do it, Jim," I urged. "The President will decide against you."
> "Why should he?" he asked.
> "For the same reason," I answered, "that the public still fears the 'trigger-happy Colonel.' Don't get yourself into a position where, for the first time in your dealing with him, the President will overrule you. If he does, the fact can't be kept secret. It's bound to leak. An important element in your authority is that the President has always backed you up in everything concerned with national defense."[11]

Despite Forrestal's intervention, Truman sided with Lilienthal, and Forrestal's influence declined, as Strauss had warned.

—*Account with the president.* Senior participants find that they can get the president to support them from time to time simply by making an issue of personal privilege. Unless there are overriding reasons not to, presidents tend to give in when their principal advisers feel very strongly about something. However, such influence must be carefully husbanded. If a senior participant draws upon his or her personal account with the president too frequently, he or she may come up short on influence when a matter of great importance comes along. In addition, senior participants discover that when they ask the president for something, he asks them for something in return. Are they prepared to pay the price?

—*Antagonizing others.* The principle of avoiding involvement for fear of losing to other senior participants is taken one step further in the principle of avoiding conflict with other participants lest they enter battle against "the troublemaker." Secretary of State Dulles was careful to stay out of areas where the powerful secretary of the treasury, George Humphrey, considered his responsibilities to be paramount. In return he expected Humphrey to stay out of foreign policy issues. Dulles drew the line very carefully, and that influenced how far he was prepared to go in fighting for the Development Loan Fund and for aid to the British at the time of the Suez crisis.[12]

—*Concept of one's role.* Some participants may stay out of an issue simply because they do not view it as part of their responsibility. For example, Charles Wilson and Neil McElroy, Eisenhower's secretaries of defense, both viewed their job as being managers of the Pentagon and did not involve themselves in foreign policy or strategic disputes.[13] Secretary of State Dean Rusk's conception of his role under Kennedy and Johnson required that he not engage in controversy with his colleagues, either in front of the president or elsewhere. He viewed his role as private adviser to the president and thus did not involve himself when issues were argued out in other forums.[14] Similarly, in late 2002, Secretary of State Colin Powell met privately with President Bush to express his concerns about the consequences of precipitating war in Iraq, rather than speaking frankly in front of other senior advisers who were pressing forward with battle plans.[15]

Often several of the motives listed above combine to explain the absence of a major figure's involvement in an important controversy. Such was the case for Henry Kissinger's failure to try to prevent starvation in Biafra following its capture and reincorporation into Nigeria:

> A major question is where the President and Henry Kissinger were through all of this. It appears that Kissinger was informed of the controversy in detail, and was deeply concerned, and backed his staff in its efforts to change State Department policy. But Kissinger is one of the busiest men in Washington, and he had other wars, literal and bureaucratic, to fight. Any official must decide his priorities, the issues on which he chooses to spend his capital, and the Nigerian case was not as important to him as were some others. Moreover, Kissinger's relationship with Richardson appears to have been an important factor. Because of the power that Kissinger has accrued, and because of Rogers' own relaxed approach to his job, the Secretary of State has become a largely irrelevant figure in the making of foreign policy. The relationship between Kissinger and Rogers is, from several accounts, strained. The axis of power and policy runs from Kissinger to Undersecretary Richardson, a cool, bright, and able man who is Kissinger's close friend. The two men

12. Neustadt, *Alliance Politics,* p. 99.

13. Snyder, "The 'New Look' of 1953," pp. 517–18; Halperin, "The Gaither Committee and the Policy Process," p. 373.

14. See the *Life* interview with Dean Rusk, "Mr. Secretary on the Eve of Emeritus," p. 62B.

15. Woodward, *Plan of Attack,* pp. 148–52.

have lunch once a week, and talk on the telephone several times a day. Richardson had charge of Nigerian policy, and Kissinger has confidence in him. Finally, the form in which the issue came up was incompatible with Kissinger's chosen role: he is the foreign policy conceptualizer, the grand strategist; this was an operational issue of a rather mundane sort—malnutrition statistics, trucks, food tonnages.[16]

Drawing the Circle

We have spoken of how officials judge whether it is in their interest to get involved in an issue. We also have spoken of their calculations as to possible allies and possible enemies. Once they become involved and once the calculations are made, a set of maneuvers for including certain participants and excluding opponents comes into play. Those efforts are constrained by the rules of the game, but within those rules there is considerable scope for maneuver, particularly by the president, to reduce the circle, widen the circle, or even change personnel.

REDUCING THE CIRCLE. We have mentioned the technique of persuading an uncommitted official that, given his interests, he should not get involved. If that fails, it may be possible to structure the procedure leading to a decision so that some potential participants are left out.

The usual rationale for excluding particular participants generally makes use of the argument that "security" must be maintained so that the planned course of action is not revealed prematurely through information given to allied governments or leaked to the press. As George Reedy explained, such arguments are likely to be received with sympathy at the White House:

> The environment of deference, approaching sycophancy, helps to foster another insidious factor. It is a belief that the president and a few of his most trusted advisers are possessed of a special knowledge which must be closely held within a small group lest the plans and the designs of the United States be anticipated and frustrated by enemies. It is a knowledge which is thought to be endangered in geometrical proportion to the number of other men to whom it is passed. Therefore, the most vital national projects can be worked out only within a select coterie, or there will be a "leak" which will disadvantage the country's security.[17]

16. Drew, "Washington," p. 24.
17. Reedy, *The Twilight of the Presidency*, pp. 10–11.

Such arguments were used effectively in the case of the Bay of Pigs invasion. Kennedy was informed by the CIA that information about covert operations of that kind should be restricted to a very tight circle of those who had "a need to know." On that basis, most of those involved in the analysis of foreign events in the CIA and the Department of State were excluded from consideration of the Bay of Pigs operation. During the second Bush presidency, Defense Secretary Rumsfeld, in the interests of secrecy, ensured that planning for the 2003 attack on Iraq was restricted to a very small circle in the Defense Department and the most senior national security officials surrounding the president, cutting out any advisers or analysts who would have raised the question of political consequences. Even when it came to postwar planning, Rumsfeld refused to allow State Department officials to participate, because he believed that they were not supportive.[18]

The second set of standard arguments for excluding potential participants relates to the notion that only those with responsibility for a particular issue need to be consulted. To an extent, exclusion can be accomplished in the way an issue is defined. In the case of the ABM program, McNamara, in effect, argued that it was a matter that concerned only his department and therefore should be settled bilaterally between the president and the secretary of defense, with only minimal consultation with other officials.

If the president is firmly committed to moving in a particular direction, the argument can be made to him that individuals who are likely to oppose the action or to raise objections should be excluded. The president may feel that he is thoroughly familiar with the arguments on both sides and does not want to waste time or to be bogged down hearing objections or pleas for consultation with allies. President Carter deliberately excluded State Department experts from his preparations to normalize relations with China. As he explained,

> Secretary Vance was conversant with every dispatch we sent and had constant access to me, so I did not give much weight to his disgruntled subordinates in the State Department, some of whom had been a constant source of complaints to the news media regarding the national security adviser's having too much influence over foreign policy. If these assistants at the State Department felt excluded from the China normalization process . . . it was because of my orders to hold information closely so that our efforts would not be subverted.[19]

18. Woodward, *Plan of Attack*, pp. 283–84.
19. Carter, letter to the editor, p. 165.

One tactic used on those to be excluded is simply not to inform them that a decision is under consideration. Obviously officials kept in the dark are not in a position even to volunteer advice or information. President Nixon apparently did not inform a number of officials of his plan to invade Cambodia in April 1970. Even more tightly held was the decision at the same time to engage in limited bombing of North Vietnam. In that case, according to the journalist Hugh Sidey, the secretary of defense was not informed of the full extent of the planned bombing operations, and the secretary of state was not informed at all.[20]

The second President Bush allowed Vice President Cheney to cut EPA director Christine Todd Whitman completely out of the White House decision to withdraw from the Kyoto Protocol on global warming in 2001. According to the biographer of former treasury secretary Paul O'Neill, the vice president got a member of Congress to send a letter requesting clarification of the new administration's policy on global warming in order to give the White House, not the EPA, the initiative in articulating policy in its response to the letter. The response, drafted by Cheney, announced the president's decision to withdraw from the Kyoto Protocol, abruptly rejecting Whitman's inclination to work with the international community.[21]

Although it is quite irregular to deny Cabinet officers information about impending decisions, officials at lower levels often are excluded. The chief of intelligence in the Department of State and the CIA's deputy director for intelligence were not informed of the impending invasion of Cuba in 1961. Refusal to inform officials can sometimes be carried to the extreme of not telling them "officially" about something that they have already caught wind of. That occurred when the senior officials of the United States Information Agency (USIA) learned from a reporter that the United States was planning to invade Cuba. Donald M. Wilson, who was then deputy Director of USIA, described the bizarre episode:

> I had little to do with the Bay of Pigs operation. USIA was not informed, and I found out about it before it happened in a strange way. I was called on the telephone by Tad Szulc of the *New York Times*. He had been down in Florida and insisted that I join him for breakfast at his father-in-law's house in Georgetown, at which point he revealed all he had found in Florida—only some of which he printed in the *New York Times*—and said that he was convinced that an invasion was about to take place, and

20. Sidey, "Nixon in a Crisis of Leadership," p. 28.
21. Suskind, *The Price of Loyalty*, pp. 120–28.

I think he talked to me because I was a friend of his and he didn't quite know what to do with it. So I went to Ed Murrow, who was my boss, and Murrow promptly called up Allen Dulles. Murrow and I went over to see Allen Dulles and told him everything Szulc had told me. Allen Dulles didn't give us a thing. He was very bland and he didn't admit that any of it was true and of course we knew it was by then—you could just tell— and Murrow was angry in a way but he was a loyal soldier and he realized, I guess, that he wasn't supposed to know about it. So we went back to USIA and pretty much operated in the dark during the Bay of Pigs thing. It was very unfortunate and poorly handled from all points of view and certainly from the propaganda point of view.[22]

Even when officials are informed or have become aware of a particular issue, they may be denied the right to comment or to prepare a study on the question involved. For example, after Roger Hilsman, who was director of the State Department's Bureau of Intelligence and Research, inadvertently learned about the planned invasion of Cuba, he confronted Secretary of State Rusk and asked for permission to have his Cuban experts prepare an analysis of the situation. Hilsman was denied permission to do the study.[23]

Preventing the circulation of documents is a tactic to forestall potential participants from drawing in officials on their staff to prepare careful comments on a proposal. Often documents are handed out at a White House meeting but then participants are refused permission to take copies back to their own agencies. That was in fact done during the Bay of Pigs preparations.[24]

Efforts also can be made to restrict the circle by failing to invite a particular participant to a key meeting. The White House staff, believing that Eisenhower was unduly influenced by the hard-line views of John Foster Dulles, tried from time to time to get Eisenhower committed to a particular course of action before the secretary of state was brought into the picture. Perhaps the most spectacular attempt occurred when Washington was informed that the Russian leader, Joseph Stalin, was dying. Robert Cutler, the president's assistant for national security, called a meeting with the president, a group of White House officials, and Allen Dulles, director of the CIA. It was decided at the meeting that the President should address a message to the Russian people. John Foster Dulles arrived at the White House after the meeting and

22. Wilson, Kennedy Library Oral History Interview, pp. 14–15. See also Thomas C. Sorensen, *The Word War: The Story of American Propaganda*.

23. Hilsman, *To Move a Nation*, p. 31.

24. Sorensen, *Kennedy*, pp. 304–05.

expressed serious reservations in an apparent effort to change the president's mind, but to no avail.[25]

While individual officials might be selectively excluded from the decision-making process, presidents also often form informal groups of top advisers to handle particular issues. President Jimmy Carter handled sensitive issues and issues still in a preliminary stage in an inner circle consisting of the secretary of state, secretary of defense, national security adviser, vice president, and select White House staff, which met regularly on Fridays.[26]

NSC adviser Brent Scrowcroft described how the decision circle around the president was reduced during the first Bush administration.

> It was becoming apparent to me that a full-blown NSC gathering was not always the place for a no-holds-barred discussion among the President's top advisors. Some might be inhibited from expressing themselves frankly with staff present and the constant possibility of leaks. I suggested that [an] opening session take place informally, in the Oval Office, and with only a select group present, in this case Quayle, Baker, Cheney, myself, Eagleburger, Gates, and Sununu. The President liked the suggestion, and it worked. This marked the beginning of a new pattern for top-level meetings (the "core group") during the rest of the Administration. While we continued to hold formal NSC meetings, an informal group became the rule rather than the exception for practical decision-making.[27]

WIDENING THE CIRCLE. Presidents, who sometimes try to reduce the circle themselves when they are sure what they wish to do, have methods to check such maneuvers by subordinates. Often they expand the circle precisely to keep certain protagonists from excluding critics. The basic argument used for enlarging the number of participants is the doctrine that the president should hear all points of view. More concretely it can be argued that others whose areas of responsibility are affected by a decision ought to be consulted and that the president should also hear "disinterested" individuals who do not have any bureaucratic responsibilities in the area under consideration. For example, following the Bay of Pigs fiasco, President Kennedy often consulted outside advisers as well as his brother Robert, then serving as Attorney General. President Johnson often consulted Clark Clifford and Abe Fortas, the former a lawyer practicing in Washington at the time and the latter then serv-

25. Cutler, *No Time for Rest,* p. 321.
26. Carter, letter to the editor, p. 164.
27. Bush and Scowcroft, *A World Transformed,* pp. 41–42.

ing as an associate justice of the Supreme Court. Sometimes the argument that an individual should be included relates not to the likelihood that he or she will provide information or options that the president will find of value but rather to the fear that his or her exclusion will entail political costs because of the belief of others, frequently others outside the executive branch, that the individual should be consulted. Presidents often feel pressure, particularly from senior members of Congress, to consult military leaders on matters concerning defense budgets or the employment of military force. For that reason General Earle Wheeler, chairman of the Joint Chiefs of Staff, was ultimately included in the Tuesday lunch at which President Johnson made his major Vietnam decisions.[28] Pressure may come from other senators and representatives to include other viewpoints. Members of the Senate Foreign Relations Committee, for example, often probe the administration as to whether officials of the Arms Control and Disarmament Agency were consulted before decisions were made. Though an individual may be brought into a discussion merely so it can be said that he or she was consulted, that individual, once involved, may affect the outcome.

There are a number of different ways in which individuals can be brought into the process. Doing so is easier when the individual concerned is anxious or at least willing to be involved, although some techniques can be effective in drawing in a participant who would prefer to remain aloof.

In some cases it is sufficient to inform participants that a decision is about to be made if they have no hesitation about being involved and the rules of the game clearly provide for their involvement. For example, State Department opponents of a proposed sale of American military aircraft to South Africa were able to block the sale by informing the U.S. ambassador to the United Nations, Arthur Goldberg, of the impending decision. Goldberg phoned under secretary of state Thomas Mann and was able to persuade him to cancel the sale.[29]

Another means of expanding the circle is to secure an invitation for a certain individual to participate in an existing forum. As indicated above, in 1966 President Johnson invited General Wheeler to participate in the Tuesday lunch discussions at which Vietnam matters were being debated. An alternative technique is to seek to move an issue into a new forum. Often those desir-

28. Sidey, *A Very Personal Presidency*, pp. 204–6. Sidey suggests that the president did not particularly value Wheeler's advice and acceded to this request only to please Congress. President Johnson in his memoirs did not deal with this question, but there is evidence to suggest that he took the military position more seriously following the major escalation of the war in Vietnam.

29. Beichman, *The "Other" State Department*, pp. 97–98.

ing to have a large number of individuals examine a question seek to move it into a formal NSC process, which typically involves a number of agencies. In general, the more formal the process, the larger the number of participants.

The number of participants also can be expanded by persuading the president to appoint an ad hoc committee, of either executive branch officials or outsiders, to examine an issue that he normally would treat by dealing directly with the principal operating agency concerned. When participants seeking a particular decision find themselves unable to obtain what they want by expanding the circle within the executive branch, they often go beyond it to bring in members of Congress or outside individuals. Often the problem is primarily to alert outside parties to an impending decision. That can be done either by providing information privately to a senator or representative, by leaking information to the press, or by arranging to have a senator or representative ask a question that can be answered in a way that provides him or her with information with which to fight presidential preferences. The latter technique is particularly effective with military officers, since Congress asserts the right to ask military leaders for their "personal" opinions on military issues. That right is jealously guarded by Congress.[30]

Congressional involvement can be used to bring pressure to bear directly on the president on the substance of the issue, or it can be used to expand the circle. If congressional pressure is not sufficient, people from the private sector who for one reason or another have influence with the president may be pulled in. Harry Truman remembered one episode when his former haberdashery partner was brought into the process in an effort to overturn a presidential decision:

> As the pressure mounted, I found it necessary to give instructions that I did not want to be approached by any more spokesmen for the extreme Zionist cause. I was even so disturbed that I put off seeing Dr. Chaim Weizmann, who had returned to the United States and had asked for an interview with me. My old friend, Eddie Jacobson, called on me at the White House and urged me to receive Dr. Weizmann at the earliest possible moment. Eddie, who had been with me through the hard days of World War I, had never been a Zionist. In all my years in Washington he had never asked me for anything for himself. He was of the Jewish faith and was deeply moved by the sufferings of the Jewish people abroad. He had spoken to me on occasion, both before and after I became President,

---

30. See, for example, the exchange between Secretary of Defense McNamara and members of the Senate Government Operations Subcommittee, reprinted in Jackson, ed., *The National Security Council*, pp. 232–33.

about some specific hardship cases that he happened to know about, but he did this rarely. On March 13 he called at the White House.

I was always glad to see him. Not only had we shared so much in the past, but I have always had the warmest feelings toward him. It would be hard to find a truer friend. Eddie said that he wanted to talk about Palestine. I told him that I would rather he did not and that I wanted to let the matter run its course in the United Nations.

I do not believe that in all our thirty years of friendship a sharp word had ever passed between Eddie and me, and I was sorry that Eddie had brought up the subject.

Eddie was becoming self-conscious, but he kept on talking. He asked me to bear in mind that some of the pro-Zionists who had approached me were only individuals and did not speak for any responsible leadership. I told him that I respected Dr. Weizmann, but if I saw him, it would only result in more wrong interpretations.

Eddie waved toward a small replica of an Andrew Jackson statue that was in my office.

"He's been your hero all your life, hasn't he?" he said. "You have probably read every book there is on Andrew Jackson. I remember when we had the store that you were always reading books and pamphlets, and a lot of them were about Jackson. You put this statue in front of the Jackson County Courthouse in Kansas City when you built it."

I did not know what he was leading up to, but he went on.

"I have never met the man who has been my hero all my life," he continued. "But I have studied his past as you have studied Jackson's. He is the greatest Jew alive, perhaps the greatest Jew who ever lived. You yourself have told me that he is a great statesman and a fine gentleman. I am talking about Dr. Chaim Weizmann. He is an old man and a very sick man. He has traveled thousands of miles to see you, and now you are putting off seeing him. That isn't like you."

When Eddie left, I gave instructions to have Dr. Weizmann come to the White House as soon as it could be arranged. However, the visit was to be entirely off the record. Dr. Weizmann, by my specific instructions, was to be brought in through the East Gate. There was to be no press coverage of his visit and no public announcement.[31]

When an official is reluctant to get involved in an issue but it is believed that if he does he will support a particular decision, participants favoring that

31. Truman, *Years of Trial and Hope*, pp. 160–61.

decision seek to force him to become involved. They may do so by urging the president to consult with him, or they may seek to establish on the record that the concerns of his agency are affected. Secretary of Defense Forrestal made a substantial effort to get Secretary of State Marshall involved in a struggle with the president over the size of the military budget in 1948. Forrestal believed that if Marshall were somehow drawn into the process, he would inevitably support a larger budget. He thus sent Marshall a letter in which he raised three questions:

> (a) Has there been an improvement in the international picture which would warrant a substantial reduction in the military forces we had planned to have in being by the end of the current fiscal year?
> (b) Has the situation worsened since last Spring, and should we, therefore, be considering an augmentation of the forces that we were planning at that time?
> (c) Is the situation about the same—that is, neither better nor worse?[32]

The ploy failed because Marshall was unwilling to get involved in opposing the president. Later, in fact, Truman brought him in on his side in the campaign to keep down defense spending.

Who Plans?

The range of options available to any participants and the degree to which they can plan depend on their position and the kind of issue involved. Every participant is constrained by the amount of time, energy, and resources available to carry out a particular objective. Some participants seem to plan often, others almost never. In general, staffs without formal operational responsibility have more time and are more likely to be involved in maneuvers to obtain a certain policy. Thus planning of the kind suggested here (to induce a decision) is often done by a "planning staff" in the second sense. For example, a small group of officials connected primarily with the policy planning staff of the State Department favored the multilateral nuclear force (MLF) and engaged extensively in systematic efforts to "sell" it to the administration. Henry Kissinger noted:

> The MLF was put over by five or six highly motivated, highly intelligent individuals, in a government where a considerable number of people were indifferent and nobody was really opposed. The process by which it

32. Schilling, "The Politics of National Defense," pp. 187–88.

was done involved, at least in its early phases, a fairly deliberate manipulation by the bureaucracy of the senior executives. For example, sentences were put into a Presidential speech which in themselves were perfectly sensible, but the full import of which was perhaps not understood. These were then used to start study groups which were subsequently used to present a new claim for a little more progress, and so on until the point where the prestige of the United States had become heavily committed to something the implications of which, in my judgment, had never been submitted to the adversary procedure.[33]

Organizations as such are most likely to carry out conscious planning in relation to matters affecting their essence. Michael Armacost reported that both the Army and the Air Force engaged in considerable systematic planning in their struggle for medium-range missile deployments.[34]

Although most senior officials are in general too busy to plan, evidence suggests that presidents and Cabinet officers do plan on a few items of very high priority. McNamara seems to have engaged in some systematic planning to prevent large-scale ABM deployment. Richard Neustadt's description of the way in which Truman succeeded in getting the Marshall Plan approved by Congress suggests a considerable amount of conscious planning on Truman's part:

The crucial thing to note about this case is that despite compatibility of views on public policy, Truman got no help he did not pay for (except Stalin's). Bevin scarcely could have seized on Marshall's words had Marshall not been plainly backed by Truman. Marshall's interest would not have comported with the exploitation of his prestige by a President who undercut him openly, or subtly, or even inadvertently, at any point. Vandenberg, presumably, could not have backed proposals by a White House which begrudged him deference and access gratifying to his fellow-partisans (and satisfying to himself). Prominent Republicans in private life would not have found it easy to promote a cause identified with Truman's claims in 1948—and neither would the prominent New Dealers then engaged in searching for a substitute.

Truman paid the price required for their services. So far as the record shows, the White House did not falter once in firm support for Marshall and the Marshall Plan. Truman backed his Secretary's gamble on an invi-

33. Kissinger, "Bureaucracy and Policy Making," p. 88. See also Steinbruner, *The Cybernetic Theory of Decision.*
34. Armacost, *The Politics of Weapons Innovation,* especially pp. 17–18, 92, 97, 169–70.

PLANNING A DECISION STRATEGY / 137

tation to all Europe. He made the plan his own in a well-timed address to the Canadians. He lost no opportunity to widen the involvements of his own official family in the cause. Averell Harriman the Secretary of Commerce, Julius Krug the Secretary of the Interior, Edwin Nourse the Economic Council Chairman, James Webb the Director of the Budget—all were made responsible for studies and reports contributing directly to the legislative presentation. Thus these men were committed in advance. Besides, the President continually emphasized to everyone in reach that he did not have doubts, did not desire complications and would foreclose all he could. Reportedly, his emphasis was felt at the Treasury, with good effect. And Truman was at special pains to smooth the way for Vandenberg. The Senator insisted on "no politics" from the Administration side; there was none. He thought a survey of American resources and capacity essential; he got it in the Krug and Harriman reports. Vandenberg expected advance consultation; he received it, step by step, in frequent meetings with the President and weekly conferences with Marshall. He asked for an effective liaison between Congress and agencies concerned; Lovett and others gave him what he wanted. When the Senator decided on the need to change financing and administrative features of the legislation, Truman disregarded Budget Bureau grumbling and acquiesced with grace. When, finally, Vandenberg desired a Republican to head the new administering agency, his candidate, Paul Hoffman, was appointed despite the President's own preference for another. In all of these ways Truman employed the sparse advantages his "powers" and his status then accorded him to gain the sort of help he had to have.[35]

Perhaps the most striking example of presidential planning, however, was the deliberate, inexorable march by the second President Bush to war in Iraq in 2003, as documented in several accounts, including most notably that by Bob Woodward. Apparently from the moment he took office, the president and several of his close advisers had made "regime change" in Iraq a central objective of his presidency, setting their plans into full gear in the wake of the terrorist attack of September 2001, which they used to insinuate a direct threat to the United States from Saddam's Iraq.[36]

35. Neustadt, *Presidential Power*, pp. 52–53.
36. The accounts of Woodward, *Plan of Attack*, Clarke, *Against All Enemies*, and Suskind, *The Price of Loyalty*, document this planning process in compelling detail.

THE LIMITS OF PLANNING

As Neustadt suggests, even presidents have to engage in considerable persuasion, bargaining, and coercion if they are to be able to make the kinds of decisions that they wish to make, particularly when they need congressional concurrence. In the next two chapters, we consider the way in which all participants struggle to affect decisions by persuading other participants to support them or by maneuvers aimed at bargaining or coercion.[37] Before leaving the subject of planning, however, we wish to reiterate that planning is a variable in bureaucratic behavior. It may or may not be present in any given struggle, and it may or may not be efficacious.

The reader should keep in mind that everything described in the next chapter occurs at the same time. Moreover, it occurs while participants are dealing with a great many other issues. Some of the participants spend a considerable amount of time on a particular issue; others devote almost no time to it and simply involve themselves episodically. Some carry out well-formulated plans. Most react on a day-to-day basis to particular events and to pressures and deadlines. Thus what might be described in retrospect as a maneuver may not actually be consciously thought out by the participants. Moreover, any effort to describe the process involves the great risk of suggesting much greater order, uniformity, and regularity than exists. Indeed, observers who have been involved in government are unanimous in emphasizing the confusion, the great pressure of deadlines, the importance of accident, misunderstandings, and lack of information in determining what occurs. If the reader keeps all of that in mind, we may proceed first to consider efforts at persuasion and then to consider maneuvering aimed at bargaining and coercion.

---

37. This discussion owes much to Caraley, *The Politics of Military Unification*, pp. 272–76. The three categories are drawn from his text.

CHAPTER EIGHT

Information
and Arguments

Recall from chapter 2 that participants in the foreign policy process believe that the United States should do what is required for national security as they define it. But they become aware that their own view of national interests, shaped as it is by organizational, presidential, or personal interests, is not necessarily shared by other participants. They therefore recognize the need to present positive, "impartial" evidence in favor of their position. Often they seek to convince other participants by putting forward information and arguments designed to demonstrate that what they advocate is objectively in the interest of the United States. Generally they relate their arguments to concepts that appeal to the majority and avoid explaining the process of reasoning and the particular interests that led to their stand.

Arguments in favor of a decision are the most important form in which information reaches the president and other senior participants. Normally a proposal for a presidential decision moves through the bureaucracy accompanied by a set of arguments initially drafted by advocates and revised to take account of criticisms and to get as many participants as possible on board. Arguments presented formally and in writing must relate to national security in the context of the shared images and rules then operating within the government.

Arguments accompanying a proposal are those that participants believe will lead others to adopt a desired position. That does not mean that they use arguments that they know to be false; rather, they choose from the wide range of plausible arguments those that seem likely to convince others. For example, in commenting in his journal on his successful effort to persuade President Truman not to turn physical control of nuclear weapons over to the military, Atomic Energy Commission chairman David Lilienthal wrote: "I had guessed right on the kind of argument that would appeal to him in his present frame of mind, and his sanguine temperament."[1] Under secretary of defense Paul Wolfowitz, a leading advocate of the invasion of Iraq in 2003, explained that he relied on the argument that Iraqi's weapons of mass destruction needed to be destroyed because that was the argument on which consensus could be reached.[2]

Other arguments designed to influence particular participants must be made privately and usually orally. It is possible that arguments designed to convince one organization that a proposal is in its organizational interest will turn off other participants; hence such arguments are made privately and directly to the organization concerned. There is the fear that foreign policy arguments that relate to domestic interests will be leaked to the press in an effort to undermine a proposal by showing that it is being put forward only for domestic political purposes.

Those who are exposed to arguments frequently support a recommended decision without accepting the reasoning with which it is put forward. In many cases they see no purpose in explaining their own motivations. Organizational calculations are best kept within the organization. Highly technical considerations are meaningful to some participants, unimportant to others. Senior participants and the president are likely to be concerned with very generalized kinds of national security arguments and (discreetly) with domestic political considerations rather than with the arguments put forward in memoranda. Thus gaps frequently develop between the arguments that the writer and the reader each find persuasive and those that appear in the memorandum proposing a decision.

Despite the fact that arguments put forward may bear very little relation to the motives of either those advocating a policy change or the senior participants who make the decision, such arguments may take on a life of their own. Frequently they are incorporated into presentations made to congressional leaders and into public statements used to justify a policy.

1. Lilienthal, *Journals*, p. 595.
2. From "Bush's Brain Trust," Paul Wolfowitz interview with Sam Tannenhaus in *Vanity Fair*, July 2003, pp. 114–18, 164–65, 168–69.

PURPOSES OF ARGUMENTS

The arguments accompanying a proposal through the bureaucracy serve a number of different purposes in addition to attempting to persuade other participants that the proposed course of action is indeed in the national interest. To indicate that policy arguments may have other purposes is not to prejudge the intellectual merits of the arguments or their soundness in terms of policy analysis. Five such purposes may be noted.

—*To fill in the blanks.* The rules of the game require that any proposal to change policy must be accompanied by arguments supporting the change. Participants advocating a change in policy must state *some* argument in favor of the change even if they do not feel free to state either the reasons that led them to favor the new policy or those that they believe would persuade others in private. Participants wish to avoid arguments that could be used against them in other situations; consequently they sometimes employ standard arguments, referred to as "boilerplate" in the bureaucracy. Such arguments are simply stated and exploit widely shared values and images. For example, during the cold war, the boilerplate artist might have written, "This action is necessary to stop the spread of Communism." After 9/11 an action might be justified as necessary in the fight against terrorism.

—*To demonstrate that there is a national security argument.* Senior players are likely to be more reluctant to support a proposal solely for organizational, personal, or domestic reasons. They must be persuaded that such a stand is also in the interest of the country. Thus one purpose of arguments is to demonstrate to those players that something that they wish to support for other reasons can be supported on national interest grounds. National interest arguments need not be totally persuasive or irrefutable; they simply must demonstrate that it is possible to support a certain outcome on national interests grounds.

For example, the service secretaries are under tremendous pressure to support the most highly valued proposals of their service. A secretary of the Air Force who opposed the construction of a new manned strategic bomber would find it very difficult to get the cooperation of his uniformed officers on other issues. Hence he would like to support a manned bomber, but he would be reluctant to do so unless he could be persuaded that a case could be made that it served the national interest. Air Force officers would thus give him such arguments as could be made with reference to the national interest and could be advanced before congressional committees and the secretary of defense. Only if the secretary can be convinced that such arguments are respectable will he support the proposal.

—*To signal policy preferences.* Some arguments simply predict the consequences of changes in policy or patterns of action without making a specific recommendation. Arguments relating only to consequences are used by participants to signal policy preferences, and those who hear arguments relating to consequences read policy preferences into them.

That function of arguments is particularly important to the intelligence community, which, under the rules of the game, is limited to predicting consequences of alternative policies and is not permitted to recommend policies. Thus only by shaping arguments about policy consequences can members of the intelligence community signal what policy they think should be adopted. In the second Bush administration, a group close to the president used intelligence estimates selectively in order to justify a U.S. attack on Iraq by claiming that Saddam Hussein posed an imminent threat to national security because he had weapons of mass destruction that he intended to employ. Other participants also find that their policy views are read into their predictions of consequences, and they choose their words accordingly. Karl Rankin, the American ambassador to Nationalist China during the 1950s, explained why he felt it necessary to exaggerate his arguments in order to accomplish his objectives:

> Some of these excerpts may sound unwarrantedly alarming or seem to support unduly the side of Nationalist China. This was done deliberately, for my pervading purpose was to assist those in Washington who shared my own sense of urgency about China and the Far East in general and who believed that a positive and active American strategy was indispensable.
>
> The milder presentation of so grave a situation could have given comfort in quarters favoring disengagement. With American responsibilities so heavy and widespread, I could not place those with whom I agreed in a position to be told, "What are you worrying about? Our man on the spot doesn't seem alarmed."[3]

—*To signal the degree of concern.* Participants, including the president, not only weigh the arguments but also take note of who makes them and how strongly the various parties feel. The arguments used are a way of indicating how strongly a participant feels about a proposed outcome. To say, for example, that a proposal is on balance probably not worth the risk signals a certain attitude; to say that the action suggested would gravely threaten the national

3. Rankin, *China Assignment*, pp. vii–viii.

interest signals quite a different attitude. Participants, recognizing that others read into arguments the intensity of commitment, tailor their presentation appropriately.

—*To report a consensus.* When participants agree on a desired outcome, they wish to appear to agree also on the reasons why the outcome is desirable. Senior participants are more likely to be persuaded to support a change in policy if they believe that there is agreement down the line. Thus participants seek to draft arguments to which all can subscribe. Because other participants will be gauging concern, such arguments must represent a "highest common denominator"—that is, they must reflect not only consensus but the seriousness with which each of the participants feels that a change in policy is either necessary or dangerous. The pressure to formulate statements to which all can subscribe frequently leads to the use of broad generalizations as arguments. As noted above, that imperative apparently led officials supporting a U.S. attack on Iraq in 2003 to stress the need to destroy weapons of mass destruction and to thwart terrorism rather than other arguments, such as that relating to democracy in the Middle East, which would not have had broad support.

When President Reagan insisted on making the Strategic Defense Initiative (SDI), a missile defense system designed to intercept nuclear weapons launched at the United States, the centerpiece of his security policy, it created sharp divisions both inside and outside government for and against SDI. To avoid challenging the president's position, to finesse sharp divisions of opinion within the administration, and to rationalize SDI with the administration's other programs, senior Defense Department officials and arms control negotiators identified three criteria with which all could agree to guide SDI deployment: effectiveness, survivability, and cost-effectiveness.[4]

CONSTRAINTS ON INFORMATION AND ARGUMENTS

In their efforts to influence others, participants are constrained by the procedures through which organizations gather and report information; the need to protect numerous long-run interests that may outweigh current issues; the need to defer to experts within the government; and shared images.

Organizational Procedures and Programs

Most of the information and options laid before senior participants are prepared by large organizations such as the Central Intelligence Agency, the Joint

4. Talbott, *Master of the Game*, pp. 217–18.

Chiefs of Staff, and the State Department and its Foreign Service bureaucracy. Key information may be gathered by a number of different agencies and individuals, some of them located in Washington and some overseas. In order for information about many countries and a variety of different issues to be disseminated to a number of different people in several large organizations, it is necessary to adopt standard operating procedures for gathering and transmitting it. Graham Allison commented on the delay, loss of detail, and filtering out that occur in the process:

> Information does not pass from the tentacle to the top of the organization instantaneously. Facts can be "in the system" without being available to the head of the organization. Information must be winnowed at every step up the organizational hierarchy, since the number of minutes in each day limits the number of bits of information each individual can absorb. It is impossible for men at the top to examine every report from sources in 100 nations (25 of which had as high a priority as Cuba). But those who decide which information their boss shall see rarely see their bosses' problem. Finally, facts that with hindsight are clear signals are frequently indistinguishable from surrounding "noise" before the occurrence.[5]

In his careful study of the Cuban missile crisis, Allison provides a systematic and detailed explanation of how information was gathered about the possible presence of Soviet missiles in Cuba and the way that information was processed within the various organs of the intelligence community. His description, filled with fascinating details, is worth quoting at length:

> Information about Soviet missiles in Cuba came to the attention of the President on October 14 rather than three weeks earlier, or a week later, as a consequence of the routines and procedures of the organizations that make up the U.S. intelligence community. . . .
> The available record permits a fairly reliable reconstruction of the major features of the organizational behavior that resulted in discovery of the Soviet missiles. Intelligence on activities within Cuba came from four primary sources: shipping intelligence, refugees, agents within Cuba, and U-2 overflights. Intelligence on all ships going to Cuba provided a catalogue of information on the number of Soviet shipments to Cuba (eighty-five by October 3), the character of these ships (size, registry, and the fact that several of the large-hatch lumber ships were used), and the character of their cargoes (transport, electronic, and construc-

5. Allison, *Essence of Decision*, p. 120.

tion equipment, SAMs, MiGs, patrol boats, and Soviet technicians).
Refugees from Cuba brought innumerable distorted reports of Soviet
missiles, Chinese soldiers, etc. For 1959—before the Soviet Union had
begun sending any arms whatever to Cuba—the CIA file of reports
devoted solely to missiles in Cuba was five inches thick. The low reliabil-
ity of these reports made their collection and processing of marginal
value. Nevertheless, a staff of CIA professionals at Opa Locka, Florida,
collected, collated, and compared the results of interrogations of
refugees—though often with a lag, since refugees numbered in the thousands. Reports from agents in Cuba produced information about the
evacuation of Cubans from the port of Mariel and the secrecy that surrounded unloading and transport of equipment (trucks were lowered
into the holds, loaded, and hoisted out covered with tarpaulins), a sighting and sketch of the rear profile of a missile on a Cuban highway heading west, and a report of missile activity in the Pinar del Rio province.
But this information had to be transferred from sub-agent to master-
agent and then to the United States, a procedure that usually meant a lag
of ten days between a sighting and arrival of the information in Washington. The U-2 camera recorded the highest-quality U.S. intelligence.
Photographs taken from a height of fourteen miles allowed analysts to
distinguish painted lines on a parking lot, or to recognize a new kind of
cannon on the wing of an airplane. U-2s flew over Cuba on August 29,
September 5, 17, 26, 29, and October 5 and 7 before the October 14 flight
that discovered the missiles. These earlier flights gathered information
on SAM sites, coastal defense missile sites, MiGs, missile patrol boats,
and IL-28 light bombers.

Intelligence experts in Washington processed information received
from these four sources and produced estimates of certain contingencies.
Hindsight highlights several bits of evidence in the intelligence system
that might have suggested the presence of Soviet missiles in Cuba. Yet the
notorious "September estimate" concluded that the Soviet Union would
not introduce offensive missiles into Cuba. No U-2 flight was directed
over the western end of Cuba between September 5 and October 4. No
U-2 flew over the western end of Cuba until the flight that discovered the
Soviet missiles on October 14. Can these "failures" be accounted for in
organizational terms?

On September 19, when the highest assembly of the American intelligence community, the United States Intelligence Board (USIB), met to
consider the question of Cuba, the "system" contained the following

information: (1) shipping intelligence about the arrival in Cuba of two large-hatch Soviet lumber ships, the Omsk and the Poltava, which the intelligence report also noted were riding high in the water; (2) refugee reports of countless sighting[s] of missiles, plus a report that Castro's private pilot, after a night of drinking in Havana, had boasted: "We will fight to the death and perhaps we can win because we have everything, including atomic weapons"; (3) a sighting by a CIA agent of the rear profile of a strategic missile; (4) U-2 photos from flights on August 29 and September 5 and 17, showing the construction of a number of SAM sites and other defensive missiles.

Not all of this information, however, was on the desk of the estimators . . .

Intelligence about large-hatch ships riding high in the water did not go unremarked. Shipping intelligence experts spelled out the implication: the ships must be carrying "space consuming" cargo. These details were carefully included in the catalogue of intelligence on shipping. For experts alert to the Soviet Union's pressing requirement for ships, however, neither the facts nor the implication carried a special signal. The refugee report of Castro's pilot's remark had been received at Opa Locka along with reams of inaccurate and even deliberately false reports spread by the refugee community. That report and a thousand others had to be checked and compared before being sent to Washington. The two weeks required for initial processing could have been shortened by a large increase in resources devoted to this source of information. But the yield of this source was already quite marginal, and there was little reason to expect that a change in procedures, reducing transmission time to one week, would be worth the cost. The CIA agent's sighting of the rear profile of a strategic missile had occurred on September 12; transmission time from agent sighting to arrival of the report in Washington typically took nine to twelve days. That report arrived at CIA headquarters on September 21, two days after the USIB meeting. Shortening the transmission time would have imposed severe cost in terms of danger to subagents, agents, and communication networks.

U-2 flights had produced no hard indication of the presence of offensive missiles. The flight over western Cuba on September 5 revealed SAM installations approaching completion. Then on September 9, a U-2 on "loan" to the Chinese Nationalists was shot down over mainland China. Recalling the outcry that followed the downing of Francis Gary Powers' U-2 over the Soviet Union on May 1, 1960, the intelligence community feared lest this incident trigger an international stage show that could force the abandonment of U-2 flights, eliminating its most reliable source of information. The Committee on Overhead Reconnaissance (COMOR), which approved each U-2 flight pattern, was quickly convened. The State Department pressed arguments about the political consequences if another U-2 should be shot down, for example, over Cuba. As a result, COMOR decided that rather than flying up one side of the island and down the other, future flights should "dip into" Cuban airspace and peer as much as possible from the periphery. COMOR also decided at this meeting that flights should concentrate on the eastern half of Cuba rather than on the western tip, where SAMs were known to be approaching operational readiness.

Given the information available to them on September 19, then, the chiefs of intelligence made a reasonable judgment in predicting that the Soviets would not introduce offensive missiles into Cuba. And the information available to them included everything that they could reasonably expect.[6]

More than forty years later, despite dramatic advances in the technology of intelligence gathering, the same weaknesses in intelligence processing, sharing among agencies, and interpretation by analysts and senior policymakers were found to have contributed to the failure to foresee the terrorist attacks of 9/11 and misreading signs of weapons of mass destruction in Iraq. The National Commission on Terrorist Threats to the United States (known as the 9/11 Commission) concluded that decision processes and rules had seriously obstructed intelligence gathering and analysis in the lead-up to the terrorist attacks of 9/11, as well as previous terrorist activity.[7] A former senior intelligence officer has described the "politicization" of intelligence that occurred when the second Bush administration was making the case for deposing Iraq's Saddam Hussein.[8]

Standard operating procedures influence the relative weight given to items of information that enter an organization. For example, in the early stages of the Vietnam War there was a tendency to take reports from South Vietnamese officials seriously. The supposition seemed to be that they were trying as hard as American officials were to get accurate information. Almost no one studied the possibility that the South Vietnamese were supplying information that they hoped would lead the United States to do what the government of South

6. Ibid., pp. 118–21.
7. *9/11 Commission Report*, especially p. 347.
8. Pillar, "Intelligence, Policy, and the War in Iraq."

Vietnam wanted.[9] Similarly, in the lead-up to the attack on Iraq in 2003, information provided by Iraqi exiles and dissidents was often presented as hard evidence in intelligence briefs, with no verification of its accuracy.

Standard operating procedures tend also to produce a mass of papers unlikely to hold the attention of senior participants or the president, particularly when routine items must compete with reports of individual visitors and the news media. George Kennan explained:

> The regular governmental machinery was designed to serve the President and the Secretary of State in two ways: first, as a source of information, stimulus, and recommendation with relation to the exercise of their responsibility, and, secondly, as a channel for the implementation of their decisions.
>
> So far as the first of these purposes is concerned, it is plain that the contribution the regular apparatus is capable of making bears no proper relation to its size and to the enormity of its effort. This is partly the result of the very limited time the senior officials have in which to absorb information and impulses of all sorts brought to them through the regular channels; but it is also partly a consequence of the inferior form in which this information is produced—inferior, that is, from the standpoint of its effectiveness in engaging and impressing the mind of anyone so busy, so overwhelmed with ulterior preoccupations, and so constituted by education and intellect as most presidents and most secretaries of state are apt to be. On countless occasions subordinates have been surprised and disappointed—sometimes even personally hurt—to find that the Secretary or the President has been more decisively influenced by some chance outside contact or experience than by the information and advice offered to him through the regular channels. Either he has talked with someone from outside whose statements seemed somehow simpler and more striking and appealing than anything he had heard from his own subordinates, or the same effect has been produced upon him by some newspaper or magazine article he read or by something he heard on the radio or saw on the news-reels or on television.
>
> There is, admittedly, a real injustice here in most instances. The statements of the fascinating outsider often prove in retrospect to have been less sound and balanced than the final product of official judgment, and the items purveyed by the mass media are found to be dangerously oversimplified and inadequate as a basis for official action.

9. Mecklin, *Mission in Torment*, pp. 100–102.

But the regular subordinates are inclined to forget or ignore the deadening effect of the bureaucracy on all forms of communication, oral and written. Whereas the products of the mass media are designed to strike and to hold briefly the attention of busy people, and whereas the statements of the outside visitor are apt to have at least the charm of the expression of a single human mind, with all its directness and freshness, the products of the official machinery are almost invariably dull and pedestrian, drafted or spoken in the usual abominable governmentese, and even, in many instances, intellectually inferior by virtue of the extensive compromising of language which has preceded their final formulation. In short, the busy senior executive frequently finds more useful and meaningful to him the product of the individual mind than the product of a tortured collective effort; and it is only the latter that he gets from his assistants.[10]

Protecting Other Interests

Participants concerned about organizational and personal interests see the face of an issue that affects those interests; that, in turn, guides their choice of what information to report or not report because of its possible effects on those interests.

Concern with organizational interests inclines participants to refuse to report or to concede facts that might be damaging in another context. The problem can be particularly acute when it involves competing parts of a particular service. Enthoven and Smith, former senior civilian officials in the Office of Systems Analysis in the Pentagon, report that trying to determine the so-called probability of kill (PK) of existing naval antisubmarine warfare (ASW) forces was quite difficult because of the struggle within the Navy between the submarine and surface faction and the aircraft faction. They explained:

Our effort to come up with a convincing analysis of ASW forces, one that everyone would accept and agree upon, failed. It failed, in part, because the U.S. Navy is made up of three competing branches, each proud of its own capabilities and traditions: a submarine Navy, a surface Navy, and an aircraft Navy. The Navy conducted ASW studies by committee, with representatives from all three branches present. When it came time to gather assumptions on which to base the PK's of the vari-

10. Kennan, "America's Administrative Response to Its World Problems," pp.18–19.

ous Navy forces, each branch competed with the others in overstating performance claims for its own preferred weapon systems. Each feared that if it did not, future studies would show that all or most of the Soviet submarine force was being destroyed by one of the other branches, which might then get more of the total Navy budget. Also, each branch felt obliged, when stating the PK's of its particular weapons, to use the numbers that it had earlier claimed would be achieved when it justified the R&D programs for these weapons. Thus, if a branch did not claim a high effectiveness for its proposed new weapons, it stood in danger of having its R&D budget cut back.

When all these inflated claims for PK's were put together and run through a total-fleet war game, the results were, predictably, that our side won handsomely with the forces already approved by the Secretary of Defense; in fact, we won not only decisively but within a very few weeks. Indeed, it often appeared that we could have won the war quickly enough with even smaller forces. Given the high PK's, it was apparent that the programmed forces were entirely adequate to do the job.[11]

Intelligence officials in the various services and agencies wish to demonstrate that they are doing a good job and that competing organizations in the intelligence field are less effective. That may lead to a determination to downgrade information provided by other agencies. One observer of the State Department has suggested that the career Foreign Service officers tend to "downgrade or ignore some of CIA'S more alarming news, particularly if it did not corroborate their own."[12]

Organizations constantly hedge against unforeseen consequences and the possibility that their private estimates are wrong. Such concerns lead intelligence organizations to predict crises continually, for when a crisis does occur, they can then point out that they predicted it. General Westmoreland, the commander of U.S. forces in Vietnam, was reported to have a favorite story that he recited whenever an intelligence officer told him that he, the officer, had accurately predicted a forthcoming enemy move. Westmoreland, visiting a unit badly hit by the Viet Cong, demanded to know why there had been no warning. The unit's intelligence officer asserted that he had predicted an attack for that day. "Yeah, he's right," interjected the weary unit commander, "but he also predicted an attack for ninety-nine straight days before—and nothing happened."[13]

11. Enthoven and Smith, *How Much Is Enough?* pp. 229–30.
12. Simpson, *Anatomy of the State Department,* p. 100.
13. Oberdorfer, *Tet!* p. 134.

Operating agencies tend to hedge by asking for larger forces or more autonomy than they believe that they need. That may make an operation look much
more expensive or much more difficult than they actually believe it to be. Yet
hedging of that kind is held down somewhat by the wariness of officials not
in the intelligence community about developing a reputation for false predictions. Joseph de Rivera put the point well:

> Within the government, the intelligence service places a high cost on fail-
> ure to report a signal. Since nobody wants to be blamed for an intelli-
> gence failure, far too many false leads swamp the information channels
> at a high level in the State Department and elsewhere. On the other
> hand, at the Assistant Secretary level, there is a high cost placed on falsely
> reporting a signal to be present when actually nothing is there. No one
> wants to bother a Secretary of State or a President with false informa-
> tion. Unfortunately, the result is a filter which may be at the wrong place
> in the system. While central decision makers have a broader view of
> world events, persons nearer the source of intelligence might be better
> judges of the accuracy and importance of information mainly relevant to
> one nation.[14]

Personal interest can also affect information that officials are prepared to
report. Career officials concerned about promotion may be unwilling to
report facts that undercut the stand taken by the organization controlling
their promotion. People appointed to the White House staff find it extremely
difficult to bring "bad news" to the President or to take positions that they
know go against the President's own desires. George Reedy, who was Lyndon
Johnson's press secretary, reports the great difficulty of saying no to a strong
President. "You know that nobody is strong minded around a President; let's
get that thing established right now. It just doesn't exist. As far as the President
is concerned, it is always: 'yes sir,' 'no sir' (the 'no sir' comes when he asks
whether you're dissatisfied)."[15]

Deference to Expertise

One notion that affects the kind of arguments that can be put forward within
the American government is the view that one should defer to expertise. In
some respects that notion complements the use of standard operating procedures. No one else need bother with a subject or area routinely "covered" by

14. De Rivera, *The Psychological Dimension of Foreign Policy,* p. 56.
15. Quoted in Hoxie, ed., *The White House,* p. 183.

an expert. When a policy move brings the area to the fore, the expert is relied upon to suggest the means for reaching whatever goal is decided upon. Robert A. Lovett, who served in the State Department and the Defense Department, believed strongly in bureaucratic specialization. As he expressed it:

> Civilian and military executives alike should stick to the fields in which they have special training and aptitudes: if they do, the chance of making the machinery work well is excellent. One of the few humans as exasperating as a civilian businessman who suddenly becomes an expert on military strategy and tactics is the military adviser who magically becomes an expert in some highly sophisticated production problem in which he has no background or experience.[16]

Many in-and-outers defer to expertise in the expectation that they will be deferred to in their own specialty. Senior business executives brought into the Defense Department as management experts have deferred to the military on what they view as strategic questions and to the State Department on political questions, the assumption being that they in turn deserve the last word on business management issues. In-and-outers without any formally defined expertise have tended to be much more skeptical of expert advice and much more willing to challenge it.

Career officials have a very strong tendency to defer to expertise. Their own involvement and influence depend in large part on other officials deferring to their expertise. To challenge the expertise of another career group is to risk retaliation. Thus Foreign Service officers have been extremely reluctant to challenge the military on strategic questions or to challenge Treasury officials on economic matters.[17]

The great difficulty in challenging what is viewed as expert advice can be seen in the debate in the ExCom (executive committee) of the National Security Council during the first week of the Cuban missile crisis in 1962 over the option of a "surgical strike" against the missile sites being constructed in Cuba. The idea of a surgical strike was appealing to a number of senior civilian officials. They were unwilling to recommend an all-out invasion, but they doubted that a blockade would be effective when the missiles were already in Cuba and undergoing deployment. The military services were thus pressed very hard to come up with a plan for a surgical strike. Nevertheless, their assertion that such a strike was impossible settled the issue and moved that option off the feasible list. President Kennedy, however, not completely satis-

16. Lovett, "Perspective on the Policy Process," p. 81.
17. See, for example, Johnson, "The National Security Council," p. 728.

fied with that information, met with the commander of the Tactical Air Command, who assured him that a surgical strike was indeed impossible. Dean Acheson, serving as an ad hoc member of ExCom, strongly favored a surgical strike and experienced great frustration in trying to overcome the military judgment that such a strike was infeasible. He was only one of many.[18]

Deference to expert opinion is based on the belief that the calculation and process of reasoning by which experts reach their conclusion is extremely complicated and impenetrable by outsiders. Frequently, however, that belief is erroneous. Expert judgments may be based on simple rules of thumb, standard operating procedures of the organization, compromises among experts determined to present a unanimous report, and in some cases guesswork.

Debate over the surgical air strike illustrates several of those points. The calculations done by the Tactical Air Command and by the Joint Chiefs of Staff were apparently based on the assumption that the Soviet missiles in Cuba were "mobile"—meaning that they could be moved within a few minutes or a few hours. In fact, the Soviet missiles were "movable" only in the sense that in weeks or days they could be moved to a new location and set up again. Once that mistake was discovered, after President Kennedy's speech announcing a quarantine of Cuba, the surgical air strike option was put back on the list of feasible options. The Tactical Air Command's original calculation that a surgical strike was not feasible was based also on the standard military doctrine that if one goes after a military target, one goes all out. TAC calculated that in the event of an attack on missile sites the enemy might send bombers and fighters aloft, and thus it would be necessary to simultaneously hit air bases. Since air bases were going to be attacked, tactical air defense sites would have to be hit as well. Moreover, the military planners felt that an invasion would probably have to follow a large air strike. Thus landing sites and other targets of relevance to a landing should be hit in the first place. In brief, the standard operating procedures by which the military gauged the feasibility of a surgical strike were heavily weighted against the kind of operation supposedly being studied.

The limitations of expert advice can be illustrated by examining the basis upon which a distinguished group of scientists set the performance goals of the first-generation American intercontinental ballistic missiles (ICBMs). They were to have "a one-megaton-warhead explosive yield, 5,500 nautical miles range, and five miles or better accuracy." As Herbert York has reported, military officers and others took these goals seriously, and the goals in fact

18. On this episode, see Schlesinger, *A Thousand Days,* p. 827; Sorensen, *Kennedy,* p. 684; Kennedy, *Thirteen Days,* pp. 48–49; and Allison, *Essence of Decision,* pp. 202–10.

determined the shape and size of the American program.[19] As is usually the case, the assumption was that those numbers could be "derived from complex mathematical formulae connecting explosive yield, damage radius, target vulnerability and other numerically defined quantities." In fact, the reality was quite different. York, who was a member of the missile science committee and served as the chief scientist in the Pentagon, revealed that the criterion of one megaton and the other numbers were picked arbitrarily through a sort of primitive reflex:

> So, why 1.0 megaton? The answer is because and only because one million is a particularly round number in our culture. We picked a one-megaton yield for the Atlas warhead for the same reason that everyone speaks of rich men as being millionaires and never as being tenmillion-aires or one-hundred-thousandaires. It really was that mystical, and I was one of the mystics. Thus, the actual physical size of the first Atlas warhead and the number of people it would kill were determined by the fact that human beings have two hands with five fingers each and therefore count by tens.
>
> What if we had had six fingers on each hand and therefore counted by twelves instead of tens? As any school child who takes modern math knows, the number one-million in base twelve is fully three times as big as the number one-million in base ten. Thus, if evolution had given us six fingers on each hand, our first ICBM warhead would have had to be three times as big, the rockets to deliver them would have threatened the lives of up to three times as many human beings, and it would have taken one or two years longer to carry out their development program. Similarly, if we had had only four fingers, like some comic-strip characters, the first warheads and missiles would have been only one-fourth as large, we could have built them somewhat sooner, and the present overkill problem would not be nearly as serious as it is. The only funny thing about this story is that it is true. It really was that arbitrary, and what's more, that same arbitrariness has stayed with us.[20]

The other two numbers were almost equally arbitrary. The 5,500 nautical miles simply made the target area equal to one quarter of the earth's surface, and the five miles or better accuracy was a compromise between those who believed that one could do much better and those who thought that five miles would be doing well. It was thus simply "a conservative estimate."

19. On this episode, see York, *Race to Oblivion*, pp. 88–90.
20. Ibid., pp. 89–90.

The reluctance of policymakers to go behind the numbers in analyses produced by experts can be found not only in military and scientific affairs but sometimes also in the case of "information" put forth by the intelligence community. David Lilienthal recorded in his journals his amazement at discovering the process by which estimates were made about when the Soviet Union would have atomic weapons:

> The thing that rather chills one's blood is to observe what is nothing less than lack of integrity in the way the intelligence agencies deal with the meager stuff they have. It is chiefly a matter of reasoning from our own American experience, guessing from that how much longer it will take Russia using our methods and based upon our own problems of achieving weapons. But when this is put into a report, the reader, e.g., Congressional committee, is given the impression, and deliberately, that behind the estimates lies specific knowledge, knowledge so important and delicate that its nature and sources cannot be disclosed or hinted at.[21]

When U.S. forces failed to find weapons of mass destruction after they invaded Iraq in 2003, it became clear that U.S. decisionmakers, particularly the president, had been presented with flawed intelligence estimates for many years. While the Clinton administration had not found the intelligence sufficient to justify unilateral U.S. action, it nonetheless believed that Iraq had weapons of mass destruction and pressed hard for Security Council resolutions and vigorous UN inspections based on that intelligence.

Expert advice is likely to be challenged only when the policy conclusions that derive from it are strongly inconsistent with the interests of participants in the policy process. Then standard maneuvers come into play. One way to challenge expert advice is to argue that there is an overlapping body of expert opinion that renders invalid the judgment of the particular experts being challenged. Thus military judgments about the proper size of the defense budget are undercut by advice from economists and bankers that the proposed expenditures would bankrupt the government and play into the hands of our enemies. In other cases, advocates of a certain policy charge that the experts have exceeded the bounds of their expertise. For example, military men often argue that scientific advice has gone beyond the realm of science into military questions. When experts disagree, then one is of course free to choose advice that fits best with the stand that one already has taken.

---

21. Lilienthal, *Journals*, p. 376.

Shared Images

By definition, most participants share the images that predominate within the government at any one time. However, even those who do not are constrained by the knowledge that the shared images influence others, and that knowledge affects the kind of arguments they put forward.

Participants have considerable difficulty getting the ordinary administrator or politician to believe facts that go against the shared images. Officials react as all individuals do to evidence that goes against their strongly held beliefs: they either ignore the evidence or reinterpret it so as to change what it seems to mean. That problem affected American perceptions of what the Soviet Union was up to in Cuba before the Cuban missile crisis. There was a widely shared view, held by the Russia experts in the Central Intelligence Agency, the State Department, and elsewhere, that the Soviet Union would never ship nuclear weapons or nuclear delivery systems beyond its borders. To the best of the knowledge of American officials at the time, the Soviet Union had never done so, even to East European countries contiguous with the Soviet Union. The shipment of missiles and nuclear warheads abroad meant running the risk that they would be taken over by unfriendly forces. In view of the Russian government's known caution about dispersing nuclear weapons and the emphasis on maintaining tight command and control over weapons even in the Soviet Union, it seemed wildly implausible to U.S. experts that the Soviet Union would ship missiles and weapons across the seas to Cuba, where they would be particularly vulnerable to an American effort to capture them. Thus evidence that the Soviet Union was installing missiles in Cuba tended to be ignored. John McCone, then the director of central intelligence, did not have an extensive background in Soviet behavior and did not himself subscribe to the notion that the Soviet Union was extremely cautious in the dispersal of nuclear weapons. Hence McCone, looking at the evidence, saw a pattern and came to believe that the Soviet Union was in fact in the process of installing missiles in Cuba. However, he was unable to convince anyone else that that was indeed the case.[22]

Colin Powell, the national security adviser in 1988, during the last year of the Reagan administration, recalled that the shared images that had guided Kremlinologists during the cold war were now hindering their ability to analyze events in Moscow accurately:

CIA Soviet specialists told me about an upcoming meeting of the Communist Party Central Committee at which, this time for sure, the hard-

22. On this point, see Wohlstetter, *Cuba and Pearl Harbor.*

liners would hand Gorbachev his head. The meeting was held, and afterward Gorbachev fired a dozen or so generals and hard-liners. I felt sympathy for our Kremlinologists. The world they had studied and had known so well for forty years was losing its structure and rules. With all their expertise, they could no longer anticipate events much better than a layman watching television.[23]

During the long cold war period, shared images were so firmly entrenched that participants learned that it was not productive to put forward a proposal or to take a stand in such a way that its acceptance required rejecting shared images. For example, to reinforce his argument against an invasion or other military action against Cuba in the opening days of the debate over how to react to the Russian missiles, Secretary of Defense McNamara at first suggested that it simply did not matter that the Soviet Union was putting missiles in Cuba. He asserted that "a missile is a missile" and that the Russians could threaten the United States just as effectively from the Soviet Union. That assertion went against the widely shared belief that the establishment of a military base by a hostile outside power in Latin America, especially in the Caribbean, posed a vital threat to the security of the United States, and it met with instant and firm rebuttal. McNamara quickly recognized that by arguing against the national security images held by the great majority of the group he ran the risk of entirely undercutting his credibility as an opponent of an invasion, which was being proposed by Dean Acheson and others. He switched without delay to different arguments.[24]

With the end of the cold war, the power of shared images diminished, as successive administrations coped with a rapidly changing world that required greater policy flexibility and innovation. The first President Bush and his national security adviser, Brent Scowcroft, deliberately encouraged debate between moderate and conservative views among senior officials in the administration to make sure that they were considering all possible motives behind the Soviets' increasingly unpredictable behavior.[25] In the aftermath of the terrorist attacks on 9/11, however, the second Bush presidency returned to a set of shared images about the threat of terrorism that were similar to those about the threat of communism during the cold war.

Many participants believe that their influence and even their tenure in office depend on their endorsement or seeming endorsement of shared images. Even those who appear invulnerable to opposition may zealously

23. Powell, *My American Journey*, p. 363.
24. See Abel, *The Missile Crisis*, p. 51.
25. Bush and Scowcroft, *A World Transformed*, pp. 154–55.

158 / INFORMATION AND ARGUMENTS

guard their reputation for accepting shared images. A number of observers
suggest, for example, that officials felt the need to go along with the use of military power in Vietnam because of the danger that they would otherwise
appear to be rejecting the shared image that the United States had to assume
the burden of "world responsibility" and hence had to be willing to use power
to oppose "international communism."[26] Officials of the second Bush presidency may have supported the war in Iraq for similar reasons.

Although fears about nonconformity may be exaggerated and are perhaps
self-fulfilling, they are not groundless. John Kenneth Galbraith maintains
with good reason that his ability to influence Vietnam policy was substantially
reduced by the fact that he was largely recognized as not sharing the belief that
the United States had to be willing to use military force against international
communism. He confided to his diary in 1961 that McGeorge Bundy "thinks
there is no occasion when I would urge the use of force. I have to admit that
my enthusiasm for it is always very low."[27] Similarly, when George W. Ball, the
under secretary of state, in 1964 warned his close colleagues against an escalation of U.S. involvement in Vietnam, his challenge appears to have been
considered more as the interesting view of a skeptic than as a viable alternative to escalation.[28] President Kennedy himself had been largely responsible for
sanctifying the widely held belief that the United States had to use force
against local insurgency because behind it lay international communism.
Having established the doctrine that native guerrilla movements backed by
Russia and China were now the threat and had to be opposed by military
force, he created a situation in which other officials felt pressure to indicate
their support for that doctrine. As students of the period, Kalb and Abel concluded that "if a high official expressed skepticism about the significance or
newness ascribed to this style of warfare, it was said, he risked shortening his
tenure in office. McNamara, Taylor, and Rostow became early converts, and
their White House standing soared."[29]

As a result of the conditions, lessons, and fears discussed here, a disingen-
uous style of argument prevails. It can become more complicated and more
wearing than the substantive issues themselves.

—*Participants shape arguments in terms of the shared images of the society
and the government even if they do not believe that those images are an accurate*

26. See, for example, Thomson, "How Could Vietnam Happen?" p. 207; Kalb and Abel,
Roots of Involvement, pp. 122–33.

27. Galbraith, *Ambassador's Journal*, p. 243.

28. Ball, "Top Secret: The Prophecy the President Rejected," pp. 36–49. This article is a
reproduction of a memorandum written by Ball on October 5, 1964.

29. Kalb and Abel, *Roots of Involvement*, p. 124.

reflection of the world. Galbraith, for example, attempting to keep himself involved in the Vietnam debate, argued that his proposals for diplomatic and economic moves would be more effective in preventing the spread of communism than proposals for the use of military force. He presented those arguments despite the fact that he did not really believe that there was much danger of the spread of communism anyway or that increased communist influence in Indochina would threaten American security interests.

—*Since participants seldom challenge shared images, regardless of their ultimate policy position, the president is rarely exposed to fresh and provocative arguments.* In the ABM debate, for instance, President Johnson was not confronted with the argument that simple numerical nuclear superiority was irrelevant, that the United States did not need any sort of an ABM system no matter what the Russians might do. In opposing the system, McNamara did not challenge the conventional notion of American superiority. He merely attempted to show that the ABM system might increase the probability of nuclear war without saving any American lives.

—*If participants believe that taking a certain stand that they think wise will be interpreted as a deviation from shared images, they will take the opposite stand for fear of losing influence or indeed their position in the government.* Arthur Schlesinger Jr. suggests that that was in fact part of the motivation for the failure of State Department officials to oppose the Bay of Pigs invasion despite their anticipation of its disastrous international consequences. "I could not help feeling," he writes, "that the desire to prove to the CIA and the Joint Chiefs that they were not soft-headed idealists but were really tough guys, too, influenced State's representatives at the cabinet table."[30]

George Ball related a similar episode that occurred during his tenure as under secretary of state. In early 1965, Ball found himself the acting secretary when the decision was being made to begin the bombing of North Vietnam. He recognized that the other participants believed that the United States needed to prevent South Vietnam from being ruled by a communist government and could do so by using force against North Vietnam. To oppose the decision to begin the bombing, was, Ball believed, to sacrifice all future influence on the Vietnam issue. Thus, as he explained it later, he supported the initiation of bombing.[31]

—*In some cases, a devil's advocate is designated or emerges who is known not to accept the shared images that shape a policy or at least agrees to act as if he or*

30. Schlesinger, *A Thousand Days*, p. 256.
31. Ball, "Vietnam Hindsight."

she does not accept it. George Reedy, who served in the Johnson White House, explained the phenomenon of token opposition:

> Of course, within these councils there was always at least one "devil's advocate." But an official dissenter always starts with half his battle lost. It is assumed that he is bringing up arguments solely because arguing is his official role. It is well understood that he is not going to press his points harshly or stridently. Therefore, his objections and cautions are discounted before they are delivered. They are actually welcomed because they prove for the record that decision was preceded by controversy.[32]

George Ball, although he did not press his dissent from the set of images guiding Vietnam policy, was soon cast into that role, according to an account written by James Thomson:

> Once Mr. Ball began to express doubts, he was warmly institutionalized: he was encouraged to become the in-house devil's advocate on Vietnam. The upshot was inevitable: the process of escalation allowed for periodic requests to Mr. Ball to speak his piece; Ball felt good, I assume (he had fought for righteousness); the others felt good (they had given a full hearing to the dovish option); and there was minimal unpleasantness. The club remained intact; and it is of course possible that matters would have gotten worse faster if Mr. Ball had kept silent, or left before his final departure in the fall of 1966.[33]

Secretary of State Colin Powell was institutionalized in the role of dissenter by the second President Bush, as he prepared for the attack on Iraq. While Powell succeeded at least briefly in drawing the administration back into negotiations at the UN in the months before the attack, he did not have any influence on the president when he described the dilemmas the United States would face in taking responsibility for a post-Saddam Iraq. Powell's arguments, however, made it possible for the president to say that he had considered the potential negative consequences thoroughly.

CHALLENGING SHARED IMAGES

As seen in chapter 2, sometimes changes in personnel or changes in perceptions of reality either at home or abroad lead to changes in shared images without any participant deliberately setting about to create change. It also

32. Reedy, *The Twilight of the Presidency,* p. 11.
33. Thomson, "How Could Vietnam Happen?" p. 201

happens on occasion that a few audacious participants tire of framing every argument in terms of some well-worn orthodoxy. Certain officials conclude that they can get the decisions they want from the government by changing the set of images by which the government operates. If they feel that they have built up sufficient credibility as reputable and reasonable participants in the policy process, they may launch a deliberate effort to change others' interpretations of reality. One such episode occurred in late 1949 and the first months of 1950. It involved an effort to convince American officials that the serious military threat from the Soviet bloc required a major buildup in American military forces. In order to bring about a substantial increase in military spending, it was necessary also to destroy the conviction that the United States could not afford to spend more than $15 billion a year on defense. President Truman was persuaded to appoint a special committee within the National Security Council system to examine threats to the United States in light of the changing international environment and to recommend the action to be taken. The committee worked slowly to form a consensus within the government. Its members made a deliberate decision to exaggerate possible dangers so that officials who discounted such documents would still feel sufficient concern to accept a change. Economic officials, particularly those on the Council of Economic Advisers, were recruited to counteract the notion that the United States could not afford to increase military spending. As Dean Acheson later explained:

> The purpose of NSC-68 was to so bludgeon the mass mind of "top government" that not only could the President make a decision but that the decision could be carried out. Even so, it is doubtful whether anything like what happened in the next few years could have been done had not the Russians been stupid enough to have instigated the attack against South Korea and opened the "hate America" campaign.[34]

A similar effort was made by Robert McNamara in seeking to prevent deployment of an American ballistic missile defense system. McNamara recognized that the prevailing set of images within the American government stressed the importance to the United States of maintaining strategic superiority over the Soviet Union. Such superiority was believed to be politically important to the United States, giving it advantages in diplomatic dealings and in crisis bargaining with the Soviet Union. Superiority was seen as requiring an American countermove to any Soviet military system and American matching of any Soviet deployment. Thus an ABM system was thought to be

34. Acheson, *Present at the Creation*, p. 374. See also Hammond, "NSC–68."

necessary because the Soviet Union had such a system and because the Russians were building a large fleet of intercontinental ballistic missiles; the United States needed a defense against such an attack. McNamara, both in his public statements and within the government, sought a fundamental change in the images that guided participants' thoughts about nuclear weapons. Though he had hesitated to challenge the standard images in the Cuban missile crisis, by 1967 he was arguing openly that the concept of nuclear superiority was essentially meaningless. If both sides have the capability to destroy each other, the only benefit that one can get from nuclear weapons is to deter a nuclear attack. He argued that it was useless to try to defend against Russian missiles, for the Russians could easily build additional missiles, fully offsetting the value of the defense. Finally, he argued that the United States did not need to match every Soviet deployment. If the Russians were wasting money on an ineffective ABM system, it did not mean that the Americans needed to do so as well. However, at the same time that he was putting forward those arguments, McNamara recognized that the prevailing sentiment in favor of superiority was so comforting to so many people that he would lose his case if it rested solely on the spuriousness of the concept. Thus he compromised by arguing that the United States was maintaining its "superiority" with the multiple, separately controllable warheads known as MIRVs.

Although McNamara ultimately lost the battle and the ABM deployment went forward, his arguments triggered a reassessment of strategic doctrine. The changes in images that he sought came to fruition in the early years of the Nixon administration, leading to President Nixon's espousal of the doctrine of nuclear sufficiency and his specific assertion that the United States would not seek to counter Soviet offensive and defensive moves in a way that might threaten the Soviet deterrent.

President Reagan later challenged the accepted orthodoxy of mutual assured destruction during his second term by introducing the concept of strategic defense, aimed at the eventual elimination of nuclear weapons, into arms control negotiations with the Soviet Union. Although many experts believed that Reagan's Strategic Defense Initiative—dubbed "Star Wars"—was unrealistic and technologically unachievable, Reagan's personal commitment to the program became a central theme in his approach to strategic arms control. It led almost inadvertently to the major negotiating breakthroughs that came at the end of his second term, in which the two superpowers agreed to eliminate medium-range nuclear weapons and greatly reduce their strategic nuclear arsenals.[35]

35. See Talbott, *Master of the Game,* for a detailed description of this period.

With the sudden collapse of the Soviet Union in 1990, the set of shared images and accepted orthodoxy that had governed U.S. policymaking for forty years, especially in Europe, began to break down. It became much easier for senior participants, particularly those coming in from outside, to establish new decision frameworks and make them credible. That was perhaps nowhere more apparent than in the case of German reunification. When the first President Bush came to office in early 1989, the accepted wisdom was that German reunification would destabilize Europe, it would be unacceptable to the Soviet Union, and it was probably impossible to contemplate in the near term, despite decades of lip service to the goal of reunification. When the Berlin Wall fell later that year, President Bush came to the conclusion that it was time to follow through on the long-standing pledge of reunification and that it was the role of the United States to guide reluctant Europeans through the process. Over the coming months, he worked systematically with European leaders and his own Cabinet to overcome their apprehensions. Within a year, against the background of rapid political evolution in Eastern Europe and the Soviet Union, German reunification became the accepted, logical course of action.[36]

It is now time to pass on to another facet of information. Assembling information to prove that what one wants to do is required by the national interest in light of shared images is only one aspect of the problem. The second is getting that information to the right people and keeping "misleading information" away from them. That sort of maneuvering is described in the next chapter.

36. Bush and Scowcroft, *A World Transformed*, pp. 184–229.

CHAPTER NINE

Maneuvers to Affect Information

A great deal of the information that reaches the president and other senior participants has been selected because it confirms the position of the officials who report it. Higher-ups in turn may digest the information at their disposal in such a way as to support a given policy line, or they may seek to "recover" facts that have been filtered out. In this chapter we focus on maneuvers commonly used at all levels to affect information in favor of a given decision.

TACTICS FOR SELECTING INFORMATION

—*Report only those facts that support the stand that you are taking.* For any complicated foreign policy issue there are a large number of facts that might be relevant in judging what should be done. A participant favoring a particular stand can and frequently does choose among facts, reporting those that back up his or her position and ignoring those that do not. Harlan Cleveland, who was the U.S. ambassador to NATO in the 1960s, reported how the issue of whether the United States could rely on a conventional defense was affected by the selective reporting of information. One example he cited had to do with the aircraft capabilities of the NATO powers compared with those of the Warsaw Pact forces:

> Similarly in air power, it is not just how many aircraft each side has on hand, but how good they are, how accurate are their maintenance crews, how well trained are their pilots, how sophisticated are the air defenses

they have to penetrate, what stocks of ammunition are within easy reach, what reserves and replacements are quickly available, how vulnerable are the airfields they propose to use, and above all how the commanders and pilots rate themselves and their opposition. If an F-4 Phantom is likely to shoot down three or four MiG-21s before it gets hit—or, what is less likely, vice versa—what does it mean to compare the numbers of strike/attack aircraft?

Yet sober and honest officers will tell you the Warsaw Pact has twice as many first-line planes as NATO and forget to mention that most of the discrepancy is in air defense, not in strike/attack aircraft. They will describe the Warsaw Pact "threat" to the central front as more than a million men, against perhaps three-quarters of a million for NATO, without reminding you of the War College dictum that the attacker needs two or three times as many men as the defender. (This conventional wisdom applies to conventional war; nobody knows about nuclear war.) They will speak of NATO manpower without explaining that the Western allies have committed to NATO varying proportions of their men under arms; some of those armed but uncommitted men, ranging from one-fifth to four-fifths of national totals, would surely be available in a real pinch.[1]

A former senior intelligence officer described another form of information manipulation that was used to bolster the case for attacking Iraq:

In the case of Iraq, there was also the matter of sheer quantity of output—not just what the intelligence community said, but how many times it said it. On any given subject, the intelligence community faces what is in effect a field of rocks, and it lacks the resources to turn over every one to see what threats to national security may lurk underneath. In an unpoliticized environment, intelligence officers decide which rocks to turn over based on past patterns and their own judgments. But when policymakers repeatedly urge the intelligence community to turn over only certain rocks, the process becomes biased. The community responds by concentrating its resources on those rocks, eventually producing a body of reporting and analysis that, thanks to quantity and emphasis, leaves the impression that what lies under those same rocks is a bigger part of the problem than it really is.

That is what happened when the Bush administration repeatedly called on the intelligence community to uncover more material that

1. Cleveland, *NATO*, p. 85.

would contribute to the case for war. The Bush team approached the community again and again and pushed it to look harder at the supposed Saddam–al Qaeda relationship—calling on analysts not only to turn over additional Iraqi rocks, but also to turn over ones already examined and to scratch the dirt to see if there might be something there after all. The result was an intelligence output that— because the question being investigated was never put in context—obscured rather than enhanced understanding of al Qaeda's actual sources of strength and support.[2]

—*Structure reporting of information so that senior participants see what you want them to see and not other information.* The quantity of intelligence information produced in the American government each day is overwhelming. Cables arrive from more than a hundred nations, field reports are sent in by military commands throughout the world, intelligence units in Washington produce long reports. Some of that information, such as the daily intelligence report for the president and the State Department summary of major cables, almost inevitably reaches the president. Other information, such as reports about country economic and social conditions sent from embassies, are unlikely to reach any senior participants at all. A participant can put information that he or she wants to reach the president into special channels that ensure that it gets to the top. Other information can be reported in more routine ways, which almost guarantees that it will not surface before senior participants. Thus one can hedge against being accused of not reporting undesired information while reporting desired information so that it reaches senior participants.

According to an official then serving in the Defense Intelligence Agency in the Pentagon, that technique was used by the U.S. military commanders in Vietnam to signal either optimism or pessimism:

> From 1964–65, when U.S. involvement in Vietnam began to be considerable, until late 1966 or early 1967, the generals in Saigon worked to build up U.S. troop strength. Therefore, they wanted every bit of evidence brought to the fore that could show that infiltration was increasing. DIA obliged and also emphasized in all reports the enemy's capability to recruit forces from the South Vietnamese population. In 1967 a second period began. The high priests of Saigon decided that we were "winning." Then the paramount interest became to show the enemy's reduced capability to recruit and a slowdown in infiltration due to our bombing.

2. Pillar, "Intelligence, Policy, and the War in Iraq," p. 23.

The tone and emphasis of reports from the field changed radically, and so did those put out by DIA.

It should not be concluded that anyone suppressed evidence. No one did. The military in Saigon sent all the facts back to Washington eventually. During the buildup period, infiltration data and recruitment data came in via General Westmoreland's daily cablegram. Data from field contact with enemy units came amid the more mundane cables or by courier up to five weeks later. Cables from Westmoreland, of course, were given higher priority in Washington. When we started "winning," detailed reports highlighting "body counts" and statistics on how many villages were pacified were cabled with Westmoreland's signature; recruitment studies were pouched or cabled with the reports on the fluctuating price of rice. It was all a matter of emphasis.[3]

—*Do not report facts that show danger.* The experts in charge of a program or an operation are frequently the only ones knowledgeable enough to report the dangers and difficulties inherent in an operation. If they are pressing for approval of a weapons system or an operation, they may well be reluctant to gratuitously inform top leaders of dangers that those leaders would otherwise not be aware of. President Eisenhower's discussion of the U-2 flights over the Soviet Union, for example, suggests that he was not informed of the increasing concern that Soviet missiles would be able to bring down a high-flying intruder in the relatively near future.[4]

In the case of the Bay of Pigs, President Kennedy was informed that if the landing failed to establish a beachhead, the invading forces would move to the nearby mountains. No mention was made of the fact that there was a virtually impassable swamp between the landing site and the mountain sanctuary.[5]

—*Prepare a careful and detailed study to present facts in what appears to be an authoritative manner and uncover new facts that may bolster your position.* Participants conduct within their own organization a detailed study of a proposed decision. In most cases they do so knowing in advance which position they support and seeking to enhance the credibility of that position by presenting in a formal and detailed manner the results of a study based on extensive expert research and careful analysis.

3. McGarvey, "The Culture of Bureaucracy," pp. 71–72.

4. Compare the account in Eisenhower, *Waging Peace,* pp. 544–59, with the discussion in Powers, *Operation Overflight,* p. 353.

5. Schlesinger, *A Thousand Days,* p. 293; Johnson, *The Bay of Pigs,* pp. 68–69, 224; Sorensen, *Kennedy,* p. 302.

General Matthew Ridgway reports, for example, that in his efforts to pre-vent a decision by the Eisenhower administration to intervene in Indochina in 1954 he had Army staff prepare a detailed study based on trips to the field and an analysis of requirements for intervention. Ridgway indicates that the study enabled him to be somewhat more persuasive with the president in arguing against allied intervention to save the French in Indochina.[6]

—*Request a study from those who will give you the desired conclusions.* In many cases it is much more effective to ask for a study from an ostensibly impartial or external body, knowing in advance that it will produce facts that support the desired stand. The United States intelligence community has a procedure to produce what is known as a National Intelligence Estimate (NIE) or a Special National Intelligence Estimate (SNIE). The estimates are pro-duced in crises or in case of unexpected developments to evaluate possible American courses of action. In some cases officials impartially request such studies. Often, however, there is a debate within the government about whether an SNIE should be requested, whether it is appropriate in the given circumstances. Frequently those arguing in favor of an SNIE have reason to believe that the Intelligence Board, which approves such estimates, will take a position favorable to the stand they are advocating, whereas those arguing against it have reason to doubt that they will be supported by the intelligence community. For example, those who believed that the United States was not doing well in Vietnam and who favored a retrenchment argued in 1968 that the intelligence community should be asked to prepare an SNIE on the paci-fication program. They knew that those who would be responsible for draft-ing the estimate believed that the pacification program was not going well. On the other hand, officials who felt that such pessimistic information would hurt their position argued that pacification was an allied program and hence should be evaluated by the operators in the field and not by the intelligence community. In the closing days of the Johnson administration an SNIE was finally produced, and it took the pessimistic position that those seeking the estimate believed that it would.

Authoritative advice can also be sought from an ad hoc group of presiden-tial advisers or from a formal presidential commission. In some cases the president himself uses the device to build support within his administration and within Congress for a desired program. For example, President Eisen-hower, desiring a new trade policy for the United States, appointed a carefully selected commission under Clarence Randall, who had recently retired as chairman of Inland Steel Company. Sherman Adams, Eisenhower's principal

6. Ridgway, *Soldier*, pp. 276–78.

assistant, explains that Randall was selected not because anyone wished to know whether free trade was a good idea but because Randall was likely to be effective in advocating free trade. "Randall's position as a capitalist was unassailable," Adams writes. "He was also a brilliantly intelligent man who had traveled widely around the world and shared Eisenhower's convictions about the need for free trade as a peace weapon. He had remarkable ability in an argument to explain a complex proposition with clear simplicity and to stick to a position with calm control."[7]

When the president's mind is not made up, one or more of his advisers may recommend a convening of a presidential panel in hopes that its recommendation will persuade him to take the desired direction. Thus during March 1968, in an effort to get President Johnson to cut back on the U.S. involvement in Vietnam, Secretary of Defense Clark Clifford proposed convening a panel of the "Wise Men." They were a group that Johnson had consulted from time to time on Vietnam, and Clifford had reason to believe that the group had moved substantially from the hawkish position that it had reported to the president some months before. After convening and listening to government briefings, the group did urge the president to "de-escalate." (In this case, LBJ said later, he discounted their views because they were based on the pessimistic mood in the United States rather than on the detailed reports that the president was receiving from the field.)[8]

Similarly, Strobe Talbott described the creation of "Team B" in 1976 as an effort by George H. W. Bush, then the director of central intelligence, to co-opt hard-liners, who were arguing that the American intelligence community had been underestimating the Soviet threat.

In June 1976, President Ford's new Director of Central Intelligence, George Bush, created a kind of visiting committee of outsiders to carry out an exercise in "competitive analysis." This meant offering a critique of, and alternative to, the CIA's assessment of Soviet capabilities and intentions. This exercise, known as Team B, was Bush's attempt to help the Administration fend off the challenge from the right, particularly from Ronald Reagan, who was doing well in the Republican primaries and piling up delegates to the party's nominating convention later that summer.[9]

7. Adams, *Firsthand Report,* p. 383.
8. Johnson, *The Vantage Point,* pp. 409, 416–18, 422.
9. Talbott, *Master of the Game,* pp. 145–46.

In other situations advisory committees may be appointed at lower levels within the departments in the hopes that their prestigious conclusions will serve to influence the president and his principal counselors. For example, in an effort to get the strategic missile program moving over the opposition of the Air Force (which was more concerned with bombers), the civilian director of the program in the Pentagon, Trevor Gardner, created a Strategic Missiles Evaluation Group whose members were appointed on the basis of their commitment to ICBMs and their influence with senior officials.[10]

—*Keep away from senior participants those who might report facts one wishes to have suppressed.* White House officials are sometimes able to control a briefing presented to the president, and they use that power to keep out undesirable information. In other cases participants maneuver to exclude individuals who are likely to report information that they do not wish to have presented to the president. Thus in the case of the Bay of Pigs, both the State Department Bureau of Intelligence and Research and the CIA's Intelligence Branch were not informed of the impending invasion and were thus unable to report to the president their own view that an invasion was unlikely to spark the uprising in Cuba that the operations branch of the CIA was promising.

Strobe Talbott described how, after arms negotiator Paul Nitze had developed a new formula for an intermediate-range nuclear forces (INF) reduction in Europe during his 1982 "walk in the woods" with Soviet negotiator Kvitsinsky, officials opposed to the formula maneuvered to suppress information going to the president that they considered to be harmful to their views.

The White House "tasked" the Joint Chiefs of Staff to study the question of whether, from a strictly military standpoint, the security of the United States and NATO would still be served by an INF deal that excluded the Pershing II. The Chiefs warned that there were risks in giving up the Pershing II, especially if cancellation of that particular program established the precedent that the United States would never, under any circumstances, be able to deploy long-range ballistic missiles in Europe. But the Chiefs also concluded that precisely because the Pershing II was a ballistic missile much feared by the Soviets, it was the principal source of leverage for the United States in the negotiations. The chairman, General John Vessey, and the Air Force chief of staff, Charles Gabriel, went one step further: They felt that while giving up the Pershing II was a large price to pay, it was a price worth paying for a major reduction of SS-20s in Europe and a limit on them in Asia. While the Chiefs' final report was

10. Armacost, *The Politics of Weapons Innovation*, p. 57.

carefully hedged and stopped short of a clear recommendation, it might have provided the basis for a presidential decision to proceed with the walk-in-the-woods formula.

However, the Chiefs' answer never reached the White House. Perle and Weinberger intercepted it, squelched it, and sent in its place one of their own which unequivocally reiterated Perle's own denunciation of the deal.[11]

Exclusion of those with contrary views was virtually a hallmark of the very highest level of the second Bush administration. As senior officials were preparing to attack Iraq, for example, State Department analysis concluding that Iraq would have to build infrastructure and political experience before it could sustain democracy was discarded by the vice president and senior Pentagon officials, who insisted that the president's vision of Iraqi democracy was the only alternative to be considered. State Department officials were largely excluded from the planning for postwar occupation and reconstruction of Iraq.[12]

—*Expose participants informally to those who hold the correct views.* Maneuvers may also be planned to see to it that senior participants are exposed to the views of those who speak authoritatively for the favored position from a different frame of reference. President Eisenhower, for example, was reported to be anxious to have all the Joint Chiefs attend National Security Council meetings because he had also invited his secretary of the treasury, George Humphrey. Eisenhower believed that Humphrey might be effective in convincing the Joint Chiefs that the fiscal requirements of the nation meant that the military spending had to be reduced.[13]

George Kennan reported an elaborate plot on the part of Kennedy to have Kennan in attendance at the White House when some senior members of Congress were present so that the president could casually introduce Kennan to them and have him explain his position on aid to Yugoslavia.[14]

—*Get other governments to report facts that are believed to be valuable.* Officials seeking to convince the president that the facts that they have reported are correct may try to get a foreign government to convey the same information to the United States. Proponents of the multilateral force (a plan for a NATO multilateral nuclear force in the 1960s), for example, used that technique to counter doubts about the intensity with which governments in

11. Talbott, *Master of the Game*, pp. 176–77.
12. Woodward, *Plan of Attack*, p. 284.
13. Snyder, "The 'New Look' of 1953."
14. Kennan, Kennedy Library Oral History Interview, p. 79.

Europe favored the American plan for a multilateral nuclear force by persuading a number of foreign officials to express support for the proposal.[15] In
other cases an effort may be made to get foreign governments to share in the
evaluation of a situation in a third country.

—*Advise other participants on what to say.* When they recognize that other
senior participants are looking to a particular official or organization for
authoritative judgment on a question, participants attempt to get that official
or organization to say the right thing. If one is not certain that the other participant shares one's stand, the effort may be subtle. For example, in the case
of the 1965 U.S. intervention in the Dominican Republic, the acting U.S.
ambassador, W. Tapley Bennett, received strong hints from Washington that
it would like him to report that "a rebel victory would probably lead to a pro-
Communist government." The hints were conveyed to Bennett by Secretary of
State Rusk and Secretary of Defense McNamara, who both asked him by telephone if he did not agree with that conclusion, which had been reached in
Washington. Bennett, who favored intervention to put a pro-American government in power, was quick to pick up the clue and report that there was
danger of communists coming to power.[16]

In some cases, career officials may have to be bludgeoned into presenting
the desired information by reminding them that their parent organization
controls their promotion. A former Defense Intelligence Agency (DIA) official recalls how General Westmoreland and other officers were able to influence the estimates prepared by the Defense Intelligence Agency, their leverage
being the control that the armed services wielded over their representatives in
the agency. According to that official:

> In one instance the Air Force Chief of Intelligence called my boss at DIA
> about a nearly completed estimate on U.S. bombing in Laos. He told him
> that he was sending a team down to change the wording of the estimate
> and that my boss had better remember what color his uniform was. Of
> course it was the same as the General's, blue. The team arrived, and, over
> the protests of the DIA analysts, a compromise was reached.
>
> The classic example of command influence on intelligence matters
> occurred just after the Tet Offensive in January 1968. In the early weeks
> of February, the JCS insisted that the offensive was total military defeat
> for the enemy—General Westmoreland told them so in his daily cables.
> DIA didn't agree with this interpretation, but it watered down every

15. Steinbruner, *The Cybernetic Theory of Decision.*
16. Martin, *Overtaken by Events: The Dominican Crises from the Fall of Trujillo to the Civil
War,* p. 659.

paper it wrote on this subject so that its position was impossible to determine. Then General Wheeler went to Saigon and came back with Westmoreland's request for 206,000 troops to "clean up" the "defeated" enemy. Suddenly it was legitimate to say that the Tet Offensive had really "set us back." Everybody on the service staffs, with DIA leading the pack, started writing gloomy estimates with unaccustomed forthrightness and clarity.[17]

—*Circumvent formal channels.* So-called back channel messages are an effective way to tell an already committed participant what line to take. Military and Foreign Service officials in Washington often send private messages to the field so that officials there will know the best way to answer questions put to them from Washington. Roger Hilsman reports one such episode. At a National Security Council meeting it was decided to pose a series of questions to General Paul D. Harkins, then the U.S. commander in Vietnam. A back channel Pentagon message advised Harkins of the most effective answers to the questions. In that case President Kennedy and State Department officials discovered the maneuver, but often it goes undetected.[18]

In some cases the problem is to get information to the president and other senior participants that one cannot move through formal channels. If members of the intelligence community refuse to accept information developed at lower levels within their organization or if Cabinet officers are reluctant to bring information to the attention of the president, it may still come to him informally, often through members of the White House staff. Arthur Larson, who served on Eisenhower's staff, reports that Foreign Service officers unable to get information past their ambassadors into Washington would often send him frantic appeals, such as one from an American official in a Southeast Asian country, which said: "For God sakes, tell John Foster Dulles that Ambassador X is backing the wrong horse here and that the situation is about to blow up!"[19]

The armed services frequently use military assistants in the White House to get information informally to the President. Dean Acheson described an episode when he was secretary of state in which information from the president's naval attaché went directly to President Truman, who in turn raised the matter with British Foreign Secretary Anthony Eden:

After dinner the President and Prime Minister withdrew to the aft saloon while the table was being cleared, in a few minutes sending for Mr. Eden

17. McGarvey, "The Culture of Bureaucracy," p. 73.
18. Hilsman, *To Move a Nation*, pp. 492–93.
19. Larson, *Eisenhower*, p. 19.

and me. The President opened by a complaint that I instantly recognized as coming from a persistent and infuriating practice of the Navy. Through his naval aide the President would be given what was known in the trade as "raw intelligence," reports not analyzed and appraised in accordance with required procedure—in this case a list of British ships, with the gross (not cargo) tonnages, said to have called at Chinese ports over the past year. The practice, as in this case, resulted in extreme and unsupportable conclusions being drawn and caused considerable trouble until the ounce or two of truth had been extracted from the blubber. Our guests were understandably disturbed by possible conclusions. I pointed out that the matter had not been brought to my attention, as it should have been, and asked that it be left to Mr. Eden and me to investigate. When fully analyzed and put together with other data, including known trade between Hong Kong and the mainland, this Navy bombshell amounted to very little.[20]

—*Distort the facts if necessary (if you can get away with it).* Participants seem to strain very hard not to say anything that they know to be false, either in internal argument or publicly. Nevertheless, when it appears necessary to secure approval of a project, they are sometimes prepared not only to use each of the maneuvers described above but also to distort the facts. Francis Gary Powers, the pilot of the ill-fated U-2, believes that Eisenhower was deceived about the ability of the aircraft that he flew over the Soviet Union to destroy itself. Eisenhower wrote in his memoirs:

> There was, to be sure, reason for deep concern and sadness over the probable loss of the pilot, but not for immediate alarm about the equipment. I had been assured that if a plane were to go down it would be destroyed either in the air or on impact, so that proof of espionage would be lacking. Self-destroying mechanisms were built in.[21]

Powers, after quoting this paragraph, asserted:

> If Eisenhower was told this, he was deceived. Had we been carrying ten times the two-and-a-half-pound explosive charge, there would have been no guarantee that the entire plane and all its contents would have been destroyed. Nor was the single mechanism "self-destroying." It would have to be activated by the pilot.[22]

20. Acheson, *Present at the Creation*, p. 598.
21. Eisenhower, *Waging Peace*, p. 547.
22. Powers, *Operation Overflight*, p. 353.

A combination of the maneuvers enumerated above can lead to a substantial distortion of the information available to the president. When there are advocates of different positions within the administration and when participants on all sides have their own access to sources of information, the president tends to be informed of the problems and difficulties of various alternative positions. When, however, the advocates of a certain policy are able to keep out of the process those with alternative sources of information and expertise, the distortions can be very great. The Bay of Pigs invasion provides an example of obvious distortion of the information available to the president when making a critical decision. Sorensen, in writing about the episode, summed up the number of ways in which the president was either misled or deceived about the facts:

1. *The President thought he was approving a quiet, even though large-scale, reinfiltration of fourteen hundred Cuban exiles back into their homeland.* . . . Their landing was, in fact, highly publicized in advance and deliberately and grossly overstated.

2. *The President thought he was approving a plan whereby the exiles, should they fail to hold and expand a beachhead, could take up guerrilla warfare with other rebels in the mountains.* . . . The immediate area was not suitable for guerrilla warfare, as the President had been assured; the vast majority of brigade members had not been given guerrilla training, as he had been assured. . . . [A move to the mountains] was never even planned by the CIA officers in charge of the operation, and they neither told the President they thought this option was out nor told the exiles that this was the President's plan.

3. *The President thought he was permitting the Cuban exiles, as represented by their Revolutionary Council and brigade leaders, to decide whether they wished to risk their own lives and liberty for the liberty of their country without any overt American support.* Most members of the brigade were in fact under the mistaken impression, apparently from their CIA contacts, that American armed forces would openly and directly assist them, if necessary, to neutralize the air (presumably with jets), make certain of their ammunition, and prevent their defeat.

4. *President Kennedy thought he was approving a plan calculated to succeed with the help of the Cuban underground, military desertions, and in time an uprising of a rebellious population.* In fact, both Castro's popularity and his police state measures, aided by the mass arrests which promptly followed the bombing and landing, proved far stronger than

the operation's planners had claimed. The planners, moreover, had no way to alert the underground without alerting Castro's forces. . . . As a result . . . no coordinated uprising or underground effort was really planned or possible.

5. *The President thought he was approving a plan rushed into execution on the grounds that Castro would later acquire the military capability to defeat it.* Castro, in fact, already possessed that capability.[23]

PRESIDENTIAL EFFORTS TO EXPAND INFORMATION

The president has available some of the same devices listed above for getting information to certain participants in order to persuade them to agree with his position on an issue. He, too, can arrange to expose other participants informally to views of persuasive individuals, and he can seek to influence what field commanders, ambassadors, or even other countries report to Washington. He can seek to suppress facts or to keep certain participants out of a particular dispute.

Presidents find, however, that the real test of their ability is to expand their own information, because they learn that the information being provided to them by subordinates is designed not so much to enlighten them as to convince them to adopt certain positions. Sometimes it may take a president a year or more to discover that he cannot rely on the information he is being given. Only by 1965 did Lyndon Johnson begin to understand that the optimistic statistics being reported to him from Vietnam were meaningless.[24] It was not until the spring of 1962 that Kennedy, addressing a group of Foreign Service officers in the State Department auditorium, remarked: "Winston Churchill once said that the secret of the survival of the British Empire was that they never trusted the judgment of the man on the spot. I never understood that until recently."[25]

When he is dissatisfied with the information reaching him, the president can do a number of things:

—*Instruct the White House staff to seek alternative sources of information on critical issues.* Every postwar American president has come to see the White House staff as a means of getting information that the departments would not wish him to have. That function was drastically expanded after the Bay of Pigs operation, when Kennedy, believing that the White House staff was not

23. Sorensen, *Kennedy,* pp. 302–03 (italics added).
24. Sidey, *A Very Personal Presidency,* p. 220.
25. Leacacos, *Fires in the In-Basket: The ABCs of the State Department,* p. 301.

in a position to keep him fully informed, instructed McGeorge Bundy, his assistant for national security affairs, to increase staff capacity substantially and to see that the president was fully briefed. As a result, Bundy arranged to have much of the raw material coming in from the field, including State Department, CIA, and military cables, sent directly to the White House situation room. Prior to that time only those cables that the departments chose to send over reached the White House. Since 1962, the White House staff has been in a much more effective position to monitor information coming into Washington and report it to the president. It is more difficult for the White House to get access to information that does not come into Washington or reaches Washington through informal channels and back channels.

—*Create new channels of reliable information.* When the president feels that he has fully tapped existing sources of information and is still receiving biased reports, he may find it convenient to create an entirely new vehicle for gathering and processing information on national security issues. President Truman proposed the creation of a centralized intelligence system to eliminate conflicting and self-serving intelligence reports from each agency.[26] President Nixon, twenty-five years later, believing that the national estimates now being produced by a centralized apparatus had become sterile bureaucratic compromises, created special panels to evaluate weapons problems and events in Vietnam.[27] Secretary of Defense Donald Rumsfeld, believing that the president's intelligence reports on Iraq did not accurately reflect Saddam's links to al Qaeda, established an office to review raw intelligence reports and draw its own conclusions. According to one observer, that office "was dedicated to finding every possible link between Saddam and al Qaeda, and its briefings accused the intelligence community of faulty analysis for failing to see the supposed alliance."[28]

—*Surround himself with divergent views.* To guard against biased information, a president may surround himself with individuals who have divergent views on particular issues and who are likely to call attention to facts supporting different positions.

—*Ask for the separate views of each adviser.* The president frequently presses his advisers for a unanimous judgment as to what should be done. However, when he has doubts about the information being presented, he may ask each adviser to give a separate view, in an effort to uncover hidden differences. Kennedy resorted to this technique when confronted with the question of

26. Truman, *Memoirs,* vol. 1, *Year of Decisions,* pp. 98–99 (cited hereafter as *Year of Decisions*).

27. Nixon, *U.S. Foreign Policy for the 1970s.*

28. Pillar, "Intelligence, Policy, and the War in Iraq," p. 24.

whether to intervene in Laos. "Thank God the Bay of Pigs happened when it did," he told Sorensen on the eve of a UN address. "Otherwise we would be in Laos by now—and that would be a hundred times worse."[29] Anxious in that case to discover whether his advisers did in fact all agree, he had pressed for the separate views of each of the Joint Chiefs. After hearing them, he discovered that they in fact had very divergent notions as to what was going on in Laos, what American forces would be needed, and what the danger of Chinese intervention was.

—*Encourage adversary proceedings.* A refinement of the techniques of developing new channels and discovering divergent views is for the president, when he feels that he needs to hear all sides of an issue, to have a group of participants with different interests and direct stakes in the issue sit down and fight it out in front of him. Presidents Truman and Kennedy frequently resorted to this technique.[30] The first President Bush also encouraged adversary proceedings when there were serious policy divisions. "Sometimes cabinet members might still have deep differences of opinion, or rival departments would feel strongly about an issue. Brent [Scowcroft] always made sure the views of every 'player' were understood by him and by me. If he could not resolve the impasse separately, then the principals would sort it out with me."[31]

—*Call middle-level officials and permit them to call.* In an effort to go beyond the information provided formally by the senior participants who have direct access to him, the president can seek to establish informal channels of communication with middle-level officials. In most cases, that is done through the White House staff. A substantial part of its job in ferreting out additional information for the president is to maintain informal contact with middle-level officials in various departments whose views are unlikely to get through the filter of each agency. In some cases, however, the president himself seeks to establish such contact. Kennedy appears to have done that more than any other president since World War II. He frequently would telephone middle-level officials or bring them into White House meetings. Often Kennedy would call the person that he thought had written the memo that came to him under the signature of the secretary of state.[32] President Clinton

29. Sorensen, *Kennedy,* p. 644.

30. George, in "The Case for Multiple Advocacy in Making Foreign Policy," pp. 751–85, expands this point into a scheme that he believes might overcome the liabilities of bureaucratic politics in the foreign policy process. In essence, he prescribes a system in which all the arguments bearing on an issue are brought into focus and fought out under the direction of a disinterested "custodian" at the special assistant level.

31. Bush and Scowcroft, *A World Transformed,* p. 35.

32. See the numerous references to this technique in the Oral History Interviews in the John F. Kennedy Library cited in part B of the bibliography.

also liked to reach down to mid-level officials and National Security Council staff in his informal foreign policy deliberations to ensure that he was considering every possible angle.

—*Contact ambassadors directly.* Presidents sometimes encourage their ambassadors to communicate directly with them or through the White House staff in addition to using formal State Department channels of communication. Again, Kennedy seems to have favored this technique more often than any other recent president, making it a point to see ambassadors when they were in Washington and encouraging them to write directly to him.[33] Ambassadors, of course, are interested in establishing that kind of direct communication, because they often feel that their side of a story does not get beyond the country desk in the State Department.[34]

—*Send representatives to the field.* Sometimes presidents come to distrust the information being sent to them through formal channels. In that case, they may send their personal emissary to the field for a direct assessment of the situation. Cabinet officials are sometimes chosen to perform that role, but, because their views are likely to be affected by the stands and interests of their organization, they are more often passed over in favor of White House officials or ad hoc personal advisers. Thus during the long history of the Vietnam War a number of different presidential emissaries were sent to assess the situation. President Nixon, for example, once sent the British counterinsurgency expert Sir Robert Thompson, and President Johnson sent Maxwell Taylor on such a mission. In one of the earliest instances, President Kennedy sent a Foreign Service officer and a general to Vietnam on an inspection trip together. The civil official came back with a deeply pessimistic report, and the military officer came back greatly encouraged by what he had seen. That led to the famous presidential response: "Were you two gentlemen in the same country?"[35]

Kennedy's dilemma in that case reflects a frequent presidential problem. If an individual with a lack of prior experience or involvement in the issue goes out, it is difficult for him to penetrate beyond the formal briefings. If, on the other hand, a career official intimately involved is sent to the field, he is likely to report back whatever serves the interests of his organization. In the days before his authorization of the Bay of Pigs invasion, President Kennedy asked a Marine colonel who was an old friend to evaluate the situation. His enthusiastic concurrence in the optimism of the CIA was apparently important in overcoming Kennedy's doubts.[36]

33. Ibid.
34. For a discussion of this issue, see Attwood, *The Reds and the Blacks*, pp. 157–58.
35. Schlesinger, *A Thousand Days*, pp. 992–93.
36. Johnson, *The Bay of Pigs*, p. 73.

The use of special envoys became even more common, for example, in communications with the Soviet Union during the final years of the cold war and for a variety of purposes in the post–cold war period. Presidents often reach outside the formal structures of government to demonstrate that special attention is being devoted to a particular problem through the appointment of a special envoy, as the second President Bush did in both Afghanistan and Iraq.

—*Go outside the government.* Finally, a president has the option of expanding his base of information by seeking opinions outside the executive branch and outside the government. One of the most common methods of getting information from beyond the confines of the bureaucracy is the presidential commission. Presidents often consult with representatives and senators from relevant committees, with former government officials, and with academic experts, and they confer with foreign ambassadors stationed in Washington.

One of the most important ways in which both the president and the other participants maneuver to affect information is by seeking to influence what is reported in the press and other news media about any particular subject. That maneuver receives more detailed treatment in the following chapter.

CHAPTER TEN

Uses of
the Press

Information that appears in the American press (including television and the Internet) plays a central role in shaping presidential decisions. Much of the information available to senior participants on any issue consists of what they encounter in the media, particularly with the recent explosion of electronic information, because the news media often set the agenda by being first on the scene. Most of the information reaches the press routinely or through the persistence of reporters, but some is put there by participants in an effort to influence presidential decisions. This chapter explores the techniques that bureaucrats employ in using the press. We do not suggest that "leaking" is the only or even the most important way that information gets into print, but we wish to discuss the use of leaks as a standard bureaucratic maneuver.

RELEASING INFORMATION

Most of the news about national security issues that reaches the press concerns formal government decisions. A decision is made, and then as a matter of routine it is announced to the press either because that is part of the process of implementation (to be discussed in the following section) or because it is simply assumed that the public should be informed about major presidential or Cabinet-level decisions and should not have to learn about them by observing implementation. However, a substantial fraction of what appears in the press is there for other reasons, some of which are related to efforts to affect presidential decisions.[1]

Most of the information about national security issues that reaches the press is released by participants in the executive branch, either in official hand-outs at meetings or in press conferences. Often such press conferences are on the record: that is, journalists are free to report that the conference was held and to identify and directly quote the officials who spoke to them. In other cases, the press conference is on a "background" basis, whereby reporters may use the information but instead of quoting directly must attribute it to some vague source, such as "senior administration officials" or "State Department officials." Only senior participants are in a position to call press conferences, whether on the record or for background, although occasionally they sponsor one conducted by a relatively junior official. During the Kennedy and Johnson administrations, Secretary of State Dean Rusk and Secretary of Defense Robert McNamara held background briefings weekly.[2] Presidential adviser Henry Kissinger frequently held background briefings following a major presidential speech or in the midst of a foreign policy crisis. Usually a conference is open to all reporters, but in some cases a specific group of journalists hold a luncheon or breakfast to which they invite an official and ask for a background briefing. Though the material given in a background press conference normally can be attributed to "senior officials," in some cases a conference is designated "deep background," and the reporter must write the information on his own initiative without attributing it to any official source. President Kennedy, for example, held such deep backgrounders at the end of each year, leading to a series of stories saying, "The President is known to believe that...."[3]

Apart from such official forms of release, an important fraction of the material supplied to the press by participants in the executive branch is in the form of "leaks." Leaking is accomplished in many ways, such as private and off-the-record interviews, vague tips to reporters to look into a particular subject, or actually handing official papers to a reporter surreptitiously.

---

1. Sigal, *Reporters and Officials,* pp. 131–50.

2. Alsop, *The Center: People and Power in Political Washington,* pp. 186–89; Weintal and Bartlett, *Facing the Brink: An Intimate Study in Crisis Diplomacy,* p. 163.

3. Public knowledge of what is said at background briefings is generally limited to news stories. For two complete texts of background briefings, see Deputy Under Secretary of State Alex Johnson's remarks on the return of Okinawa to Japan in U.S. Congress, *United States Security Agreements and Commitments Abroad,* pp. 1439–46; and presidential assistant Henry Kissinger's remarks on the Indo-Pakistani war of 1971 in Kissinger, Background briefing, pp. 45734–38.

Most White House leaks occur at the president's initiative. However, some reporters seek to establish a general relationship with the White House so that they may be provided with leaks in return for a promise to report the information in a way that will accomplish the objectives of the president in leaking the material. Joseph Alsop, a Washington syndicated columnist, was frequently successful in establishing such relations and apparently took the initiative in seeking to do so. Robert Cutler, President Eisenhower's special assistant for national security affairs, reported being approached by Alsop early in the Eisenhower administration in an attempt to set up such an arrangement.[4] Bob Woodward of the *Washington Post* seems to have enjoyed a position of trust with the second President Bush after he published a book lauding Bush's post-9/11 leadership in Afghanistan.

Another ploy reporters use on their own initiative is to call officials, act as if they know that something has occurred, and get implied confirmation from them, often in the form of a refusal to discuss the subject. Thus on one occasion, alerted almost inadvertently by McGeorge Bundy to the fact that there was a major news story waiting to be discovered, Chalmers Roberts and Murray Marder of the *Washington Post* began calling administration officials and asking them, "What was in the message from Khrushchev to Kennedy about the Il-28s?" On one call Roberts finally got the response, "For Crissakes, how did you know about that? I can't tell you what was in the message."[5] On that basis, the *Post* was able to print a story indicating that Khrushchev had sent a message to Kennedy on the Il-28s in the closing days of the Cuban missile crisis.

Less often, officials describe a document in detail to favored journalists or actually let them see the document or take a copy away—with or without their superior's knowledge. Presidential assistant Walt Rostow, for example, would frequently call in a group of reporters on Johnson's orders and permit them to read intelligence reports on the Vietnam situation.[6] Following the Indo-Pakistani war of late 1971, some officials gave to Jack Anderson, a syndicated columnist, the full text of a number of documents, including three reports of meetings of the Washington Special Actions Group, a senior-level group chaired by Henry Kissinger.[7]

Leaks come from many different sources, but it is the judgment of most reporters that the greatest single source of leaks is the White House.[8] Reporters

4. Cutler, *No Time for Rest*, pp. 317–19.
5. Alsop, *The Center*, pp. 165–67. See also Roberts, *First Rough Draft*, p. 207.
6. *Newsweek*, July 5, 1971, p. 21.
7. The three documents were reprinted in the *Washington Post*, January 5, 1972.
8. See, for example, Reston, *The Artillery of the Press: Its Influence on American Foreign Policy*, p. 66.

themselves have told of receiving highly sensitive information directly from the president. Both Max Frankel and Benjamin Bradlee were briefed by President Kennedy on his meeting with Nikita Khrushchev in Vienna in 1961.[9] In other cases the source of a story may be Congress or a foreign embassy.[10] For example, one of the most famous leaks of the Johnson administration, of the fact that General Westmoreland had requested an additional 206,000 troops to be sent to Vietnam following the Tet offensive, was apparently leaked to the press from Capitol Hill.[11]

Senior officials have a choice of revealing information through leaks, background press conferences, or on-the-record statements. They may choose to use a background press conference or a leak because they do not have authority from the president to reveal the information and they fear being fired or, more likely, cut out from the circle of participants involved in a particular issue. Because of the same fears, junior participants take elaborate precautions to protect themselves when they leak material. Another reason for resorting to leaks or background press conferences is to conceal the source of information so as to make it appear to be some more authoritative or expert source. In other cases, a participant is concerned about "multiple audiences." He or she may desire to make clear to a domestic American audience or to the bureaucracy what the position is without making a formal statement to a foreign government, or he or she may wish to launch a trial balloon or to give guidance to the bureaucracy without making a formal commitment on the part of the president. For all those reasons, officials resort to leaking, background press conferences, and other techniques of putting information into the press without first securing the president's agreement that such material should be released. What specifically do participants hope to accomplish in providing material to the press?

WHY INFORMATION IS LEAKED

In general, information is provided to the press either to affect bureaucratic maneuvers directly or to alert and bring into the process participants from outside the bureaucracy. A leak, for example, can inspire further investigative reporting or attention from members of Congress. Leaking is a time-honored means of getting information to the president outside formal channels.

9. *Washington Post*, June 22, 1971; *Washington Post*, July 9, 1971. See also Krock, *Memoirs*, p. 27.
10. Cater, *The Fourth Branch of Government*, p. 125.
11. Kalb and Abel, *Roots of Involvement*, p. 238.

—To get the message through. Providing material to the press is often designed to expose senior participants to a certain view of what is happening and the likelihood of certain developments. Much of the information about the world that reaches senior participants comes through the press. The feeling is that "everyone" in Washington reads the *New York Times* and the *Washington Post.* They also follow CNN and TV network news. The reality reflected in newspapers and on radio, television, and the Internet helps shape the way senior participants see the world. Therefore participants may talk to reporters in a manner designed to get them to present their stories in a particular light, hoping that the daily reading of the press and electronic media gradually leads senior participants to interpret an issue in a given way. For example, during the early 1960s different officials in Saigon leaked conflicting reports about the Vietnam War to American reporters in the hope of convincing senior participants in Washington either that the war was a civil war or that it was essentially an invasion from the north. Those conflicting notions of what was going on in South Vietnam implied quite different policy stands.[12]

—To undermine rivals. Leaks often are used in an effort to drive a participant entirely from the executive branch or to reduce his or her influence substantially by trying in a variety of ways to bring his or her behavior into question. One technique is to try to show that a participant is in favor of a policy that lacks any support in the country. Following the Cuban missile crisis, opponents of UN ambassador Adlai Stevenson hinted to reporters that Stevenson had favored appeasement of the Soviet Union by advocating a trade of missiles in Cuba for missiles in Turkey. The intent was to show that Stevenson was so "soft" that his views could not be taken seriously. If that could be shown, Stevenson's enemies believed, then President Kennedy would feel pressed to remove him from office or to ignore him.[13]

A closely related technique is to try to have the press portray a particular participant as not being a loyal supporter of the president. As with other aspects of leaking information to the press, the machinations can become quite involved. Following the Bay of Pigs invasion, news stories appeared indicating that Chester Bowles, the under secretary of state, was one of the few officials who had opposed the operation. Opponents of Bowles charged that he had deliberately leaked the story in order to ingratiate himself with the left wing of the Democratic party but that in doing so he had undercut the president's effort to maintain a united front. It is not impossible that the initial sto-

12. Hilsman, *To Move a Nation,* p. 499.
13. Beichman, *The "Other" State Department,* pp. 146–47; Schlesinger, *A Thousand Days,* p. 835.

ries were leaked by opponents of Bowles in order to put them in a position to make the charge.

Secretary of State Colin Powell was subjected to similar innuendo during the second Bush administration when he was seen to be contradicting Vice President Cheney in stating the president's position on war with Iraq. Powell had told the BBC that the president was in favor of getting the UN weapons inspectors back into Iraq. Cheney then gave a major speech to press the case for attacking Iraq, arguing that a return of inspectors was futile, if not danger-ous. Shortly thereafter, "stories began appearing that Powell was contradict-ing Cheney. He was accused of disloyalty, and he counted seven editorials calling for his resignation or implying that he should quit. How can I be dis-loyal, he wondered, when I'm giving the President's stated position?"[14]

Leaks also may be designed to show that a particular participant is incom-petent or doing a poor job. Such leaks frequently occur when two senior par-ticipants are in a feud with each other and each is prepared to use any available means to undercut the other's position. Thus when Harold Stassen and John Foster Dulles competed for the ear of the president on disarmament matters and when Secretary of State Dean Acheson and Secretary of Defense Louis Johnson feuded, the press was full of stories about the positions of each of those officials.[15] The running policy feuds between National Security Coun-cil adviser Brzezinski and Secretary of State Vance during the Carter admin-istration and between Secretary of Defense Rumsfeld and Secretary of State Powell during the second Bush administration were often reflected in press accounts inspired by one against the other. Participants may also seek to undercut the position of an opponent by showing that he does not have the support of the president. Often the president himself engages in such leaks as a way of advising other participants that they need not take the views of a par-ticular individual or organization as seriously as they had in the past. James F. Byrnes, Truman's first secretary of state, believed that he was subjected to such a move on the part of the president.[16] President Kennedy sought to undercut the position of the Joint Chiefs of Staff following the Bay of Pigs operation by telling Arthur Krock, the Washington correspondent of the *New York Times,* that he had "lost confidence" in the Joint Chiefs and permitting Krock to publish that statement on his own authority.[17]

Leaks may be utilized to indicate that a participant has lied to the public, thereby making it an embarrassment to the president to keep him in office.

14. Woodward, *Plan of Attack,* p. 164.
15. Cohen, *The Press and Foreign Policy,* p. 197.
16. Byrnes, *Speaking Frankly,* p. 238.
17. Krock, *Memoirs,* p. 371.

That was one explanation offered for the leak of documents relating to American policy during the Indo-Pakistani war of 1971. The leaks seemed to show that presidential assistant Henry Kissinger had lied to the press in describing American policy, and some observers believed that the purpose of the leak was to discredit Kissinger.[18]

Accusing an official of leaking something is itself a way of discrediting his reputation within the bureaucracy. John Mecklin, the U.S. public affairs adviser in Vietnam in the early 1960s, reports that because he was friendly with two reporters, Neil Sheehan of UPI and David Halberstam of the *New York Times,* he was accused of leaking stories to them. Such complaints were conveyed by Secretary of State Dean Rusk and CIA director John McCone to the head of the U.S. Information Agency. Mecklin concluded that "the damage done to my reputation at such a level also severely compromised my future with the government."[19]

Machiavellian use of the press to discredit one's opponents attains its highest levels within the White House staff itself. George Reedy described the atmosphere:

> The only aspect of "palace-guard" politics which requires subtlety is the use of the press. The inexperienced courtier may make the mistake of using his press contacts (which it takes a positive effort of will not to acquire) to secure favorable mention of his name in public. But the wilier practitioners of the art of palace knife-fighting take a different tack. They seek to feature their competitors' names in a context which will displease the man who holds the real power. This reverse-thrust technique is somewhat more complex than it appears on first glance. It is not inconceivable, for example, that a newspaper story speculating on the promotion of an assistant to higher office may be the death knell of that assistant's governmental career. It all depends upon the psychology of the president, but whatever that psychology, there will always be people around him who are willing to play it for whatever it is worth.[20]

Leaks to the press can be designed to affect relations between organizations as well as individuals when that is believed necessary to attain a desired outcome. The Army, attempting to get permission for development of a medium-range missile, at one point sought to cement an alliance with the Navy by inflaming relations between the Navy and the Air Force. Army colonels leaked

18. See, for example, Kraft, "Undermining Kissinger," *Washington Post,* January 11, 1972.
19. Mecklin, *Mission in Torment,* pp. 184–86.
20. Reedy, *The Twilight of the Presidency,* pp. 90–91.

to the Pentagon reporter of the *New York Times* an Air Force staff paper that deprecated the contribution of Forrestal-class carriers to the overall strategic mission. The aim was to deceive the Navy into thinking that the Air Force was leaking papers prejudicial to the Navy's interest.[21]

—To attract the attention of the president. Getting a story into the news media sometimes is a way of bringing issues to the attention of the president. As one former official observed: "The amount of high-level interest in an issue varies with potential press interest."[22] Particularly when preparing for a press conference, the president is informed by his aides regarding what questions reporters are likely to raise. In the process he may learn of issues that would otherwise remain buried in the bureaucracy. One clue that aides use in determining what questions reporters are likely to raise are leaked stories that have recently appeared in the press. Thus an official anxious to bring an issue to the attention of the president may plant a story with the expectation that the subject will then come up in the preparation for a press conference.

—To build support. Presidents may use press leaks to issue what bureaucrats call a "hunting license"—meaning that they let their inclination in favor of a particular proposal be known as it is winding its way through the bureaucracy. By having reporters write stories saying that the president favors moving in a particular direction, the White House strengthens the hand of those advocating that move. Advocates point to the story as an indication of presidential concern justifying movement.

—To ensure implementation. Many times a leak follows a presidential decision and is designed to enforce implementation. This aspect of leaking is discussed in Part 3.

—To alert foreign governments. In some instances, press leaks are used to bring the influence of foreign governments to bear on a policy question. During the cold war period, NATO countries were likely targets for such operations. Officials in those countries read the American press carefully and were sensitive to American actions that they thought might undercut the NATO alliance. George Kennan explained in his memoirs how a leak, by a person still unknown, was used to kill a plan for a partial withdrawal of American forces from Europe in the period immediately after World War II.[23] Maxwell Taylor stated that a leak also undercut a plan by Admiral Arthur Radford during the latter's term as chairman of the Joint Chiefs of Staff to withdraw a substan-

21. *New York Times*, May 20, 1956, cited and explained in Armacost, *The Politics of Weapons Innovation*, p. 93.

22. Quoted from an anonymous former official by Holbrooke, "The Machine That Fails," p. 72.

23. Kennan, *Memoirs, 1925–1950*, pp. 444–45.

tial number of American forces from Europe. The report in the press that such a plan was afoot led German Chancellor Konrad Adenauer to send the chief of the German armed forces to Washington to express Germany's great concern[24] and resulted in intense complaints from other European allies, forcing the U.S. government to suspend consideration of a reduction of forces. One of the first notorious leaks of the Kennedy administration involved such a maneuver. Secretary of State Rusk had sent a memorandum to Secretary of Defense McNamara on February 15, 1961, outlining the American military forces that he believed were required to support the proper foreign policy objectives. In the course of the memorandum Rusk emphasized the need for general-purpose forces, an emphasis that could be construed as supporting the Army's budget against that of the Air Force. The memorandum was leaked to the press within two weeks in a badly distorted form, suggesting that Rusk favored abandonment of the nuclear deterrent in Europe. The episode was typical in that what finally reached the press was a distorted version designed to create the maximum sense of fear in the intended audience.[25]

Going Outside the Executive Branch

Most leaks are designed to put information into the public domain that would not otherwise be available, and the purpose of putting it there is to influence Congress or the public as a whole and thereby to influence presidential decisions. The decision to leak information to the press is taken by those who are dissatisfied with the decisions being made within the executive branch and who have reason to believe that public attitudes are likely to be more favorable to their position. Participants who recognize that public and congressional views are likely to be even more opposed to their position have no incentive to alert the news media despite the expectation of an adverse presidential decision. Thus the sort of information disclosed changes from time to time in light of the executive branch's views of public and congressional attitudes. Leaks may be designed simply to alert participants outside the executive branch in order to enable them to bring influence to bear, or they may be designed to affect the information that Congress and the public have and to lead them to make up their mind in a particular way on a particular issue. Frequently the stand that a particular group or individual has taken on an issue is made known through leaks when it is believed that knowledge of that stand will affect the attitudes of leading members of Congress and important

24. Taylor, *The Uncertain Trumpet*, pp. 41–42.
25. Kraft, *Profiles in Power*, pp. 115–18; Cater, *Power in Washington*, p. 48.

groups. Finally, leaks related to domestic politics may be designed to create the expectation that something that is favored by important segments of the public will in fact occur.

Alerting Outside Supporters

In some situations participants recognize that a number of supporters of their position hold key congressional positions or belong to influential interest groups. The problem is simply that those potential allies are not aware of the fact that a presidential decision is about to be made. In such instances, the purpose of leaks is to inform the individuals that an issue is up for decision, so that they can make their views known. Officials find it more difficult to act to the contrary after they have been informed in advance about the strong views of individuals whose support they need on a wide range of issues. Roger Hilsman, who was then the director of the Bureau of Intelligence and Research (INR) at the State Department, described an episode in which he had the agreement of State Department officials to transfer to the Central Intelligence Agency what he viewed as certain peripheral functions then being performed by INR with funds transferred from the CIA:

> But I had not reckoned on Congress. I had Rusk's approval, but before the decision was final I had to touch base with the Bureau of the Budget, the CIA, and others. Before I could complete the rounds, there was—inevitably—a leak, and a leak designed to block the move. A national newsmagazine reported that I was about to sell half the personnel of the bureau "up the river"—literally up the Potomac River to the CIA headquarters at Langley, Virginia. Wayne Hayes, Chairman of the Subcommittee on State Department Organization, and the entire membership of the House Foreign Affairs Committee were furious at what they thought was a further enhancement of the power of CIA. For the Foreign Affairs Committee shared many of the State Department's resentments of the CIA, and for many of the same reasons. Knowledgeable and sensitive to the political considerations in our dealings abroad because of their work on the committee, the members decried the growth of the CIA, its ubiquitousness, and the political handicaps which the United States' seemingly excessive reliance on secret agents and cloak-and-dagger techniques brought in their wake. They also resented the fact that the CIA had a special relationship with a secret subcommittee consisting of members from the Appropriations Committee and the Armed Services Committee—

bypassing the Foreign Affairs Committee on a number of matters they considered their proper responsibility. I was ordered to appear before the subcommittee the next day.[26]

If outside opponents of a favored line of action are known to exist, strenuous efforts are made to keep a matter from leaking before a presidential decision is announced. For example, in planning his trip to Peking, President Nixon went to great lengths to keep the matter from leaking to supporters of the Chinese Nationalist regime in the United States until he could announce that he had accepted an invitation from Chairman Mao. Similarly, great efforts were made to prevent any leaks of the proposed American plans to support an invasion of Cuba in 1961.[27] The Clinton administration later went to great lengths to conceal the secret negotiations between Cuba and the United States leading to an agreement that Cuba would accept the return of Cubans seeking to enter the United States illegally.

Affecting Public Information

In other cases the problem is more complicated. Participants believe that there is potential support for their position among the public but that they need to focus that support by providing information that will make clear why their position is important to national security. In such cases the leaks, besides alerting the public to the fact that an issue is up for debate, must also present information that will galvanize outsiders into action. The information leaked to the press may be designed to warn the public of the great dangers that would flow from a decision that participants fear the president will make. Their aim is to increase the domestic political cost of the decision to the president by generating public fears. Admiral Arthur Radford may have resorted to this technique as part of the campaign to get Eisenhower to approve military intervention in Vietnam in 1954. According to one study:

> An important section of the military led by Admiral Arthur Radford, the Chairman of the Joint Chiefs of Staff, increasingly identified the Indochina War with centralized Communist planning in Moscow and Peking. The French, in this view, were fighting to defend the free world, to hold back the yellow hordes of Communist-indoctrinated peasant guerrillas bent on conquering all of Asia—first China, then Vietnam, and which country next? The analogy of a line of falling dominoes was used

26. Hilsman, *To Move a Nation*, p. 71.
27. Schlesinger, *A Thousand Days*, p. 261.

to illustrate the danger confronting the American defense system based on a chain of islands from Japan to Formosa and the Philippines. It was argued that intervention to meet the threat, either alone or in concert, was preferable to a negotiated surrender. As the *New York Times* put it in a dispatch printed on May 2, the Radford school argued that there should be "no agreement to cease firing or to an armistice or to any settlement that will permit the Communist Viet Minh to build up their strength and resume fighting more effectively later." The article concluded that "In essence, any solution in Indochina short of outright military defeat of the Viet Minh rebels is opposed by the men responsible for the military security of the United States."[28]

Many leaks relate to supposed "enemy" capabilities. The military services seek to generate support for their proposed weapons systems by leaking information to the press about enemy capabilities. In some cases the estimates leaked may be wildly exaggerated or even totally false. One example of the latter was the story put out surreptitiously by the military that the Soviet Union had tested a nuclear-powered bomber. In fact no such test had taken place, and no information existed that suggested that it would.[29] Many leaks relating to Russia's capabilities occurred during the SALT and subsequent arms control negotiations.

Other leaks are aimed at extolling the virtues of one military capability opposed to another. These show up especially when the services are developing two closely related systems, such as the Polaris and Minuteman missiles.[30] Leaks are also devised to emphasize "gaps" in U.S. capabilities if it is thought that the gaps may then be "overcome" to the advantage of the armed forces. Thus when the military were denied operational control over nuclear weapons by President Truman, they leaked the fact to the press along with hints that his decision interfered with the operational readiness of the Air Force.[31]

Informing a Constituency

Matters of allegiance and personality sometimes lie behind leaks. The position taken by a key individual or organization on a particular issue may be made known through a leak if important groups outside the executive branch take their cues from the stands of specific participants within the executive branch.

28. Dommen, *Conflict in Laos*, p. 47.
29. Lambright, *Shooting Down the Nuclear Plane*, p. 17.
30. James Baar and William Howard, *Polaris*, pp. 215–16.
31. Davis, *Lawrence and Oppenheimer*, p. 287.

If participants have no following, their position is rarely leaked. Thus one seldom learns what the career officials in the various State Department regional bureaus think about an issue. When, however, groups with prestige outside the executive branch fear that the president will not accept their positions, they are likely to see to it that their supporters know what is happening. In some cases the leak originates with other officials anxious to get the support that may come from letting it be known that a prestigious group has supported their position.

Because of the prestigious position that the military services have had in most of the period since World War II, their views on a number of issues are leaked to the press in an effort to increase the domestic cost to the president of overruling the military. For example, in the early postwar period the fact that the Joint Chiefs of Staff favored German rearmament was made known to Congress in an effort to pressure the State Department to support that position.[32] The objections of the services to limitations imposed by a president on defense budgets are also frequently reported in the press. The views of particularly prestigious military leaders also may be made known. General Douglas MacArthur frequently resorted to this technique in an effort to pressure President Truman. MacArthur, rather than resorting to leaks, simply made public statements, on one occasion announcing plans to withdraw a substantial number of American military forces from the occupation of Japan and in another announcing that he thought a Japanese peace treaty could come fairly soon.[33] During the Korean conflict, MacArthur revealed in a letter to Representative Joseph Martin, which the latter made public, that he favored an expansion of the war.[34]

Leaking the views of one prestigious group or individual can be countered by leaking the position of another. Counter-leaking was a key part of the effort to use the press to influence a decision by President Nixon in the spring of 1971 on the number of troops that he would withdraw from Vietnam. The maneuvering began on March 16, 1971, with Secretary of Defense Melvin Laird asserting that the Nixon administration was committed to continuing its current rate of withdrawal from Vietnam through late 1972. Laird was quoted in the next day's newspapers as saying that the president would withdraw at least 12,500 men a month from Vietnam "from now on."[35] Two days later, the New York Times published a story out of Saigon reporting the con-

32. Laurence Martin, "The American Decision to Rearm Germany," p. 651.

33. Truman, *Year of Decisions*, p. 520; Dunn, *Peace–Making and the Settlement with Japan*, p. 63.

34. The episode was described by Truman in *Years of Trial and Hope*, pp. 445–46.

35. *Washington Post*, March 17, 1971.

cern felt by the U.S. military command in Vietnam that budget restraints and troop force ceilings were forcing withdrawals from Vietnam faster than would be dictated by the president's "Vietnamization" program.[36]

As the leaking and counter-leaking continued over the next month, President Nixon faced a dilemma. If he acceded to the Joint Chiefs' request to delay troop withdrawals, he would do so with the public knowing that his own Secretary of Defense believed that troop withdrawals would go forward on schedule. Thus the doves would be aroused. On the other hand, if he announced that he was withdrawing troops on the current schedule, it would be known that he was doing so over the strong recommendations of the Joint Chiefs of Staff and of the American commander in Vietnam. Thus the hawks would be aroused. The president pulled a rabbit out of the hat by announcing the withdrawal of 150,000 men from Vietnam over the next twelve months (thus maintaining the current rate of withdrawal) but then apparently agreeing privately with the military that they could postpone any withdrawals during the first sixty days of the twelve-month period.[37]

The arms control talks with the Soviet Union during President Reagan's administration provided fertile ground for warring factions to engage in bureaucratic maneuvering, which often broke out in the press as they fought over the future of the Strategic Defense Initiative and the ABM treaty. Strobe Talbott chronicled the cross fire that took place on the eve of the Geneva Summit in November 1985:

> Every presidential mention of the ABM treaty [in public] was a point for Shultz, McFarlane, and Nitze in their struggle against Weinberger and Perle. Now they were about to carry that struggle to the summit. With the help of the White House chief of staff, Donald Regan, Shultz and McFarlane arranged for Weinberger to be left out of the entourage that would accompany the President to Geneva.
>
> On the very eve of the meeting, the Pentagon struck back. The *New York Times* and the *Washington Post* carried front-page articles about a letter drafted by Perle and sent to Reagan over Weinberger's signature, recommending that the President not commit the United States to continued compliance with the ABM treaty. The letter rehearsed the case that the Pentagon had been making for the broad interpretation of the ABM treaty: "In Geneva, you will almost certainly come under great pressure ... to agree formally to limit SDI research development and testing to only that research allowed under the most restrictive interpre-

36. *New York Times*, March 18, 1971.
37. *New York Times*, April 22, 1971.

tation of the ABM treaty, even though you have determined that a less restrictive interpretation is justified legally."

Acceding to such pressure—which the letter implied would come not just from the Soviets but from the State Department—would be to play into the hands of SDI opponents on Capitol Hill: "The Soviets doubtless will seek assurances that you will continue to be bound to such tight limits on SDI development and testing that would discourage Congress from making any but token appropriations."

As the President set off for his first meeting with the leader of the Soviet Union, the letter was a dramatic display of dissension within the ranks of his Administration. McFarlane, in the guise of an unnamed official aboard Air Force One who was quoted in the newspapers the next day, fumed that "someone" was trying to "sabotage" the summit. He left no doubt that Perle was the leading suspect. In Geneva, Perle denied the charge and suggested that the State Department had leaked the letter to make the Pentagon look bad.[38]

Announcing a Policy

The press can be used to create the impression that a decision has been made. If the news is well received by the public, the president must go along or else appear in the unwelcome role of an executive reversing a popular policy. The announcement of a policy in hopes of pressuring the president to accept it may be done in a backgrounder or in a press leak, but it is much more effective when done on the record.

The technique is limited to senior participants such as Cabinet officers who are in a position to call a press conference. When maneuvering in this way, a senior participant announces to the press on the record that the government has made a particular decision. He does so only if he has tried and failed to get the president to make that decision, only if he feels very strongly that the proposed decision is in the national interest, and only if he thinks that by publicly announcing the policy he can change the consequences for the president sufficiently so that the president will not publicly challenge him or otherwise revert to the previous decision.

Naturally, also, the official who tries this ploy must choose a time when there is strong and widespread public support for the decision that he or she announces.

38. Talbott, *The Master of the Game*, pp. 284–85.

Secretary of Defense Clark Clifford used this maneuver in the spring of 1968 after he had sought and failed to get President Lyndon Johnson to change his Vietnam policy in several respects. Clifford had recommended to the president that the United States declare that it would send no additional troops to Vietnam. During March 1968 the president decided not to meet General Westmoreland's specific request for 206,000 men, but he was unwilling to announce categorically that no additional troops would be sent.

Nevertheless, in the weeks following President Johnson's March 31 speech, Clifford announced to the press (largely in response to reporters' questions, so there was no prepared text that had to be cleared in advance) that the United States had decided to put a ceiling on its effort in Vietnam, that it would no longer pour troops into a bottomless pit, and that as a matter of fact it did not intend to send any additional troops to Vietnam.

Obviously, in rejecting Clifford's advice that he announce such a decision, the president sensed the great domestic popularity the announcement would have, but he apparently felt that the adverse consequences for national security outweighed the possible domestic gains. However, once Clifford announced the policy, the president's choice was either to go along or to publicly engage in a hassle with his secretary of defense over the question of whether he would send additional troops to Vietnam. Having said that he had renounced another term as president to work for peace in Vietnam, Johnson was not in a very strong position to argue in public that additional troops might have to be sent to Indochina. Clifford's maneuver changed the domestic political consequences for President Johnson to the point that they outweighed his estimate of foreign policy consequences, and he went along with the change in policy.[39]

Trial Balloons

In some situations the press is used in an attempt to learn more about the likely domestic consequences of a proposed course of action. Thus what is known as a trial balloon may be floated, on the record by a Cabinet officer, in a background briefing, or through a leak. The public debate generated by the news that a proposed decision is under consideration gives the president additional information regarding its likely domestic consequences. Often after a decision has been made, the press is used to test various ways of softening feared adverse domestic consequences.

39. Goulding, *Confirm or Deny*, pp. 323–33.

PRESIDENTIAL SPEECHES

The president himself can use each of the techniques listed above. He can command much more press attention than anyone else, whether he is speaking on the record or offering background information or carefully leaking something. Presidents often obtain press coverage by delivering a major foreign policy speech.

The great advantage of this device for a president is that he can in effect implement decisions himself soon after making them. Presidents often find that the most effective way to settle an ongoing bureaucratic squabble is with a public statement. "Faced with an administrative machine which is both elaborate and fragmented," Henry Kissinger has written, "the executive is forced into essentially lateral means of control."[40] Thus many public speeches, though ostensibly directed to outsiders, may perform a more important role in laying down guidelines for the bureaucracy. The chief significance of a foreign policy speech by the president may be that it settles an internal debate in Washington. A public statement is more useful for that purpose than an administrative memorandum because it is harder to reverse.

In some cases the president may be unwilling to settle a bureaucratic conflict definitively but may wish to give a hunting license to a particular group. To do that he may give a speech that indicates his general support for a particular policy approach. He thereby avoids putting himself in the position of having definitively overruled a major part of the bureaucracy, while he increases the probability of getting the outcome that he desires. The hunting license serves the purpose only if important elements in the bureaucracy attach high priority to the proposal to which the president has given impetus and are prepared to pick up his hunting license and move with him.

In some cases the president seeks in a speech not to settle an ongoing bureaucratic dispute or to issue a specific hunting license but to set an entirely new direction for the foreign policy of his administration. He realizes that he is going to be moving against the strongly held views of a number of factions in his bureaucracy. Many presidents have made such speeches, and they have followed a strikingly similar pattern. Avoiding the usual procedure of informing the bureaucracy that the president plans to give a major speech and requesting inputs to it, the White House keeps to itself the fact that a speech is being contemplated. A draft is put on paper in secret, after consultation among a few key White House advisers. Only after the draft is discussed with the president and he has given it his approval is any effort made to notify the

40. Kissinger, *American Foreign Policy*, p. 22.

bureaucracy. At that time, the coordination usually takes place at very high levels. A senior White House official conveys the speech to the secretary of state and the secretary of defense, informing them that the president has already approved the text and that he plans to give the speech in a very few days. Under obligation not to show the text to their subordinates, key officials almost always go along with the president's proposed text, because any suggestion for change means challenging a presidential decision that has already been made. Thus speeches clear quickly at high levels.[41]

Early in their respective administrations President Reagan and the second President Bush seized on the device of speeches to set a clear tone for their attitudes toward perceived enemies. With his famous "Evil Empire" and "Star Wars" speeches, Reagan served notice that he was not prepared to accept the concept of mutual assured destruction and he embarked on an ambitious program to intercept ballistic missiles by asking one question: "What if free people could live secure in the knowledge that their security did not rest upon the threat of instant retaliation to deter a Soviet attack, that we could intercept and destroy strategic ballistic missiles before they reached our own soil or that of our allies?"[42] Remembering the power of the simplicity of Reagan's phraseology, the second President Bush used his first State of the Union address, only six months after the 9/11 attack, to coin a phrase of his own that would set the mood of his administration. Singling out North Korea, Iran, and Iraq, he said, "States like these, and their terrorist allies, constitute an axis of evil, arming to threaten the peace of the world. By seeking weapons of mass destruction, these regimes pose a grave and growing danger."[43]

Senior participants and representatives of organizations quickly come to recognize the importance of major presidential speeches. Those who are frustrated in their efforts to get the bureaucracy to adopt a policy frequently recommend that the president give a "new directions" speech. Others seek to slip a key idea into a paragraph of a speech being drafted. They hope to affect future decisions within the bureaucracy by being able to cite a presidential source for endorsement. The aim, for example, may be to set the tone of deliberations on an issue that is up for decision, such as the American stand in an

41. For examples of this approach, see Hughes, *The Ordeal of Power*, p. 107, relating to a major peace speech by President Eisenhower delivered in April 1953. See Schlesinger, *A Thousand Days*, p. 900; Sorensen, *Kennedy*, pp. 73–31; and Brandon, "Schlesinger at the White House," on President Kennedy's American University peace speech. President Nixon resorted to this technique more often than any of his predecessors. He appears to have employed it first in delivering his initial major speech on Vietnam in May 1969.

42. Talbott, *The Master of the Game*, pp. 5–6.

43. Woodward, *Plan of Attack*, p. 92. Woodward also describes the impact that this speech had on various senior officials in the administration.

ongoing negotiation. George Kennan related just such an episode, which occurred after he was appointed to chair an interdepartmental committee to try to settle differences between Treasury Secretary John Snyder and the State Department about how to deal with a British request for a substantial loan shortly after the end of World War II:

> Three days later, while my interdepartmental committee was still at work, the department received the draft of a speech the President proposed shortly to give which included a paragraph addressed to the forthcoming arrival of the British statesmen. It seemed to me cold and wholly devoid of sympathy or understanding for the British position. I therefore dictated a paragraph for inclusion in it; the Secretary read this over the phone to Clark Clifford in the White House; and to my own surprise it found its way into the speech. It was to the effect that the British statesmen would find the usual warm welcome in our country; that we would not forget our wartime associations with Britain or the strains and stresses to which the British people had been subject in the postwar years; that we would regard the matters under discussion as a common problem and would sit down to the discussions in a spirit of friendliness and helpfulness. When this speech appeared in the papers, on August 30, the general reception was highly favorable, but I later heard that it was the occasion of much anguish, and even phone calls of protest to the President, on the part of Secretary Snyder, to whom a friendly word of this sort appeared to harbor sinister dangers.[44]

Because officials are always on the lookout for opportunities to insert in the president's speeches statements that they can later cite to serve their special purposes, he must be wary. "The executive thus finds himself confronted by proposals for public declarations," Henry Kissinger wrote, "which may be innocuous in themselves—and whose bureaucratic significance may be anything but obvious—but which can be used by some agency or department to launch a study or program which will restrict his freedom of decision later on."[45]

George Ball, under secretary of state in the Kennedy administration and one of those in favor of creating a multilateral nuclear force, related one episode that demonstrates the high value placed on even the most tenuous presidential hunting license inserted into a speech. In May 1961, when a speech by Kennedy was scheduled, there was much opposition within the government to the American proposals for creating an interallied nuclear

44. Kennan, *Memoirs, 1925–1950*, pp. 460–61.
45. Kissinger, *American Foreign Policy*, p. 23.

force. Thus the best that Ball and his colleagues were able to get was a presidential statement that "beyond this we look to the possibility of eventually establishing a NATO seaborne force, which would be truly multilateral in ownership and control, if this should be desired and found feasible by other allies, *once NATO's nonnuclear goals have been achieved* [emphasis added]."[46] Opponents of the MLF viewed that statement as entirely innocuous, since everyone understood that NATO's nonnuclear goals would in fact never be achieved. Nevertheless, as Ball himself explains, the statement was exploited as a presidential "mandate" and formed the basis for an effort by Ball and his colleagues within the State Department to convince the Europeans to support the MLF proposal.[47]

Astute bureaucrats thus view major presidential speeches both as a danger and as an opportunity. Dean Acheson, writing from the vantage point of his experience as secretary of state, summed up the perspective of the senior participants on this aspect of maneuvering within the government:

> The Secretary, if he is wise, will join the fray himself, with his own draft, and try to guide and direct it. He can carry more weight than any of his associates, particularly in the final stages when the President himself, as I knew the procedure, joins the group and makes the final decisions.
>
> It may seem absurd—and doubtless is—for a Secretary of State to be spending his time as a member of a Presidential speech-writing group. But this is often where policy is made, regardless of where it is supposed to be made. The despised speech, often agreed to be made months beforehand without thought of subject, a nuisance to prepare and annoyance to deliver, has often proved the vehicle for statements of far-reaching effect for good or ill. As both a junior and a senior official, I have fought this guerrilla warfare; sometimes to get things done which would otherwise be stopped, and sometimes to prevent others from doing the same thing.[48]

In some cases, the White House may view presidential speeches as a means of formulating policy in the absence of timely recommendations from the cumbersome foreign policy bureaucracy. Early in the first Bush administration, the White House became concerned about mounting criticism of its seeming failure to find new policy responses to the rapid political change engulfing Eastern Europe. Recognizing that the formal policy reviews initiated

46. Presidential address at Ottawa on May 17, 1961, quoted in Ball, *The Discipline of Power*, p. 207.
47. Ibid., pp. 206–09.
48. Acheson, "The President and the Secretary of State," p. 44.

USES OF THE PRESS / 201

at the beginning of the administration were not going to provide a creative basis for new approaches, the president turned instead to a small core group of senior officials to work out a new strategic framework. The NSC decided to lay out that framework in a series of four presidential commencement speeches during the late spring, effectively preempting the formal policy process and setting the administration's agenda for addressing the new European order.[49]

IMPLICATIONS FOR DECISIONS

At the top levels of the American government the belief is that anything of importance, especially if it touches on domestic political interests, will be leaked to the press by some participant unhappy with the drift of a presidential decision. Because that belief is so widely held, it tends to influence significantly the way that issues are handled in the executive branch. Often an option under consideration is rejected on the grounds that to be effective, it has to be implemented before it is leaked, but it is likely to be leaked before it is implemented.

The extremes to which a president may conclude he has to go to keep things from leaking is illustrated by the preparations for the trip by presidential assistant Henry Kissinger to Peking to arrange a visit by Nixon. Apparently no more than four or five Americans, inside or outside the government, at any level, were aware of the preparations. All the departments of the government, including the State Department (with the possible exception of the secretary of state himself), were kept in the dark. Although the secret was kept, it entailed a substantial cost. The president was denied the expertise of the bureaucracy in designing the probe toward China, and allied governments could not be informed, an omission that caused a crisis in American relations with Japan. This secret probe was possible only because the president had great confidence in his national security adviser and therefore was prepared to move without the advice of the State Department and the intelligence agencies and only because the action to be carried out was one that could be performed by a very small number of people. Ironically, when President Carter was preparing to normalize relations with China several years later, he came to the same conclusion as President Nixon: that the move was best entrusted to his national security adviser without the advice of the State Department.

In some situations the calculation that a leak will occur and would be disastrous leads a president and other senior participants to reject proposed

49. Bush and Scowcroft, *A World Transformed*, pp. 46–56.

courses of action. Knowing of the fear of leaks, participants opposed to a particular course of action sometimes seek to prevent it by warning participants higher up that, if the action is taken, it will quickly be leaked, with detrimental effects. For example, during the Indo-Pakistani war of 1971, the White House was pressing for an anti-Indian position, which was being resisted by the bureaucracy. When Henry Kissinger informed the senior USAID official that the president wished to tightly restrict aid to India, the following exchange took place:

> *Kissinger*: The President wants no more irrevocable letters of credit issued under the ninety-nine million credit. He wants the seventy-two million PL 480 credit also held.
>
> *Williams*: Word will soon get around when we do this. Does the President understand that?
>
> *Kissinger*: That is his order, but I will check with the President again. . . .[50]

The threat is always made in impersonal terms: not "I will leak it," but "It will leak." When they feared that President Kennedy might cancel the Bay of Pigs invasion, CIA officials pressed him very hard with the argument that, if the invasion were called off, the fact would certainly leak from the Cuban refugees, who would provide a highly distorted view of the probability of success of the operation and the American reasons for cancellation. Arthur Schlesinger reported the arguments as they were put to the president:

> As [Allen] Dulles said at the March 11 meeting, "Don't forget that we have a disposal problem. If we have to take these men out of Guatemala, we will have to transfer them to the United States, and we can't have them wandering around the country telling everyone what they have been doing."[51]

Since a president believes that anything of importance may leak, he is concerned about the possibility of a leak even if no explicit threat is made or the possibility is not pointed out by other participants. Apparently one of President Johnson's concerns in considering whether to continue with the Vietnam policy that he inherited from President Kennedy was the fear that if he changed course, his advisers—whom he also inherited and who had framed the policy in the first place—would contrive leaks to imply that the new president was jeopardizing the security of the United States.[52]

50. *Washington Post*, January 5, 1972.
51. Schlesinger, *A Thousand Days*, p. 242.
52. Wicker, *JFK and LBJ*, pp. 203–4; Halberstam, "The Very Expensive Education of McGeorge Bundy," p. 31.

When a revealing story does appear in the press, a president sees it as a confirmation of his view that participants with different objectives will leak things through the press. Presidents tend to ignore the possibility that the leak resulted from some source outside the executive branch or that the story appeared as a result of a reporter's initiative. At one point, in a desperate effort to convince President Johnson that many of the stories appearing in the press did not get there as a result of deliberate leaks by his staff, presidential assistant McGeorge Bundy asked Philip Potter, who had just written an accurate account of President Johnson's policy on aid to India, to explain how he had gotten the story. "Would you mind giving me a memorandum on how you came to write that story?" he asked. "I'd like to show it to the President. I know you got the story legitimately, but this President never believes a reporter can get a story like that unless the secret paper is filched or a Cabinet member suborned."[53]

Because of the importance of the press in the policymaking process as a whole and because of the analytical value of considering the press's role in a single chapter, we have diverted somewhat from our effort to trace a particular issue, the ABM program, through the government to a presidential decision. Recall, then, where we are. Participants with varying interests and constrained by the rules plan strategies to get the decisions that they want. Part of the strategy relates to information content and dissemination of information. It is this aspect that we have been concerned with thus far and that led us to a discussion of the role of the press. The second strand of the process relates to how the issue moves through the system toward the president and toward a decision.

53. Quoted in Alsop, *The Center*, pp. 203–04.

CHAPTER ELEVEN

Involving
the President

As we saw in chapter 7, ascertaining whether the president is to be involved in a decision is one of the crucial steps in planning to obtain the decision that one wants. The rules of the game, particularly those set by the president, may necessitate the president's involvement, or they may specify that the issue be decided at another level of the bureaucracy. Often, however, the rules are sufficiently flexible that they do not prescribe the exact progress of a decision through the bureaucracy. This chapter first discusses the reasons why participants prefer to achieve consensus without involving the president, then it deals with the options open to participants to affect the way that issues reach the president in those cases in which his involvement cannot be avoided (or, less frequently, when a participant decides that presidential involvement is more desirable). Finally, it considers two key elements in securing a presidential decision: securing a consensus and creating a deadline.

AGREEING WITHOUT THE PRESIDENT

When there is a choice, participants prefer to reach a consensus and a decision without involving the president. This is true for a number of reasons. Participants recognize that they are likely to have much more *control over what is decided* if it is the result of a compromise among the organizations and individuals directly involved in an issue. If an unresolved issue is taken to the president for a decision, the White House might shape its own compromise, taking into account the president's domestic political concerns, and that compromise might substantially reduce the autonomy of an organization with operating responsibilities. Moreover, sending an issue up to the president for a decision, calling on him to overrule one or another organization, runs the risk of shifting the locus of decisionmaking in general toward the White House, thereby reducing the autonomy of all organizations in the bureaucracy.[1]

In some cases, participants have a strong *need or desire to get a decision quickly* that will permit them to go forward with various actions. They recognize that it may be difficult to persuade the president to involve himself in an issue or that in any case it may be a substantial period of time before he makes a decision. Thus there is strong pressure to compromise in order to get a unanimous decision that will permit actions to go forward. In such cases participants who are less eager for action frequently can get their way by threatening to take the matter to the president. John Kenneth Galbraith, for example, reports that while he was ambassador to India, he quarreled with the State Department and the White House about the text of a letter to go in the president's name to Indian Prime Minister Nehru. Galbraith, receiving a draft unacceptable to him, sent it back with his recommended changes, "asking that my recommended changes, or my reasons for them, be sent to the President himself." He noted that he got his way by relying on the fact that "since getting his [the President's] attention was difficult, the alternative would be to accept them. So it happened."[2]

Fear of losing, and thus of hurting their reputation, is another reason why participants are reluctant to take issues to the president. Also, they recognize that when they ask the president to overrule another official, they are using up one of the limited number of occasions on which the president will go to such lengths for them. For example, when Secretary of State John Foster Dulles clashed with Secretary of the Treasury George Humphrey about a proposal for a development loan fund (under which the United States would provide loans on lenient terms to developing countries), both felt under strong pressure to reach an agreement so that neither of them had go to the president and ask him to overrule the other. By invoking foreign policy considerations of high importance, Dulles was able to get Humphrey to retreat from the position that the fund would have to be financed by annual appro-

---

1. As Alexander George observes in "The Case for Multiple Advocacy in Making Foreign Policy," p. 753: "Left to their own devices, those subunits which share responsibility for a particular policy area often adapt by restricting competition with each other. As a result, policy issues may not rise to the presidential level, or when they do, they often take the form of concealed compromises that reflect the special interest of actors at lower levels of the hierarchical system."

2. Galbraith, *Ambassador's Journal,* p. 516, n. 28.

priations. At the same time Dulles accepted Humphrey's position that appropriations would have to be requested for the first year. As Russell Edgerton has observed in his careful study of the loan fund, despite the fact that the agreement was not fully satisfactory to either official, "Neither man went to the President."[3]

The considerations involved here are the same as those that lead participants to stay out of an issue. When they cannot, those considerations lead them to consider a compromise below the level of the president.

GETTING TO THE PRESIDENT

It may happen that participants have no choice but to go to the president. Perhaps he has asked that an issue be referred to him for a decision, or a matter has arisen that, according to the rules of the game, requires a presidential decision. The importance of an issue is a factor, as when someone wishes to send troops into combat in a conflict that is just developing or when successful implementation of a policy would require a presidential commitment that can be revealed to other governments. In other cases, a participant may elect to take an issue to the president because he or she is dissatisfied with the compromise negotiated below the president and prefers to take his or her chances on a decision from above. If an issue is to be taken to the president, participants have a number of choices about how to do so.

Through Channels

The most straightforward way of bringing an issue to the president is to do so through the prescribed formal channels. In some cases that calls for introducing the question into a formal National Security Council system such as that established by presidents Eisenhower and Nixon. If there is no formal NSC system or if the issue does not warrant introduction into the system, the procedure calls for a memorandum from the relevant heads of departments, generally the secretary of state and the secretary of defense and/or the secretary of the treasury, with a recommendation for a particular course of action or a memorandum from the national security adviser to the president that informs him of the views of the key agencies and then makes a recommendation.

The rules of the game prescribe whether in the formal procedures the president is to be presented with a single recommended option or a variety of options from which to choose. When a single option is called for, an effort is

3. Edgerton, *Sub-Cabinet Politics and Policy Commitment*, pp. 140–41.

made to negotiate a compromise with which all the relevant departments and participants are satisfied. Where the rules of the game call for several options, participants seek to arrange the options so that the package of options presented contains only one viable option acceptable to all of them. If that cannot be done, then the president may be confronted with real options, each advocated by different parts of the bureaucracy.

Often that path appears to be extremely risky. Participants, uncertain of how the president will react to various options, do not know how to shape their proposal and take their stance so as to get him to make the desired decision. For that reason, a participant who has control of the action often tries to get to the president by a different route in order to maximize his or her chances of getting the desired decision. Senior participants have a number of routes open to them, some of which also are open to junior participants intent on circumventing their nominal superiors.

Going Solo

The ideal situation for a senior participant is to be able to take a controversial issue to the president and get him to decide it without further recourse to other participants. An official whose relationship permits him or her to bring issues forward in this way nevertheless uses the privilege sparingly, recognizing the price that the president will pay with other participants. Officials with direct access to the president are most likely to take issues to him in hopes of a quick decision when there is substantial disagreement or when others plan to act without informing the president. Dean Acheson recounted a number of occasions when he acted this way in the face of intense squabbling within the government, particularly when the Pentagon refused to accept his judgment on political matters. Acheson reported that he saw the president alone each Monday and Thursday and had an opportunity to bring up such matters.[4]

Few officials, however, have the confidence of the president to the extent that he is prepared to decide a controversial issue simply upon hearing one side of the story and without at least pretending to have a formal review of the matter through regular channels. More often an issue is taken privately to the president for his tentative judgment subject to review and confirmation when the issue comes through formal channels.

Acheson used this technique frequently when he was secretary of state. He would discuss an issue with Truman to assure himself of the president's support and then orchestrate with the president how to handle the more formal

4. Acheson, "The President and the Secretary of State," p. 45.

meeting with other officials. He reports that he tried this again under President Kennedy when Kennedy assigned him to try to work out a solution to the American balance-of-payments problem. In that case, as Acheson relates, it did not work as well, apparently because there was no commanding figure under the president to whom others were prepared to defer. According to Acheson:

> After I got this down, I had another talk with the Treasury, and I got the impression that Roosa would go along with this perfectly well, and I talked with Doug Dillon about it, talked with people in State. Then I had another session with the President, and I said, "You know, I think that if you study this, then call everybody together and say, let every man now speak if he wants to but later hold his peace—then decide what should be done." He thought that was a good idea, and we had such a meeting. It just didn't turn out the way I thought it was going to.[5]

Nevertheless, members of the White House staff often work with sympathetic Cabinet officers and with the president to determine in advance how he wishes to decide an issue and to help to conduct a meeting so as to minimize tensions.

In other cases, senior participants may go to the president separately in the hope that by explaining the issue in their own way they can get the president firmly on board before others present their side of the issue. In some cases, it is important to participants to learn what the president's position is likely to be so that they can find out whether they would be better off compromising or standing firm with the confidence that the president will support their position.

When David Lilienthal was head of the Atomic Energy Commission, he frequently used this technique. He relates one episode when he was fighting with the military about the degree of control that the Atomic Energy Commission (AEC) would have over weapons laboratories. He was relieved to find that Truman appeared to fully support his position:

> Well, of course, we were "charmed" by this clearheaded and simple talk. I went on to explain how we planned the transfer, that he would be asked to sign certain orders. "Send them along; I'll sign whatever you recommend." I said that we might as well mention the fact that, though we hoped for agreement with the War Department, there might be some differences we couldn't adjust that would have to come to him. "I expect that. The Army will never give up without a fight, and they will fight you

5. Acheson, Kennedy Library Oral History Interview, p. 33.

on this from here on out, and be working at it in all sorts of places. But you can count on it, I am your advocate."

"No, you're not an advocate, Mr. President," I said, "you are the judge—and it's a lot better to have the judge on your side than the most persuasive advocate." This seemed to amuse him a lot, and he said, "Well, I know how they are, they are trained never to give up. I know because I am one of them." "Well," I said, "if you are, you are a lay brother." This was all lighthearted, but very, very important. It meant that in our negotiations with the Army about transferring Sandia and so on we could draw the line where we thought it wise, rather than where we thought we must as a compromise.[6]

Knowledge of such private meetings is often kept from other participants, who might complain of unfair treatment if they heard that the president had already talked to one of the parties and reached at least a tentative decision. For that reason, there are very few reports of such meetings on the public record, although one suspects that they occur frequently.

In a few instances a participant seeks to inform others of his or her private meeting with the president in an effort to get them to go along without having to bring the issue back to the president. William Attwood, U.S. ambassador to Guinea at the time, succeeded in getting President Kennedy on board with a proposed program and then went out of his way to contrive circumstances in which others would learn of the president's support:

After talking to McGeorge Bundy—at the President's suggestion—I returned to the State Department to find the task force already arguing over the draft of my instructions. With things about to get unraveled, I picked up the phone, called Rostow at the White House, and, with the task force silently attentive, told him about my talk with the President and said we nevertheless seemed to be running into problems. It didn't take too long after that to get the instructions approved, and I left Washington that night.[7]

Going through the White House Staff

Often participants bring issues to the president through the White House staff rather than going to him themselves or going through formal channels. In some instances senior participants use White House staff simply as a

6. Lilienthal, *Journals*, p. 118.
7. Attwood, *The Reds and the Blacks*, p. 40.

quicker and less conspicuous route to the president than asking for an appointment. As head of the AEC, Lilienthal frequently went through the White House staff to get a presidential reading on an issue before taking it to the president through regular channels. He used this technique, for example, in dealing with the requests from the military and Defense Secretary Louis Johnson to have custody of nuclear weapons turned over to the military. After assuring himself of the president's support through Clark Clifford, the president's counselor, and Jim Webb, the director of the Bureau of the Budget, Lilienthal recommended that the president receive the issue formally and send back a formal response.[8]

Senior participants recognize that they pay a price by going alone to the president without informing their colleagues. Rather than do that, they may seek to interest a member of the White House staff in a proposal and have him or her carry the ball to the president. For example, when Secretary of Defense Robert McNamara reached the conclusion that the United States government was not giving sufficiently serious attention to getting a treaty banning the spread of nuclear weapons, he was reluctant to carry the issue to the president. Since it was primarily a foreign policy matter, the major responsibility for making recommendations to the president in this area lay with Secretary of State Dean Rusk. For McNamara to bring the issue to President Johnson would appear to be undercutting Rusk and would complicate his relations with the secretary of state. Therefore McNamara avoided this route by having his assistant secretary for international affairs, John T. McNaughton, speak privately to presidential aide Bill Moyers. McNaughton explained to Moyers the importance of preventing proliferation and quietly pointed out the ways in which the State Department was failing to give the issue top priority. Moyers, convinced, went to the president, who upon being convinced himself called in Dean Rusk and gave the orders that led to a change in American policy and eventually to a nonproliferation treaty.[9]

In other cases, participants may attempt to reach the president through the White House staff when they urgently need a means of preventing another part of the government from acting and they do not feel that they have the personal standing to take the issue to the president themselves. Lilienthal resorted to a call to Clark Clifford to prevent the Joint Chiefs of Staff from releasing a report on an American nuclear test that the Joint Chiefs apparently planned to make public without getting presidential approval. Clifford brought the report to the president, who then insisted on clearance.[10]

8. Lilienthal, *Journals,* pp. 376–77, 384.
9. Anderson, *The President's Men,* p. 344.
10. Lilienthal, *Journals,* pp. 233–34.

In some cases, senior participants find it difficult to get through to the president on a particular issue and resort to friends on the White House staff who they believe are likely to be sympathetic to their position. While serving in the State Department, Averell Harriman used this technique on several occasions to get the president's attention, often going through Arthur Schlesinger Jr., who, though he had no formal role, was able to reach the president. While negotiating on Laos, Harriman received instructions from the State Department that he was not to talk to the Chinese. He informed John Kenneth Galbraith, the U.S. ambassador to India, who in turn communicated with Schlesinger, who informed the president. As a result Harriman was given instructions to talk to anyone he wished. Harriman used the same technique during the Cuban missile crisis, going through Schlesinger to get across his interpretation that Khrushchev was desperately seeking for a way out.[11]

The Joint Chiefs of Staff are likely to pass the word quietly through a White House staff member when they are unhappy about being overruled by the secretary of defense and are prepared to take their case to the Congress. For example, in preparing for the fiscal year 1972 defense budget, several staff members in the Bureau of the Budget persuaded the budget director that the defense budget could be cut by almost $2 billion. The budget director, George Shultz, in turn convinced the secretary of defense, Melvin Laird, to go along with the cuts. When informed of that, the Joint Chiefs went to the president's assistant for national security affairs, Henry Kissinger, and persuaded him to take the issue to the president, at which point the funds were restored to the budget.[12]

Junior staff members frequently take issues to White House staff when they cannot get their superiors to make a formal recommendation to the president. They hope that the president will act or instruct departments to act on a matter that might not otherwise gain presidential attention. This technique shaped the Point Four Program, under which President Truman, in his inaugural address, proposed technical assistance to developing countries. State Department officials who had long favored such a program found it impossible up to that point to gain any support within the department. In preparing for his inaugural address, Truman had instructed the White House staff to seek fresh ideas that he could talk about. In searching for ideas, White House staff assistant George Elsey came upon the proposal for a technical assistance program. Working with State Department staffers who favored the proposal, Elsey developed a paragraph for the president's speech. When the draft was

11. Schlesinger, *A Thousand Days*, pp. 821–22; Brandon, "Schlesinger at the White House."
12. *New York Times*, April 9, 1971.

sent to the State Department for comment, the paragraph was removed; however, Elsey put it back, and the president delivered the address with Point Four intact.[13]

Senior participants sometimes calculate that, by choosing which White House staff member handles the issue and what face of the issue the president sees, they can influence the outcome of a presidential deliberation. For example, as head of the Mutual Security Agency, Harold Stassen recognized that the White House staff member most friendly to his cause was Eisenhower speechwriter Emmet John Hughes. Therefore, instead of seeking to gain approval through normal budgetary procedures for a proposed level of spending, Stassen simply put the figure he desired into a draft of a presidential text on mutual security and sent it off to Hughes's office. Hughes reports that he edited the message in the morning and then quotes from his diary about what happened afterward. His description is worth quoting in full, not only to illustrate this use of White House staff but also to guard against the tendency of the reader to assume that the processes being described are orderly ones:

> On returning to my office from lunch, I find a huge hassle on. The issue, boiled down: does the Administration really want $5.8 billion—or would, say, a billion dollars less do just as nicely? Incredible—but no one has made a decision. And I quickly gathered a few other incredible facts. One: The State Department had neither seen the message nor knew its contents till this noontime. Two: Joe Dodge at the Budget Bureau likewise had not seen it. Three: State thinks the message is too weak, asks for not enough. Four: Budget thinks the message is too strong, asks for too much. Five: Neither Dulles nor Adams can be reached till the end of the day, for they are locked in a conference of state governors in the old State Department building. Six: Committee hearings on the request— whatever it turns out to be—start on the Hill at 10 A.M. tomorrow morning.
>
> It took a while—and maybe a dozen phone calls—to piece together a coherent picture of all this incoherence. On one side, Douglas MacArthur at State lamented to me: "I'm terribly worried about this. There's no water in the $5.8 billion figure, and if we don't get all of it, we're in real trouble." (And Dulles somehow sent me a note, perhaps by carrier pigeon, from his closed conference with the governors to the same effect.) From the other side, came the voice of Joe Dodge: "Nonsense! State's going to have to have a lot of unspent funds at the end of

13. Bingham, *Shirt-Sleeve Diplomacy*, p. 10; Halle, *The Society of Man*, pp. 21–23, 29–30.

this year. I just don't want to see the President getting out on a limb asking for so much money as a must when he may damn well take a licking on the request." To compound confusion, Herb Brownell somehow learns of the clash. Shows up in the White House, and corners me in the corridor to back Dodge vehemently, adding: "What the hell, if we do need more money later, we can always ask for it then." A remarkable theory: call it "Planning for Yesterday?" Finally, to cap all, Jerry Persons emerges from the President's office, vaguely reporting this and other business, to advise that the President wants Dodge to be the deciding voice. At best, this seems odd, for I'm sure no one had briefed the President on the substance of the disagreements.

After some hours of this nonsense, and running between the White House and State, carrying the crumpled message-draft—by now it is beginning to have the feel of a battered and half-unfeathered shuttlecock—I decided to get Adams out of his conference. As he glowers kindly at the interruption, I tell him: "This is all too damn serious to be decided in a series of side-of-the-mouth corridor conversations. We just have to hold it till the morning when we can get to the President directly and quietly." Garrulously, he grunts: "Okay."

The circus continues after sundown. I finally locate Stassen, Stassen heads for Dodge's office, and after some three-way phone-negotiating we all reach agreement of a sort on the message language—roughly close to original, with the dollar figure intact. No sooner is this compact contrived than Dulles' office phones to suggest to me still stronger language in the request. Arbitrarily I decide to put it in and leave it to State to so advise Dodge and Stassen.

We come full circle next morning, when Adams and I see the President. He buys "strong" message as I've written it, even though we report both Brownell's (political) and Dodge's (fiscal) aversion to it. With marvelous disregard of his nomination of Dodge yesterday to be deciding voice, he shrugs off such reservations. Message swiftly typed in final form and rushed to the Hill.

How reassuring it would be to all governments of our allies around the world if they could see the disciplined and dedicated way we plan and provide our economic assistance![14]

14. Hughes, *The Ordeal of Power*, pp. 82–83.

Taking Other Paths

The most frequently used paths to the president are described above. Other things being equal, participants prefer to take a consensus position to the president, or when he demands options, they prefer to structure a series of options so that only one is truly viable. When it is not possible to put together a consensus, or when certain senior participants are unwilling to take an issue to the president, other participants may resort to either going alone to the president and attempting to arrange things with him or working through members of the White House staff believed to be friendly to a given position. When none of these methods succeeds, alternative routes to the president may be tried.

One such method is to work through individuals in Washington known to have direct access to the president. Most presidents have a few Washington advisers from outside the government. If those individuals can be persuaded to interest themselves in a problem, they provide a route to the president. In addition, senior leaders of Congress have access to the president and often are asked to bring up with him issues that are known to interest them. And, as we saw in chapter 10, the press can be used as a way of getting issues to the president.

Foreign governments, too, can be used for this purpose. If a foreign government can be persuaded to raise a question or request that a proposal be considered at the highest levels of the American government, then that can be a route for forcing an issue to the attention of the White House. Often an American ambassador in the field can stimulate such a request.

Negotiating teams sent out by the United States often are in a position to raise issues that they could not get to the president in any other way. While W. Averell Harriman worked in Washington as the president's special representative for Vietnam negotiations, he had to channel his proposals through the secretary of state. When he went to Paris as the head of the Vietnam negotiating team, however, his cables from Paris automatically went to the president and other senior officials. Thus, from the vantage point of Paris, Harriman was able to get through to the president with proposals that otherwise would not have reached him.

Another technique is to propose the creation of a commission on a general subject in the hope that the commission members will make the proposal that one is advocating.

SECURING A PRESIDENTIAL DECISION

Even when an issue reaches the president, participants continue to maneuver to get him to make a decision and the right decision. That may involve promoting as broad a consensus as possible for the desired decision and establishing a deadline so that the president feels a need to decide.

Building a Consensus

Because of concern about maintaining the support of his principal subordinates and because of his recognition of the need for widespread support in order to gain congressional and public acceptance of a proposal and its implementation by the bureaucracy, a president is reluctant to overrule key individual supporters or major institutions such as the Joint Chiefs of Staff. Participants, discovering that over time, feel the need to forge a consensus in order to increase the probability that the president will act and act in the way that they desire. Therefore, at the crucial time, proponents intensify their efforts to get all the key participants on board, hopefully with participants' active support or at least with their agreement not to report their dissent to the president. This is primarily a bargaining process.[15] A number of techniques are used by participants in pursuing a broad consensus.

PERSUASION. Persuasion involves an effort, without changing a proposal, to convince a participant that it is in his or her interest to support it. That can be done, as we suggested earlier, either by relating arguments to the national interest (conceived in terms of the shared images of the participants) or by appealing to particular organizational, personal, or domestic political interests of the participants.

When the appeal is to interests other than national security, care must be taken to see that the arguments are presented only to those who will be influenced by them. That must be done because certain forms of argument—for example, those relating to domestic politics or personal interests—are considered questionable, and there is a danger that they will be leaked to the press. Moreover, arguments relating to one set of organizational interests may underline the disadvantages of a particular proposal to other organizations.

The need to avoid broad dissemination of arguments related to other interests means that they are almost always made orally. Participants recognize that almost anything put in writing will be duplicated and widely distributed within the government and that it is likely to be leaked if leaking will help the argument's opponents. In some cases the arguments are stated orally and privately to a single individual in an effort to persuade him or her to support a particular position. Thus there appears to be no written record of any discussion

15. See Schilling, "The Politics of National Defense," p. 22.

about the impact of an ABM deployment on domestic politics and in particular on the presidential election of 1968. Certainly none of the papers coming
from the Pentagon to the president discussed the matter. It appears that all such
discussions, assuming that they took place, were confined to private conversations between President Johnson and Secretary of Defense McNamara, in
which the president sought to convince McNamara or at least explain to him
why he felt that some sort of ABM was necessary if the president was to be
reelected and to avoid the charge of a ballistic missile defense gap.

Participants who do not have an opportunity to speak with the president
privately may have to bring up their arguments relating to other interests in
meetings that include others. In that case they are likely to speak in a veiled
and elliptical manner. For example, one of the strongest arguments that the
CIA had for going forward with the Bay of Pigs invasion was that cancellation
would weaken the political position of President Kennedy, since he had promised during the election campaign to assist Cuban refugees in seeking to "lib-
erate" their homeland. The CIA leaders simply pointed out that if the invasion
were cancelled, the Cuban brigade would disperse, and many of its leaders
would return to the United States. They did not have to spell out the fact that
these people would talk to their friends and ultimately to the press, making it
known in Washington that the president had prevented what these leaders
would of course describe as a sure-to-succeed invasion. Kennedy no doubt got
the point without needing explicit reference to domestic politics.

The appeal to organizational interests frequently takes the form of suggesting a delayed benefit. For example, in trying to make the case for Army control
of a medium-range missile, the Army explicitly adopted Navy doctrine. The
admirals had long argued that they needed to have offensive missiles in order
to destroy targets of particular concern to the Navy, such as Russian submarines.
The generals now argued that they needed to have offensive missiles to destroy
targets such as enemy staging areas and enemy launching sites for missiles aimed
at troops. The Army appealed to the Navy for support on the grounds that the
proposal would reinforce the principle that each service should have the offensive forces to deal with threats to its own particular mission.[16]

COMPROMISE. In bargaining, a participant offers to alter his or her proposal
in order to make it more palatable to another participant or to change the consequences of accepting or rejecting the proposal. One way in which proposals frequently are changed in order to seek consensus is by omitting items
that are known to be controversial even though they seem to go to the heart

16. Armacost, *The Politics of Weapons Innovation*, p. 94.

of what is being recommended. For example, in preparing "NSC-68," a 1950 study that advocated substantial American rearmament in order to deal with what was seen as a growing Russian military threat, a conscious decision was made to omit costs and the details of what the increases in military capability should be. That was done explicitly to avoid conflict among the armed services and to provide a document to which all the services would give their support. That was felt to be necessary if there was to be any hope of securing the support of the secretary of defense, who had been asked by President Truman to hold down defense spending.[17]

An alternative way to create a consensus is to add items to the package so that there is something in it for everyone. That is what is typically done in creating what is known somewhat humorously in the bureaucracy as Option B. If the president has asked for a statement of alternatives, he may receive two extreme options, A and C, both of which are clearly unacceptable and impossible to carry out, and a consensus Option B, the item around which the bureaucracy has coalesced and which it is urging the president to implement. Often a consensus has been attained for this option by including in it many of the things that each organization wishes to do and stating the principle or "policy" in such general terms that each organization is free to continue behaving as it had in the past. This maneuver seemingly was much used in Washington during the Vietnam War. For example, in the debates in late 1964 and early 1965 over what to do about the rapidly "deteriorating" situation in South Vietnam, some argued for a substantial bombing campaign against North Vietnam and others argued that the only way to save the situation was to send large numbers of ground troops into South Vietnam. In the end the president was confronted with a compromise Option B, which called for both a bombing campaign against North Vietnam and the introduction of substantial ground combat troops into South Vietnam.[18]

A similar process occurred in an attempt to develop a unified proposal for President Truman regarding the beefing up of the defense of Europe after the outbreak of the Korean War. The State Department, believing that it was necessary to make some symbolic gestures quickly, urged the appointment of an American Supreme Commander and the creation of an integrated military force. The Joint Chiefs, more concerned with actual military capability than with symbols, were pressing for early rearmament of Germany. Even though Secretary of State Dean Acheson recognized that a proposal to rearm Germany would meet stiff opposition not only in France but in Germany itself, he

17. Hammond, "NSC-68," pp. 319–20. Nitze, *From Hiroshima to Glasnost*, pp. 93–98.
18. Thomson, "How Could Vietnam Happen?" p. 208.

agreed to take the proposal to President Truman, who ultimately approved what Acheson referred to as the "one package" decision.[19]

Generally speaking, changes in the wording of proposals to secure the support of a particular participant or organization have more to do with getting them accepted than with altering what is proposed. In some cases the change is perceptible only to those involved in the bureaucratic infighting. Acheson tells of a typical incident, which occurred among the members of the U.S. delegation to a NATO meeting in which the principal protagonists were Averell Harriman, then an assistant to President Truman for national security affairs, and General Omar Bradley, chairman of the Joint Chiefs of Staff. Acheson explained:

> Almost at the beginning of the Lisbon week a heated disagreement in our own delegation between Harriman and General Bradley showed me how thin was the ice we had to cross. Harriman pressed the General to endorse the view that the military forces which the Temporary Committee report recommended as being within the economic capability of the European countries would provide an adequate defense for Europe. Bradley refused to do so. I listened to the discussion until it seemed to be getting out of hand and then adjourned the delegation meeting, asking the disputants to meet alone with me. Pointing out that General Bradley was being asked to lend his great reputation to the support of a proposition that one could see was, at least, open to doubt, I asked whether he thought the forces recommended were better than what we had, were the best we could get, and, taken together with our nuclear capacity, would have a strong deterrent effect upon any desire to test their adequacy. The General said that he most certainly did think so. Harriman, I urged, ought to be able to find language that Bradley could accept and would carry the desired meaning. This was done.[20]

ABM deployment and the Bay of Pigs invasion stand as more complicated illustrations of the same tendency. In the ABM case, President Johnson was seeking to get McNamara to agree to some sort of deployment. For Johnson to achieve his purpose—heading off a domestic political struggle—he needed only a token ABM deployment that the Joint Chiefs and ABM's leading supporters in Congress could describe for their own satisfaction as the first step toward the large anti-Russian system that they wanted. His problem was that

---

19. Acheson, *Present at the Creation*, pp. 437–38, 440, 459; Martin, "The American Decision to Rearm Germany," pp. 656–67.
20. Acheson, *Present at the Creation*, p. 623.

McNamara was strongly opposed to any actual large anti-Russian system and would not agree to a deployment that was the beginning of such a system. The compromise that Johnson offered McNamara was to permit the secretary of defense to describe the proposal any way that he chose and to accompany it with as strong a warning as he wished to make against a large system, provided only that the actual deployment that he authorized was one that the generals and senators such as Richard Russell could urge be made the first step toward a major system. In turn, Johnson appears to have authorized the Joint Chiefs to condition their acceptance of the proposed deployment with a statement to congressional committees that they were going along with it only because they viewed it as the first step toward the large anti-Russian system that the secretary of defense was simultaneously resisting. Thus, without altering in any significant way the actual physical first-stage deployment of the ABM system, Johnson was able to secure consensus by letting McNamara and the Joint Chiefs describe it as they chose, which kept his secretary of defense from resigning and kept the Joint Chiefs from coming out against him.

In the case of the Bay of Pigs, the problem for the CIA was to convince President Kennedy that the invasion should be authorized. In order to do so, they agreed in principle to cut back the size of the invasion and to eliminate any overt U.S. involvement. There appears to have been very little change in what they actually planned to do, but a substantial change occurred in the president's perception of what he was authorizing.[21]

CHANGING THE CONSEQUENCES. If the proposal itself cannot be sufficiently altered to secure the support of key participants, it may be possible to gain their support by altering the consequences to them of the proposal. The change of consequences may relate either to their perception of national security interests or to other interests. One device frequently used to change consequences is to give a friendly foreign government some crucial information. For example, in the case of an argument within the American government about whether to respond to an increase in Russian military power, the consequences will be seen as very different if the increase is known to allies of the United States. If American allies are informed, it will be argued that failure to respond to the Russian move could increase their concern about whether the United States intends to meet its commitments.

21. How far this change went is not entirely clear, but it is worth noting that Secretary of State Dean Rusk assured his under secretary, Chester Bowles, who had great qualms about the proposed invasion, that the planned operation had been reduced to the point that it would not be reported on page one of the *New York Times*. See Bowles, *Promises To Keep: My Years in Public Life, 1941–1969*, p. 239, n. 2.

A second frequently used technique is to arrange for an issue to come up in an international forum. It is one thing for the United States to avoid taking a position publicly on an international issue; it may be quite another to vote or speak against a stand that has wide support. For example, when the second President Bush agreed to speak at a UN conference on financing for development, the bureaucracy wanted him simply to reiterate the view that private investments were the key to development. However, the White House staff felt the need for the president to be perceived as responding in a way that showed concern and that supported Vicente Fox, the Mexican president, who was hosting the meeting. The result was a presidential announcement of a major new American initiative that came to be known as the Millennium Challenge Account, which was administrated by a new corporation and which focused on providing substantial new assistance to democratic governments that have sensible economic policies and show concern for the health and education of their people.

The chief obstacle to changing national security consequences is the difficulty of getting other governments to take action. For that reason participants may have to seek to manipulate consequences in relation to other interests. In some cases the other interest may be an extremely narrow one of convenience. For example, the military services have been known to persuade an ambassador to permit a military attaché section to be added to an embassy by indicating that an airplane goes with an attaché's office and would be at the disposal of the ambassador.[22] In other cases the consequences are more substantial. Typically an effort is made to convince a participant that to withhold support for a proposal moving toward the president is to isolate himself from everybody else in the government and create a situation in which he is in effect asking the president to overrule everybody else and support him. Participants are reluctant to do that, recognizing that there are only a few occasions when they can ask the president to support them against everybody else. If a participant can demonstrate the likelihood of presidential support, he or she can change the consequences for other participants by putting them in the position of seeking to oppose what the president wants to do. In an effort to affect consequences in this way, participants seek to get a presidential speech that suggests support for the principle involved in a particular proposal, hence creating in people's minds the increased likelihood that the president will support the participants who influenced the speech. Or bureaucratic strategists may seek to gain the support of all other relevant officials before approaching an official known to be likely to oppose a particular proposal.

22. See, for example, Attwood, *The Reds and the Blacks*, p. 152.

That was done with some skill in the case of NSC-68. Secretary of Defense Louis Johnson was known to be strongly opposed to any substantial increase in defense spending. Thus it was clear from the start that Johnson would be the principal opponent of the report, which advocated a major buildup of military forces. In the words of Paul Nitze, the principal architect of NSC-68, "Johnson had promised Mr. Truman that he would hold the military budget to thirteen billion dollars, a figure that was becoming more unrealistic with each passing day. He believed the State Department was conspiring with the armed services to make it impossible for him to carry out his promise." By Nitze's account, Secretary Johnson allowed military officials to work on the report but deliberately divorced himself from day-to-day oversight, perhaps hoping that without his endorsement it would never see the light of day. As the study was being completed, a meeting was arranged between Johnson and Secretary of State Acheson to ensure that Johnson would be briefed on the report before it moved on to the NSC for the president's consideration. When Johnson refused to be stampeded by the meeting and left the room in anger, the supporters of the proposal resorted to a different technique. The finished report was circulated for approval while Secretary Johnson was attending a NATO meeting in the Hague. When he returned, he found that the secretary of state, the three service secretaries, and each of the Joint Chiefs had already endorsed it. He had no choice but to endorse it himself, if he was to avoid looking foolish with the president.[23]

Another technique to change consequences for a participant is to link a particular issue to other issues and to promise support to him on those issues in return for his support on the issue under discussion. In some cases this type of logrolling can be done by actually joining two issues and bringing them up to the president simultaneously. In other cases, the technique used is to implicitly threaten that one will fight another participant on issues of concern to him or her if he or she fights on the issue at hand.

Still another stratagem is to inculcate pessimistic beliefs about what may be done if a particular proposal, though not really welcome itself, is rejected. If participants come to believe that the alternative will be even worse in terms of their perception of national security interests, they may be prepared to go along with a proposal that they would otherwise vigorously oppose. Participants feel that they cannot fight every suggestion, and they tell themselves that they have to support the lesser of two evils. President Johnson recalled using this technique on the U.S. ambassador to Vietnam, Ellsworth Bunker. During

23. Nitze, *From Hiroshima to Glasnost*, p. 95; Acheson, *Present at the Creation*, pp. 373–74; Hammond, "NSC-68," pp. 325–26.

March 1968, when he was considering a partial bombing halt, Johnson sent Bunker a cable outlining what he described as two pending suggestions. One proposed a complete halt to bombing and the other proposed a partial halt. As Johnson predicted, Bunker came back with a reluctant acceptance of the partial halt while strongly opposing a complete halt.[24]

Deadlines and Delays

Getting an issue on the president's desk with a consensus supporting a particular position is only a part of the battle. The president must make a decision. Presidents and senior participants have time to do only what they think they must do. Richard Neustadt has well described the world of executive pressure:

> A President's own use of time, his allocation of his personal attention, is governed by the things he has to do from day to day: the speech he has agreed to make, the fixed appointment he cannot put off, the paper no one else can sign, the rest and exercise his doctors order. These doings may be far removed from academic images of White House concentration on high policy, grand strategy. There is no help for that. A President's priorities are set not by the relative importance of a task, but by the relative necessity for him to do it. He deals first with the things that are required of him next. Deadlines rule his personal agenda. In most days of his working week, most seasons of his year, he meets deadlines enough to drain his energy and crowd his time regardless of all else. The net result may be a far cry from the order of priorities that would appeal to scholars or to columnists—or to the President himself.
>
> What makes a deadline? The answer, very simply, is a date or an event or both combined. The date set by MacArthur for a landing at Inchon, or the date set by statute for submission of the budget, or the date set by the White House for a press conference, these and others like them force decisions on a President, pre-empt his time. And statements by MacArthur, or a Humphrey press explosion, or a House appropriations cut, or Sputniks overhead, may generate such pressure inside government or out as to affect him in precisely the same way. Dates make deadlines in proportion to their certainty; events make deadlines in proportion to their heat. Singly or combined, approaching dates and rising heat start fires burning underneath the White House. Trying to stop fires is what Presidents do first. It takes most of their time.[25]

24. Johnson, *The Vantage Point*, pp. 408, 411.
25. Neustadt, *Presidential Power*, pp. 155–56.

Thus participants who are seeking a presidential decision must find a way to attach a deadline to their issue or attach the issue to a preexisting deadline. In the first case they must find a way to convince the president of the necessity of deciding the issue now. In the second, they must convince the president that an already recognized problem can be solved by their proposal. As mentioned before, those in the State Department who favored a major American technical assistance program were able to get the president to announce such a program because it was an answer to his problem—finding something new and dramatic to say in an inaugural address. Such opportunities crop up from time to time—the president or a Cabinet officer is giving a speech or testimony before Congress, or is attending an international meeting, or is feeling pressure to demonstrate that he or she is resolute. At such times, participants with a favorite proposal put it forward in the hope that the president or a department chief will consider it the solution to his or her problem.

Some issues carry a deadline that forces the president to make a decision. The president's budget message carries the most inexorable deadline. Each year, by early February, the president must present a budget to Congress, in which he must take at least an implied stand for or against those items in the budget that are of public or congressional concern. That means that any part of the bureaucracy that is vitally concerned about an issue can stimulate public or congressional interest in the issue and thereby force it into the open at budget time. Since there was great congressional and public interest in the ABM, Lyndon Johnson could not duck the issue in his annual budget messages. Instead, he had to discuss the subject and state clearly why he was for or against the ABM. Because it was an annual budget issue, proponents of the deployment of an ABM system had no difficulty in reaching the president and getting him to make a decision. For the same reason, opponents could present their case each year, as long as they suggested a plausible public anti-ABM stand that could be elaborated by the secretary of defense under congressional questioning. Thus at each budget cycle the proponents of ABM had a natural deadline and opponents had to devote considerable effort and energy to finding a rationale that the president could use to explain why he was not going forward with deployment.

In some cases a deadline arises out of a scheduled international meeting. For example, the debate within the U.S. government about whether to seek the permission of European governments to deploy Thor and Jupiter intermediate-range ballistic missiles (IRBMs) in Europe came to a head in preparations for a NATO summit meeting in mid-December 1957. Because of the importance of the IRBM issue in the wake of the Sputnik launching, the

United States could not go to that meeting without raising the issue. Thus a decision had to be made.[26]

Congressional hearings also can impose a deadline on decisions. If a committee is known to be strongly interested in a question and if a Cabinet officer can therefore expect to be intensely drilled, there is strong pressure to establish an administration position before he or she testifies. For example, Secretary of State Dulles found himself about to face the Senate Foreign Relations Committee on the subject of foreign aid. He was informed that the committee was particularly interested in a proposal for long-term financing and would press him on the creation of the proposed development loan fund. Knowing that the committee would demand something new from him and informed of its support for this particular proposal, Dulles decided to go forward and announce administration support for the fund.[27]

An event abroad also may create a deadline. Thus the death of Stalin, which clearly required some sort of presidential statement, posed the question of what kind of initial appeal Eisenhower would make to the new Russian leaders. The decision could not be delayed.

In some situations a scheduled presidential speech is inevitably related to a particular subject. If the president is to address the United Nations General Assembly, it is difficult for him not to comment on major issues of concern to the assembly; thus a deadline is imposed for taking a position on such issues.

As he approached his decision to go to war in Iraq in 2003, the second President Bush and his most senior advisers apparently became preoccupied with the question of what constituted a deadline for the decision. Secretary of Defense Rumsfeld is said to have advised the president that the decision to move forward would be made when the United States asked other countries to put themselves at risk for the United States. Thus they identified the day that the president told the Saudi ambassador that he had decided to move against Iraq as the point at which the decision had been made. As soon as he had talked with Prince Bandar, the president called in the secretary of state to inform him that he had decided to attack Iraq.[28]

To keep such examples in perspective, it may be well to close this discussion of deadlines with a reminder that nearly every bureaucratic maneuver is subject to counter-maneuvers. Participants who favor delay, for instance, find ways to evade deadlines. Frequently, they do nothing, counting on the fact that their opponents will not be able to establish a deadline or attach their proposal

26. Armacost, *The Politics of Weapons Innovation*, p. 187.
27. Edgerton, *Sub-Cabinet Politics and Policy Commitment*, pp. 129–31.
28. Woodward, *Plan of Attack*, pp. 260–68.

to a deadline. If those favoring a decision seem to be succeeding, those who favor delay can and will propose a number of procedural devices to put off a decision. They may, for example, suggest that a document has not been fully cleared with all of those concerned and that a decision should be postponed until additional agencies and individuals are consulted. Alternatively, they can argue that the proposal should come through a different channel and should be delayed until it does. For example, the existence of a formal National Security Council system permits participants to argue that a proposal cannot simply go from one Cabinet officer to the president but that it must go through formal consideration not only by the National Security Council but also by its subordinate organs. Proponents of delay also can call for further study, claiming that additional information is needed before a sensible decision can be made. They may promise to provide additional information themselves, insist that proponents provide it, or propose the creation of a special study group. If all else fails, they may put forward arguments against acting now. They may suggest that the process is moving too quickly and that there is danger in acting hastily, or they may argue that the current international situation does not permit taking the proposed actions.

By examining these and many other maneuvers and counter-maneuvers, we have traced the policy process through to a presidential decision, but in doing so we have assumed, more or less, that all of the maneuvers described are equally available to all of the participants. Clearly that is not the case. Influence is unequally distributed, and that inequality affects what issues get to the president and how he decides them.

CHAPTER TWELVE

Influence
and Decisions

We have discussed shared images, interests, the rules of
the game, and stratagems for both advancing proposals and blocking them.
A great number of officials operate within this framework, subject to the same
constraints. What personal characteristics enable some of them consistently
to influence decisions more than the rest? In brief, the list reads as follows:

—They have the ability to gain the confidence of the president.

—They are willing to assume responsibility.

—They exercise finesse in threatening to leak information or to resign.

—Their staff is skilled in performing the functions of the bureaucracy.

—They have an aptitude for mobilizing support outside the bureaucracy.

To fully understand politics inside government, it is useful to examine each
of these characteristics in action.

RELATIONS WITH THE PRESIDENT

The single most important determinant of the influence of any senior official
is his or her relationship with the president. Indeed, a main topic of conversation in Washington is who is "in" with the president now.[1] "Confidence" is
the key concept in establishing a good relationship. As Dean Rusk explained:

> The real organization of government at higher echelons is not what you
> find in textbooks or organizational charts. It is how confidence flows

1. See, for example, Attwood, *The Reds and the Blacks,* p. 108.

down from the President. That is never put on paper—people don't like it. Besides, it fluctuates. People go up—and people go down.[2]

To win the president's confidence, officials generally must demonstrate both that they have mastered their area of responsibility and that they have the president's interest at heart. By following his own precept regarding the president's confidence, Rusk himself gained more power in Washington than most observers realized. That is borne out in the recollections of George Christian, Lyndon Johnson's press secretary, who commented:

> Johnson's faith in Rusk never wavered. He listened to Clifford, McNamara, George Ball, and others who sometimes differed with Rusk on specifics, and he might blend these views into a decision; but mainly it was Rusk's judgment he wanted in the end, and Rusk's judgment he followed.[3]

Confidence leads to the feeling on the part of the president that he should defer to a particular individual. The feeling is reinforced when an issue falls into that individual's area of responsibility. Presidents come to feel that, having made a person secretary of state or secretary of defense, they owe that person their support and ought not to undercut him or her. Several of President Eisenhower's closest advisers, including Sherman Adams, reported that Eisenhower frequently felt obliged to yield to Secretary of State John Foster Dulles on what he viewed as a diplomatic question even though Eisenhower was more eager for detente and arms control agreements with the Soviet Union than was Dulles. Eisenhower speechwriter Arthur Larson told of one key episode, which revolved around a proposed speech to the American Society of Newspaper Editors:

> President Eisenhower had practically decided to call off the Editors' speech. The main reason was that he was in disagreement with John Foster Dulles on the content and tone of the speech. Dulles wanted to stress our accomplishments in the past in working toward peace. President Eisenhower wanted to stress how dark things were at that very moment and why all-out efforts were needed to get at the cause of tension. He showed me his exchange with Dulles and said, "I don't like to make a speech on foreign policy that my Secretary of State disagrees with." Moreover, Dulles had pooh-poohed his idea of inviting several thousand Soviet students and had raised many objections. The letter to Bulganin,

2. Rusk, "Mr. Secretary on the Eve of Emeritus," p. 62B.
3. Christian, *The President Steps Down*, p. 115.

as far as I know, was never actually sent, and the idea of bringing in three thousand Russian students was never followed up.[4]

The power of individuals close to the president, either personally or by virtue of their position, is increased by the fact that they are better able to predict what arguments will be most persuasive with him. Other participants rely on those key officials for a judgment as to whether it is worth taking an issue to the president and, if so, in what form. Success in gauging the president's likely response increases the probability that an individual will be consulted on other issues and have his or her views taken into account in shaping options for the president.

A participant who has the president's ear quickly acquires a reputation for being able to win. Not only is that person's support sought, but proposals will be dropped rather than brought forward against his or her opposition. The great strength of Dean Acheson and John Foster Dulles was the widely held perception in Washington that they would win if others carried a diplomatic or foreign policy issue to the president over their objections. Similar considerations affect the influence of junior participants in relation to their principals. Thus, if a Cabinet officer feels confidence in a particular individual or feels that he should defer to the individual because of his or her position—or if that person has the ability to predict what the secretary is likely to do and what will persuade him to do something—he or she will come to have substantial influence within the bureaucracy.

It was suggested at the beginning of this section that there is nothing that Washington officials watch more closely than the relationship of particular individuals to the president. When a participant's standing is going up, the sense that one should defer to that individual rather than take an issue to the president increases. When the reverse occurs, when an individual's or an organization's standing with the president is seen as declining, then the sinking party begins to find it necessary to compromise and yield to other groups whose status has, at least by comparison, risen. Roger Hilsman, who was then director of intelligence and research in the Department of State, described the working of this rather subtle process following the decline in presidential respect for the Central Intelligence Agency after the Bay of Pigs fiasco:

What no one in Washington had failed to notice was that the Bay of Pigs debacle, the public display of the CIA's feet of clay, and, within the administration, the President's obvious disenchantment were all having

4. Larson, *Eisenhower,* pp. 72–73. See also Adams, *Firsthand Report,* p. 87.

an effect. On May 15, 1961, Allen Dulles called me to say that although he still had a few qualms, he was withdrawing his objections to the State Department's plan to consolidate its staffs and procedures for "co-ordinating" intelligence and political action proposals. More importantly, the letter to the ambassadors from the President giving them clear authority over all United States agencies abroad was cleared and shortly thereafter, on May 29, 1961, dispatched. Over the next few weeks, the ambassadors at all our missions overseas received briefings on the operations of all the agencies represented at their posts. Another, more subtle change also became apparent—everyone had been burned so badly by the Bay of Pigs that fewer of the "political action" kind of operations were now being proposed for interdepartmental approval, and fewer still were approved. Not all of this became known immediately, but it was not long before even those of our allies who were most dependent on CIA saw the way the Washington wind was blowing. Finally, our ambassadors in those countries began to feel the change reflected in the officials with whom they dealt. When notables from these countries visited Washington, for example, they paid far fewer calls on the Director of Central Intelligence than had once been customary. CIA's power had been at least slightly reduced, in other words, even though no formal organizational changes had actually been made.[5]

During the last decade of the twentieth century, a curious trend began to emerge: the rise of the vice president as a major policy influence on the president. President Clinton gave Vice President Al Gore his own role in foreign policy, allowing Gore to carve out large areas of policy where he would take the lead. Gore formed his own foreign policy staff, which operated in tandem with the NSC staff in directing the bureaucracy. This trend was accelerated by the second President Bush when he chose Vice President Cheney, an accomplished Washington infighter, as his running mate precisely to function as his alter ego and compensate for Bush's lack of Washington experience. As vice president, Cheney rightly or wrongly came to be seen as the *éminence grise* behind the president's major policy decisions. In fact Cheney took full advantage of his extensive political and bureaucratic experience, as well as his unique access to the president, to leave an indelible mark on the president's policy predilections.

5. Hilsman, *To Move a Nation*, pp. 80–81.

WILLINGNESS TO ASSUME RESPONSIBILITY

When asked by a former colleague in the State Department to name the quality that he thought was most necessary in a secretary of state, Dean Acheson reportedly replied, without hesitation, "The killer instinct."[6] Acheson was not thinking of foreign adversaries in making his remark. Rather, he was referring to the secretary's relation with officials from other departments and members of the White House staff. One key component of the killer instinct is a drive for power. Because many do not have that instinct, those who do can wield substantial influence. In addressing the senior officials of the State Department at the beginning of the Kennedy administration, Secretary of State Rusk noted, "The processes of government have sometimes been described as a struggle for power among those holding public office." But, Rusk continued, that is true only in the sense that people struggle for formal bureaucratic trappings, such as "water bottles." He argued that in fact most officials shy away from power and that the struggle is far more "the effort to diffuse or avoid responsibility." Therefore, he said, "Power gravitates to those who are willing to make decisions and live with the results."[7] Coupled with the drive for power must be an understanding of what makes for influence in Washington. Acheson and Dulles, for example, both understood the critical importance of maintaining the president's confidence and the perception in Washington that they had that confidence. They thus avoided fights that they knew that they would lose and were careful to check with the president before undertaking a major battle.

Another element affecting personal power is an individual's ability to get mad, to display a temper. Referring to his experience as ambassador to India, John Kenneth Galbraith observed that "a bad temper, real or contrived, serves as a 'No Trespassing' sign."[8] One must be willing to confront those who seek to usurp one's power and to dispense with etiquette in dealing with them. One can thereby head off attempts by power seekers to move into one's domain and have them move on to others who are less assertive. For example, after the appointment of former Texas congressman George Bush as President Nixon's representative to the United Nations, a number of officers in the State Department feared that Bush might move into their territory. After Bush made a comment about Middle East policy at his first press conference, Joseph Sisco, the assistant secretary of state for Near Eastern affairs and a man with a rep-

6. Kraft, *Profiles in Power,* p. 178.
7. Rusk speaking to the policymaking officers of the Department of State, February 20, 1961, as quoted in Hilsman, *To Move a Nation,* p. 15.
8. Galbraith, *Ambassador's Journal,* p. 106.

utation for having an instinct for power, reportedly called Bush and told him "politely but firmly that he would give out the news about this area, including any leaks."[9] No doubt Bush got the message. If he sought to move in on Sisco, he would have a brawl on his hands.

A reputation for chutzpah also helps. Acheson related an incident in which he dealt with an attempt by the Department of the Interior to discredit the State Department's adviser on petroleum problems:

> So when Mr. Hull, during the oil-to-Spain controversy, received a letter from his Cabinet colleague bitterly attacking our Petroleum Adviser, Max Thornburg, I intervened. The letter, copies of which had been sent to the President, Vice President, and others, charged that Thornburg, one of the officers principally concerned with the Spanish oil problem, was improperly influenced by connections in the oil industry. It was true that Thornburg, like Churchill, was in favor of a more liberal oil allowance to Spain than were most of the rest of us, but he was no more moved to judgment by improper influences than Churchill was. While Harold Ickes' charges were quite unfounded, the source of the argument ad hominem was not obscure. The Petroleum Adviser to Ickes had been a rival officer in the same company with Thornburg. Their opinions of one another were not laudatory, and this was not the first spat they had had. Since the oil controversy provided enough inflammable material without added charges of this nature, I asked Mr. Hull to allow me to handle the matter, and he, glad to be rid of the whole disagreeable business, assented.
>
> Max Thornburg agreed to my plan. I telephoned Harold Ickes, told him that Mr. Hull had demanded an investigation of his charges, and said that one would be held that afternoon, with witnesses to be sworn and their testimony reported.
>
> "Investigation!" he roared. "Before whom?"
>
> "Before you," I said.
>
> "What in hell is going on?" he demanded. "Are you crazy?" I explained that I was not; that, although it was well known that he was a curmudgeon, I was betting that he was an honest curmudgeon and would be willing to hear and decide upon the evidence my contention that he was mistaken about Thornburg. As the enormity and, at the same time, the humor of my effrontery sank in, he murmured, "Well, I'll be damned," and set an hour to receive us.
>
> We went through with the judicial farce: witnesses sworn by a court reporter, testimony taken stenographically, and cross-examination

9. *Washington Post*, March 18, 1971.

offered to the Solicitor of Interior—now an eminent justice. The substance of the charges was disproved. No improper interest in conflict with Thornburg's duty had influenced his advice. Ickes agreed to this and was about to dismiss us when I pointed out that the retraction, like the charges, should be in writing and go to the same people. He agreed to this, also, and called a secretary and dictated an ungrudging letter saying that on further investigation he found that he had been mistaken and withdrew what he had said. A copy was given to the reporter.

We had risen to leave when in an audible sotto voce Harold added, as a postscript, "Anyway, I still think he's a so-and-so."

"Mr. Thornburg," I said, "resume the stand. Do you know the ordinary and usual meaning of the term Secretary Ickes has just used?"

"Oh my lord," Harold shouted, "skip it. I withdraw that, too. Now get out of here and let me do some work."

"Good-bye," I said, as we filed out. "I'll see you at six o'clock." And I did.[10]

Though Acheson has written more clearly than almost any other former bureaucrat about the need to assert oneself in the bureaucracy, President Truman evidently feared that Acheson was no match in that regard for Secretary of Defense Louis Johnson. Truman took aside his newly appointed budget director, James Webb, and told him: "Acheson is a gentleman. He won't descend to a row. Johnson is a rough customer, gets his way by rowing. When he takes out after you, you give it right back to him."[11]

A special case of willingness to take responsibility—sometimes the source of it and sometimes a manifestation of it—is passion and devotion to an issue. If power in general depends on relations with the president, power on a particular issue may depend much more on the amount of time, energy, and interest one is prepared to devote to it. A senior official who is prepared to devote substantial energy to a problem can exert influence far beyond his ordinary performance. The same is often true of a junior official who has the confidence of his principal and devotes himself passionately to any one issue.

THE THREAT OF RESIGNATION

Even if a president does not warm up to particular senior participants or does not feel that their standing entitles them to great deference, he may feel

---

10. Acheson, *Present at the Creation,* pp. 62–63.

11. Lilienthal, *Journals,* p. 565. In recording this episode, Lilienthal writes: "mystified Webb; doesn't me."

obliged to take their views into account because of the fear that otherwise they may resign and embarrass him politically. Presidential sensitivity on this score is well known inside the government. Theodore Sorensen, speaking while still a White House senior adviser, commented:

> Whenever any President overrules any Secretary, he runs the risk of that Secretary grumbling, privately, if not publicly, to the Congress or to the press (or to his diary), or dragging his feet on implementation, or, at the very worst, resigning with a blast at the President. It is rare, of course, for any appointee leaving office to have more public appeal than a President in office. The whirlpools he expects to stir up with his dramatic resignation and published exposes are soon lost in a tide of other events over which the President continues to ride.
>
> Nevertheless, the violent resignation of almost any Secretary of State, Secretary of Defense, or Secretary of the Treasury could cause his chief considerable trouble; and other appointees could cause trouble in their own circles.[12]

The resignation of a senior cabinet official is often a sign that the president is in trouble. Secretary of State Cyrus Vance resigned in opposition to President Carter's decision to send a military mission to rescue the American hostages held in Iran in 1980, after Vance had advised the president that the mission was likely to fail. The embarrassment of the failed mission and Vance's resignation dealt a severe blow to the Carter administration on the eve of an election. Similarly, Elliot Richardson's resignation as Attorney General in October 1973 to protest President Nixon's decision to fire Watergate special prosecutor Archibald Cox when he ordered the White House to make the president's tapes public was a clear sign that Nixon was vulnerable. Indeed, Nixon himself was forced to resign less than a year later.

Even when the president *asks* for the resignation of a senior participant, he does so in a way that avoids a public break, particularly if the senior participant is seen to have his own following outside the executive branch. Thus when President Kennedy decided that he needed to replace Chester Bowles as the under secretary of state, he went to great lengths to persuade Bowles to take a different job in the government and ultimately to leave quietly without expressing his great misgivings about the current direction of Kennedy's foreign policy.[13]

Knowing of presidential sensitivity on this score, senior officials on occasion explicitly threaten to resign if their views are not somehow accommo-

---

12. Sorensen, *Decision-Making in the White* House, p. 80.
13. Bowles, *Promises to Keep,* pp. 352–64.

234 / INFLUENCE AND DECISIONS

dated. Secretary of Defense James Forrestal recorded in his diary a conversation with President Truman in which he stated what he would have to do if his views on defense reorganization were not taken into account:

> I said I also wanted to make it clear that while I recognized that the genius of our government made it necessary for the President to have the support of his Cabinet members, I could not get myself into the position of agreeing to support by testimony before committees of Congress a bill which did violence to the principles which I outlined above. I said I recognized clearly that a member of the President's Cabinet should support his policies and that therefore I did not wish to set myself up as any source of embarrassment to him in the carrying out of his policies, and that, if I could not support with conviction and sincerity a bill introduced by the administration, I would have to ask him to accept my resignation. The President said in response to this that he expected no such necessity need arise.[14]

Warner Schilling later expressed the conventional opinion on why Truman chose to compromise in such a case. "The President," Schilling wrote, "was far better suited to cope with the arguments of an acting Secretary in private than he was to risk hearing them from an ex-Secretary in public, especially in an election year."[15]

An interesting question remains, however, concerning civilian officials. Resignations by senior officials followed by a statement of disagreement with current policy are extremely rare. Not even the Vietnam War, which provoked substantial disagreement within the Kennedy and Johnson administrations, produced a civilian resignation followed by a blast at the president's policies. Does that mean that the risk of embarrassment exists mostly in the president's mind and that it simply is exploited from time to time by adroit bureaucrats? Or does it mean that the risk assumes such importance that every president brings all his powers to bear to prevent an open break?

The one group that clearly has been prepared to follow up on threats to resign in protest is the military. American military officers feel strongly about the organizational interests of their branch of the service. They have often had broad support among the public and in Congress and have demonstrated a willingness to resign "noisily" if overruled on key issues. That combination has made the threat of resignation of prominent military officers a very real one to every president.

14. *Forrestal Diaries*, p. 205.
15. Schilling, "The Politics of National Defense," p. 158.

The decision to resign depends in part on the perception of the likely public reaction to the resignation. Thus, in the late 1940s, General Omar Bradley considered resigning but held off because of his belief that his plea for increased spending on the Army would fall on deaf ears in a period when Congress and the public favored a drive for economy.[16] A number of admirals outraged by Truman's refusal to build large carriers did resign in the so-called "revolt of the admirals" because of their strong feeling on the issue. Although they recognized that they could probably not win with the public, they perhaps expected some shift of attitudes in their direction. During the Eisenhower administration both Matthew Ridgway and Maxwell Taylor resigned from the post of Army Chief of Staff because of their opposition to the doctrine of massive retaliation. They took their case to the public, though without any great expectation of winning in the short run.

The most potent threat that the military can make is to threaten to have all of the Joint Chiefs of Staff resign en masse. President Johnson was apparently confronted with such a threat in 1966. The chiefs, sensing that Secretary McNamara's standing with the public and the president had begun to fall, pressed the White House for higher budgets and threatened to resign en masse unless the programs of each service—the ABM system, the new manned bomber, and ship construction—were carried forward.[17] Johnson, deciding that he could not tolerate a mass resignation of the chiefs in the middle of the controversy about the Vietnam War, apparently took steps to mollify them, including by deciding to go forward with the Sentinel ABM system.

STAFF SKILL

Bureaucrats can make use of the skills of their trade in increasing their influence. Staff skill is in part a matter of knowledge, of "understanding" in detail how the system works—how various components such as the Joint Chiefs and the intelligence bureaus make their decisions, what arguments are likely to influence them, and how to time the release of new information. Staff skill also involves knowing the position of different individuals, knowing to whom one should go for a particular stand on a particular issue or to get a particular fact that others may be seeking to bury. It means knowing whom to call in a particular agency, because that individual is likely to favor what one wants done and can exert the necessary influence. It means knowing when to ques-

16. Ibid., pp. 160–61.
17. Hoopes, *The Limits of Intervention*, p. 90; Korb, "Budget Strategies of the Joint Chiefs of Staff," pp. 14, 17. Korb cites as his source an interview with the chief of naval operations, Admiral McDonald.

tion the expertise of others and how to do so.[18] A key component of bureau-cratic skill is knowledge of how to make planning effective. Adam Yarmolin-sky explained how that was done in the Office of the Secretary of Defense, in which he served:

> In the area of direct relations with State, the planning function was simi-larly integrated with operations. Within the Office of the Assistant Secre-tary of Defense for International Security Affairs, the Assistant Secretary set up a policy planning staff as a kind of free-wheeling adjunct to the regional and subject-matter specialized units within the office to work on whatever problems might be assigned to it from time to time. This staff examined the long-range planning implications of immediate deci-sions facing the department, but it did so always in the context of a mat-ter that was very much at the top of the Assistant Secretary's immediate priority list. It did not produce policy papers in vacuo, but rather made recommendations for action in areas where the Assistant Secretary and the Secretary were prepared to act.
>
> By contrast the policy planning function in the State Department has been lodged in a policy planning council, a group of senior foreign ser-vice officers assigned for this purpose, who have largely generated their own agenda, but whose work product has had very little visible impact on the decision-making that goes on at the other end of the building.
>
> The Defense Department approach to policy planning in the foreign area has the obvious defect of limiting the opportunities for the planning staff to raise questions that are wholly outside the current concerns of decision-makers. But this function is one that, realistically, must be per-formed outside government if it is to be performed effectively and if the result is to draw the attention of busy men at the top of any government structure. On the other hand, the Defense Department approach to the planning process reinforces the effectiveness of the department in gener-ating immediate policy proposals, and particularly in taking a more active and less reactive position on matters that are on the joint State-Defense agenda.[19]

One key skill is the ability to write short and concise memos that explain an issue in a way that is likely to seem persuasive to the president and other senior officials. McGeorge Bundy, special assistant for national security to

18. On these points see, for example, McGarvey, "The Culture of Bureaucracy," p. 75; Anderson, *The Presidents' Men*, p. 330; Johnson, "The National Security Council," p. 727; Yarmolinsky, "Bureaucratic Structures and Political Outcomes"; Hilsman, *To Move a Nation*.
19. Yarmolinsky, "Bureaucratic Structures and Political Outcomes," p. 232.

Kennedy and Johnson, had a reputation for writing excellent memorandums.[20] The State Department, on the other hand, has always had a reputation for writing memos that are much too long and lack persuasiveness. Under Secretary of State George Ball, for example, is reported to have wondered aloud on one occasion "why State Department officials never seemed to be able to write anything under ten pages."[21] A former White House official noted the following episode in which State lost the battle of the briefings:

> When he called for briefing papers on short notice from State for a Presidential overseas trip, his first deadline passed without any response. He then turned to the office of International Security Affairs at Defense, which responded with a complete, concise, and thoroughly indexed briefing book. State finally crashed through with several cardboard cartons of unsorted cables on the countries listed in the President's itinerary.[22]

The effective bureaucrat takes considerable time on an important memo in an effort to make it both short and persuasive to the president. David Lilienthal, then director of the Tennessee Valley Authority (TVA), described one working session:

> Owen had been working several days on such a memo. It was very long and quite preachy, and full of a tone of preoccupation with ourselves that doesn't seem to me very persuasive. But it had the essential points. I suggested a different approach: one that I thought built upon the President's own experience and interests. This was to assert that TVA was still in danger from its enemies, but that this time the danger came from efforts to break down the autonomy and freedom from red tape that provides our chief armor against attacks; namely, our ability to do a good job and one that evokes the approval and support of the people. So I drafted a rough statement along that line. By the time Owen and Clapp rewrote it, it was again obscure and much too long, I thought. By this time it was 10:30 p.m. This went on and on. At 12:40 a.m. we had another draft, briefer, but still not too good. I was so whipped down that I would have accepted it, but Owen saw its weaknesses and insisted on doing something with it. At two o'clock we quit, still without a memorandum. I didn't get to bed until 3 a.m.

20. Halberstam, "The Very Expensive Education of McGeorge Bundy," pp. 28–29.
21. Attwood, *The Reds and the Blacks,* p. 106.
22. Yarmolinsky, *The Military Establishment,* p. 34. Though this example may be extreme, it is not atypical. See, for example, the first memorandum presented to President Truman by the Department of State and reprinted by him in *Year of Decisions,* pp. 14–17.

I got off by myself at 9:15 and wrote the introductory part on a new basis, in longhand, and revised the balance; Clapp made some suggestions, and at 2:45 I was with the President's special counsel, Captain Clifford, with a copy of a 5 1/2 page, double-spaced draft.

This tale of a memo is almost incredible—that's why I have taken the trouble to tell its story in such fullness. No one seeing the memo would believe that it represented so much work.

But it appears that the care was worth it. For the President did read it, and he began our meeting this morning by pointing to it on his desk and saying, "I've read your statement and I agree completely. But where are we going to get someone to take your place so TVA can go on that way, the way I want it?"[23]

ABILITY TO MOBILIZE OUTSIDE SUPPORT

A major form of influence within the bureaucracy is the ability to mobilize the support of influential groups outside the executive branch. These are groups that matter to the president, either because they affect his ability to pursue the particular policy under discussion or his more general ability to function effectively and to be reelected. The most potent such groups are leading representatives and senators, as well as major groups within the president's political party and interest groups whose support the president needs to have. The ability to mobilize outside groups comes in part from their perception that particular participants within the bureaucracy should be deferred to in defining the national interest. It also may come from a belief that the particular participants inside represent the interests of the outside group.

The substantial influence of senior military officers has rested in part on the prestige and influence that military leaders have enjoyed in the past with leading figures in Congress. Many members of Congress have defined the national interest in terms of what the military believes is necessary for national security. Other groups in society, including some newspaper editors, and leaders of veterans' groups such as the American Legion have also defined the national interest largely in terms of deference to military perceptions. The influence of the military services has been enhanced by their willingness and ability to make their views known outside the executive branch. In testifying before congressional committees, senior military officers will make clear where their judgment differs from that of the president, particularly as

23. Lilienthal, *Journals*, p. 93.

reflected in budget decisions. Military officers also are quite willing to talk to members of the press about their views on security matters. Presidents are aware that, if the military is unhappy, Pentagon press reporters will report their disaffection. For example, for many years Hanson Baldwin, the military editor of the *New York Times,* accurately reported the views of the Joint Chiefs and particularly of the Navy. On some issues the influence of the military has virtually amounted to a veto. On the matter of reorganizing the Defense Department, for example, both President Truman and President Eisenhower carried on extensive negotiations with the military, recognizing the fact that they were unlikely to get Congress to accept any reorganization plan that did not have military support.

The military services offer perhaps the best example of achieving influence within the American government through the ability to call on outside groups of importance to the president. But such influence has not been limited to the military. Bernard Baruch, for instance, despite Truman's impatience with him, had considerable influence within the Truman administration, without holding any official position, because it was recognized that he had important influence with congressional leaders and with the business community.[24]

The Elusiveness of Decisions

Our effort to describe the process by which decisions on national security issues are made within the U.S. government is at an end. What is contained in these past six chapters may be misleading, insofar as it gives the reader too great a sense of orderliness. In reality, as we have hinted from time to time, there is much confusion, much that occurs by accident and without the intent of any particular participant. There is much also that remains inscrutable. All close observers of presidential decisions have warned of the difficulty of analyzing decisionmaking in the White House. In John F. Kennedy's words: "The essence of ultimate decision remains impenetrable to the observer—often, indeed to the decider himself. . . . There will always be the dark entangled stretches in the decision-making process—mysterious even to those who may be most intimately involved."[25] And George Reedy, a close observer of President Johnson, warned:

> The fact is that a president makes his decisions as he wishes to make them, under conditions which he himself has established, and at times of his own determination. He decides what he wants to decide, and any stu-

24. See, for example, Lilienthal, *Journals,* p. 163.
25. Sorensen, *Decision-Making in the White House,* pp. xi–xiii.

dent of the White House who believes that he is making a contribution to political thought when he analyzes the process is sadly mistaken. At best—at the very best—he can only contribute to human knowledge some insights into the decision-making process of one man.[26]

The president does make decisions on major issues. But, as we suggest in part 3, by no means is the process then over.

26. Reedy, *The Twilight of the Presidency*, p. 31.

PART III

Actions

CHAPTER THIRTEEN

Decisions and Implementation

The reader has every right to expect to be at the end of this book. For one thing, it is already quite long. For another, we have reached the end of the topic as it is normally discussed. We have traced the process of making foreign policy inside the bureaucracy to the point of presidential decisionmaking.

But the process is by no means over. If our question is not "How do presidents decide?" but "How does the United States act?" then we need to explore the relationship between presidential decisions and the subsequent actions of government officials.

PRESIDENTIAL DECISIONS

Presidential decisions vary in specificity. They often are conveyed only in policy statements expressing a sentiment or intention. The statements may indicate in general terms that certain kinds of actions should be taken but not say who should take them. Even if they do specify the actor, they seldom indicate when the action should be taken or the details of how it should be done. In fact, the instructions are often so vague as to leave all the actors free to continue behaving as they have in the past.[1]

Even if a decision results from a long struggle among the president's advisers—indeed, especially when it results from such a struggle—the president

---

1. On this general point, see Taylor, *The Uncertain Trumpet,* pp. 82–83; and Rostow, "The American Agenda," p. 17.

tends to delay decisions and then to decide as little as possible.[2] Furthermore, the president seldom makes a single comprehensive decision covering a wide range of interrelated issues. More often he decides a series of questions discretely, each one on its own merits, compiling a series of diffuse and, on some occasions, contradictory guidelines to the bureaucracy about what should be done.

There are a number of reasons why a president may not want to state definitely what should be done to implement a decision that he has made. In many cases, the consensus on which the decision was built may depend on its vagueness. In the case of the ABM, Secretary of Defense McNamara was prepared to go along with a limited deployment provided that he could announce it as anti-Chinese and express strong opposition to erecting any large system supposedly designed to counter a Russian missile attack. At the same time, the Joint Chiefs of Staff and Senate leaders, such as Richard Russell, the chairman of the Senate Armed Services Committee, were prepared to go along with limited initial deployment provided that they could describe it as the first step toward a large anti-Russian system. In order to keep this "coalition" together the president's decision had to be vague enough so that participants on both sides could believe that he had decided in their favor—and in any case so that they were free to describe his decision as they chose. President Truman was confronted with a similar problem, that of differing views on whether the United States should begin to develop a hydrogen bomb. With Atomic Energy Commission chairman David Lilienthal against any deployment, the military in favor of proceeding with a deployment, and the State Department in favor of exploring the options, Truman settled on a tentative, minimal decision that kept everybody on board by both giving Lilienthal no target to shoot at and moving in the direction of the military enough that they were prepared to acquiesce.[3] During the first term of his presidency, Ronald Reagan announced his Strategic Defense Initiative (SDI), committing his administration to the pursuit of a missile defense system that he believed would make it possible to eliminate nuclear weapons. While Reagan's commitment to that goal never wavered, senior members of his Cabinet, who were deeply skeptical of its feasibility, proceeded to use SDI as a bargaining chip in arms control negotiations with the Soviet Union. One faction saw SDI as something that could be traded for significant Soviet concessions on missile deployment. The other saw SDI as a means of ensuring that the arms control talks would go nowhere.[4]

2. On this point, see Schilling, "The H–Bomb Decision: How to Decide without Actually Choosing." Our description here draws heavily on this article as well as Schilling's "The Politics of National Defense."

3. Schilling, *The H–Bomb Decision*, pp. 38–42.

4. Talbot, *The Master of the Game*, pp. 18–19.

A president's desire not to be committed to the details of a decision often reinforces his desire to maintain a semblance of harmony by expressing his decision in vague terms. Presidents typically confront an issue on a very general, theoretical level without much discussion of the details of the best way to implement a decision. When he has not spent time on details and has not looked into the possible problems buried in one kind of decision or another, the president prefers to express only a general desire to move in a particular direction and leave it to his subordinates to battle over the details. He is likely to assume that important issues will be brought back to him for a further decision.

In many cases, after making a decision a president wishes to keep it secret for a while in order to head off attacks before implementation of the decision is under way. He recognizes that the further down the line the information gets, the more likely it is to be leaked. In Washington what the president decides is news, and lower-level officials are eager either to show that they know what the president wants or to undercut a policy that they oppose. When he decided in 1978 to normalize relations with China, President Carter came to believe that the State Department would be an impediment to faithful implementation of his instructions. In his words,

> I was leery of channeling my proposals through the State Department, because I did not feel that I had full support there and it was and is an enormous bureaucracy that is unable and sometimes unwilling to keep a secret. It seemed obvious to me that premature public disclosure of our intensifying diplomatic effort could arouse a firestorm of opposition from those who thought that Taiwan should always be the "one China." I decided that no negotiating instructions to Ambassador Leonard Woodcock would ever be channeled through the State Department; they would be sent directly from the White House.[5]

In addition, the president may feel that his time must not be squandered in providing specific instructions. Robert Cutler, at one time the assistant to the president for national security affairs, reported that that was Eisenhower's view:

> Eisenhower believed that policy decisions at the apex of Government should afford general direction, principle, and guidance, but should not be spelled out in detail. The Council dealt with strategy, not tactics. A Supreme Commander's orders are directed to Army groups and armies; they do not deal with battalions and companies. The last throw of

5. Carter, Letter to the editor, pp. 164–65.

Ludendorff in 1944 [sic] failed, in part, because his orders meddled with the battle movement of small elements. President Eisenhower was as impatient with too much detail as he was with lack of clarity in stating general policy.[6]

Whether he considers attention to "details" appropriate, when a president is new in office he tends to assume that faithful subordinates all down the line will labor to put his policies into practice. One of President Eisenhower's speechwriters commented on Eisenhower's initial faith of this kind: "Nowhere did the lack of civilian experience so betray itself as in this system's cheerful assumption that, once the Chief Executive had pointed in a certain political direction, the full force of government would move in that direction, in concert as precise and as massive as battalions and divisions wheeling through field maneuvers."[7]

Even when he comes to understand that specification of detail is necessary if one wishes to have faithful implementation, a president does not have on tap at the White House experts to draft decisions in specific terms in all areas. Nor does the White House staff, whatever its own expertise, have time to prepare detailed instructions on many issues.

Because presidential decisions are seldom formulated in a way that conveys in detail what should be done and because the president himself seldom carries out the decision, only in very special cases are presidential decisions self-executing. Usually, in fact, they begin a process. The president often announces a policy decision in conversation with the senior officials who head the organizations that will be responsible for implementing his decisions. The first steps toward concrete action depend on their understanding or recollection of what was said. When he wanted to explore the options for attacking Iraq, the second President Bush took his secretary of defense aside in November 2002 and asked for optional war plans. Bob Woodward quoted the president as saying, "I have no idea what it takes to cause the Pentagon to respond to a request since I've never been there. I presume Don Rumsfeld . . . was making sure that the product got done and the process didn't linger."[8] In fact, Rumsfeld understood clearly that the president wished to handle the decisionmaking process in strict confidence, dealing directly with the military commander who would implement the decision to go to war.

In other cases, the president makes a decision alone or in the company of White House officials and the decision is then conveyed (sometimes orally) to

6. Cutler, *No Time for Rest*, p. 300.
7. Hughes, *The Ordeal of Power*, p. 153.
8. Woodward, *Plan of Attack*, p. 30.

the heads of the departments concerned or to a subordinate official believed to be responsible for supervising the required actions. They in turn issue instructions to those who, according to the rules of procedure, are responsible for actually carrying out the decision. Frequently that involves not only distributing directives to subordinates in Washington but also sending out cables to American ambassadors and military commanders in the field. This is not a trivial matter. Turning the sketchy language of a presidential decision into precise terms that can be understood and acted on in the field is extraordinarily difficult and may have to be done at high speed. During the opening days of the Korean War, for example, the senior civilian and military officials, after meeting with the president and getting his oral instructions, would move to the Pentagon or the State Department and improvise written instructions to the field.[9]

Once orders are written and sent to the individuals who should act, one might at last expect faithful implementation of the presidential decision, but that does not occur either. Why it does not is our next subject.

Limits on Faithful Implementation

There are three basic causes for the failure of officials at the operations level to comply with presidential or other directives:

—They may not know what senior officials want them to do.

—They may be unable to do what they believe that they have been ordered to do.

—They may resist doing what they have been ordered to do.

UNCERTAINTY ABOUT ORDERS. In approaching the question of why presidential orders may not be obeyed, it is important to keep in mind the vast size and diversity of the federal government. Few officials see the president at all. Even fewer see him often enough to have a good feel for his approach to problem solving. Many of those who have to implement decisions are not privy to conversations between the president and his principal advisers or between those advisers and their subordinates. The orders that they receive, in writing or orally, are not only very general but often are the only clues they have. Thus the ambassador or first secretary in the field, the commander of a bomber squadron, an assistant secretary in Washington, a Treasury official vis-

9. This process and the difficulty of translating orders into operational form in the opening days of the Korean War are described in Paige, *The Korean Decision*, pp. 138–39, 142, 161, 163, 245–47, 250–51, 321–23. See also Smith, "Why We Went to War in Korea," p. 80.

iting a foreign government—all may have little information with which to determine what the president wants them to do.

In some cases, officials at the operations level may not even know that the president has issued orders in a particular area. After an American U-2 plane was shot down over the Soviet Union, a public affairs officer in the National Aeronautics and Space Agency held a press conference at which he asserted that the plane had accidentally drifted over Russian territory. That happened long after President Eisenhower and his senior advisers had decided that only the State Department would make any comment.[10] Senior officials, too, may sometimes be unaware of the president's plans. For example, Secretary of Defense Melvin Laird, while visiting Japan, made a number of statements that led the press to report that the United States favored Japan's development of nuclear capability. Laird unknowingly made his statements at precisely the time that presidential assistant Henry Kissinger was in Peking negotiating with Chou En-lai about the possibility of a trip by Nixon to China. It is believed that Laird's comments greatly complicated Kissinger's mission. Laird was not disobeying orders. He was simply uninformed about Nixon's approach to China and therefore was unaware that what he was saying might halt or at least complicate progress.

Misunderstanding about what a subordinate is ordered to do crops up. One of the most dramatic cases on record of a pure misunderstanding resulted in President Eisenhower's invitation to Soviet Premier Nikita Khrushchev to visit the United States. Eisenhower had decided that he would be prepared to invite Khrushchev to the United States *only if* there was progress at the ongoing foreign ministers' meeting that would justify convening a four-power summit conference. The invitation to the Russians was to be conveyed by Under Secretary of State Robert Murphy, who was to meet Soviet Deputy Prime Minister Kozlov during the latter's visit to the United States. Murphy's instructions were given him directly by the president, but they were oral. Evidently, even direct communication did not prevent misunderstanding. Murphy conveyed through Kozlov an unconditional invitation to Premier Khrushchev, rather than the one that the president wished to transmit (contingent upon progress in the four-power talks), and Eisenhower felt obliged to honor the invitation.[11]

A similar incident occurred in the run-up to the Gulf War during the first Bush administration, when Secretary of State Baker was drawn into a joint statement with the Soviet foreign minister offering a cease-fire if Saddam

10. Wise and Ross, *The U–2 Affair*, pp. 78–84.
11. Eisenhower, *Waging Peace*, pp. 405–8.

Hussein withdrew from Kuwait. Because the president had been demanding *unconditional* withdrawal from Kuwait, he was furious when he learned of Baker's statement. As Brent Scowcroft, the national security adviser, recalled, "Without knowing what Baker was up to, we agreed the right tactic was to say there had been no change in policy and simply brush it off. In the end that worked."[12]

More often, it is not that officials are totally uninformed or that they completely misunderstand their orders. Rather, they have no way of grasping the nuances behind decisions, no guidance as to exactly why they were told to do what they were told to do. That makes it very difficult for them to implement the policy, to make day-to-day decisions that conform to the president's desires. George Kennan explained:

> In the execution of policy, we see the same phenomenon. Anyone who has ever had anything to do with the conduct of foreign relations knows that policies can be correctly and effectively implemented only by people who understand the entire philosophy and world of thought of the person or persons who took the original decision. But senior officials are constantly forced to realize that in a governmental apparatus so vast, so impersonal, and lacking in any sort of ideological indoctrination and discipline, they cannot count on any great portion of the apparatus to understand entirely what they mean. The people in question here are in large part people they do not know personally and cannot hope to know in this way. Considerations of security alone would make it difficult, in many instances, to initiate into the reasons of action all those who might be involved if one were to use the regular channels. The expansion of the governmental apparatus has led to a steady inflation of titles roughly matching that of the growth of the apparatus itself.[13]

The problem has gotten even more acute since 1957, when Kennan wrote. An examination of the State Department prepared by a group of Foreign Service officers in 1970 related this problem to the Nixon National Security Council system:

> Specific decisions are generally communicated promptly and clearly to the implementing units. On occasion, however, the implementing unit is not specified precisely, and the system suffers. More often, the specific decision is transmitted without reference to the broader objectives which

12. Bush and Scowcroft, *A World Transformed,* p. 461. How this happened is explained in detail in Beschloss and Talbott, *At the Highest Level,* pp. 330–31.
13. Kennan, "America's Administrative Response to Its World Problems," p. 19.

should guide the action office in carrying it out. Action offices thus must rely on rather rough and ready guidance of their own making, extrapolating from the specific decision and the very broad-brush generalizations contained in public pronouncements by the President and the Secretary. The result can be either inconsistency in implementation or excessive caution. One reason for this lack of guidance is that Departmental inputs to NSSMs [National Security Study Memoranda] are often not framed in such a way as to produce it. Also the Department usually does not participate in drafting NSDMs [National Security Decision Memoranda] it is required to implement.[14]

While the decision process varies from one administration to another, it has continued to become more complex with the expansion of senior positions and changes in national security responsibilities to adjust for the end of the cold war and the rise of terrorism. The problem of determining what one is supposed to do is further complicated by the fact that no official receives just one order. The directive comes as one item in a flow of paper across an official's desk. He is receiving instructions to do things because other officials have made decisions. He is receiving requests from his subordinates for authority to take actions within existing directives. He is receiving reports of ongoing activities. Whatever effort he makes to implement a particular directive must be within the context of his attempt to implement other directives that have come to him before. He may see a conflict between two very specific directives—a conflict of which senior officials may not be aware. He may perceive a contradiction between a specific directive and a more general policy statement that was received in writing or that he gleaned from public presidential and departmental statements. Such a conflict accounts in part for the failure of the State Department to remove American missiles from Turkey in 1961 after President Kennedy had ordered them removed. But he had also ordered the State Department to invigorate the NATO alliance, and, indeed, one of his campaign pledges had been that he would bolster NATO. At the same time, his secretary of defense, Robert McNamara, was engaged in an effort to persuade the NATO countries to take conventional military options more seriously. The State Department officials concerned were well aware of the fact that that effort was causing great difficulties within the alliance. The officials who received the directive to remove the missiles from Turkey also felt themselves to be operating under a more general presidential directive to strengthen the troubled alliance. They did not believe that the order to remove

14. Macomber, *Diplomacy for the 1970s,* pp. 556–57.

the missiles from Turkey was intended to contradict the order to strengthen NATO. They raised the issue in a tentative way with the Turkish government. When the government registered strong objections, they held off obeying the order to remove the missiles.

Whereas missiles remained in Turkey because of conflicting directives from the president, in other cases uncertainty arises from the fact that an official receives conflicting orders from two or more of his superiors. The president may in effect tell him to do one thing, and the secretary of the navy or the chief of naval operations seemingly tells him to do another. In such cases, the official often makes his own judgment about which orders have higher priority.

THE DIFFICULTY OF IMPLEMENTATION. Some orders direct an official to achieve a certain outcome but do not specify any particular action. For example, an official may be told to secure ratification of a nonproliferation treaty by a particular government, or he or she may be told to persuade a certain country to increase its military forces. In such cases, the implementation of the order depends on the cooperation or at least the acquiescence of a foreign government. In other cases, implementation may depend on the cooperation of Congress or of other groups outside the executive branch and beyond the control of the official given the order. Under those circumstances he or she may find it impossible to comply.

In still other cases, limits on compliance arise from the fact that most presidential orders must be carried out by large complex organizations. Some presidential decisions can be carried out by a relatively small number of presidential advisers without regard to the capability of large organizations. When President Nixon decided that he wished to establish contact with the People's Republic of China, he was able to dispatch Henry Kissinger, his assistant for national security affairs, to Beijing. Kissinger could carry on discussions in China without reference to the standard operating procedures of the Department of State. However, when the action to be carried out requires the cooperation of large numbers of people in the major organizations of the American government, what the president can order done is much more limited. For example, when North Korean forces attacked South Korea in June 1950, President Truman could only order into the fight those forces that already existed and that could reach the battlefield; those were the occupation forces in Japan under General Douglas MacArthur. When President Kennedy in 1961 wished to step up the number of American "advisers" in Vietnam, he could send only those "counterinsurgency" specialists who had already been trained by the government, either in the CIA or in the armed services.

The organization designated to carry out an action uses its standard operating procedures (SOPs)—routine methods that facilitate coordinated and concerted actions by large numbers of individuals—to do so. For that purpose the rules need to be simple in order to allow easy learning and unambiguous application. Clusters of standard procedures constitute a program for dealing with a particular situation. A set of programs related to a particular type of activity constitute an organization's repertoire. The number of programs in a repertoire is always quite limited. Thus activity undertaken according to standard operating procedures and programs does not constitute a farsighted, flexible adaptation to the president's decision. Detailed implementation of actions by organizations is determined predominantly by organizational routines. Since the programs cannot be tailored to the specific situation, the organization, when striving to obey presidential decisions, uses whatever program in the existing repertoire seems most appropriate, given its limited understanding of the purposes of the decision.[15]

Again, we can cite Kennedy's experience with Vietnam. When he increased the number of American military personnel in Vietnam from 685 in 1961 to 30,000 in 1962, one observer noted that "there was no change in the advice provided by the advisor; there were just more advisors."[16] In general, the American troops later sent to Vietnam performed very much as they would if they had been sent to fight a large-scale military battle on the plains of central Europe, toward which most of their training had been directed. The State Department, AID, and USIA missions likewise performed in accordance with their standard procedures.[17]

In 2004, the 9/11 Commission found similar problems in how Washington agencies tried to cope with the new challenges of terrorism:

> Yet at least for the CIA, part of the burden in tackling terrorism arose from the background we have described: an organization capable of attracting extraordinarily motivated people but institutionally averse to risk with its capacity for covert action atrophied, predisposed to restrict the distribution of information, having difficulty assimilating new types of personnel, and accustomed to presenting descriptive reportage of the latest intelligence. The CIA, to put it another way, needed significant change in order to get maximum effect in counterterrorism.[18]

15. Allison, *Essence of Decision,* pp. 67–100.
16. Corson, *The Betrayal,* pp. 45–46.
17. Cooke, "Organizational Constraints in U.S. Performance in Vietnam."
18. *9/11 Commission Report,* p. 93.

Large organizations find it extremely difficult to develop new plans quickly or to implement plans developed for a different purpose. When the Soviet Union constructed the Berlin Wall in 1961, Kennedy found that his advisers suggested no options for action. All the contingency planning had been directed to other possible provocations, such as closing the access routes between West Berlin and West Germany.[19] Routine behavior is followed even when it appears foolish to an outsider. During the Cuban missile crisis, for example, intelligence officers reported that Russian and Cuban planes were inexplicably lined up wingtip to wingtip on Cuban airfields, making perfect targets. Kennedy, recognizing that as standard military practice, had a U-2 fly over the American airfields in Florida and discovered that American planes were similarly lined up.[20]

When a senior official gives an organization an order to carry out an action, he or she is likely to have an idealized picture of what will occur. The official assumes that the organization will quickly grasp what he or she is trying to accomplish and adapt its behavior creatively to the particular purpose. The truth is, however, that action, when it involves large numbers, may turn into something quite different from what the official had in mind. One such episode occurred during the summit meeting of 1960. Secretary of Defense Thomas Gates, who had accompanied Eisenhower to Paris, learned that Khrushchev was making rather strong demands and became convinced that the summit conference was about to end in disagreement. He therefore decided on Sunday night to order a worldwide alert of American military forces, feeling that it would be prudent to have local commanders alerted at battle stations all over the globe. He sent a message to the Pentagon calling for a "quiet" alert on a "minimum need to know basis." The secretary, however, was not familiar with the set of alert patterns that had been developed and did not specify which alert, among alternatives numbered one to five, he wished to have implemented. The Joint Chiefs, feeling the pressure of time and having to guess what Gates wished to accomplish, concluded that alert number three was in order but adhered to Gates's injunction about restricting information. Gates evidently had not visualized that there would be any movement of weapons or troops, but the Pentagon announced that both the continental air defense command and SAC had conducted "limited routine air alert activities." The alert quickly became visible throughout the country and undoubtedly was visible to the Soviet Union as well, sending a signal far dif-

19. Sorensen, *Kennedy*, p. 594.
20. Kennedy, *Thirteen Days*, pp. 59–60.

ferent from Gates's simple desire to have the military ready in case the situation should deteriorate.[21]

Resistance

Thus far we have explored why presidential decisions may not be implemented even though participants seek faithfully to do what the president or his principal associates have ordered them to do. For that reason, the discussion has been somewhat artificial, for in fact those who are assigned to implement presidential decisions often do not feel obliged to execute their orders. Neither career officials nor political appointees necessarily feel that a presidential decision settles the matter. Participants still have different interests and still see different faces of an issue and have different stakes in it. They may believe that their conception of what is in the national interest is still correct and resist efforts to do things that they feel are contrary to the national interest or to their own organizational or personal interests, even if they have been directed to do them by the president. Henry Kissinger explained the problem to a journalist after serving for several years as President Nixon's assistant for national security affairs:

> The outsider believes a Presidential order is consistently followed out. Nonsense. I have to spend considerable time seeing that it is carried out and in the spirit the President intended. Inevitably, in the nature of bureaucracy, departments become pressure groups for a point of view. If the President decides against them, they are convinced some evil influence worked on the President: if only he knew all the facts, he would have decided their way.
>
> The nightmare of the modern state is the hugeness of the bureaucracy, and the problem is how to get coherence and design in it.[22]

This problem is not a new one. It has confronted every American president in the modern period, and they have reacted either by seeking to concentrate power in the White House or by trying to get the departments under control. In his memoirs, Truman revealed his strong feelings on the subject:

> The difficulty with many career officials in the government is that they regard themselves as the men who really make policy and run the government. They look upon the elected officials as just temporary occupants. Every President in our history has been faced with this problem:

21. Wise and Ross, *The U–2 Affair*, pp. 146–47.
22. Pett, "Henry A. Kissinger: Loyal Retainer or Nixon's Svengali?" p. B–3.

how to prevent career people from circumventing presidential policy. Too often career people seek to impose their own views instead of carrying out the established policy of the administration. Sometimes they achieve this by influencing the key people appointed by the President to put his policies into operation. It has often happened in the War and Navy Departments that the generals and the admirals, instead of working for and under the Secretaries, succeeded in having the Secretaries act for and under them. And it has happened in the Department of State.

Some Presidents have handled this situation by setting up what amounted to a little State Department of their own. President Roosevelt did this and carried on direct communications with Churchill and Stalin. I did not feel that I wanted to follow this method, because the State Department is set up for the purpose of handling foreign policy operations, and the State Department ought to take care of them. But I wanted to make it plain that the President of the United States, and not the second or third echelon in the State Department, is responsible for making foreign policy, and, furthermore, that no one in any department can sabotage the President's policy. The civil servant, the general or admiral, the foreign service officer has no authority to make policy. They act only as servants of the government, and therefore they must remain in line with the government policy that is established by those who have been chosen by the people to set that policy.

In the Palestine situation, as Secretary Lovett said to me after the announcement of the recognition of Israel, "They almost put it over on you."[23]

The view that one knows what is best for national security affects not only career officials but also political appointees, even when they clearly understand the president's perspective. When at the first meeting of his Cabinet, even before inauguration, General Eisenhower expressed his strong support for increased trade with the Soviet Union, Secretary of Defense Charles Wilson said, "I am a little old fashioned. I don't like to sell firearms to the Indians." Eisenhower then explained in detail why he thought that such trade was good. Obviously, however, he failed to convince Wilson to go along, for the discussion concluded with Wilson saying, "I am going to be on the tough side of this one."[24]

One of the reasons that the president is overwhelmingly busy is that so many officials maneuver to line him up on their side of an issue. Then, pre-

23. Truman, *Years of Trial and Hope*, p. 165.
24. Adams, *Firsthand Report*, p. 68. See also Hughes, *The Ordeal of Power*, p. 76.

cisely because of the heavy demands on his time, Cabinet members and staff officers get away with ignoring his orders. One observer commented succinctly on the game of outwaiting the president:

> Half of a President's suggestions, which theoretically carry the weight of orders, can be safely forgotten by a Cabinet member. And if the President asks about a suggestion a second time, he can be told that it is being investigated. If he asks a third time, a wise Cabinet officer will give him at least part of what he suggests. But only occasionally, except about the most important matters, do Presidents ever get around to asking three times.[25]

As a president discovers that his decisions are being resisted, he tends more and more to keep the bureaucracy in the dark and to work through outside channels. That further reduces loyalty as well as contributes to inadvertent disobedience, which in turn reinforces the president's inclination toward secrecy. Henry Kissinger, writing before he became an assistant to President Nixon, described the vicious circle that results:

> Because management of the bureaucracy takes so much energy and precisely because changing course is so difficult, many of the most important decisions are taken by extra-bureaucratic means. Some of the key decisions are kept to a very small circle while the bureaucracy happily continues working away in ignorance of the fact that decisions are being made, or the fact that a decision is being made in a particular area. One reason for keeping the decisions to small groups is that when bureaucracies are so unwieldy and when their internal morale becomes a serious problem, an unpopular decision may be fought by brutal means, such as leaks to the press or to congressional committees. Thus, the only way secrecy can be kept is to exclude from the making of the decision all those who are theoretically charged with carrying it out. There is, thus, small wonder for the many allegations of deliberate sabotage of certain American efforts, or of great cynicism of American efforts because of inconsistent actions. In the majority of cases this was due to the ignorance of certain parts of the bureaucracy, rather than to malevolent intent. Another result is that the relevant part of the bureaucracy, because it is being excluded from the making of a particular decision, continues with great intensity sending out cables, thereby distorting the

---

25. Daniels, *Frontier on the Potomac*, pp. 31–32.

effort with the best intentions in the world. You cannot stop them from doing this because you do not tell them what is going on.[26]

The first President Bush, who came to office with years of experience in various parts of both the legislative and executive branches as well as in positions in the field, was perhaps as aware of the relationship between the presidency and the bureaucracy as any U.S. president in history. Having been vice president in the preceding administration and knowing from the outset that as the Soviet empire disintegrated and the cold war came to an end, he would be presiding over a historic period, President Bush established an inner circle of trusted decisonmakers to manage the actions of the bureaucracy and avoid impediments to the policy changes that would be required.

The second President Bush, who incorporated many of his father's advisers in his administration, followed that pattern, retreating into an even smaller inner circle, dominated by his vice president. In the words of former NSC staff member Richard Clarke, "the second Bush administration was like his father's: NSC Staff saw the President infrequently and always with a chaperon."[27]

The Struggle over Implementation

What has been said thus far should explain why a presidential decision, rather than settling the question of what is to be done, simply opens a new round of maneuvers. The process that occurs after a presidential decision is made proceeds in much the same way as the efforts to get a presidential decision. Indeed, in many areas the two processes overlap, since a presidential decision may be followed by a simultaneous struggle over its implementation and the drafting of new decisions. The participants are often the same as those who were involved in framing the decision, although many more lower-level officials may be involved in actual implementation and senior officials are likely to devote less attention to it. The participants bring to the process the same range of conceptions of what is in the national interest, and they tend to see different faces of the issue, have different stakes, and fight for different kinds of action. Participants have to decide again whether to get involved in the process, and some develop strategies designed to secure the implementation of the president's decision if they favor it or to resist implementation if they do not. They are constrained by the rules of the game, which determine who has responsibility for implementing the decision, whose concurrence is needed on any orders given, and who has the right or responsibility to mon-

26. Kissinger, "Bureaucracy and Policy Making," p. 89.
27. Clarke, *Against All Enemies*, p. 243.

itor compliance with the decision. If they favor the action, officials charged with implementation are likely to be able to proceed despite the opposition of other groups. If they resist action, then the problem of securing implementation is much more difficult. However, the president's problem is difficult even when officials at the operations level favor his policy.

OVERZEALOUS IMPLEMENTATION. When the president makes a decision urged on him by those who will be responsible for its implementation, they often feel that he has not gone far enough or they may choose to interpret the decision as giving them more license than he intended. They then are likely to act in a way that from the president's point of view appears to be overzealous. Truman recalled how that happened to him in connection with his agreement to terminate lend-lease aid to America's European allies following the surrender of Germany:

> Leo Crowley, Foreign Economic Administrator, and Joseph C. Grew, Acting Secretary of State, came into my office after the Cabinet meeting on May 8 and said that they had an important order in connection with Lend-Lease which President Roosevelt had approved but not signed. It was an order authorizing the FEA and the State Department to take joint action to cut back the volume of Lend-Lease supplies when Germany surrendered. What they told me made good sense to me; with Germany out of the war, Lend-Lease should be reduced. They asked me to sign it. I reached for my pen and, without reading the document, I signed it.
>
> The storm broke almost at once. The manner in which the order was executed was unfortunate. Crowley interpreted the order literally and placed an embargo on all shipments to Russia and to other European nations, even to the extent of having some of the ships turned around and brought back to American ports for unloading. The British were hardest hit, but the Russians interpreted the move as especially aimed at them. Because we were furnishing Russia with immense quantities of food, clothing, arms, and ammunition, this sudden and abrupt interruption of Lend-Lease aid naturally stirred up a hornets' nest in that country. The Russians complained about our unfriendly attitude. We had unwittingly given Stalin a point of contention which he would undoubtedly bring up every chance he had. Other European governments complained about being cut off too abruptly. The result was that I rescinded the order.[28]

28. Truman, *Year of Decisions*, pp. 227–28.

President Kennedy was confronted with an example of overzealous implementation in the case of a proposed multilateral force. A group of officials in the
State Department favored the creation of a jointly manned and jointly owned
nuclear force of surface ships to be operated by the NATO alliance. Upon securing a decision by Kennedy to ask the European allies of the United States whether
they favored such a force, the advocates took it as an indication that the president
wished them to seek to persuade others to join the force. Their own reasoning
was that the president knew that "nothing happened" in Europe unless the United
States forcefully advocated it. Therefore, from their perspective, simply asking the
Europeans whether they were interested guaranteed that nothing would happen.
Kennedy, on the other hand, apparently assumed that he had authorized only
quiet exploration of the possibility and was surprised to discover that the Europeans believed that he was pressing hard for the multilateral force.[29]

One of the most notorious cases of overzealous implementation took place
during the presidency of Ronald Reagan, when his White House staff engi-
neered a complex arrangement to use the funds from clandestine arms sales to
Iran to finance the right-wing Contras in Nicaragua, subverting congressional
legislation. President Reagan at first refused to believe that that could have
happened without his knowledge, but he later announced in a speech to the
nation that it had indeed happened right under his nose.

> A few months ago I told the American people I did not trade arms for
> hostages. My heart and my best intentions still tell me that's true, but the
> facts and the evidence tell me it is not. As the Tower Board reported, what
> began as a strategic opening to Iran deteriorated, in its implementation,
> into trading arms for hostages. This runs counter to my own beliefs, to
> administration policy, and the original strategy we had in mind. There are
> reasons why it happened, but no excuses. It was a mistake. I undertook
> the original Iran initiative in order to develop relations with those who
> might assume leadership in a post-Khomeini government.
>
> It's clear from the Board's report, however, that I let my personal con-
> cern for the hostages spill over into the geopolitical strategy of reaching
> out to Iran. I asked so many questions about the hostages' welfare that I
> didn't ask enough about the specifics of the total Iran plan.[30]

DISREGARDING ORDERS. As noted above, officials find ways to overlook,
twist, or resist orders. Franklin Roosevelt once gave a classic description of
how that is done in general:

29. Sorensen, *Kennedy,* p. 569; Schlesinger, *A Thousand Days,* p. 875.
30. Speech by President Reagan from the White House, March 4, 1987.

The Treasury is so large and far-flung and ingrained in its practices that I find it is almost impossible to get the action and results I want—even with Henry [Morgenthau] there. But the Treasury is not to be compared with the State Department. You should go through the experience of trying to get any changes in the thinking, policy, and action of the career diplomats, and then you'd know what a real problem was. But the Treasury and the State Department put together are nothing compared with the Na-a-vy. The admirals are really something to cope with—and I should know. To change anything in the Na-a-vy is like punching a feather bed. You punch it with your right and you punch it with your left until you are finally exhausted, and then you find the damn bed just as it was before you started punching.[31]

Orders often are disregarded more or less openly. Participants may make no effort to disguise the fact that they do not favor a presidential decision and will do what they can to thwart it. For this purpose they set in motion one or more of the following maneuvers.

—*Do not pass on orders.* One technique available to senior participants is not to pass the president's order on to those who actually have to carry it out. "Forgetting" and "overriding circumstances" serve as excuses. During the preparations for the Bay of Pigs invasion, for example, President Kennedy directed that if the invading forces failed to establish a beachhead, they should move quickly to the mountains and become a guerrilla force. However, the CIA did not pass his instruction on to the leader of the brigade. CIA officials later explained that they felt that to do so might weaken the brigade's resolve to fight and that the brigade might choose the alternative plan when the going got rough, even when the invasion still had a chance of success.[32] More than once a secretary of defense has kept a presidential directive to himself in the belief that to pass it on would greatly complicate the problem of dealing with the Joint Chiefs of Staff. Both Secretary of Defense Charles Wilson under Eisenhower and Secretary of Defense James Forrestal under Truman failed to deliver presidential directives establishing ceilings on force levels.[33]

—*Change "cosmetics" but not reality.* A second technique is to change the formal procedures regarding what is to be done but make it clear to subordinates that the reality is to remain the same. Eisenhower during the course of his presidency became increasingly aware of the limited authority of the "uni-

31. Eccles, *Beckoning Frontiers*, p. 336.
32. Johnson, *The Bay of Pigs,* p. 86.
33. Lilienthal, *Journals,* p. 355; Larson, *Eisenhower,* p. 23; Hammond, "Super Carriers and B–36 Bombers," p. 478.

fied" military commanders who were supposed to be in charge of all of the American forces overseas in areas such as Europe and the Far East. He therefore devoted considerable energy to persuading the services to accept and Congress to enact a change in procedure that would strengthen the area commander's authority. In presenting the 1958 defense reorganization act to Congress, Eisenhower stated that "each Unified Commander must have unquestioned authority over all units of his command. . . . The commander's authority over these component commands is short of the full command required for maximum efficiency."[34] At the time that Eisenhower sent his message to Congress, the authority of area commanders was known as "operational control." The 1958 act invested in the area commander "full operational command," indicating Congress's intent to overcome the deficiency pointed out by Eisenhower. However, as a blue ribbon defense panel subsequently concluded, "[With respect to] Unified Action Armed Forces (JCS Pub. 2), which sets forth principles, doctrines, and functions governing the activities and performance of Forces assigned to Unified Commands, the JCS now define 'Operational Command' as being synonymous with 'Operational Control.'" According to the panel, the command arrangements remained "substantially unchanged," and "the net result is an organizational structure in which 'unification' of either command or of the forces is more cosmetic than substantive."[35] Thus there was a change in wording but no change in reality, despite a clear presidential and congressional directive.

—*Do something else.* A more blatant form of disobedience is to simply ignore a directive and do something else that either runs contrary to it or simply does not take into account what the president sought. On August 15, 1945, for example, Truman sent a formal memorandum to the secretaries of state, war, and the navy, to the Joint Chiefs of Staff, and to the director of the Office of Scientific Research and Development. In that memorandum he directed them to "take such steps as are necessary to prevent the release of any information in regard to the development, design, or production of the atomic bomb."[36] Soon thereafter, those agencies released the so-called Smyth Report, which contained considerable information about the design and production of the atomic bomb!

Truman was confronted with similar disobedience from the State Department during his efforts to take charge of American policy toward Israel. Truman had directed that the United States should support the partition of

34. Cited in Blue Ribbon Defense Panel, *Report to the President and the Secretary of Defense,* p. 50.

35. Ibid., p. 50.

36. Truman, *Year of Decisions,* p. 524.

Palestine. The American delegate to the UN, Warren Austin, despite the fact that he was aware of the presidential directive, declared in public at the United Nations that the United States was no longer for partition. That step was taken with the concurrence of the State Department but without Truman being informed.[37] Nor was Truman the only president treated in that way by his subordinates. Eisenhower related one episode when Secretary of State John Foster Dulles, who on the whole bent over backward to follow specific presidential directives, probably ignored one:

> In the period between the Summit Conference and the Foreign Ministers' meeting, I became ill. Before Foster left to attend the meeting he came to Denver so that we could confer in my hospital room. He had prepared a draft of a reply to Mr. Bulganin, who had asked us for a further explanation of my July proposal for exchanging "blueprints" of military establishments. *Inadvertently*, Foster had omitted my statement to the Soviet delegation at Geneva that if they would accept an aerial inspection system, I was quite ready to accept their proposition for ground teams. With this correction made, I signed the letter to Bulganin.[38]

It is difficult to believe that the omission was in fact inadvertent.

Vice President Cheney, in the second President Bush's administration, made a habit of superimposing his own views on administration policy on sensitive and controversial issues. In one notable instance, Cheney decided to preempt administration policy toward Iraq in a speech to the Veterans of Foreign Wars in August 2002, declaring that the United States had already found UN weapons inspections futile and was prepared to attack Iraq, months before the president had taken a formal decision to do so. Subsequently, Cheney issued his own national intelligence statement:

> "Simply stated, there is no doubt that Saddam Hussein now has weapons of mass destruction [and] there is no doubt that he is amassing them to use against our friends, against our allies and against us." Ten days earlier the president himself had said only that Saddam "desires" these weapons. Neither Bush nor the CIA had made any assertion comparable to Cheney's.[39]

—*Delay*. Another technique to avoid implementing a presidential decision is simply to delay, either not taking the action that the president has

37. Steinberg, *The Man from Missouri*, p. 307.
38. Eisenhower, *Mandate for Change*, p. 527 (italics added).
39. Woodward, *Plan of Attack*, p. 164.

ordered or moving very slowly toward implementing it. A view of this technique at work in a specific setting is offered by a former high official of the CIA, who reported on CIA resistance to a presidential directive:

> Despite that, shortly thereafter a National Security Council directive ordered the Agency to implement certain of the recommendations. I remember having lunch with Najeeb Halaby and discussing the report and directive. Jeeb Halaby, who later became nationally known as the administrator of the Federal Aviation Administration, was then serving in the office of the Secretary of Defense on matters that later were organized under the assistant secretary for International Security Affairs. He had considerable dealings with the CIA and was anxious to see it develop into a strong agency. I recall the conversation vividly because we both agreed that the report and directive were an important step forward, but I predicted that they would not be implemented at that time. Halaby expressed incredulity, noting that it was a Presidential Directive, but I maintained that bureaucracy grinds exceeding slow and if a directive was unpopular with the bosses it could grind even slower.
>
> Such proved to be the case. When General Smith arrived in Washington in October 1950, nearly a year later, to take over from Hillenkoetter, who had gone on to another naval assignment, little had been done to implement the report.[40]

—*Obey the letter but not the spirit of the order.* Because orders are expressed in generalities and the implementing instructions themselves tend not to be very precise, officials at the operations level frequently have some leeway to implement decisions as they choose. They often do that in ways that follow the letter but not the spirit of what they are told to do, even insofar as they understand that spirit.

That sort of behavior occurred on March 31, 1968, when the American military officers, in planning the first bombing of North Vietnam after President Johnson's speech announcing a cutback of the bombing, chose to obey the letter of their instructions rather than the spirit of the president's address. Johnson had publicly declared:

> I am taking the first step to de-escalate the conflict. We are reducing—substantially reducing—the present level of hostilities . . . unilaterally and at once. Tonight, I have ordered our aircraft and our naval vessels to make no attacks on North Vietnam, except in the area north of the

40. Kirkpatrick, *The Real CIA*, p. 89.

Demilitarized Zone where the continuing enemy buildup directly threatens allied forward positions.[41]

The unmistakable implication of what he said was that the remaining bombing would be related to tactical targets in order to provide protection for U.S. ground forces immediately below the demilitarized zone. Later press reports made it clear that the orders to the field directed the military simply to cease all bombing north of 20 degrees, but presumably the text of the president's speech was also available, at least informally, to those planning bombing raids. Nevertheless, much of the weight of the first bombing raids on April 1, 1968, was directed at the only large city below 20 degrees in North Vietnam. The ultimate "message" conveyed not only to the North Vietnamese but also to the American people was one of selected devastation rather than de-escalation. Thus the credibility gap widened, even though the commander-in-chief of U.S. forces in the Pacific, who directed the bombing raids against North Vietnam, was acting fully within his orders in carrying out the strikes on North Vietnam.[42]

Whereas the military can generally stretch orders involving combat operations, the State Department often has such flexibility in drafting cables. Elizabeth Drew described one episode in a fight by the State Department to resist White House orders to step up American economic aid to the secessionist province of Biafra in Nigeria:

When Biafra fell, the White House announced that the President had placed on alert, for relief purposes, transport planes and helicopters, and was donating $10 million. This was done on White House initiative. . . .

This difference was fought out, as such issues usually are, in seemingly minor bureaucratic skirmishes over such things as the wording of cables, and the tone of statements to the press. State, for example, drafted a cable instructing our representatives in Lagos to emphasize that the helicopters and planes were only on standby, and that the $10 million had only been made available because British Prime Minister Harold Wilson had told President Nixon that there was concern over the relief effort. The White House rewrote the cable, deleting the apologetic tone and emphasizing the President's concern that the Nigerians speed relief. It is in such ways that the United States government's posture in a crisis can be determined.[43]

41. *New York Times*, April 1, 1968.
42. Kalb and Abel, *Roots of Involvement*, p. 255.
43. Drew, "Washington," pp. 6, 10.

CHANGING DECISIONS. The maneuvers discussed so far involve finding ways not to do what one is ordered to do. Different maneuvers exist for resisting a decision by seeking to get it changed by the president or, in spite of the president, by Congress.

—*Insist on a personal hearing before obeying.* Most often presidential orders are passed on to other officials either in writing or through a member of the White House staff. When they do not like such orders, senior officials can demand a hearing from the president and insist that, before accepting his orders, they must be sure that he has heard their side of the argument and that the orders are being transmitted accurately to them. As part of this ploy, they are likely to claim that the president may well have been misunderstood and they may enlist the support of a friendly member of the White House staff.[44] According to Bob Woodward, when Secretary of State Colin Powell sensed that momentum was building inexorably around the president to mount an attack on Iraq in 2003, Powell "realized that he had not laid out his own analysis to the president directly and forcefully. And at least he owed Bush his understanding and his views on all the possible consequences of war." The secretary enlisted the assistance of Condoleezza Rice, the national security adviser, to get a private meeting with the president to lay out his reservations about going to war.[45]

— *Suggest reasons for reconsidering.* A related technique that can be used even when one has gotten an order from the president is to insist on going back to him to "report unforeseen implications." This technique is easiest to use when the president has turned down a request for permission to do something, but it also can be used when the president very specifically orders a certain action to be carried out. In his memoirs, Dean Acheson described in vivid detail the aftermath of a presidential decision to send a cable to General MacArthur ordering withdrawal of a message that MacArthur planned to make public regarding the terms for peace in Korea:

> For some time the President had had a meeting scheduled with the Secretaries of State, Treasury, and Defense, Harriman, and the Joint Chiefs of Staff for nine-thirty on that morning. When we filed into the Oval Office, the President, with lips white and compressed, dispensed with the usual greetings. He read the message and then asked each person around the room whether he had had any prior intimation or knowledge of it. No one had. Louis Johnson was directed to order MacArthur from the

44. One such episode, involving the fiscal 1958 foreign aid bill, is described in Edgerton, *Sub-Cabinet Politics and Policy Commitment,* pp. 121–122.

45. Woodward, *Plan of Attack,* p. 149.

President to withdraw the message and report that he (MacArthur) had done so. The President himself would send directly to MacArthur a copy of Ambassador Austin's letter to Trygve Lie, from which he would understand why the withdrawal order was necessary. The business for which the meeting was called was hastily dispatched.

When we left the White House, nothing could have been clearer to me than that the President had issued an order to General MacArthur to withdraw the message, but Secretary Johnson soon telephoned to say that this could cause embarrassment and that he (Johnson) thought it better to inform MacArthur that if he issued the statement "we" would reply that it was "only one man's opinion and not the official policy of the Government." I said that the issue seemed to be who was President of the United States. Johnson then asked me an amazing question—whether "we dare send [MacArthur] a message that the President directs him to withdraw his statement?" I saw nothing else to do in view of the President's order.

At Johnson's request, I asked Averell Harriman whether he was clear that the President had issued an order. This shortly resulted in another call from Johnson saying that the President had dictated to him this message to go to MacArthur: "The President of the United States directs that you withdraw your message for National Encampment of Veterans of Foreign Wars, because various features with regard to Formosa are in conflict with the policy of the United States and its position in the United Nations."

Still Johnson doubted the wisdom of sending the order and put forward his prior alternative. Stephen Early, his deputy, came on the telephone to support him, raised the question of General MacArthur's right of free speech, and proposed that the President talk to General MacArthur. At this point I excused myself and ended the conversation, duly reporting it to Harriman, saying that if Johnson wished to reopen the President's decision, he should apply to the President to do so. The President instructed Harriman that he had dictated what he wanted to go and he wanted it to go. It went. MacArthur's message was both withdrawn and unofficially published.[46]

—*Go to the Hill.* Another way to fight a presidential decision is to bring the matter to Congress, either in open testimony or in private. This maneuver is, of course, most effective when the presidential decision requires congres-

46. Acheson, *Present at the Creation*, pp. 423–24.

sional concurrence, such as when it concerns the appropriation of funds, approval of a treaty, or enactment of legislation permitting government reorganization. The channel of communication usually runs between career officials of an organization in the executive branch and staff members of congressional subcommittees. Members of Congress often see it as their duty to protect the permanent bureaucracy against encroachments by the president and Cabinet officers.[47]

The undercutting of the president can be done quite subtly, for example, by simply not showing the necessary enthusiasm to get a proposal through. Sherman Adams, President Eisenhower's principal White House assistant, described one such episode during Eisenhower's long campaign to get the reorganization of the Defense Department approved by Congress:

> Unfortunately for the President, his Secretary of Defense, Neil McElroy, did not appear to share Eisenhower's spirited dedication to the reorganization plan when he appeared to testify on it before the House committee. In sending his recommendations to Congress, the President had drafted most of the wording of the bill himself. This was a rare procedure. Usually the President left the drafting of a bill to the ranking member of his party on the appropriate committee to work out with the department head concerned. This time, because Eisenhower had drafted himself, almost word for word, the legislation that he wanted enacted, it was assumed in the House that he was taking an unshakable no-compromise stand on it. But McElroy gave the committee the impression that the administration would be willing to make concessions. He was unable to give the inquiring Congressmen any specific examples of the "outmoded concepts" that Eisenhower had cited as the main reason for the need of unification. He indicated that the terms of the bill were in some respects broader than was necessary, but the President was in some degree responsible for McElroy's comment since he had said that he did not regard the exact language of the bill as necessarily sacrosanct. This weakened the President's case somewhat and gave Uncle Carl Vinson the opening to drive in objections to some of the key provisions.
>
> After McElroy left the door open, the President jumped up fast to close it, but the room was already filled with snow. McElroy admitted to Uncle Carl's committee that the Secretary of Defense did not actually need the sweeping powers to assign and transfer that the bill conferred upon him. The President reversed the Secretary and came back strongly

47. For an account of a "protective" episode involving the State Department and USIA, see Larson, *Eisenhower*, p. 24.

to assert that any retreat from this position of demand for supervisory control would make unified strategy impossible. Eisenhower sent word to Congress that no concessions would be made because they had already been made before the bill was submitted. What they were considering were the bare essentials, he declared.[48]

Military officers more often than others have resorted to Congress—in part because of the automatic support that they have found there for their views. Many legislators insist that Congress has a duty to hear the views of career military officers who disagree with the president. The White House naturally opposes that outlook, and over the years efforts have been made to reduce the freedom of the military to testify independently before Congress. Under Truman, military officers had the freedom to volunteer the information that they disagreed with an administration proposal and, after making the administration's view clear, to express their personal views against it. Secretary of Defense McNamara in the 1960s sought to impose a much more restrictive rule: that the military reveal differences only if pressed and then, in admitting disagreement, to give the administration's side of the case as well.[49] That practice has continued, with Congress pressing to learn the views of the military and civilian leaders seeking to discourage the practice.

—*Go public.* One way to alert Congress as well as the public is to provide information to the press. Here the hope is that news of disagreement over a decision will stir up public or congressional opposition, forcing the president to back down. In 1961, for example, the Army, concerned about the fact that President Kennedy was forcing on the military a counter-guerrilla strategy in Vietnam that would impair the ability of the South Vietnamese forces to resist a conventional invasion from North Vietnam, leaked news of Kennedy's action and the Army's objections to the press.[50]

—*Go to another government.* If all else fails, those seeking to oppose implementation of a decision can go to another government and try to get it to intervene. When the presidential directive requires officials to try to persuade a second government to do something, it can be resisted by quietly urging that government not to go along with the U.S. demands. Averell Harriman believes that that was done during his efforts to negotiate an agreement concerning Laos. He maintains that the head of the right-wing forces, General Phoumi, was advised by some U.S. officials to hold out against U.S. pressures for a compromise settlement.[51]

48. Adams, *Firsthand Report*, pp. 418–19.
49. *Forrestal Diaries*, p. 119; Korb, "Budget Strategies of the Joint Chiefs of Staff," n. 15.
50. Hilsman, *To Move a Nation*, pp. 415–16.
51. Harriman, *America and Russia in a Changing World*, p. 112.

Another such incident occurred in 1986, when, at the behest of conservatives in the Defense Department, President Ronald Reagan was preparing to send a letter to Soviet leader Gorbachev proposing the elimination of all nuclear ballistic missiles. Chief negotiator Paul Nitze feared that that would not only impede congressional funding for a new generation of strategic missiles but would seriously anger NATO allies. When Nitze was dispatched to consult with British and French allies, he got the negative reaction he expected. In Strobe Talbott's words, "After his consultations, Nitze could, in good conscience and with some satisfaction, report that the allies wanted no reference to the ballistic missiles of third parties in whatever letter Reagan finally sent to Gorbachev."[52]

RESISTING REQUESTS FOR PROPOSALS. Thus far we have considered mainly those cases in which the president gives an order to do something, often something that may affect the behavior of another government. Occasionally, however, the president orders his staff to work up a proposal for doing something in a certain area. In such cases, the bureaucracy's ability to ignore presidential demands is probably greater. Among the techniques commonly used are the following.

—*Do not respond.* Presidents often make requests for imaginative or new proposals in a particular area. Such requests are often ignored, and then, when the president inquires, he is told that the problem is so difficult that a proposal is not yet ready. This technique is particularly convenient when the president insists that he receive a proposal unanimously agreed to by all his advisers. President Eisenhower, for example, apparently believed strongly that the United States should put forward more imaginative proposals in the arms control field, and he continuously pressed his advisers to come up with proposals for his approval. But he also expected his advisers to agree with each other, and such proposals were seldom forthcoming.[53] The no-response technique can be used even when the president's request is a relatively simple and straightforward one and he asks not for opinions but simply for a procedural plan to implement a proposal already decided upon. One example is the way the State Department delayed action on President Kennedy's wish to create the post of under secretary of state for Latin American affairs. As Arthur Schlesinger Jr. related the incident,

The President was more troubled than ever by the organization of Latin American affairs within our own government. Late in October he dis-

52. Talbott, *The Master of the Game*, p. 309.
53. See, for example, Hughes, *The Ordeal of Power*, pp. 203–04.

cussed with Richard Goodwin and me the old problem which Berle had raised in 1961 of an Under Secretaryship of State for Inter-American Affairs, embracing both the Alliance and the political responsibilities of the Assistant Secretary. Kennedy, remarking sharply that he could not get anyone on the seventh floor of the State Department to pay sustained attention to Latin America, dictated a plainspoken memorandum to Rusk saying that he wanted to create the new Under Secretaryship. "I am familiar," he said, "with the argument that, if we do this for Latin America, other geographical areas must receive equal treatment. But I have come increasingly to feel that this argument, however plausible in the abstract, overlooks the practicalities of the situation." Historically Latin America was an area of primary and distinctive United States interest; currently it was the area of greatest danger to us; and operationally it simply was not receiving the day-to-day, high-level attention which our national interest demanded. "Since I am familiar with the arguments against the establishment of this Under Secretaryship," his memorandum to the Secretary concluded somewhat wearily, "I would like this time to have a positive exploration of its possibilities."

He had in mind for the job Sargent Shriver or perhaps Averell Harriman, whom he had just designated to lead the United States delegation to the São Paulo meeting. We later learned that Rusk sent the presidential memorandum to the Assistant Secretary for Administration, who passed it along to some subordinate, and it took Ralph Dungan's intervention to convince the Secretary that this was a serious matter requiring senior attention. Receiving no response, the President after a fortnight renewed the request.[54]

—*Not now.* An alternative to not responding at all is to plead for postponement. State Department officials often caution the White House that the timing is wrong for a particular initiative because of the delicate political situation. John Foster Dulles was able to use this technique with great effectiveness because of President Eisenhower's feeling that he should defer to Dulles on diplomatic issues. As Eisenhower implied in an interview shortly after leaving office, it was that maneuver that kept the United States from withdrawing any troops from Europe despite the president's strong feelings that they should come out and despite his expertise as a former commander of those forces.

54. Schlesinger, *A Thousand Days*, pp. 1001–02.

Though for eight years in the White House I believed and announced to my associates that a reduction of American strength in Europe should be initiated as soon as European economies were restored, the matter was then considered too delicate a political question to raise. I believe the time has now come when we should start withdrawing some of those troops.[55]

—*Come back with a different proposal.* A further technique for stalling is to come back and present the president with a proposal that is significantly different from his directive. Often the proposal takes account of the organizational interests of the bureau or department involved. When President Kennedy was preparing to ask General Lucius Clay to go to Berlin as the president's principal adviser, reporting directly to Kennedy and taking overall charge of the situation, the State Department and the Defense Department combined to change the draft so that Clay became simply an adviser with no operational control over the military or diplomatic mission in Berlin.[56]

A classic example of bureaucracy attempting to resist and divert a president's policy objectives is the case of the Strategic Defense Initiative (SDI), which provided enough bureaucratic intrigue to occupy an entire book. As the author of that book described it,

> For five years, between 1983 and 1988, . . . the drama was played out between him and members of his government, many of whom felt compelled to feign enthusiasm for an idea that they considered extremely dubious. In the face of Reagan's stubborn attachment to SDI, his Administration became the scene of one of the most extraordinary episodes in the annals of American defense policy and diplomacy.
>
> It was a bizarre instance of covert action, carried out almost entirely within the executive branch. The broad outlines of the operation, as well as the identity, motivation, and modus operandi of the various protagonists, were largely evident, almost a matter of public record. Yet the nature of what was going on remained obscure, the object of official obfuscation and therefore of public confusion.
>
> This deception was deemed necessary largely because the President had his own objective in SDI, and it was compatible with neither of the competing ones that his advisors were trying, covertly, to impose on him. Ronald Reagan continued to believe very much in the original

---

55. Interview with Eisenhower, *Saturday Evening Post,* October 26, 1963, as quoted in Percy, "Paying for NATO," p. 36.

56. Clay, Kennedy Library Oral History Interview, pp. 5–6.

vision of March 1983: population defense so comprehensive and so close to being impregnable that the Soviet Union would have no choice but to cooperate in a transition to a new order in which defense would be the dominant, and eventually the sole, basis of Western security.

That was the President's sincere hope for SDI. Almost no one in his immediate employ shared that hope. So the objective of the game within the Administration—this deepest game that went on for five years between the two factions—was to finesse the longer-term impact of the program in such a way as either to advance arms control or to stop it in its tracks.[57]

Thus far we have emphasized the ability of participants in Washington to resist presidential orders, but the president is not without resources to combat resistance. Before looking into that aspect of foreign policy, however, we devote a chapter to how decisions from Washington are treated in the field.

57. Talbott, *The Master of the Game*, pp. 18–19.

CHAPTER FOURTEEN

Actions in
the Field

Foreign policy decisions made by the president often must be implemented in the field by ambassadors and their subordinates or by military commanders. The relationships between officials in the field and the president are similar to those between Washington agencies and the White House, but there are enough differences to merit a separate discussion.

We begin with a discussion of the structure of field operations and why and how the perspective of those in the field differs from that of officials in Washington; then we consider the range of specific maneuvers open to those in the field to resist Washington's decisions or to act in the absence of them.

PERSPECTIVES FROM THE FIELD

The core of an embassy, as most ambassadors conceive it, is the "country team," which consists of senior officers from embassy units representing the various agencies present in the embassy, especially the State Department, CIA, Defense Department, Commerce Department, and the Agency for International Development (USAID). Large embassies have large country teams, because the number of other Washington departments represented in embassies grew significantly during the post–cold war period as the requirements imposed on embassies by Congress and the executive branch became increasingly diverse. Most embassies have a defense attaché office (DAO), representing the Department of Defense. Embassies in countries with which the United States has a significant military sales relationship also have a separate office representing the Defense Department to handle those transactions. The Central Intelligence Agency, the FBI, the Department of Agriculture, the Department of Commerce, the Department of the Treasury, and other departments and agencies with international functions, such as the Federal Aviation Administration (FAA), may have representatives in many embassies, particularly those embassies that have been designated as regional centers. The United States Information Agency used to manage public outreach operations in U.S. embassies, but it was incorporated into the State Department in the late 1990s and its functions are now performed by the State Department's public diplomacy service. The Agency for International Development has missions in many developing and transitional countries, as well as a few large regional centers. Thus an ambassador in a large embassy that also serves as a regional center may find him- or herself presiding over a small-scale replica of the Washington bureaucracy. Many ambassadors, therefore, tend to rely on the deputy chief of mission, who is always a Foreign Service officer, and other key Foreign Service officers, such as the heads of the political, economic, administrative, security, and public diplomacy sections of the embassy, as the essential management team.

A regional military command in the field, such as CINCPAC (Commander in Chief Pacific) and CINCEUR (Commander in Chief Europe), consists of a commander-in-chief and staff plus subordinate commanders for each of the services whose personnel are involved in the area. All of those officials see the national interest partly in terms of the interests of their organization and their own interest in promotion. The key to promotion lies in their home agency in Washington, and they are responsive to its commands and its interests.

The different interests and perspectives of the various groups in an embassy or military command thus reproduce the situation in Washington. The military commander or ambassador is only nominally in full control of those beneath him. Ambassadors and field commanders often strive to maintain control over channels of communication between their post and Washington, and many were able to do so when overseas posts had limited means of communication. However, controlling communications became impossible with the rapid advances in communications technology at the end of the twentieth century, which now allow all agencies to have direct private channels of communication with their officials in the field. Thus an ambassador must rely above all on persuasion and authority to maintain coherence and discipline in an overseas mission.[1]

1. On communications between an agency and its officials in the field, see, for example, Galbraith, *Ambassador's Journal*, pp. 465–66, and Sebald, *With MacArthur in Japan*, pp. 120–21.

Subordinate officials use all the techniques in dealing with orders from their ambassador that are used by officials in Washington in dealing with the president. For example, they often say things to their counterparts in the host government that violate the ambassador's instructions.[2] Even outright disobedience is not uncommon. A Marine colonel who served in Vietnam described one such episode during that period:

> Before we begin our discussion on Phong Bac, it should be noted that the course of action selected was and is contrary to the spirit and intent of every directive, regulation, or order issued by COMUSMACV (Commander U.S. Military Assistance Command Vietnam) and the U.S. Embassy in Saigon, all of which require U.S. forces to serve as a forerunner of GVN control. For this breach of discipline the responsibility is mine. The men who participated in Phong Bac's pacification carried out my orders and plans because they were good Marines and because they believed in and understood what they were doing. My primary purpose was to protect American lives and property-pacification was the means. The secondary goal was to enable the people of Phong Bac to become strong enough to resist the predatory incursions of both the GVN and the Vietcong.[3]

Some ambassadors, particularly those appointed by the president, who are more interested in the ceremonial aspects of their position, may prefer not to know what is going on within the mission. During the cold war period, for example, some ambassadors were not interested in AID programs and gave the AID director virtual autonomy in dealing with the host government. In the case of the CIA, ambassadors often preferred not to know about certain of its activities so as not to be embarrassed in case of disclosure—for example, if CIA communications with antigovernment leaders in the country were to be exposed. The CIA often operates simply without informing the local ambassador, as may well have been the case with the agency's renditions of terrorist suspects from European countries during the Iraq war.[4] Earl Smith reported that the CIA established relations with Castro's rebel forces while he was ambassador to Cuba during the late 1950s and that he did not learn of it until much later, when there was a court-martial of some Cuban naval officers who participated in an early Castro revolt.[5]

2. See, for example, Martin, *Overtaken by Events,* p. 389.
3. Corson, *The Betrayal,* pp. 155–56.
4. "CIA Holds Terror Suspects in Secret Prisons," *Washington Post,* November 2, 2005 (www.washingtonpost.com/wp–dyn/content/article/2005/11/01/AR2005110101644_pf.html).
5. Smith, *The Fourth Floor: An Account of the Castro Communist Revolution,* pp. 31–34. For a description of a similar incident in an unnamed country, see Holbrooke, "The Machine That Fails," p. 66.

At the same time, the members of the diplomatic team or military command tend to share a common bias against "interference" from Washington. They are likely to be strongly motivated to improve relations with the country to which they are assigned and to take actions that accomplish that goal even at the cost of hurting relations with neighboring countries. Officials in the field often are persuaded that improving relations with their host country is vital to the security of the United States, whereas priorities decided on in Washington seem out of touch. In the journal that he wrote while serving as ambassador to India, John Kenneth Galbraith provided a typical perspective:

> Yesterday an incredible telegram came from the Department washing out the C-130 offer I was to come back to India and try to sell as a substitute for MiGs. And likewise any suggestion of military aid. All in craven reaction to the Congress and, I fear, to the President's displeasure with India. The Department was so obviously off base that I decided on a soft answer and spent most of the day on it. For the rest, I am beginning to contemplate a quiet withdrawal.[6]

Believing that they are much more adept at dealing with the local government and understanding its complexities, officials in the field feel that they should make policy decisions and that Washington should simply support them. They assume that Washington does not understand "the problem" in substantive terms or the difficulty of running an embassy and dealing with the local government. John Harr's study of the American career foreign affairs official concluded as follows:

> A familiar theme in the literature on public administration is the set of problems often found in relationships between a home office and its field posts—lack of understanding, faulty communication, distrust, poor coordination. A normally bad situation is compounded in foreign affairs by remoteness and some of the other problems already discussed—the intangibility of goals, the multi-agency mix, and the lack of systematic tools. The feelings run worse from the field to Washington than vice versa. Operators in the field are prone to see Washington as a great bureaucratic sludge which is either unresponsive when something is wanted or bristling with bright ideas that no one needs. The lack of a systematic, meaningful dialogue between Washington and the field is a severe handicap to effective coordination. Repeated so often that it has

---

6. Galbraith, *Ambassador's Journal*, p. 399.

become a cliche is the view that Washington should have a Country Team set-up like the field does.[7]

The general perspective on Washington—that the home office has the wrong priorities, that it does not understand the local situation—applies in reaction to specific Washington decisions communicated to the field. Officials in the field, whether military commanders or ambassadors, are remote from the Washington decisionmaking process. They may from time to time be called back for consultation or receive cables indicating that Washington is contemplating a particular decision and asking for their comments on it. But they do not have the benefit of sitting in the meetings where the new policy has been worked out. They are not always informed about the context in which a decision was made, of the national security considerations that influenced the president, or of the bureaucratic factors that also affected his decision. When the problem of arriving at a decision is tortuous, officials are reluctant to bear the further burden of attempting to clear a cable explaining to the field just why the decision was made. With such an incomplete idea of how a decision was reached, those in the field may feel little commitment to implementing it.

Efforts to keep in touch with what is going on in Washington have been greatly assisted by the revolution in information technology. Whereas ambassadors and field commanders during most of the cold war period had to return to Washington repeatedly to learn what was going on, the advent of multiple channels of electronic communication, as well as around-the-clock worldwide TV news coverage, expanded their ability to keep in touch with many different sources in Washington and to understand the context for decisions without having to make the long trip home.

During the cold war period, top officials in the field relied heavily on cable correspondence, known as "official-informal," with the country director in Washington. In such letters, the country director tried to give the ambassador a sense of the context in which policy decisions had been made and an explanation of the cables that he received or was about to receive. The ambassador, in turn, could use the official-informal channel to provide the desk officer with embassy input to a policy decision. Within the embassy the official-informal cable was strictly controlled by the ambassador and deputy chief of mission (DCM) in an attempt to restrict the embassy's "back channel" communication with Washington. The development of classified e-mail and tele-

7. Harr, *The Professional Diplomat*, pp. 301–02.

phone lines, however, expanded the back channel and greatly complicated the problem of disciplining an embassy's policy input.

Ambassadors and their senior management staff must rely heavily on personal persuasion, convincing senior members of their mission that the embassy can achieve the right policy decisions if it carefully coordinates its communications with Washington. Many ambassadors never achieve that coordination. A few do succeed in making their embassies the focal point for policy initiatives, particularly in countries where knowledge of rapidly shifting local conditions is essential to policy decisions. Former ambassador Peter Galbraith, describing the performance of the U.S. ambassador to Iraq, Zalmay Khalilzad, in 2005, said:

> There's a common misunderstanding that American Ambassadors go and have tea and carry messages that have been formulated in Washington. But, really, the Ambassador is in charge of policy in that country. You have the expertise, the knowledge, and know the people, and ultimately it's your position that gets carried. You have an advantage over the people in Washington. Khalilzad understood this in Afghanistan and he understands it in Iraq. And he's in the business of shaping his own instructions. So when he's going out and talking with Sunni sheikhs, or delaying the constitution to allow compromises to be made, that's him doing it, not Washington.[8]

Ambassadors look to American newspapers, news magazines, and cable TV news to supply a context for policy decisions.[9] They sometimes speak with officials of the country to which they are posted who have been to Washington. John Kenneth Galbraith, as ambassador to India, commented on one such episode: "B. K. Nehru is back for consultation. By querying him on a recent conversation with the President and Secretary, I got an improved view of American policy. One must use the available channels."[10]

When an ambassador receives a message, the ambassador and staff must determine how high up the cable went for clearance. Since all cables are signed officially with the name of the secretary of state, the message itself must indicate whether it is a directive from the president, secretary of state, assistant secretary, or simply the country director under pressure from other agencies. Occasionally the origin of an instruction may not be explained, and the ambassador is left guessing whose wrath he risks incurring if he ignores the instruc-

8. Jon Lee Anderson, "American Viceroy," *New Yorker*, December 19, 2005, p. 58.
9. See, for example, Hughes, *The Ordeal of Power*, p. 157.
10. Galbraith, *Ambassador's Journal*, p. 315.

tion.[11] In most cases, the embassy has wide latitude to decide how and at what level in the host government to carry out an instruction from Washington.

It is not surprising, therefore, that ambassadors and military commanders in the field can easily come to feel that it is their responsibility in certain situations to effectively shape policy toward the country to which they are assigned or the zone of conflict where their forces are engaged. They may view "Washington" as an irrelevant meddler rather than the source of instruction and guidance. Career ambassadors in particular tend to trust only the country director in the State Department (and the country directors in a few major countries), feeling that senior department officials and White House staff are ignorant and constitute an obstacle to be overcome. Political appointee ambassadors, on the other hand, often disregard the department desk officers in the belief that they do not know what the president wants.

One way or another, most officials in the field come to believe that Washington has to be handled with care but circumvented to maintain flexibility for independent action in the field. Bedell Smith, a retired military officer who served as American ambassador in Moscow in the early postwar period, expressed that attitude:

> We knew, of course, that there would be difficulties. The time difference between Moscow and our several capitals was one source. I think we also were conscious of the fact that back in the Foreign Offices at home there were a lot of very able young experts who would feel quite sure (possibly with some reason) that they could conduct the negotiations far better than we could. For this reason we agreed that we would have to be tactful but firm with our own Foreign Offices in order to maintain some freedom of maneuver. Most important of all was the necessity to safeguard carefully the position of our military commanders in Germany, who did not operate directly under Foreign Office or State Department instructions. I had, from the time I arrived in Moscow, been in close touch both officially and personally with General Clay and Ambassador Murphy in Berlin.[12]

Note the comments of former career ambassador Ellis Briggs on the incompetence of Washington and the need for ambassadors to save Washington from ineptness as well as folly:

> Consider the widely believed statement that "an ambassador is merely a Washington messenger boy." That was clearly invented by someone who

11. Dulles, *American Foreign Policy in the Making*, p. 59.
12. Smith, *My Three Years in Moscow*, pp. 241–42.

never served in an embassy. The person who is content to carry messages is in fact a messenger boy, but he has no business being an ambassador. How an envoy delivers a message can be as important as the communication itself. What the ambassador says when he delivers the views of his government can cause the representations to prosper or to fail, regardless of the eloquence of the prose confected in Washington. . . . There are many awkward or infelicitous Washington messages that are rescued from failure by experienced ambassadorial handling. It is the responsibility of the ambassador, as his government's senior agent abroad, to protect his principal from the effects of his folly as well as his wisdom—and always to have Washington think it has cornered the market on clairvoyance.[13]

With recent advances in communications enhancing the ability of an overseas mission, either military or diplomatic, to keep in close contact with Washington, the ability of the missions to affect policy has increased, especially in the case of embassies. Because embassies tend to be a more manageable image of the larger policy bureaucracy in Washington, they often are able to surmount Washington's complex bureaucratic differences—and thus policy stalemates—more easily. An ambassador who can unite the essential elements of the embassy in pursuit of a policy objective in that country can often manage to dictate Washington's position on a given policy issue.

Perceptive officials in Washington, catching glimpses of this attitude, come to understand how little control they have. Dean Acheson wrote that "authority fades with distance and with the speed of light."[14] George Kennan offered a warning on military commands established abroad:

Whoever in Washington takes responsibility for placing a major American armed establishment anywhere beyond our borders, particularly when it is given extensive powers with relation to civil affairs in the area where it is stationed, should remember that he is not thereby creating just an instrument of American policy—he is committing himself seriously to the insights, interests, and decisions of a new bureaucratic power structure situated far from our shores and endowed with its own specific perspective on all problems of world policy; and to this extent he is resigning his own power of control over the use to be made of America's resources in the process of international life.[15]

13. Briggs, *Farewell to Foggy Bottom*, pp. 5–6.
14. Acheson, *Sketches from Life*, p. 48.
15. Kennan, *Memoirs, 1925–1950*, p. 372.

EVADING INSTRUCTIONS

In addition to inadequate information and conflict over control versus autonomy, field operations bear the burden of conforming to standard operating procedures. When given an order from Washington, organizations in the field typically begin to function according to the standard operating procedure that applies most closely to what they are ordered to do. The simple application of existing routines, once Washington accepts or condones a general policy, often leads to a situation in which Washington finds that the constraints that it wished to impose are ineffective. McGeorge Bundy explained how this process led from authorization for a very narrow use of tear gas and herbicides in Vietnam to almost complete freedom on the part of the military in the field to use these weapons as they chose:

> There is, however, one specific lesson from the past which seems to me worth holding in mind. Both in the case of herbicides and in that of tear gas, the initial authorizations for military use in the early 1960's were narrowly framed, at least as understood by civilians in Washington.
>
> The first authorized use of herbicides, as I recall it, was for defoliation along narrow jungle trails. I remember no talk of crop destruction at the beginning. The initial use of tear gas was for situations involving the need to protect civilian lives, in conditions closely analogous to those of a civil riot at home, and indeed in his first public statement on the subject Secretary Rusk made it clear that it was the policy of the administration to authorize the use of such agents only in such riot control situations. But as time passed, increasingly warlike uses were found for both kinds of agents, and in testimony before Congress senior military officials have made it clear that in their view both herbicides and tear gas are now legitimate weapons for use wherever they may do some military good. For example, in authoritative testimony in 1969 before a subcommittee of the House Committee on Foreign Affairs, a senior Pentagon official identified six varied battlefield uses of tear gas, and five separate classes of military use of herbicides. Thus under the pressure of availability and battlefield urgency, the initial authorizations from Washington have been steadily widened. This is not a matter of bad faith or deception. Nor is it primarily a failure of command and control, although tighter and more explicit guidelines could have been useful in limiting the use of these agents. What happened here is what tends to happen quite remorselessly in war: unless there are very sharp and clear defining lines against the use of a given weapon, it tends to be used. Our experi-

ence in Vietnam with herbicides and tear gas is a compelling specific demonstration of the weakness of partial and ambiguous limitations. The only reliable way to keep chemical warfare off any future battlefield is to keep it off in all its forms. And the best way to do that, I repeat, is for the United States to accept the prevailing international view of the meaning of the Geneva Protocol.[16]

Thus Washington lost control over a major issue without a conscious effort by those in the field to usurp presidential prerogatives. In many cases, however, there is conscious maneuvering by officials in the field because of their belief that they know better than Washington what should be done. These maneuvers are similar to those in Washington, but field officials have the enormous advantage that their actions are much more difficult to monitor. Moreover, there is a strong feeling in Washington that field commanders should be given wide latitude in carrying out combat operations. Foreign Service officers also tend to feel that ambassadors should be given latitude, although that view is not generally shared at the top levels of the government.

In describing implementation in general and the perspective from the field, we have already mentioned the techniques employed, but it is worthwhile to emphasize further the effects of great distance and Washington's unfamiliarity with the local situation.

—*Do something else.* Specific instructions to officials in the field often are ignored, and sometimes the actions taken are actually contrary to those instructions. For example, despite President Kennedy's explicit instructions that no Americans were to be included in the force invading Cuba at the Bay of Pigs, an American, in fact, was the first to land.[17]

In many cases, an action taken in violation of instructions comes after an official in the field has pleaded for new instructions and has been refused. For example, many attempts were made in Washington to change the famous JCS 1067 directive, which excluded a number of former Nazis from key job categories in Germany following World War II. According to Robert Murphy, when those attempts had failed, General Lucius Clay, the American commander in Germany, simply "went out on a limb and announced that thereafter we would employ ex-Nazis in skilled jobs. The American government never did cancel this JCS 1067 prohibition; it merely refrained from repudiating Clay's action."[18]

16. Bundy, "The Consideration of the Geneva Protocol of 1925," p. 186.
17. Johnson, *The Bay of Pigs,* p. 101.
18. Murphy, *Diplomat among Warriors,* p. 284.

John Kenneth Galbraith, as ambassador to India, persisted in telling the Indians that the United States was no longer seeking military alliances in that part of the world, and he did so despite clear instructions from Washington, including a personal cable from the secretary of state, instructing him not to say any such thing.[19]

Action in the face of repeated refusal by Washington to change policy may not occur until frustration has built up in the field over an extended time. But in a crisis officials in the field may act as they think best because they believe that Washington simply does not understand the situation. John Bartlow Martin, ambassador to the Dominican Republic during a coup designed to overthrow the popularly elected Juan Bosch, reported that he sent a cable to Washington urging that he be authorized to take strong action to support the Bosch government. He related what happened next:

> And then the cable we had been waiting for came in. It said that the Department could do little more to save Bosch in view of his past performance despite all my efforts to persuade him to govern effectively. The forces arrayed against him were largely of his own creation. Now he must save himself. The Department did not oppose the moves I had already recommended to him but warned me not to tie such moves to any commitment by the United States. It suggested that perhaps he also should take some "positive" steps. (I wondered how.) As for the aircraft carrier, the Department refused to intervene militarily unless a Communist takeover were threatened. A show of force that we were not prepared to back up would only be a meaningless gesture, ineffective in a situation which had gone so far.
>
> I presumed the cable had been cleared with the White House. I showed it to King and Shlaudeman and told them that *nevertheless we would do everything we could to save Bosch tonight.* I went up to the Residence, telling the Marine to put any calls through to me there.[20]

Ambassadors engaged in negotiations also often feel that the situation is breaking too quickly to permit them to accept Washington's instructions. That often is the case at the United Nations when votes have to be cast on resolutions. Moreover, many American delegates to the UN, including Henry Cabot Lodge and Adlai Stevenson, have not felt bound to accept State Department instructions.[21] The temptation is especially keen if ambassadors engaged

19. Galbraith, *Ambassador's Journal,* p. 150.
20. Martin, *Overtaken by Events,* p. 570 (italics added).
21. Murphy, *Diplomat among Warriors,* p. 367; Attwood, *The Reds and the Blacks,* pp. 140–41; Beichman, *The "Other" State Department,* passim.

in negotiations judge that by stretching their instructions they can attain an agreement. They believe that if they do get an agreement, Washington will overlook the fact that they ignored their instructions. If the effort fails, the consequences can be serious for the negotiator. In one famous case, Harold Stassen, U.S. representative at an international disarmament conference, had instructions not to make any proposals to the Russians without clearing them first with Britain and France. Stassen, believing that he was close to a dramatic agreement with the Russians, advanced a proposal without consulting either of the two allies. However, before the Russians could react to the proposal, the British and French learned of the maneuver and complained to Washington. Stassen was quickly recalled to Washington and removed from his post because of the incident.[22]

The technique of stretching instructions in a gamble to get an agreement was evidently common at the meetings of the permanent delegates of the North Atlantic Council. Harlan Cleveland, who was U.S. ambassador to the council during most of the 1960s, gave the following account:

> The advantages of consultation are bound to be more obvious to the full-time consulters, such as an Ambassador at NATO headquarters, than to officials preoccupied with executive decision-making and congressional salesmanship in Washington. Indeed, the best reason for conducting consultations multilaterally in the North Atlantic Council and its subordinate bodies is that the full-time practitioners of multilateral diplomacy develop a "habit of consultation"—that is, they get in the habit of moving slightly beyond their formal instructions.
>
> In a typical case the discussion starts with known governmental positions that are clearly inconsistent with each other and will, if maintained, create a stalemate. But the study of these positions, when they are all laid on the same conference (or luncheon) table, enables each representative to make a judgment about how much his own instructions would have to be bent in order to meet his colleagues'—if they succeed in bending their instructions too. Each representative then reports to his government that a new proposition, not contained in anybody's instructions, might just make it possible to secure agreement. Each representative, in the elementary exercise of bureaucratic caution, attributes this composite formula to one or more other governments, and most of our allies are likely to attribute it to the United States. Without representatives who are willing to operate in that diplomatic no-man's-land beyond their formal

22. Larson, *Eisenhower*, pp. 77–78.

instructions, the efficiency of collective diplomacy would be greatly reduced, and governments might just as well send messages directly from capital to capital even on issues that involve many nations.[23]

Officials who stretch or distort their instructions may or may not report that fact to Washington. They may go so far as to suggest that they took the action as instructed. Washington often has difficulty learning the truth. Even if an official reports that he or she disobeyed instructions, Washington may have to accept it as a fait accompli, or perhaps nobody in Washington will be prepared to expend the energy necessary to send a second cable instructing the ambassador to correct his actions. Indeed, the extreme opposition demonstrated by the ambassador may weaken the coalition that managed to get the first cable out to the point that it cannot clear a second one.

—*Delay.* When an embassy receives a specific instruction that it does not wish to carry out, often the most effective technique is simply to delay taking the action. If pressed, the embassy can report that it plans to move but at an appropriate time and in an appropriate way. Washington often is not in a position to specify when an action should be taken. It frequently is at the mercy of the ambassador or the field commander to determine at what speed and in what form the action should be carried out. George Kennan, at the end of a long description of the process by which the National Security Council reached some fundamental decisions on occupation policy in Japan, wrote with skepticism about how much difference those decisions made with regard to what was done in Japan:

> These recommendations were passed on by the Secretary of State to the Far Eastern Division for its critical comment and clearance. The division accepted them with only one or two minor modifications. But because they involved so heavily our military interests and because their implementation had to proceed primarily through our military authorities, they had also to be submitted to the National Security Council, on which the armed services were powerfully represented, and thus to receive presidential sanction. This took time. Not all of the recommendations were agreeable to all echelons of the armed services whose responsibilities were engaged. Some of the recommendations would interfere, not only with existing armed service policies, but with cherished personal privileges, amenities, and advantages. Nevertheless, the recommendations met after some delay with practically complete acceptance in the National Security Council, and thus became, with presidential approval,

23. Cleveland, *NATO*, pp. 28–29.

the basis for orders issued—mostly at the end of 1948 or the beginning of 1949—by the service departments to the occupational headquarters in Tokyo.

How, at what stages, and in what degree these decisions finally found realization in the actions and practices of SCAP, I cannot tell. I think it likely that General MacArthur, being largely in agreement with them and well informed of the deliberations in Washington that led to their final adoption, anticipated them at many points by the exercise of his own great executive powers. Part of them were no doubt well on the way to implementation before Washington had even finished its deliberations. If, on the other hand, there were certain features that did not meet with General MacArthur's full approval, he had ample means of delaying, if not frustrating, their execution. For these reasons the effect of the decisions in Japan was probably a gradual and to many an almost imperceptible one. Mr. Sebald says nothing in his memoirs to indicate that he ever heard of these decisions, though he does refer to a number of the changes pursuant to them that took place in 1949. The memoirs of General Willoughby, too, reveal no awareness on his part of any of the above. One has at times the feeling that Washington did not loom very large on the horizons of this highly self-centered occupational command.[24]

—*Do nothing.* Rather than taking a different action or implementing a decision slowly, officials in the field may simply do nothing when they receive a cable. On occasion they count on the fact that Washington will find it difficult to force action or indeed even to monitor noncompliance. For example, in the midst of one of the many Laotian crises, the U.S. ambassador to Vientiane, Winthrop Brown, received a cable advising him to take such action as would remove Kong Le, who had then seized power, from the scene as expeditiously as possible. Since the message gave no specific orders as to how Brown should accomplish that objective and since in his view it was impossible to do so, he simply ignored the cable and made no move against Kong Le.[25]

—*Obey the letter but not the spirit of the instructions.* Following the letter of instructions but ignoring their spirit can take a number of different forms in the field. A diplomat who is under orders to press a foreign government to carry out some action may go through the motions but slant his conversation

24. Kennan, *Memoirs, 1925–1950,* pp. 392–93. See also Dunn, *Peace-Making and the Settlement with Japan,* pp. 74–78, where Kennan's analysis of the very gradual pace of the implementation of this policy change and the ability of General MacArthur to resist change is corroborated in detail.

25. Dommen, *Conflict in Laos,* pp. 157–58.

in a way that makes it clear to the foreign official that he does not agree. Alternatively, one can convey information to a foreign government through a channel that makes it almost certain that the message will be ignored. Elizabeth Drew described one such episode during the period following the collapse of Biafra:

> Another interagency meeting was convened on January 2, and it adopted most of the proposals that had been deferred almost a week earlier. Ten days had passed since the collapse of Biafra. The embassy in Lagos was instructed to bring the Western report to the attention of the Nigerian government. Two days later, the embassy sent word back that the report was given to the Ministry of Health by an AID doctor who, it added, could not be expected to support its findings. The embassy said that it believed another survey was necessary. This transmittal of the report— routine, at low levels, with no sense of urgency—was not what Washington had in mind. The Ambassador, William Trueheart, reported that despite Washington's instructions he did not believe that 10,000 tons a week was necessary, and that he could not be expected to convince the Nigerians of the revised, higher need. He argued that the problem needed more study, and that there was a better chance of getting the Nigerians to act if they were not "nudged."[26]

One can also report that the official to whom one was told to speak was not available and that therefore one has taken up the matter with a lesser official who will report the information to the senior official.

A subtle way of obeying the spirit but not the letter of instructions is to "overachieve." Galbraith described an incident when as ambassador to India he thwarted the will of the State Department by pressing even harder than the department wanted him to on making concessions that would ease the Kashmir dispute.

> Actually, one thing was accomplished. Until last week, the Department had felt I was dragging my feet. In the course of the week, there was increasing alarm that I was pressing Nehru too hard. A telegram questioned my "all or nothing" approach. They felt I left inadequate room for retreat. This is one of many cases where the element of personal strategy enters diplomacy. My instinct was against pressing Nehru too hard. We stood to lose some of the character we gained last fall, make cooperation on other matters more difficult and probably accomplish nothing. But if I did not press

26. Drew, "Washington," p. 21.

hard, the failure would be blamed on me. "Galbraith was reluctant to come to grips with the great man; another ambassador protecting his client." Apart from being bad for me personally, this would have meant pressure for a new effort later on. So I made the best of a bad situation and tried too hard. I won't be blamed for failure, and won't be asked for more effort. I have the feeling these may be the last of the talks.[27]

—*Ask them to reconsider.* If an ambassador in the field is reluctant simply to disobey or ignore an order, he or she can send Washington a cable explaining why the action proposed would not be sensible and asking for a new decision. For reasons indicated above, that often works. The narrow coalition put together in Washington to get a proposal through may be shattered by a strong cable from the ambassador asking for reconsideration. Tired by the first battle, those who press for a particular decision often do not have the energy to renew it. They sense that even if they get out a reaffirming cable, the ambassador may then resort to one of the other techniques to avoid putting the decision into effect. They also must allow for the possibility that the ambassador may be correct in saying that the action he or she opposes will not accomplish the purpose intended.[28]

ACTIONS IN THE ABSENCE OF A DECISION

Field missions, like agencies in Washington, prefer if possible to act without presidential decisions. Karl Rankin, a career official who was ambassador to Taiwan, reflected the prevalent view:

An unwritten law in the Foreign Service is: Never ask for instructions from Washington if you can help it. It is presumed that the officer in the field is familiar with official policy; in most cases he is in a better position than anyone else to decide how a given problem should be handled in the light of that policy, and whether circumstances demand that he ask for instructions.[29]

Emissaries may feel that they have no choice but to respond immediately to a question put to them by a foreign leader. Failure to respond, they fear, will demonstrate their own lack of knowledge of policy (and hence reduce their

27. Galbraith, *Ambassador's Journal,* p. 564.
28. For examples of reclama, see Attwood, *The Reds and the Blacks,* pp. 92–93; Hilsman, *To Move a Nation,* pp. 488–89; Beichman, *The "Other" State Department,* pp. 8–81.
29. Rankin, *China Assignment,* p. ix.

effectiveness as an envoy) or will reveal that Washington has no policy. Alternatively, they may fear that Washington's answer, although it would authorize them to respond as they would like, would come too late to be effective. Dean Acheson related one such incident when he was briefing French president Charles de Gaulle on the Cuban missile crisis:

> "Suppose they don't do anything—suppose they don't try to break the blockade—suppose they don't take the missiles out—what will your President do then?" When I left Washington nobody had told me the answer to that question. I don't know whether a plan existed, but if it did, I didn't know it. But I thought it would be most unwise to indicate to General de Gaulle that we were not absolutely clear as to what we were going to do in each stage of this—and I said, "We will immediately tighten this blockade and the next thing we would do is to stop tankers—and this will bring Cuba to a standstill in no time at all." He said, "That's very good" again. I said, "If we have to go further why, of course, we'll go further." He said, "I understand."[30]

William Attwood reported a similar episode, when, as ambassador to Guinea, he had no instructions but would not admit it and nevertheless responded affirmatively to a request for help. "I made this offer on my own, knowing that Washington would have approved, but also would have been bureaucratically unable to get the approval to me in time had I requested it."[31]

One reason for taking action without requesting approval is, of course, to avoid the refusal that might ensue. Adlai Stevenson made such a move while ambassador to the United Nations, in an effort to break a deadlock over Article 19, which provided that countries in arrears in their payments to the UN could not vote. Stevenson on his own arranged a meeting with the Soviet Union's ambassador to the United Nations. During the course of the meeting Stevenson and Ambassador Fedorenko worked out an arrangement under which the General Assembly would meet but postpone any vote about the status of the Soviet Union. Stevenson reported their arrangement to the State Department, which felt under pressure to go along.[32]

If ambassadors are not prepared to act without instructions, they can take steps that maximize the probability of getting the decision that they want. The mildest form of this maneuver is simply to send a cable to Washington proposing the instructions that one would like to have, recognizing that the cable

30. Acheson, Kennedy Library Oral History Interview, p. 28.
31. Attwood, *The Reds and the Blacks,* p. 63.
32. Beichman, *The "Other" State Department,* pp. 149–58.

is likely to become the basis for drafting instructions and that one has gained a substantial advantage by having others work from one's draft.

A stronger version is to indicate the course of action that one plans to take and to state that one proposes to act by a certain date unless the department advises to the contrary. That puts the supporters of the proposed action in Washington in a strong position, since they only have to find ways to delay sending out a cable in response.[33]

Even ambassadors who ask for instructions sometimes find that they must act before instructions arrive. Henry S. Villard, a career Foreign Service officer who was then Ambassador to Libya, told of a typical episode in which he was involved:

> The [Libyan] Prime Minister had resigned and flown off to Rome, his nerves frayed by the thankless task of guiding a newborn state. The King was ill, in seclusion; there was a rumor in the bazaars that he might abdicate. The whole government structure seemed about to collapse. I had just reached a vital point in negotiations for an air-base agreement. So when the Libyan cabinet asked me to fly to Italy and persuade the Prime Minister to return, I cabled the Department urgently for permission to make the try.
>
> Time was of the essence, yet the hours ticked by without response. In Washington, the wheels ground methodically. Committee met with committee, weighing the pros and cons of my recommendation. The Pentagon had to be consulted. Policy factors had to be considered; so did tactics, in the light of progress to date on the air-base negotiations. Suggestions at a lower level had to be referred to a higher level for further discussion. I sent a second cable. No reply.
>
> Finally, I decided to act on my own. I boarded the plane of my Air Attache, flew to Rome, and called on the Prime Minister at his hotel. With all the eloquence I could muster, I urged him to come back and steer the ship of state through the storm, pointing out that the fate of his country—and our delicate negotiations—rested in his hands alone. He heard me in silence, still smarting from the political wounds which had caused him to resign. He would think it over; he would give me his answer that evening.
>
> At eight o'clock I was again at the Prime Minister's door. His face was wreathed in smiles. He would do as I asked, and to mark the occasion he invited me to dine with him downstairs. With a load like lead off my

---

33. Galbraith describes one such episode in *Ambassador's Journal*, p. 391.

mind, I was enjoying the repast when I spied an officer of our Rome Embassy discreetly waving a piece of paper from behind the potted palms. I made my excuses, rose, and went over to receive the message—a priority cable to Tripoli, repeated to Rome for information. At long last, Washington had moved. There were my orders. Under no circumstance was I to follow the Prime Minister to Rome, for that, the Department feared, might be interpreted as interference in the domestic affairs of a sovereign country.[34]

Having explored some of the reasons why participants, both in Washington and in the field, neglect to implement policy and having outlined techniques available to them to resist presidential or department directives, we are ready to consider the options left to the president for gaining compliance.

34. Villard, "How To Save Money: An Open Letter to Congressman John J. Rooney," pp. 2–22. For a similar episode, see Attwood, *The Reds and the Blacks*, pp. 200–202.

CHAPTER FIFTEEN

Presidential Control

According to some standard accounts of how the U.S. government works, the only time the bureaucracy can ignore presidential orders is when the president is uninterested or unconcerned in a matter. If the president devotes his personal attention to a matter, it is said, the bureaucracy and his principal subordinates have no choice but to obey. Yet the evidence indicates the contrary. Even when the president does devote his time and effort and the issue is critical, disobedience can occur.

The Cuban missile crisis is often taken as the extreme example of presidential involvement. President Kennedy did almost nothing during the period of the Cuban missile crisis but work on the crisis, devoting his attention to even the most minute details. In Robert Kennedy's words:

> Despite the heavy pressure on the big decisions, President Kennedy followed every detail. He requested, for instance, the names of all the Cuban doctors in the Miami area, should their services be required in Cuba. Learning that a U.S. military ship with extremely sensitive equipment (similar to the Liberty, which was struck by Israel during the Israeli-Arab war) was very close to the coast of Cuba, he ordered it farther out to sea, where it would be less vulnerable to attack. He supervised everything, from the contents of leaflets to be dropped over Cuba to the assembling of ships for the invasion.[1]

Yet during that period, the president's orders on a number of critical issues were not obeyed in the manner that he had intended. At one point a tentative

1. Kennedy, *Thirteen Days*, p. 86.

presidential decision that he would authorize bombing of Cuba if an American U-2 was shot down was taken by the Air Force as sufficient authority to proceed with bombing when an American U-2 was attacked. It was only at the last minute that the Air Force's interpretation was discovered and the attack called back. Although the president had given no orders that would permit American vessels to attack Soviet submarines and believed that there had been no contact between Soviet and American forces, in fact throughout the period the American Navy was forcing Soviet submarines in the Caribbean to surface. Despite the president's order to put forces on the alert in case of military confrontation, American aircraft remained lined up wingtip to wingtip on airfields in the southern part of the United States. Despite an explicit presidential order, issued over intense Navy opposition, to move the blockade line closer to Cuba, the line remained where the Navy wanted it. Despite a presidential order to avoid provocative intelligence operations, an American U-2 strayed over Soviet territory at the very height of the crisis.[2]

President Truman fared little better during the opening days of the Korean War, despite his personal attention to the matters at hand. American pilots failed to attack invading tanks in the Seoul area, despite Truman's explicit decision that they should be permitted to do so. Without authorization from Washington, General MacArthur ordered an attack on an airfield in North Korea.[3]

Such resistance can extend to even the most trivial items. For example, President Kennedy was unsuccessful in his desire to choose the names for American ships. As Theodore Sorensen explained:

> On the other hand, a President's personal interests may draw to him decisions normally left for others. Roosevelt, for example, took a hand in deciding postage stamp designs. I have seen President Kennedy engrossed in a list of famous Indian chiefs, deciding on an appropriate name for a nuclear submarine. (Inasmuch as most of the chiefs had earned their fame by defying the armed might of the United States, it was not an easy decision. In fact, when he finally decided on Chief Red Cloud, the Navy protested that this name had undesirable foreign-policy implications.)[4]

2. See Allison, *Essence of Decision*, p. 137–42; Abel, *The Missile Crisis*, pp. 193–94; Schlesinger, *A Thousand Days*, p. 828; Hilsman, *To Move a Nation*, p. 221.

3. Paige, *The Korean Decision*, pp. 181, 364–65.

4. Sorensen, *Decision-Making in the White House*, p. 17.

As Truman summed it up in his often quoted remark about Eisenhower: "He'll sit here and he'll say, 'Do this! Do that!' *And nothing will happen.* Poor Ike—it won't be a bit like the Army. He'll find it very frustrating."[5]

PRESIDENTIAL STRATEGIES TO GAIN COMPLIANCE

Even if the thrust of Truman's observations is correct, nevertheless it is not true that nothing ever happens. The resistance of the bureaucracy to implementation has a vital effect on the way that decisions are made in the first place, and presidents, as they become accustomed to resistance, tend to develop ways to deal with it.

By the authority of his office and the position from which he plays the game, the president enjoys certain powers that make it possible for him to break down some bureaucratic resistance. Richard Neustadt's study of presidential power provides a cogent summary of what those assets are:

> Governmental power, in reality not form, is influence of an effective sort on the behavior of men actually involved in making public policy and carrying it out. Effective influence for the man in the White House stems from three related sources: first are the bargaining advantages inherent in his job with which to persuade other men that what he wants of them is what their own responsibilities require them to do. Second are the expectations of those other men regarding his ability and will to use the various advantages they think he has. Third are those men's estimates of how his public views him and of how their publics may view them if they do what he wants. In short, his power is the product of his vantage points in government, together with his reputation in the Washington community and his prestige outside.[6]

By virtue of the assets peculiar to his position, the president may maneuver in a number of ways to increase the probability that his orders will be obeyed.[7] His demonstrated willingness to maneuver increases the likelihood that in the future his orders will be obeyed without his implementing some

5. Quoted in Neustadt, *Presidential Power,* p. 9.
6. Ibid., p. 179.
7. Most of these maneuvers will be familiar to the reader because they are similar to those discussed in the section on the decision process. The distinction being made here is the effect of resistance to implementation on the way that a president maneuvers to gain compliance. It is obvious that the processes of decisionmaking and implementation are so interrelated that it is impossible to separate one from the other completely.

of the more drastic measures. The maneuvers available to the president include the following:

Persuasion

One of the president's most important assets is his ability to persuade his principal associates that something that he wishes to do is in the national interest. Most participants believe that they should do anything that is required to ensure the security of the United States. They recognize that the president is the only government official chosen in a national election and that he therefore has a much stronger mandate than they do to define the national interest. Moreover, the president is seen as having a wider area of responsibility. Thus participants take the president's arguments very seriously, particularly when he delivers them personally and when he invokes national security considerations. In fact, every president spends a good deal of time capitalizing on the aura of his power to convince principal associates that they should do what he has decided should be done. As President Truman once put it, "I sit here all day trying to persuade people to do the things they ought to have sense enough to do without my persuading them. . . . That's all the powers of the President amount to."[8]

A president is most persuasive when he makes his pitch personally in direct conversation with those involved. That may mean that he must meet with officials with whom he does not normally confer or with those who must implement a decision to ensure that they have a chance to argue with him personally and hear directly from him what he wants them to do. President Truman, for example, determined to reassert civilian control over atomic energy, called in the officer he was about to appoint as the Army's director of the nuclear weapons program to replace the legendary General Groves, who had run the program during World War II. Although there was no question of whether he would approve the appointment, Truman recognized the importance of laying down his own position in person. David Lilienthal, then chairman of the Atomic Energy Commission, described the scene:

> Talked to Secretary Royall and Col. Nichols outside the President's office; they said they didn't know what the meeting was about, that Royall hadn't asked for it.
>
> The President said he had before him the recommendation of the promotion of Col. Nichols as head of the Armed Forces Special Weapons

8. Quoted in Neustadt, *Presidential Power,* pp. 9–10.

Project, that he wanted to have a talk with us before acting on it. "I don't want another General Groves incident." Royall injected to say that he saw after his trip West that that situation was as I had said it was, quite impossible.

The President said, "I want it clearly understood before I act on this appointment that this is a civilian-run agency, and I thought I ought to say this to you directly. It requires cooperation between the civilian and the military, of course." Nichols said, "You can count on 100 percent cooperation." I said, "You have a team, Mr. President."⁹

Unless the president can succeed in persuading his principal associates to do as he wishes, he is likely to find that his decisions do not turn into effective actions.

Negotiation

When the president cannot persuade, he must seek to negotiate. His principal associates and the career organizations of the government constantly need things from the president and wish to avoid an all-out confrontation with him. Thus if they are not willing simply to obey his directives on an issue about which the president feels very strongly, they are likely to be willing to compromise. A president who is prepared to negotiate and to throw other issues into the pot can often persuade others to go along with what he wants. However, in the absence of such negotiations, he is unlikely to get cooperation in seeking to override strong organizational interests.

President Eisenhower in his conversation with President-elect Kennedy during the transition period was amazed to discover that Kennedy seemed unaware of the limitations on presidential power to enforce decisions. Kennedy had raised with Eisenhower questions about the desirability of a rather sweeping reorganization of the Department of Defense that had been proposed to him by a task force. Eisenhower, who had spent the better part of his second term using all his prestige as a war hero and former five-star general to get enacted a much more limited reorganization, was appalled at Kennedy's assumption that the only issue was whether the reorganization made sense. He was conscious that any such reorganization would require endless negotiations and compromise. In a memorandum to himself describing the conversation, he put the point well:

9. Lilienthal, *Journals,* p. 303.

I did urge him to avoid any reorganization until he himself could become well acquainted with the problem. (Incidentally, I made this same suggestion with respect to the White House staff, the National Security Council, and the Pentagon.) I told him that improvements could undoubtedly be made in the Pentagon and the command organization, but I also made it clear that the present organization and the improved functioning of the establishment had, during the past eight years, been brought about by patient study and long and drawn out negotiations with the Congress and the Armed Services.[10]

Concerns expressed by friendly foreign leaders about U.S. policy, however, can sometimes be easier to assuage. In 1983, when President Reagan took his Cabinet by surprise with his Star Wars speech, which announced his intention to put an end to the threat of nuclear weapons by developing a space-based missile defense system, he met strong objections from key officials who would be responsible for implementing such a program—the Joint Chiefs of Staff, the secretary of defense, and the secretary of state. Reagan's intense commitment to the program, however, forced all of them to find a way to accommodate his wishes, some more than others. Not the least of the skeptics was his good friend British prime minister Margaret Thatcher, who saw its potential for splitting the NATO alliance and pleaded with Reagan not to jettison the ABM treaty. To allay her concerns, Reagan agreed to endorse her statement that SDI was only under research and would not be deployed without negotiation. Nonetheless, as one observer concluded, "All Reagan's own subsequent statements and decisions made clear that he had not meant to confine SDI to the laboratory. Nor had he meant to deliver a ringing reaffirmation of the ABM treaty. He had simply wanted to tell Margaret Thatcher what she wanted to hear, to let her say what she wanted to say, and to cast SDI in the terms most acceptable to an important ally."[11]

Abusive Behavior

Some chief executives switch from persuasion to bullying and hectoring to keep subordinates in line. The president in ceremonial terms stands above his colleagues in a way that no prime minister in a parliamentary system does. He is "Mr. President" even to those who have known him long and intimately prior to his election, and he is treated with the deference of a head of state

10. Eisenhower, *Waging Peace*, p. 713.
11. Talbott, *The Master of the Game*, p. 207.

while functioning as a head of government. If he is prepared to use the leverage that his status accords him and exploit the extreme reluctance of others to engage in a rough-and-tumble argument with him, he can gain some control over his senior associates. Presidents Truman, Kennedy, and Nixon are in general identified with considerate treatment of subordinates, though exceptional incidents might be cited. On the other hand, the famous Eisenhower temper exploded occasionally, and Lyndon Johnson was well known for his abuse of subordinates. Philip Geyelin described one of the first such occasions, when Johnson and his principal advisers were preparing for a visit of British prime minister Harold Wilson to Washington to seek agreement to move forward on the MLF:

> In the course of the protracted conferences in preparation for the Wilson visit, Johnson assailed the men around him, questioning their competence as well as their counsel. It was at one of these sessions that Johnson ticked off each man in turn. Ball was upbraided for the "disgraceful" caliber of ambassadorial candidates served up by the State Department. Dean Acheson, sitting in as private consultant, was needled "as the man who got us into war in Korea" and had to "get Eisenhower to get us out of it." McNamara was derided for his easy assurances that the MLF could be sold to Congress; commended, sarcastically, for his command of Senate politics; and reminded that if MLF was to be sold to Congress, the job would have to be done by the President himself. Acheson, according to reports, finally broke the mounting tension by declaring: "Mr. President, you don't pay these men enough to talk to them that way—even with the federal pay raise."
>
> Rough as some of the sessions apparently were, they were also instructive. Few who were there or heard about it would thereafter make any quick assumptions about what would be palatable and what would not when presented to Lyndon Johnson. Few would come unprepared to present their case in minute and, if possible, irrefutable detail. And few would presume to speak for the President without being quite certain where he stood. It was a memorable object lesson in Johnson decision-making, a major development in the President's move towards mastery of the "processes," a significant turn in the U.S. approach to Alliance policy.[12]

---

12. Geyelin, *LBJ and the World*, pp. 162–63.

Taking Over as Desk Officer

Another source of power that the president has is the ability to personally take charge of as much of the execution of policy as possible. When the president makes a decision to communicate certain information to another government or to the American public and then does so himself in a speech, he is combining the roles of decisionmaker and practitioner in a way that gives him maximum control over the implementing process. That is also the case when the president calls in a foreign ambassador resident in Washington and conveys his views on a particular subject. As Theodore Sorensen explained, that is what Kennedy did in dealing with the Berlin crisis:

> His second basic decision was to take complete charge of the operation. For months he saturated himself in the problem. He reviewed and revised the military contingency plans, the conventional force build-up, the diplomatic and propaganda initiatives, the budget changes, and the plans for economic welfare. He considered the effect each move would have on Berlin morale, Allied unity, Soviet intransigence, and his own legislative and foreign aid program. He talked to Allied leaders, to Gromyko, and to the Germans; he kept track of all the cables; he read transcripts of all the conferences; and he complained (with limited success) about the pace at the Department of State, about leaks from Allied clearances, and about the lack of new diplomatic suggestions.[13]

The second President Bush chose to become directly involved in the development of war plans for the 2003 attack on Iraq, confining his deliberations to a small group including only the secretary of defense and the military commander charged with responsibility for the plans. The Joint Chiefs of Staff were brought into the president's confidence only well after the plans had been developed.[14]

The president, of course, pays a price for taking direct charge of operations. He and his staff may lack all of the relevant facts. More important, the president uses up time that could be employed to become more intensively involved in several other issues. Consequently he may limit his involvement somewhat, especially when negotiations need to be conducted overseas, by appointing a trusted agent and in effect playing the role of desk officer with respect to that agent. That is what Kennedy did in the test ban negotiations,

13. Sorensen, *Kennedy,* pp. 586–87.
14. Woodward, *Plan of Attack,* pp. 205–208.

sending Averell Harriman and taking personal charge of communications with him.[15]

An active president not only makes speeches and issues press statements but also, on occasion, becomes a "working member of the bureaucracy" by making announcements in the name of his press secretary or a Cabinet officer or arranging leaks to the press in order to communicate to his own government as well as foreign governments. Thus, determined to put an end to excessive American pressure for a multilateral force, Lyndon Johnson first had his advisers prepare a precise memorandum laying out what could and could not be done. Then he not only sent it to senior participants but leaked the entire memorandum to the *New York Times,* thereby communicating it to lower-level officials who supported his position as well as to foreign governments. The implied message was that any American official who applied pressure on behalf of the MLF was acting without the president's support.[16]

Changing Personnel

The president has almost unlimited legal power to appoint and replace his principal advisers. In the case of military advisers, he is constrained to appoint career people from the established services, but even then he has latitude regarding whom he appoints and whether people are kept in a position. A president determined to enforce a particular policy can do so in part by systematically removing from office anyone who opposes that policy. President Truman, battling against the pressure for preventive war in the early postwar period, removed Secretary of the Navy Francis P. Matthews from the Cabinet and named him ambassador to Ireland after Matthews made a speech calling for preventive war, and Truman retired the commandant of the Air War College, who also made such a proposal.[17] After Admiral George W. Anderson resisted Kennedy's orders during the Cuban missile crisis, he was appointed ambassador to Portugal.[18]

As those examples suggest, an official who has influence with an important group in the bureaucracy or elsewhere usually receives another post rather than outright dismissal. When President Kennedy decided that he had to replace Chester Bowles, a leader of the Democratic Party's left wing, as under secretary of state, long negotiations ensued to be sure that Bowles would not

---

15. Sorensen, *Kennedy,* p. 735.

16. Geyelin, *LBJ and the World,* pp. 175–76.

17. Acheson, *Present at the Creation,* p. 478. See also Truman, *Years of Trial and Hope,* pp. 383–84, on the decision to relieve General MacArthur.

18. Korb, "Budget Strategies of the Joint Chiefs of Staff," p. 6.

resign with a blast at the president's policy. Bowles ultimately was persuaded to accept the position of special presidential adviser on developing nations.[19]

When President Reagan's second administration became enmeshed in the Iran-Contra scandal, which was brought on by the president's National Security Council (NSC) staff, one of the main elements of Reagan's remedy was to replace several key staff members, including the national security adviser himself, Admiral John Poindexter.

Appointing an Agent

Rather than seeking to fill an existing position with a new official, a president often resorts to the technique of appointing a special agent who does not have commitments to a particular bureaucratic organization and is free to cut across the concerns of various departments. Henry Kissinger, writing before he joined the Nixon administration, explained the maneuver:

> The executive [is driven] in the direction of extrabureaucratic means of decision. The practice of relying on special emissaries or personal envoys is an example; their status outside the bureaucracy frees them from some of its restraints. International agreements are sometimes possible only by ignoring safeguards against capricious action. It is a paradoxical aspect of modern bureaucracies that their quest for objectivity and calculability often leads to impasses which can be overcome only by essentially arbitrary decisions.[20]

President Nixon often relied on Henry Kissinger in precisely this way, and John F. Kennedy relied on Averell Harriman to negotiate both the Laos agreement and the test ban treaty. Harriman was given wide discretionary powers and authority to deal directly with the president, and his appointment signaled to the Russians a serious intention to negotiate.[21] President Truman resorted to a special agent to break a logjam on the question of a Japanese peace treaty. With the State Department pressing for an early treaty and the Joint Chiefs of Staff and the secretary of defense resisting, Truman decided that he wanted to move forward and recognized that the only way to do so was to give a person with influence and energy the mission of getting a peace treaty. As Dean Rusk recalled the episode:

19. Bowles, *Promises to Keep*, pp. 36–67.
20. Kissinger, *American Foreign* Policy, p. 511.
21. Brandon, *Anatomy of Error*, p. 16; Schlesinger, *A Thousand Days*, pp. 902–03.

One of the most effective task-force exercises was the practically one-man task force that John Foster Dulles constituted in getting the Japanese Peace Treaty. I think that had we tried to handle that problem on an interdepartmental committee basis, we could never have gotten that peace treaty negotiated and ratified. He simply took it on with a two-page letter from the President, saying, "Dear Mr. Dulles: I want you to get a peace treaty of this sort with Japan." On the basis of that, he could cut away the stacks of materials that had developed over the years in the departments. He concentrated on a simple treaty of reconciliation. My job then, as Assistant Secretary of Far Eastern Affairs, was not only to support him, but to block off interference from all the other agencies. They knew that if they wanted to interfere they had to go to the President, and this was difficult to do.[22]

Henry Kissinger reprised his role as agent early in the administration of the first President Bush, when he convinced the president-elect, even before his inauguration in January 1989, to dispatch him to Moscow to sound out Gorbachev on the notion of arriving at a confidential agreement for managing political transition in Eastern Europe. In the end, President Bush decided to engage directly with Gorbachev on the sensitive transition issues, without using an intermediary.[23]

Though it was a truly unique role, Ambassador L. Paul Bremer's tenure as presidential envoy to Iraq from May 2003 to June 2004 is indicative of the increased bureaucratic strain that can be caused by a special envoy's extrabureaucratic position and the president's direct interest in an issue. As administrator of the Coalition Provisional Authority, Bremer was given "all executive, legislative, and judicial functions" in Iraq, serving as a modern viceroy with the task of stabilizing Iraq after the U.S.-led invasion. Bremer worked regularly with Secretary of State Colin Powell and spoke with his official boss, Defense Secretary Donald Rumsfeld, on a daily basis, but he also would often meet alone with the president on trips back to the United States. Bremer recalled that before leaving for Iraq, he met privately with President Bush immediately before a larger meeting with Powell; Rumsfeld; the White House chief of staff, Andrew Card; and the national security adviser, Condoleezza Rice. When the others were ushered in, "Bush waved me to the chair beside him and joked, 'I don't know whether we need this meeting after all. Jerry and I have just had it.'. . . His message was clear. I was neither Rumsfeld's nor Powell's man. I was the president's man."[24]

22. Rusk, "The Secretary of State," p. 269. See also Acheson, *Present at the Creation*, p. 432; Cohen, *The Political Process and Foreign Policy*, p. 127.

23. Beschloss and Talbott, *At the Highest Levels*, pp. 13–20.

24. Bremer, *My Year in Iraq*, pp. 12–13

Despite a direct line to the president, Bremer's position, reporting to both the Pentagon and the White House, wreaked havoc with the normal bureaucratic channels. As a result, the White House attempted to reassert control. Bremer recalled how, during one of his trips back from Iraq, Andrew Card had to fight to make sure that Bremer's access to the president was not being hindered by the bureaucracy:

Andy Card caught my arm as we left the Situation Room. "Got a minute, Jerry? I'd like a quick chat." We went up one flight of stairs to the office of the chief of staff. Card closed the door behind us.

"I want to help you in any way I can," he said. "But you've got to be absolutely frank with the president about your views. I've got the impression that people in Washington are 'gaming' you."

I knew what he meant: when a policy failed, it was handy for the senior bureaucrats to find scapegoats.

Well, we're not going to fail, I thought.

"Don't worry. I'll be absolutely frank with the president. I always have been."

[After Bremer expressed his concerns about the policies], Card said he agreed and wondered if I should have a private meeting with the president. I replied that this would be awkward, given that my boss Rumsfeld disagreed with me.

The next day, after another NSC meeting, the president asked Bremer for a private meeting. Over a one-on-one lunch, the president asked me about my relationship with Rumsfeld. "What kind of a person is he to work for? Does he really micromanage?"

"I like Don, Mr. President," I said. "I've known him thirty years, admire him, and consider him highly intelligent. But he does micromanage."

This seemed to surprise the president.

"Don terrifies his civilian subordinates, so that I can rarely get any decisions out of anyone but him. This works all right, but isn't ideal," I said. . . .

"Frankly, I'm concerned that a lot of the Pentagon's frenetic push on the political stuff is meant to set me up as a fall guy."

He looked surprised. "What do you mean by that?"

"Well, in effect the DOD position would be that they'd recommended a quick end to 'occupation,' but I had resisted, and so any problems from here on out were my fault."

"Don't worry about that," the president said as we got up from lunch. "I'll cover you here."[25]

Creating a New Institution

When the president wishes to negotiate with a foreign government, he may be able to do so himself or pick an individual from outside regular channels in order to accomplish his purpose. However, when he wishes to use military force or have another large, complicated project carried out, he must rely on a major formal organization. If the president realizes that the existing organizations are not carrying out his decisions, he may seek to alter the organizations or create a new one. Doing so is a difficult and time-consuming task that a president undertakes, if at all, only after much hesitation. Tired of receiving conflicting intelligence reports from different agencies, Truman insisted upon the creation of a central intelligence agency following World War II. President Eisenhower agreed to the creation of the National Aeronautics and Space Agency after the military services showed they were not willing to concentrate on the scientific aspects of space exploration. President Kennedy sought, in effect, to create a new institution in the form of the Army Special Forces, converting them from a guerrilla force for a large war in Europe to an organization that would have a strong counterinsurgency mission. Arthur Schlesinger described the great difficulties and resistance that Kennedy encountered:

> Guerrillas were also an old preoccupation of Walt Rostow's [sic]. When Kennedy read Lansdale's report about guerrilla success in Vietnam, he asked Rostow to check into what the Army was, in fact, doing about counterguerrilla training. He was soon informed that the Special Forces at Fort Bragg consisted of fewer than a thousand men. Looking at the field manuals and training literature, he tossed them aside as "meager" and inadequate. Reading Mao Tse-tung and Che Guevara himself on the subject, he told the Army to do likewise. (He used to entertain his wife on country weekends by inventing aphorisms in the manner of Mao's "Guerrillas must move among the people as fish swim in the sea.") He asked General Clifton, his military aide, to bring in the Army's standard anti-guerrilla equipment, examined it with sorrow and ordered Army research and development to do better. Most important of all, he instructed the Special Warfare Center at Fort Bragg to expand its mission, which had hitherto been largely the training of cadres for action

25. Ibid., pp. 206–209.

behind the lines in case of a third world war, in order to confront the existing challenge of guerrilla warfare in the jungles and hills of under-developed countries. Over the opposition of the Army bureaucracy, which abhorred separate elite commands on principle, he reinstated the SF green beret as the symbol of the new force.[26]

DEGREES OF CONTROL

In previous chapters we surveyed the array of maneuvers available to the bureaucracy and its representatives in the field to resist presidential orders or to carry on without them. In the present chapter we have covered countervailing maneuvers open to the president. What determines the outcome of the struggle? And how does the determining factor reflect back on the decision-making process?

The relative weight in the decisionmaking process of the president's influence, the interests of subordinates, and standard operating procedures depends on several factors. One is the degree of presidential involvement, which can vary enormously. Obviously the deeper the president involves himself in operations, the more influence he has over what is done. In part, that is simply because he is able to do more of it himself, but it is also because by devoting a substantial amount of time to an issue, the president makes it clear to his subordinates that it is something that he cares a great deal about. Officials recognize that to fight the president on such an issue is likely to cost them dearly in terms of their relations with the president. They also recognize that the president is much more likely to learn of a failure to implement a decision on an issue that he is closely monitoring than one on which he made a single decision and then assumed that it was being followed. When the president is actively involved in an issue, he also is likely to speak out publicly on it, thereby committing his prestige in Washington, the country, and the world to its outcome.

The second major factor affecting the line between presidential influence and that of other participants is the nature of what the president wants to have done. At one extreme, if an action is a simple one that can be carried out by a single individual in Washington without detailed technical expertise or training, presidential influence is likely to be overwhelming. To the degree that an action is a complicated one, requiring the cooperation of large numbers of people, many of them stationed outside Washington, presidential influence on

26. Schlesinger, *A Thousand Days*, p. 341.

implementation fades. Two of President Nixon's decisions in regard to U.S.-China policy illustrate the point. The first involved the president's determination to arrange for a trip to Peking, and the other involved his decision to make an effort to keep the Chinese Nationalists in the United Nations. In the first case, while effective action depended on the cooperation of the People's Republic of China, it required very little cooperation from the American bureaucracy. The president was able to entrust the task to one man, Henry Kissinger, who could operate almost independently of the existing bureaucratic organizations. In the other case—of seeking to persuade a hundred and six governments in the United Nations that they should permit Taiwan to remain in the UN—implementation depended on a large number of officials in the State Department and a substantial number of American ambassadors. The president was dependent on them to convey the message as he wished—in a way that would persuade other governments to support the American decision. The State Department, in turn, could proceed only according to its standard operating procedures in carrying out such a complicated operation.

Finally, the degree of presidential control is determined by whether the action can be carried out by different organizations—whether the president has the flexibility to choose among implementers and can find one in sympathy with what he wishes to have done. Presidential control over military operations tends to be more limited than control over diplomacy precisely because in the military field the president has few options. Furthermore, as we saw in the last chapter, the president's influence is greater if the officials carrying out an action are in Washington. Those in the capital can be summoned easily into his presence, and they may get a better feeling for what he wants done.

With the help of his unusually powerful vice president, the second President Bush was successful in employing various strategies available to the presidency to manipulate Washington's complex national security bureaucracy to pursue his goal of deposing Saddam Hussein. He persuaded his senior officials that attacking Iraq was necessary to fight terrorism, he took personal control of the development of military plans to attack Iraq, he included those who bolstered his argument and isolated those who did not, he encouraged the intelligence community to shade its estimates of the Iraqi security threat and Saddam's relations with al Qaeda, and he led the public affairs campaign with the American public and foreign governments to present the case for attacking Iraq.[27]

---

27. Bob Woodward describes all these maneuvers in great detail, as he gleaned them from firsthand interviews with the officials involved, in his book *Plan of Attack*.

Thus far we have been considering instances in which the president wishes to have something done and his subordinates resist doing it. There are, however, times when the president rejects a proposal for action but certain officials are still eager to take it. If the prospective implementers agree with the president's decision, then it is almost impossible for others to get the action that the president has rejected. On the other hand, if the implementers were turned down, they may be able to find a way to take the action even without presidential concurrence. The military services in particular have often found ways to keep projects alive after they have been cut out of the budget by the president and the secretary of defense. The most spectacular such instance occurred with the Army space program. The Army, ordered not to engage in the development of a missile that could place objects in orbit around the earth, nevertheless proceeded with its program and ultimately put the first satellite in orbit after the authorized Navy program failed on several occasions. General John P. Medaris, who was in charge of the Army program, described in his memoirs just what was done:

> Gen. H. N. Toftoy, who was in charge of Redstone Arsenal at that time, came up with what for those days was an outrageously ambitious project to build such a complex on the top of a hill at the Arsenal. The Army had no mission beyond the Redstone missile itself, which was well along in development, and there was no possible way that the research people could finance such a test complex because they could find no real excuse for it. Yet if anything significant were to be done in the future, the construction of such a complex would have to start right away. Construction time would be a couple of years at least, and in the meantime nothing bigger, or more advanced, could be undertaken. It was the old story that still haunts the programs of the Army, where you can't get what you need for future work until the work itself is approved, and when that happens it is too late to build what you needed in the first place.
>
> If anything was to be done, it seemed to us that it would have to be accomplished with production money. Now the rules say that production money cannot be used for research and development projects. Yet there was a fair amount of money available in the production budget for building or acquiring facilities, and there was none in the Research and Development budget. Finally we cooked up a plausible story of needing the test tower and other test facilities in order to carry on the required quality control and inspection testing that would be needed when the Redstone missile went into production. On the basis that the facilities

were to be used for the testing of items in production, rather than for development tests, we could legally use production money.

I do not think anyone in the Army knew what we were up to, but I watched the campaign carefully and finally wangled it through with approximately 13 million dollars as an initial increment. I very carefully avoided even mentioning any R&D work that might be done on these facilities, because I knew this would prejudice our chances. The people who were responsible for approving these projects were, I am afraid, not too well informed with respect to the guided missile area, and they swallowed our story. It is interesting to note that had not this project been rammed through and approved when it was not really justified by either the ground rules or the needs of the moment, there would have been nothing available to make possible the rapid development of the Jupiter missile or the test work that made the satellites possible.

I was convinced by this time that the future of the Ordnance Corps was in large part in guided missiles. Few were interested in old-fashioned munitions, and getting money to build modern tanks or new rifles or develop new vehicles was very difficult indeed. On the other hand, missiles were beginning to capture the public imagination, and support could be had for additional work and new projects.[28]

Many of the actions taken by officials of the American government do not result from explicit presidential decisions. As suggested above, many of them are the result simply of individuals continuing to do what they have done before. When asked about the impact of the transition from Johnson to Nixon, outgoing Secretary of State Dean Rusk suggested the importance of continuity and consistency in government behavior.

A transition is not so earth-shaking. Of the thousand or so cables that go out of here every day, I see only five or six and the President only one or two. Those who send out the other 994 cables will still be here. It is a little bit like changing engineers on a train going steadily down the track. The new engineer has some switches he can make choices about—but 4,500 intergovernmental agreements don't change.[29]

Sometimes actions result from more generalized presidential decisions that no one foresaw would promote a particular action in a particular area. Presidential budget cuts, for example, often lead to unpredictable changes in

28. Medaris, *Countdown for Decision,* pp. 63–64. See also Armacost, *The Politics of Weapons Innovation,* pp. 54, 114; York, *Race to Oblivion,* pp. 105, 135.
29. Rusk, "Mr. Secretary on the Eve of Emeritus," p. 62B.

military behavior. It was a reduction in the Navy budget that led the Navy to cease patrolling the Taiwan Strait, an event that may have been read as an important signal by the People's Republic of China.

In other cases, an organization may initiate a change in its own behavior because of its perception of its organizational interests, and it may be in a position to do so on its own without securing presidential approval. Often changes in personnel brought about through routine rotation and retirement lead to substantial changes in the behavior of the United States government. Most often such changes occur in the field, through a change of ambassadors or military commanders who have substantial freedom.

Thus we can see that most government actions, which look to the casual outside observer as the result of specific presidential decisions, are more often an amalgam of a number of coincidental occurrences: actions brought about by presidential decisions (not always those intended), actions that are really maneuvers to influence presidential decisions, actions resulting from decisions in unrelated areas, and actions taken at lower levels by junior participants without informing their superiors or the president. If one is to explain a series of actions, one must consider not only the relevant presidential decisions but also various other sources.

At this point, we add another dimension to our discussion by providing in part 4 an analysis of the bureaucratic role of Congress in making foreign policy.

PART IV

Congress

CHAPTER SIXTEEN

Congress and Bureaucratic Politics

We have now completed our exploration of the process of making foreign policy in the executive branch, with only occasional mention of Congress's role in affecting foreign policy decisionmaking and implementation within the executive branch. This chapter turns then to considering how Congress itself functions and presents a brief look at Congress as a bureaucratic entity. First it gives a brief overview of how Congress impacts the foreign policy–making process of the executive branch, then proceeds to its primary topic, how Congress's bureaucratic perspective affects the views and actions of its members.

CONGRESS AND THE EXECUTIVE BRANCH

On July 26, 1947, with the stroke of a pen, President Harry Truman swept away the U.S. national security infrastructure that had carried the United States to the top of the global power hierarchy. The signing of the National Security Act of 1947 gave birth to the foreign policy–making apparatus that would help nurture and expand American power through the end of the cold war and beyond, into the untrammeled territory of American preeminence. It authorized a monumental reorganization of the national security bureaucracy, one designed to accompany the epochal transformations in the international system.

Only an act of Congress could so profoundly influence the bureaucracy that shapes U.S. foreign policy. Much of the discussion throughout this book has focused on the methods by which the national security bureaucracy shapes foreign policy, but all of the processes and activities involved take place within a congressionally determined structure. The 1947 act created the National Security Council and the Central Intelligence Agency, and it exchanged the Department of War for the Department of Defense to oversee the military services, including what was then the newly independent Air Force. From Kennedy and Bundy to Nixon and Kissinger to George H. W. Bush and Brent Scowcroft and beyond, each administration's national security team operates uniquely. But Congress sets the stage for presidents and national security officials in their attempt to use this apparatus in formulating and controlling U.S. foreign policy decisionmaking.

Since the inception of the modern national security bureaucracy, Congress has also toyed with its composition and structure. Numerous reorganizations of the infrastructure have been dictated by congressional amendments to the 1947 act. In 1986, the Goldwater-Nichols Act created the largest shake-up of the Defense Department since 1947.

These acts and amendments are manifestations of Congress's power to create and reorganize the structure of the federal government. The impact on the foreign policy–making process in the executive branch implicit in these acts is tremendous. However, the power to reorganize the executive branch is only one of many tools that Congress employs to influence foreign policy decisions in the executive branch; especially since the end of the cold war, Congress has also used numerous other methods.

Congress can shape the perception of the national interest held by the bureaucracy and can shape shared images of national security. For example, in 1998, Congress passed and persuaded the president to sign legislation proclaiming that the national interest of the United States required regime change in Iraq. Thus, when the second President Bush decided to invade Iraq, he could build on the shared image that removal of Saddam was necessary. Those opposed to war could not argue that the national interest would not be served by regime change; they were left to argue only that he could be removed more effectively by other means.

Congress also has the power to change the players in the executive branch bureaucracy and therefore to affect their perception of their interests. In 1947, when it passed the National Security Act, Congress created a host of new players with key roles in the national security process, including the secretary of defense, the Joint Chiefs of Staff and their chairman, and the director of central intelligence. Later, the Goldwater-Nichols Act fundamentally redefined the role of the chairman of the Joint Chiefs of Staff so as to make him an independent actor and not simply a representative of the Joint Chiefs' collective judgment. It also created the Special Forces as an independent command in the armed forces. After the 9/11 terrorist attack, Congress once again altered the cast of key players when it created the positions of secretary of homeland security and director of national intelligence.

The roles of various organizations can be affected by congressional action that changes their mission. By creating a director of national intelligence with his or her own staff, for example, Congress significantly altered the role of both the director of central intelligence and the Central Intelligence Agency.

Congress can rewrite the rules of the game. Its powers are exhibited by congressionally mandated requirements that specific agencies and offices be consulted on certain decisions. Wanting human rights to play a larger role in American foreign policy, Congress created a human rights office in the Department of State, later elevated it to a bureau, and mandated its role in the decisionmaking process by requiring the production of annual human rights reports and the assignment of human rights officers to embassies. Similarly, the 1998 International Religious Freedom Act mandated that consideration of religious freedom abroad have a similar role in the decisionmaking process. It created a position for a special adviser to the National Security Council to deal with religious freedom and an office in the State Department with an at-large ambassador to promote "religious freedom as a core objective of U.S. foreign policy."

Participants in the executive branch frequently attempt to manipulate Congress to further their own ends. For example, officials will provide classified information to Congress, knowing that it is then more likely to become public—either because members of Congress or their staffs leak it or because executive branch officials, knowing that Congress will be blamed, can leak the information with impunity. That helps to widen the circle of players both inside and outside the executive branch.

Finally, Congress can be used in the maneuvering that follows a presidential decision. Members of Congress can be quietly encouraged to enact legislation that blocks a presidential decision or to deny the appropriations needed to implement it. When President Clinton decided to loosen the embargo against Cuba, Congress passed the Helms-Burton Act to restrict the president's legal authority to alter the existing embargo. When the United States entered into an agreement with North Korea to provide it with nuclear fuel in return for its freezing its plutonium production process, Congress provided far less money than was needed, preventing the United States from meeting its obligations under the agreement.

The role of Congress in shaping executive branch decisions is discussed throughout this book. In this chapter, however, we want to do something different. Here we wish to provide a brief exposition of *how* Congress makes its national security decisions, applying the same bureaucratic perspective that we use in the rest of the book to explain the executive branch's actions. We begin with a discussion of the institutional prerogatives of Congress, followed by a discussion of national security interests as perceived by members of Congress. Then we discuss the interests of members and their "organizations" (the congressional committees) and, finally, we show how decisions are affected by the rules of the game.

BUREAUCRATIC POLITICS OF CONGRESS

Congress was not spared the confusion and controversy over the meaning of McNamara's announcement of the ABM deployment in 1967. Richard Russell, chairman of the Senate Armed Services Committee, described the deployment as the beginning of an anti-Soviet ABM system even though McNamara specifically ruled out that use. Melvin Laird, then head of the GOP Congressional Policy Committee, decided to make the ABM a campaign issue in the 1968 elections to challenge Lyndon Johnson's strategic policies. In 1969, an effort to kill the ABM lost in the Senate by a razor-thin margin, with the vice president breaking a tie. What forces were pulling members of Congress in different directions? Les Aspin, who had been a Pentagon systems analyst in the late 1960s and would be elected to Congress shortly after the ABM debate, described this event years later as a congressman:

> Congress rarely adds or subtracts a major new weapons system in votes on the floor. This results partly from lack of time but mainly from lack of expertise among members of Congress. Most congressmen serve on committees that deal with matters other than defense. They worry about health issues, welfare problems, or the economy, and think about defense matters twice a year, when the military authorization and appropriation bills reach the floor. It is difficult for these congressmen to say no if the executive branch, with all its military and civilian expertise massed behind it, says the country must have a particular weapons system.
>
> This is not to say there are no congressmen who will take the lead and oppose the Pentagon. There are several, but they come from the thin ranks of those who specialize in defense. It is exceptional if they can persuade a majority of the House and Senate to differ with the administration on a major weapons system.

This is a judgment borne out by history. No major weapon has ever been defeated in either house. The closest call was the 1969 vote on the Antiballistic Missile (ABM). The effort to kill the ABM failed on a tie vote in the Senate. It is easy to forget what a unique political event the ABM debate was. Several influences converged: the arms control community argued that the ABM would not work, and numerous spokesmen for it were ready to come to Washington to explain to congressmen why it would not; peace groups said the ABM was destabilizing and were concerned enough to lobby intensely; hostile constituent pressure (almost unheard-of on a weapons system issue) was brought to bear by people living near proposed ABM sites; and, finally, the weapon was not then in production, so that members of Congress did not face pressures from large numbers of workers fearful of losing their jobs. The ABM controversy brought together a constellation of forces that is not likely to be repeated by chance and is almost impossible to put together by design.[1]

Though most members of Congress, like their executive branch counterparts, shared the national security image that military superiority and hence strategic strength was necessary to oppose the Soviets, they too differed with one another on whether the ABM was the best method of defending the United States against the Soviet nuclear threat. Aspin's recollection of the congressional decision on the ABM shows that congressional views on foreign policy are affected by myriad interests, including domestic needs that rarely weigh heavily in determining the views of officials in the executive branch. When confronted with a foreign policy question, however, members of Congress and officials in the executive branch attempt to answer the same question—what is the best interest of U.S. national security? The bureaucratic politics of Congress and the unique perspectives of its members help shape members' answers.

National Security Interests

Members of Congress, like officials of the executive branch, are constrained by shared images of what the national security requires. Because there is constant interaction between the two branches, they usually perceive the same requirements; however, they often advocate different approaches to meet them. Like officials in the executive branch, members of Congress and their staffs are

1. Aspin, "The Power of Procedure," pp. 43–44.

influenced by their own personal experiences as well as their intellectual and psychological inclinations in dealing with uncertainty about what is going on in the world and how potential actions will affect American interests.

When shared images shift, the views of members often mirror the movement. As is true within the bureaucracy, numerous factors can cause shared images to shift. Outside events, for instance, can provoke an immediate reaction from Congress. Within days of the 9/11 attacks, Congress authorized the president to use force against those responsible, authorizing the "war on terror"; not long thereafter, it passed the Patriot Act. Shared images of national security can also be affected by personnel changes in Congress. Underlying the shifts in congressional perceptions is the shifting nature of public opinion. Though often images are shared by the executive branch and Congress, public opinion can cause a shift in congressional treatment of national security without necessarily affecting the bureaucracy. Beginning in 1994, when Republicans gained control of both houses of Congress, there was a shift in congressional views toward national security, including increased hostility toward international organizations such as the United Nations at the same time that the Clinton administration was attempting to strengthen such institutions. Shifting control of the houses results in new committee chairs and players, thereby affecting congressional prerogatives.

Senators and House members and their staffs are also influenced by their position within the congressional structure. Whether they work for a member or a committee affects how congressional staffers view issues; their perceptions vary, for example, with the function they perform for a member or which committee they work for and what role they play on that committee. For instance, a senator's staff and the staff of the Senate Foreign Relations Committee (SFRC) view issues differently: the senator's staff has to consider all of the senator's domestic and personal interests, while a SFRC staffer is most likely to be influenced by the interests of the committee. Likewise, the SFRC staff director, who usually represents the chairperson's views, and a senator's designated staff on the committee approach issues from the different perspectives of the senators that they represent.

The views of members are in effect determined by their affiliations. For our purposes, their participation in the decisionmaking process can be seen as being influenced by the role that dominates their thinking on national security issues. The most important perspectives are those of committees and the personal interests of each member, such as getting reelected and being elected or appointed to higher office.

Sometimes, however, members look to protecting the broader interests of Congress as an institution with an important part to play in foreign policy making.

Institutional Interests

The first instinct of any organization is self-preservation. We have discussed how each executive branch organization comes to see the national interest as synonymous with its own interest. The agencies and departments within the executive branch may struggle with one another for influence and dissent from the presidential view, but the institutional prerogative and general direction of foreign policy lies with the president. Without a presidential equivalent in Congress, it is nearly impossible for Congress to take a unified institutional position on an issue. Nevertheless, some members speak about foreign policy issues in terms of congressional interests. While members' views of their interests are usually determined by their place within the structure of Congress, members often realize that in order to safeguard the ability of Congress as a whole to affect the foreign policy decisionmaking process, they must defend their institutional interests first.

For members struggling to maintain what they perceive as congressional prerogatives, there is no issue more salient or controversial than the power to go to war. While the Constitution grants Congress the power to "declare war," most uses of the military in combat, especially since the end of World War II, have not been stamped with official congressional approval. Congress often passes resolutions empowering the president to use force, such as the Gulf of Tonkin resolution, which enabled the Vietnam War, or the Iraq resolution in 2002 that preceded Operation Iraqi Freedom. The battle between the executive and legislative branches over who has the power to send U.S. troops into combat has a long and complex history that continues to this day. The War Powers Act of 1973 was a congressional attempt in the wake of Vietnam and unlicensed U.S. military activity in Cambodia to curtail presidential power in using the military. Though Congress overrode Nixon's veto, the act has in effect done little to shift that power to Congress.

Our purpose here is not to delve into the history of this battle between the legislative and executive branches, but to examine it through the eyes of members of Congress. Despite the fluctuations in the balance of power over the decades—and even with frequent congressional acquiescence—there are members who stalwartly defend the right of Congress to determine when to wield the sword. No matter what their particular view of a specific instance of presidential deployment of troops, members usually oppose such presidential exercise of power by invoking the sanctity of the Constitution and the integrity of the nation. With a touch of the dramatic, in September 1993 Senator Robert Byrd (D-W.Va.) rose to address the chamber in an attempt to sober the conversation over President Bill Clinton's support of UN involvement in Somalia:

> In the late summer of 29 B.C., Octavian came back to Rome after the Battle of Actium in 31 B.C. The Roman Senate gratefully—gratefully, gratefully—ceded its powers to someone who would plan and take responsibility and lead, because the Roman Senate had lost its will to make hard decisions. It had lost its will to lead. It had lost its nerve. It had lost its way. . . .
>
> No Senator has gone on record by voting any commitment for the course we are now pursuing in Somalia, and under the Constitution, Congress is not bound to uphold any such commitment by the President—not until it votes to do so. And we have run from the issue up to this point. We have preferred to be left out of tough decisions. All we have to do is to look at a bit of Roman history and see exactly where we are going.[2]

Senator Byrd's opposition to the expansion of the U.S. military role in Somalia was based in part on his belief that if congressional deference to seemingly unhampered presidential control over using force continued, the American republic would soon come under the control of a presidential emperor and disintegrate. Byrd's worry was not merely presidential usurpation of what he saw as a congressional power, but that Congress was willingly accepting its hat as it was shown its way out of the decisionmaking process.

A couple of years earlier, with the decision to eject Iraqi forces from Kuwait in 1991 pending, Speaker of the House Thomas Foley's plea for congressional power emphasized a division of power in these decisions:

> This debate is not about who supports the President of the United States and who does not. I honor and respect the President. I know his determination and I also know the awful loneliness and terrible consequence of the decisions that he must make.
>
> In a letter to Thomas Jefferson, James Madison wrote: "The Constitution supposes what the history of all governments demonstrates, that the

2. As quoted in Weissman, *A Culture of Deference: Congress's Failure of Leadership in Foreign Policy*, p. 1.

Executive is the branch . . . most interested in war, and most prone to it. It has accordingly . . . vested the question of war in the legislature."

I do not believe that the President wants war. I believe that he devoutly wishes peace and will continue to hope and work for it. But it is wrong to suggest that we who have taken our own oath can burden him further by giving to him alone the responsibility that also must be ours today. We must share in this decision. We have been elected to do it. The Constitution mandates it, and we would shirk our duty if we easily acquiesce in what the President decides. That is unfair to him, as it is to our constituents and to our responsibilities.[3]

Foley believed that the institutional integrity of Congress and its role in foreign policy is driven not only by constitutional imperatives but also by the need to serve one's constituents and by the need to share the burden of the awesome responsibility of war that cannot possibly be prudently wielded by one person.

Clearly, the floors of Congress are conducive to noble monologues decrying the exclusion of Congress from the decisionmaking process when going to war. But beneath the lofty rhetoric and the alarming analogies lies the institutional struggle for influence and relevance. Members invoking these arguments see Congress—and hence themselves—as an integral and powerful player in determining when the nation goes to war. They view a usurpation of congressional power in this arena as detrimental to national security because, in their view, it compromises the very constitutional principles intended to secure the nation. While politics is supposed to end at the water's edge, some in Congress perceive the journey to the water's edge as potentially dangerous to national security.

The decision to go to war is a unique one, and is not meant to be representative of all decisions made by members. Many members of Congress view decisions of war and peace as a matter of conscience, as Senate Majority Leader Tom Daschle did in 2002 when voting for the resolution to authorize President Bush to use force against Iraq. Rather, this issue is intended to show that, in certain circumstances, members view the interests of Congress as their own, because without a congressional role in the decisionmaking, individual members are also rendered impotent.

3. As quoted in Peters, ed., *The Speaker: Leadership in the U.S. House of Representatives*, p. 115.

Committee Interests

However, as is true within the executive branch, views on national security issues are affected more often by one's place within the institutional structure.

Committee interests in Congress are the equivalent to organizational interests in the executive branch. In order to understand the interests of committees it is necessary to understand how Congress is organized and the role that committees play in the process by which Congress enacts legislation, especially the budget. We present here a brief explanation.[4]

Both the House and Senate have several authorizing committees and an appropriations committee with subcommittees to deal with various categories of issues. Authorizing committees, such as the foreign relations committees, are involved in approving programs within their jurisdiction. Appropriations committees approve the actual funding. Although there are some differences between the two houses, on the whole, the authorizing committees dealing with national security cover the same matters. Below are brief descriptions of the jurisdiction of the committees.

—*Senate Foreign Relations Committee and House International Relations Committee.* These committees have responsibility for foreign policy in general and for oversight of the State Department and USAID. The Senate Foreign Relations Committee also has responsibility for all treaties, ambassadorial nominations, and appointments to senior positions in the agencies that it oversees. The principal piece of legislation for which the two committees have responsibility is the State Department authorization bill, which is usually enacted once during each Congress and covers a two-year period. The committees also have jurisdiction over the bill authorizing foreign aid programs, but this bill is seldom, if ever, actually passed by both houses and signed into law and, as of 2005, it had not been signed into law since 1986.

—*Armed services committees.* These committees have oversight of the Defense Department and responsibility for military policy. The Senate Armed Services Committee also has responsibility for the confirmation of those nominated to senior military positions, as well as senior officials of the Department of Defense. The principal legislation for which the armed services committees have responsibility is the Department of Defense authorization bill. The committees also share responsibility for those parts of the intelligence authorization bill that deal with the intelligence activities of the Defense Department.

—*Intelligence committees.* In contrast with the foreign affairs and armed services committees, the House and Senate intelligence committees are rela-

---

4. See Congressional Quarterly's *Guide to Congress.*

tively recent creations, formed by Congress in the aftermath of the intelligence scandals of the 1970s. These committees have responsibility for intelligence matters and oversight of the Office of the Director of National Intelligence and the CIA, as well as the intelligence components of other agencies, which they share with the committee that has jurisdiction of the agency as a whole. The Senate committee has responsibility for approving appointments to senior positions in the Office of the Director of National Intelligence and the CIA. The principal legislative vehicle for which the committees have responsibility is the annual intelligence authorization bill.

—*Appropriations committees.* On the appropriations side, the longtime symmetry between the House and the Senate was altered in 2004 when both houses revamped the structure of the subcommittees to react to recommendations proposed by the 9/11 Commission to improve oversight of intelligence and homeland security. On the Senate side, one subcommittee (the State, Foreign Operations, and Related Programs Subcommittee) was given responsibility for most foreign policy issues, including the operating budgets of the State Department, USAID, and the Peace Corps, as well as for foreign assistance. The House committee structure for foreign affairs budget matters remains as it has been in both houses since World War II, with a separate Foreign Operations Subcommittee and a subcommittee that covers the State Department budget and also handles the Commerce and Justice Departments.

In both houses the defense subcommittees handle most defense and intelligence appropriations, with some issues, such as defense construction, handled in a different subcommittee. The only bills handled by the appropriations committees are the annual appropriations bills and any supplemental appropriations bills that Congress might consider.

Other authorizing committees can have some foreign affairs jurisdiction depending on the responsibilities of the executive branch agencies for which they exercise oversight. For example, issues relating to debt relief are handled by the Treasury Department and therefore by the Finance Committee in the Senate and the Financial Services Committee in the House, and some issues related to international health are handled by the Department of Health and Human Resources and its authorizing committees in both houses.

Just as career executive branch officials believe that their organizations' welfare is vital to the national security, some members of Congress, particularly chairs and senior members of committees, along with their committee staff, come to believe that the welfare of the committee is synonymous with the national interest. To the extent that congressional participants come to equate national security interests with the interests of the committee or subcommittee with which they are associated, what stands do they take and how do their stands relate to committee interests?

Committees, like agencies, have a mission to perform. They try to enact into law the bills for which they have responsibility, conduct oversight of the executive branch departments over which they have jurisdiction, and in the case of the Senate, they deal with presidential appointments and treaties.

Committees cannot fulfill their perceived missions without influence. Since a significant part of the legislative function concerns authorizing and appropriating funds, committees jockey with one another for control of the purse. Each committee's operations are funded in the legislative appropriations bill and they can be expected as a rule to seek more funding and hence more ability to perform their oversight functions. However, the more important funding issue is that of providing money to the executive branch. Since committee interests and influence are intricately linked with the welfare of the agencies that they oversee, committees come to equate their welfare with the welfare of these agencies. Thus members of the Foreign Relations Committee prefer policies that require greater reliance on diplomacy and foreign assistance programs, while members of the Armed Services Committee prefer policies that require larger appropriations for the armed services. Members of a committee see robust funding and greater authority for the agencies under their supervision as advancing the national interest and also as providing greater scope for the committee to influence the behavior of the executive branch.

Authorizing committees affect the capabilities of the executive branch agencies by authorizing and funding programs and by prescribing rules for the conduct of programs. The foreign relations committees, for example, authorize specific assistance programs to a country or continent, such as Africa, or for a specific purpose, such as women's rights. The armed services committees authorize procurement of weapons systems and legislate rules that make it more likely that the systems are manufactured in the districts of committee members.

Appropriations committees influence executive branch actions not only by determining how much money they spend but also through riders, earmarks, and limitations. The subcommittee on foreign operations of the Senate Appropriations Committee has influenced American policy on human rights by attaching riders to legislation requiring that countries adhere to human rights standards. Senator Leahy from Vermont became the ranking Democrat on the committee in 1989, and he and his key staffer, Tim Rieser, used this process to affect American policy toward a number of countries around the world.

Because committees use their legislation to increase their influence, they come to see the passing of the bills under their jurisdiction as important to the national security.

JURISDICTION. Just as executive branch agencies struggle over roles and missions, congressional committees clash over jurisdiction. The "jurisdiction" of a committee defines the matters over which it has control and the executive branch agencies whose budget it legislates and over which it exercises oversight. Committees seek to maintain and, if possible, to expand their jurisdiction. They resist concurrent jurisdiction—sharing jurisdiction over a program or agency with another committee. Committees struggle to keep agencies under their jurisdiction and to have programs that they care about administered by agencies under their jurisdiction. Executive branch reorganizations often affect the jurisdiction of committees by moving activities from one agency to another or by creating a new entity. Committees' decisions on issues often are affected by how such potential changes would affect their jurisdiction.

Many long-running battles within Congress and between Congress and the executive branch are in fact struggles over jurisdiction. One of the continuing struggles concerns the organization and control of intelligence activities and another involves the transfer of funds to foreign governments by the Department of Defense. These are discussed in turn.

—*Intelligence organization.* The struggle among congressional committees over control of intelligence operations and the organization of the intelligence community has erupted periodically since the end of World War II. It has had a major impact on the structure of the intelligence community and on the agencies within it.

When Congress established the CIA under the National Security Act of 1947, it was basically restructuring the Office of Strategic Services, the World War II–era intelligence agency, parts of which had been parceled out to the Departments of State and War after the war. The CIA was placed under the jurisdiction of the two armed services committees and of the Defense Appropriations Subcommittee. The armed services committees were able to maintain control over intelligence activities, as well as authority for the intelligence programs within the Department of Defense (DoD), which were far larger in size and expenditures. In practice, the CIA budget and the budgets for other large intelligence agencies within DoD, including the National Security Agency and the National Reconnaissance Office (established later, in 1960), were approved by very small subcommittees of each committee and hidden within the defense budget. The intelligence units of other agencies, such as the Bureau of Intelligence and Research (INR) in the State Department and the FBI's intelligence activities, remained under the jurisdiction of the authorizing and appropriating committees that had authority over their parent agencies.

Senator Mike Mansfield, the Democratic majority leader of the Senate from 1961 to 1977, periodically proposed the creation of an intelligence committee for the Senate. The idea was met by resistance from every committee that had jurisdiction over any portion of the intelligence community. It finally began to gain traction with the intelligence scandals of the 1970s. As information became public about intelligence abuses in the CIA, FBI, NSA, and other agencies, Mansfield was able to get agreement on the need for at least a temporary committee to review the operations of those agencies. When what became known as the Church Committee (named for its chairman, Senator Frank Church, Democrat of Indiana) detailed a range of abuses and recommended the creation of an intelligence committee, the pressure to create such a committee grew.

Still there was strong resistance. A split grew between members of the Senate who were concerned about the prerogatives of their committees and those who viewed the issue through other lenses. Leading members of the armed services, foreign relations, and judiciary committees led the fight against the bill, with the members of each committee arguing that, at the very least, intelligence matters under their jurisdiction should remain where they were. Those senators invoked the principle that all of the components of an executive branch department should be under the supervision of one committee—a principle dear to most senators because it protects the jurisdiction of the committee on which they serve. Members of the Armed Services Committee insisted that one could not decide how much to spend for intelligence programs to support military operations without considering the trade-off with expenditures on weapons systems and military personnel. Members of the Judiciary Committee argued that policy matters related to FBI intelligence activities could not be separated from policy questions related to law enforcement. The Foreign Relations Committee argued that policy issues, such as whether the United States should conduct covert operations, were within its jurisdiction and should remain there since they had a direct impact on U.S. relations with other nations. Members of all of the committees argued that they had the expertise and the best staff to perform the oversight function.

Senators also argued against sharing jurisdiction. They noted that the Senate, with good reason, had adopted a provision in its rules creating a strong presumption against two committees having concurrent jurisdiction over the same program or activity. Creating a new intelligence committee would only duplicate efforts since both committees would need to hold hearings and mark up the same bill.

The legislation was stalled in the Senate, despite the public outcry about intelligence abuse and the consensus among most experts and observers that only a dedicated committee could perform effective oversight of the intelligence community and that trade-offs needed to be made among intelligence programs. Members of the affected committees were insisting on long debate, consideration of multiple amendments, stripping jurisdiction from the proposed intelligence committee, and holding out the threat of a filibuster.

To rescue the bill the Senate adopted what became known as the "Inouye compromise," named after the Democratic senator from Hawaii. The resolution, as adopted, provided for the CIA to come under the sole jurisdiction of the new Senate Intelligence Committee. Intelligence units of other departments engaged in national intelligence activities came under the concurrent jurisdiction of the new committee and the committee that had oversight of the agency. What were called tactical intelligence programs in the Department of Defense were kept under the sole jurisdiction of the Armed Services Committee. The bill also provided that no committee would lose subject matter jurisdiction as a result of the creation of the new committee. So, for example, matters that concerned both foreign affairs and intelligence would fall under the jurisdiction of both the Foreign Relations Committee and the Intelligence Committee. The Intelligence Committee would consider nominations for the director of central intelligence and senior officials of the CIA, but not intelligence officials of other agencies.

The primary legislative vehicle of the Intelligence Committee would be a new intelligence authorization bill, which would authorize all national intelligence activities. Once approved by the Intelligence Committee, the bill would be referred sequentially to other committees to review those portions related to programs in departments under their supervision. This process resulted in the perpetuation of a situation in which the director of central intelligence had very little authority over anything but the CIA itself. The other intelligence units remained under the control of their respective departments.

The fight over the organization of the intelligence community was reinvigorated after September 11, 2001. Once again the congressional reaction was dictated in large part by the face of the issue seen by leaders of congressional committees. At first, most members of Congress resisted any reorganization of the government. Those seeking change focused first on the question of creating a Department of Homeland Security. For many members of Congress the creation of a new department would mean that agencies would be pulled out of departments over which they had jurisdiction and transferred to the new department. As the pressure to deal with the perceived errors of 9/11 built up, the president finally acceded to calls for creation of a new Department of Homeland Security and Congress passed the Homeland Security Act, establishing the new cabinet agency. However, no intelligence functions were placed within the new department, nor were any intelligence agencies moved into the new department.

When pressure for intelligence reform intensified with the release of the report of the bipartisan 9/11 Commission in 2004, Congress passed the Intelligence Reform and Terrorism Prevention Act, signed by the president in December 2004, creating a new organization, the Office of the Director of National Intelligence (DNI) and a National Counterterrorism Center (NCTC) to coordinate the work of various intelligence agencies in the executive branch. The new DNI (as the director quickly became known in the jargon of the intelligence community) assumed all the responsibilities of the Office of the Director of Central Intelligence except those related directly to the management of the CIA and was given greater control over the intelligence agencies of the Department of Defense and the intelligence activities of the FBI. Although the bill also gave the new DNI substantial authority over the intelligence budget, it did not streamline the jurisdiction of a plethora of congressional committees (some forty-four) over intelligence budgets and operations. The 9/11 Commission's recommendation to unite authorization and appropriations functions within the intelligence committees was rebuffed because members of the appropriations committees in both houses refused to cede their authority.

The clash came, as it had before, over the question of the division of responsibility between the Defense and Justice Departments and their respective oversight committees, on one hand, and the intelligence committees and the DNI on the other. The leading members of the armed services committees supported the efforts of the military to restrict the authority of the DNI just as the judiciary committees supported the efforts of the FBI to remain free of the authority of the DNI. The congressional compromise left the jurisdiction of the committees and the procedures for authorizing intelligence activities essentially unchanged, while giving the DNI some greater role in the operation of the DoD intelligence agencies and the FBI intelligence functions.

Arguing that the refusal of Congress to reform itself thus doomed the intelligence reforms in the executive branch to having only marginal impact on many of the shortcomings that had led to the 9/11 intelligence failures, Helen Fessenden concluded:

> The failures of congressional reorganization received little press coverage, but the implications are serious. First, the continuation of the status quo keeps intact the unusual degree of control over the intelligence budget by appropriators (who write the checks in the end) rather than authorizers (who write the bills outlining their respective budgets), even though only the latter have a full staff of experts at their disposal. Second, the continuation of the status quo makes it more difficult for [DNI] Negroponte and his successors to count on a unified budget process, since it forces the DNI to deal with multiple actors rather than a few individuals. That splintering of jurisdiction, in turn, will make any future attempts at intelligence reform more difficult to push through Congress. Third and last, the decision to keep the intelligence budget split up among separate, classified accounts means that appropriators themselves cannot transfer money among their respective subcommittees—say, from Defense over to the State Department's Bureau of Intelligence and Research to the FBI to aid its counterterrorism efforts—even if they decide that such a transfer reflects an important priority. Coordination of the intelligence budget, in short, remains as unwieldy as it was before.[5]

—*Funding for foreign government activities.* The transfer of funds to other governments is another arena in which the struggle between congressional committees for jurisdiction has had an important impact on the conduct of American foreign policy. As noted above, a committee's jurisdiction turns largely on what agency performs a particular task. The armed services committees normally authorize Defense Department programs and funding. However, committees also have jurisdiction over certain kinds of activities, regardless of which agency performs the function. Often those two principles are in conflict. The dispute with the greatest consequence for foreign policy concerns programs administered by the Defense Department that involve transfers of funds to foreign governments and their military forces. The armed services committees claim jurisdiction because agencies under their jurisdiction carry out the programs and the committees often seek to contribute funding to the programs in order to strengthen their claim to jurisdiction. The foreign affairs committees (the Senate Foreign Relations Committee and the House International Relations Committee, which has been known by various names since World War II) take the position that any transfer of funds to a for-

5. Fessenden, "The Limits of Intelligence Reform," p. 115.

eign government is a foreign affairs function under their jurisdiction no matter how it is funded. Recognizing that control often follows funding, they have often insisted that funding must come from the so-called 150 account, which pays for foreign affairs expenses, rather than from the Defense 050 account, which is controlled by the armed services committees. The defense and foreign operations subcommittees have had a similar conflict.

As with all disputes over foreign affairs, the debate takes place in the context of the U.S. national interest and does not touch on the influence of the committees themselves. Arguments are made about why funding a program in one way or another would advance the national interest. Thus the leaders of the foreign affairs and foreign operations committees promote the need for consistency in U.S. relations with other countries and often champion respect for human rights and support of specific foreign policy goals. The armed services and defense appropriations committees emphasize the nation's defense needs and the way in which other nations can help.

This dispute has manifested itself in numerous areas. Here we consider three: foreign military training, payments for base rights, and protection of nuclear stockpiles.

—*Military training.* The International Military Education and Training (IMET) program has been a continuing source of conflict between the defense and foreign affairs committees. The activity must be conducted by members of the armed forces since it involves military training of foreign military forces, including attendance at U.S. military training facilities. At the same time it involves the transfer of resources to a foreign government. The compromise has been to have the funds for the program authorized by the foreign affairs committees and appropriated by the foreign operations subcommittees from the 150 account. The funds are then transferred by the State Department to the Defense Department, which manages the program consistent with policy laid down by the foreign affairs committees. This jerry-rigged system has ensured that the foreign affairs committees can impose requirements on the program as a whole, for example, by requiring human rights training as a component of military training. The committees have also prohibited the inclusion of specific countries in the program because of their human rights record or failure to cooperate with the United States on other issues. In some cases they also have required the president to issue a waiver and make a report to Congress before going forward with the program in a particular country.

This process has often produced frustration in the defense committees, spurring efforts to minimize the restrictions. The committees focus on the value of the training in creating foreign military forces that can complement those of the United States in combat operations. They also argue that the training is the best way to create military leaders who will not be tempted to carry out coups or to violate human rights. Ultimately, the amount of funding available for IMET is relatively small since it must compete with all of the other demands on the 150 foreign affairs account, including foreign assistance and participation in international organizations. If taken from the 050 account, it would be an insignificant amount and far greater funding almost certainly would be available for the IMET program, at least in countries where there is no dispute about the training. Yet the foreign affairs committees resist the use of DoD funds because shared funding would mean ceding partial control over the programs to DoD.

The defense committees have also sought to authorize additional programs within the DoD budget to permit the military to provide training and education to foreign militaries. They rationalize the programs by arguing that their primary purpose is to support U.S. military operations and not to provide assistance to foreign governments. Thus, the military can conduct joint training exercises with other countries and pay the full cost if the goal is to improve the readiness of U.S. forces. Each regional military commander (the regional commanders in chief, or CINCs) has a contingency fund that he can use for various activities, including the transfer of funds to foreign governments to assist in his mission. The foreign affairs committees have sought to prevent such programs, and when that has not been possible, they have insisted that the programs must operate with the same limitations as programs funded from the foreign affairs budget. The war on drugs, which gained momentum in the 1980s, placed more control of foreign assistance funds in the hands of the Defense Department in order to train foreign nations to combat the drug trade. That too was seen in light of its supposed benefit to the United States by hampering the flow of drugs. Enacted in 2002, the Counterterrorism Fellowship Program (CTFP), like IMET, allows the Defense Department to train foreign militaries, particularly in counterterrorism operations. Despite objections by some, this "militarization of foreign aid decision-making" caused the Defense Department to make a FY 2006 budget request for even more latitude in training "military and security forces," which, in addition to militaries, include "border security, civil defense, infrastructure protection, and police forces." That request represents a clear example of an attempt by DoD to expand its purview over foreign assistance and justify it by claiming that it is necessary to fighting the war on terror.[6]

6. Withers, "Who's in Charge? Foreign Assistance Responsibilities Shift from State to Defense."

—*Payment for base rights.* Payments to foreign governments to secure rights to establish bases in their country raise the same set of issues. Here the debate often is complicated by the unwillingness of any of the parties to admit that a payment is being made explicitly for the use of bases. Foreign governments often offer the "free" use of bases, which they justify to their own people as contributing to the common defense. The U.S. government justifies the assistance programs on their own merits and denies that they are, in effect, payment for use of bases. In part it fears that other countries will insist on payments as well.

Nonetheless, the interests of the Defense Department and its committees often diverge from those of the State Department and its committees. The foreign affairs committees argue that the payments are made to foreign governments and are therefore within their jurisdiction and subject to both worldwide and specific limitations. The Defense Department, focused on the cost savings from being able to use the bases, would generally prefer to have the flexibility to pay larger sums and avoid any restrictions or conditions. During the cold war this debate focused especially on authoritarian regimes that were willing to provide facilities valuable to the fulfillment of the containment doctrine. Since 9/11 the dispute has focused on authoritarian governments, such as the Central Asian "Stans," willing to support the war on terror and specifically the combat operations in Afghanistan and Iraq. The complex relationship between the State Department's diplomatic efforts and the military maneuverings of the Defense Department are in part played out in such committee battles over funding and jurisdiction.

—*Securing nuclear stockpiles: Nunn-Lugar.* An enduring source of conflict between the defense and foreign affairs committees has involved the so-called Nunn-Lugar program, which was created after the cold war to safeguard nuclear materials in the former Soviet Union.

With the collapse of the Soviet Union, many recognized the danger posed by the lack of security for the nuclear materials and other weapons of mass destruction that were widely scattered over its former territory. There also was concern that even within Russia itself the materials and "loose nukes" were not being properly protected. Russia, in any case, had far more weapons-grade material than it needed, but it lacked the capacity to safely store and destroy the material.

Recognizing the danger, Representative Les Aspin, then the chair of the House Armed Services Committee, proposed a program to assist the nations of the former USSR in protecting and destroying the material. For many participants, the paramount consideration was the urgent national security need to prevent the acquisition of the material by rogue states or terrorist groups. However, to the leaders of the foreign affairs committees and the foreign operations subcommittees the issue was their ability to impose the conditions that they felt necessary on the programs and to retain control over what they expected to be a major source of funding to foreign governments.

Thus a long and continuing struggle began over which committees would authorize the program and provide funding and oversight. One of the first responses to Aspin's proposal was from a fellow Democrat from Rhode Island, Senator Claiborne Pell, then the chairman of the Senate Foreign Relations Committee. Pell, though normally viewed as laid back and not very aggressive in defending the prerogatives of his committee, argued forcefully that his committee would have to authorize and fund any such program. Leaders of the Foreign Operations Subcommittee similarly staked out their claim to the program. As the debate progressed, it became clear that the magnitude of the need would require funding far beyond the means of the 150 foreign affairs account alone, and the 050 defense account had to be brought into play. Thus it is no accident that the program came to be known as Nunn-Lugar, after Senator Sam Nunn, the long-time Democratic chair of the Armed Services Committee, and Senator Richard Lugar, long a senior Republican on the Foreign Relations Committee and committee chairman after the retirement of Senator Jesse Helms.

Personal Interests

Thus far we have explored the ways in which national security, institutional prerogatives, and the interests of committees are the face of an issue seen by some members of Congress. For others, the face of the issue that they see relates to their personal interests, which can include reelection, enhancing their personal influence and legacy, and election or appointment to higher office. Some members of Congress also see their role as supporting the president if he is from their political party and hence view issues through that lens. Others have strong ideological positions that affect how they see specific issues.

REELECTION. With few exceptions, members of Congress are interested in getting reelected. Thus, one face of any issue that they see is whether how they vote on the issue might affect their chances of reelection. In many cases a foreign policy issue's influence on their election prospects is seen as remote and other faces of that issue are viewed as more important. In other situations, however, the impact on reelection may be critical.

Votes on whether to go to war or to continue to support a particular military operation are often seen as having a significant impact on reelection prospects. As the Vietnam War became more controversial, members of Congress felt pressure from their constituencies to alter their positions. Representative Tip O'Neill, later the House Speaker famous for the aphorism "All politics is local," began to express concern about the war when his constituency began pressing for a resolution cutting off funding. Many members thought that their votes to authorize the use of force against Saddam Hussein prior to the Gulf War in the first Bush administration and against him in Iraq a decade later in the second Bush administration would affect their reelection prospects. Some felt pressure to vote against the resolutions and some to vote for them, according to the views of the people of their district or state.

Members believe that securing defense contracts for their district and fighting to keep military bases and other government facilities in their district or state open are critical to their reelection. As with executive branch officials, members of Congress seek to state national security reasons for their stands, but a senator who thinks that a weapons system made in his or her state is not vital to the national security is very rare indeed. In fact, members often trumpet their role in bringing contracts to their district. The website of Representative Jim Saxton (R-N.J.), a member of the House Armed Services Committee, is a prime example of how members try to portray themselves as pro-military:

> Mr. Saxton has a reputation as a tireless legislator who responds promptly and conclusively to his constituency regarding issues of importance to the district.
>
> **Mr. Saxton's Biggest Victories**
> **HELPED SAVE FT. DIX, MCGUIRE AFB & NAVY LAKEHURST.** He is also widely recognized in the Garden State for taking on the Pentagon in a trio of battles to save Fort Dix (1988, 1991) and McGuire Air Force Base (1993), as well as neighboring Lakehurst Naval Air Engineering Station (1995) during Base Realignment and Closure hearings. In all three cases, the Pentagon was reversed, and today Fort Dix and McGuire are busier than they have ever been in peacetime.
> **BRINGING HOME THE "BIG J."** Also notable was winning the federal competition to bring home the Battleship USS *New Jersey* to the Delaware River in South Jersey in 2000. The victory paved the way for a major naval museum that opened in 2001 and has drawn thousands of visitors annually.

STRENGTHENING & GROWING MCGUIRE AFB. In 2001, an eight-year plan to bring ultramodern Boeing C-17 Globemasters to McGuire AFB came to fruition when the Air Force announced it intended to send a squadron of the cargo planes to McGuire, helping to ensure McGuire's role in the 21st century. In September 2004, the Congressman helped welcome the first of McGuire's C-17s, which are still arriving straight from the California factory through mid-2005. The base has seen more than $150 million of new construction in the 2000–2003 federal budgets, the most in base history. The base has seen over a half-billion dollars in new construction over the past 10 years. In the 2005 defense budget, Mr. Saxton helped steer over $50 million to Fort Dix, McGuire AFB, and Navy Lakehurst.

CONGRESS' AIR MOBILITY ADVOCATE. Ever a watchdog of overspending, Mr. Saxton helped Congress purchase 60 more C-17s in 2002 for 25 percent less than previously estimated costs. The plane is widely viewed as the best cargo transport aircraft ever built in the history of aviation. In 2005, he is seeking authorization for the Air Force to negotiate to buy another 42 C-17s. Working with other senior members of the House Armed Services Committee, he added the language to the FY2006 defense authorization bill.

YEARS OF MILITARY BASE MODERNIZATION BEAR FRUIT. As chairman of the Military Construction Subcommittee between 2001–02, he brought millions of dollars to every one of New Jersey's main military installations, a total of over $200 million in new construction in the state. These projects are critical in that they were all funded and constructed prior to the May 2005 BRAC list.

Congressman Saxton designed a 10–12 year plan to modernize Fort Dix, McGuire AFB, and Navy Lakehurst. He worked closely with base commanders to support important projects in defense budgets that enhanced existing missions and attracted new missions. Working with DoD officials from the Army, Navy, and Air Force, he has spent the past 10 years highlighting and promoting multi-service projects that improved "jointness" between the bases. On May 13, 2005, that strategy seemed to pay off when the Pentagon specifically recommended that the three bases be combined and dubbed "Joint Base McGuire-Dix-Lakehurst," along with 11 other bases. Joint Base McGuire-Dix-Lakehurst remains the only Army-Navy-Air Force base in the country.

Decisions about foreign policy also are often affected by domestic ethnic constituencies. Some members of Congress represent districts with many voters who identify with a particular foreign country because their ancestors come from that country or they themselves are recent immigrants. In such cases, members know that what stand they take, how active they are, and how they vote can affect their reelection prospects with that constituency. Reelection also requires members to raise large sums of money. Ethnic or national groups with an interest in foreign policy are an important source of funds. Members may court groups such as the Jewish community or the Indian-American community as a source of funding even if such groups are not represented in large numbers in their district or state.

ELECTION TO HIGHER OFFICE. It is said that every representative looks in the mirror and sees a senator, while every senator looks in the mirror and sees a president. Members frequently determine their stance on an issue by determining how it would affect their prospects for securing their party's nomination and being elected to higher office. For example, when the second President Bush sought congressional support for the war against Iraq, Democratic members of Congress who were considering seeking their party's nomination to run against Bush needed to consider how the vote would affect both their prospects for nomination and subsequent election. Several potential candidates had voted against the Gulf War and believed that they needed to demonstrate that they were not always against the use of force.

Some members see their future within the house in which they are serving and aspire to leadership positions, with the pinnacles being Speaker of the House and House minority leader or Senate majority and minority leaders. Members need to ask how a vote or a position will affect their ability to be elected to a leadership position.

ENHANCING PERSONAL INFLUENCE AND LEGACY. While leadership positions usually garner at least temporary fame for a member, decisions often are impelled by the temptation of achieving greater personal influence and an immortal legacy.

As in the case with the Nunn-Lugar program or the Goldwater-Nichols defense reorganization, often bills are known by their creators and key proponents. In the twilight of his Senate career, Barry Goldwater, scion of the conservative movement and stalwart defender of the armed services, decided that he "would not retire from the Senate without giving reorganization my best shot." Upon the 1984 retirement of Senator John Tower, the Republican chairman of the Armed Services Committee, Goldwater assumed the chairmanship. Although proposals for reorganization had been stalled for years due to back-and-forth wrangling with Congress and the defense community, in December 1984, Gerald J. Smith, staff member to Senator Goldwater, called committee staffer James Locher to say that Goldwater "has decided to make defense reorganization his number-one priority. He views Pentagon reform as a critical issue and one where he might be able to make a lasting contribution before he retires."[7] Along with the able stewardship of Senator Sam Nunn, ranking Democrat on the Armed Services Committee, Goldwater helped steer the bill through the political minefield of the Senate and the military establishment. After passage of the Goldwater-Nichols Act in 1986, Goldwater kept his word and retired, but the act transforming the defense community still bears his name.

A member's calculus is not confined to such considerations; they are merely a few of the more influential general factors that members weigh when deciding where they stand on issues. Other interests also play a role. For example, the need to support the president can play a major role in shaping a member's stance on an issue—and in determining how hard he or she fights to defend that stance. In 1985, with Congress mounting an attack on President Reagan's support of the Contras in Nicaragua, Democratic Representative Charlie Wilson—in a hospital in Germany suffering the effects of years of alcohol abuse and unable to stand—was called back to the United States by the president to support the Contras by voting on the House floor from his wheelchair. As author George Crile depicted it, "Not even Tip O'Neill would ask this famous war hawk to turn down a direct appeal from the president."[8] Supporting the president often plays a large role, as doing so can help garner personal influence for a member and help his or her chances for reelection if the president is of the same party and campaigns on behalf of the member.

Personal experiences often affect how members view an issue, such as Senator John McCain's experience as a P.O.W. in Vietnam and his subsequent championing of anti-torture legislation. The pressure to fall in line with the party position on an issue can also influence a member's decision; such pressure is an important consideration because the party helps fund reelection campaigns and determines party leadership and committee assignments. Those who run afoul of the party can be assured of a cold shoulder when they need its help. Across the board, ideological interests always tint a member's view of an issue. Moral repugnance toward human rights abuses can spur a

7. As quoted in Locher, *Victory on the Potomac*, p. 220–21, 213.

8. Crile, *Charlie Wilson's War: The Extraordinary Story of the Largest Covert Operation in History*, pp. 381–82.

member to support U.S. participation in interventions in humanitarian crises, or a strong religious opposition to abortion can result in a member voting for the "global gag rule," preventing U.S. funds from being used abroad for activities relating to abortion.

RULES OF THE GAME

Once members have determined their interests and views on a particular issue, they must begin to play by the rules of the game in furthering their views. Just as in the executive branch, decisional outcomes in Congress are influenced by the rules of the game, as well as by the positions of the key players. The Constitution provides the basic structure. To be enacted into law a bill must be passed in identical form in both houses and then presented to the president for his signature. If the president vetoes the bill, it is returned to the house from which it originated and, if passed by a two-thirds vote in both houses, becomes law over the president's veto. Executive branch officials of high rank (as designated by Congress) as well as ambassadors and senior military officers are appointed by the president and must be approved by the Senate. Treaties must be approved by a two-thirds majority of the Senate.

The Constitution also lays out rules and procedures meant to govern how the nation goes to war. It requires Congress to declare war and designates the president commander in chief of the armed forces. Over time the understanding of these clauses has changed so that in practice presidents often have taken the nation into war without seeking congressional approval. Before the Persian Gulf War and the war in Iraq, each President Bush asked for Congress's authorization but nevertheless made it clear that he did not think that he needed it.

To implement and complement the rules laid out in the constitution, Congress has created additional procedures. Some of these, such as the Budget Act and the War Powers Resolution, are statutes enacted into law with the approval of the president. Rules also are enacted by each house to govern its own activities: they determine which committees have jurisdiction over particular matters, how bills are referred to committees and brought to the floor, and how debate proceeds on the bills. Still other rules determine whether matters can be added to a bill when it is being considered in committee or on the floor.

The House of Representatives has a set of rules providing for the consideration of bills on the floor. From time to time a bill comes to the floor "without a rule," which means that the standing rules apply. In almost all cases, however, when bills are ready to go to the floor, they first go to the House Rules

Committee, which crafts a "rule" for consideration of the bill. When the bill comes to the floor, the House first adopts the rule (by simple majority vote) and then considers the bill under that particular rule. Only the imagination of the leadership limits how the rule can shape the outcome of the debate on an issue.

In the Senate the standing rules more often apply, and they permit unlimited debate (unless limited by the invocation of cloture, which requires the affirmative votes of sixty senators) and any item can be added to the bill; that means that in most situations there are no germaneness rules limiting amendments to the bill. The alternative in the Senate is to seek unanimous consent to bring up a bill under agreed special procedures, which also can affect the outcome of the debate on legislation.

However, the informal rules of each house have come to govern much of their operations. For example, it is understood in the Senate that only the majority leader can seek to bring a bill to the floor. In the House that prerogative belongs to the majority leadership collectively, with the Speaker having the ultimate authority. Each set of informal rules determines where the locus of authority and both formal and informal power rest. Over the years Congress has moved between three models of informal rule sets—systems dominated by the leadership, committees, or the floor. The balance of power typically swings from one extreme to the other, and finally moves back toward a mixed system in which powers are shared by the leadership, the committees, and the floor.

The style that came to typify Congress at the turn of the twenty-first century was a leadership-centered system. Under that system the leadership in each house controls the system in part by controlling the way members are assigned to committees and how the committee leadership is chosen. Bills come to the floor when the leadership is ready to consider them and in the form desired by the leadership, rather than by the committee of jurisdiction. The leadership takes responsibility for rounding up the votes, which come almost entirely from the majority party. One of the great examples of the potential power of the leadership system—though rare during the cold war—was Lyndon Johnson's reign as Senate majority leader in the 1950s. In pushing through legislation, such as the hard-fought Civil Rights Act of 1957, LBJ was able to mitigate the control often exerted by committees and regional caucuses. Under the iron-fisted leadership of Speaker Dennis Hastert and Majority Leader Tom "the Hammer" DeLay, the Republican leadership of the House during President George W. Bush's first term was reminiscent of LBJ's domination of the Senate.

Under the committee-centric system in effect during much of the cold war period, when the Democrats controlled the House and usually controlled the Senate, the leadership role was much reduced. Bills came to the floor only when reported by the committee of jurisdiction and in the form reported by the committee. Bills often had bipartisan support within the committee and committee leaders from both sides of the aisle were responsible for rounding up the needed votes. Often the leadership could take no position on a bill because the party caucus was badly divided on the issue. Here, opposition to legislation often came from members of other committees with overlapping authority and alternative solutions to problems.

In this system, the committee chair often wields tremendous power. The support of Democrat Les Aspin, chairman of the House Armed Services Committee, was instrumental in obtaining congressional approval for President George H.W. Bush's plans for ejecting Iraq from Kuwait in 1991. When Senator Barry Goldwater, newly appointed chairman of the Senate Armed Services Committee, took the lead in reorganizing the defense establishment, he was not shy about using his power as committee chairman to round up committee members' votes. James Locher reports that when Goldwater asked for Senator Dan Quayle's vote on the bill, "Goldwater played political hardball, warning Quayle that if the Indiana senator failed to support him he would first take the chairmanship of the Defense Acquisition Policy Subcommittee away from him. Then he would get him kicked off the Armed Services Committee. And then he would work for his defeat in the next election."[9] Quayle capitulated.

Sometimes, however, the floor itself is king. Rather than being controlled by the leadership or committee leaders, legislative battles are fought out on the floor among coalitions based on regional concerns or ideological positions that cut across party lines.

Often the systems clash. After 9/11, for example, the House Judiciary Committee crafted a version of what became known as the Patriot Act, which passed the committee unanimously. The administration decided that it could not accept the text as reported out by the committee. Instead of bringing the bill as reported to the floor and seeking to amend it, the House Republican leadership introduced a different bill and brought it directly to the floor under a rule that permitted few amendments. In 2005, when leading Republican members of the Senate Armed Services Committee sought to legislate limits on interrogation techniques used with suspected terrorists, the Senate Republican leadership, at the urging of the administration, sought to invoke cloture

9. Locher, *Victory on the Potomac,* p. 407.

in order to end debate on the bill before the amendments could be considered, but it failed to get the support that it needed on the floor. Trade bills often are adopted on the house floor, with a majority of members voting for free trade based on regional and local economic interests despite disagreement between the committee of jurisdiction and the leadership of both parties.

Another set of rules determines how Congress appropriates funds for various activities, including those related to national security and foreign policy; those rules have a major impact on the actions taken. The congressional budget process starts when the president submits his budget in February of each year, which is followed by the drafting of a budget resolution in each house, setting a funding level for defense (the 050 account) and foreign policy (the 150 account). The fact that defense and foreign policy are in separate accounts probably leads to less spending on nondefense foreign policy issues. Many members want to see the 050 account as large as possible since it leaves more room for funding for defense contracts and bases in members' districts or states. Most members also think that it improves their prospect for reelection or promotion to higher office if they are seen to be voting for more money for defense. The opposite is true for the 150 account. Although it encompasses many items, including funding for agencies that facilitate trade and investment, it is generally viewed as the foreign aid account. Most members think that voting for less funding for foreign aid advances their political interests.

Once each house approves the budget resolution, it is reconciled in a conference and approved by both houses; however, it is not sent to the president, because it is merely guidance to the two houses, not binding legislation. On the basis of the numbers in the approved resolution, the appropriations committees get a figure for total discretionary spending. Those funds are in turn reallocated to the ten subcommittees of the appropriations committees, which are then limited to spending no more than that amount. One of the many anomalies of the budget process is that the appropriations subcommittees do not line up with the budget categories in the budget resolution. Because the 050 account is so large, it is broken into three parts. The bulk of the funding falls within the defense appropriations bill, but the part of the budget allocated for nuclear weapons programs goes to the subcommittee for the Energy Department and another portion goes to a separate Military Construction Subcommittee.

Until 2005 both the House and the Senate Appropriations Committees divided the 150 account into three parts. Foreign assistance programs went to a separate Foreign Operations Subcommittee. Most of the rest of the 150 account went to a subcommittee that also had jurisdiction over the Justice and Commerce Departments and related programs. That meant that funding for foreign policy competed with the much more popular programs in the other two agencies, including the FBI. In 2005, the Senate, but not the House, consolidated almost all of the 150 programs in a single subcommittee, and for the first time the appropriations subcommittees of the two houses did not have the same jurisdiction. The implications for foreign policy spending were not clear.

In theory, before the Appropriations Committees act, authorizing committees should authorize the programs to be funded. Congress almost always passes a defense authorization bill and usually passes what is popularly known as the State Department authorization bill (usually for two years) but almost never passes a bill authorizing the foreign aid program. Because the defense authorization bill is viewed as "must pass" legislation, it often becomes the vehicle through which Congress expresses its views and legislates restrictions on foreign policy activities. That is especially true in the Senate, where the rules permit amendments on any subject to a pending authorization bill.

The importance of rules in affecting outcomes in Congress can be illustrated most graphically by the issue of base closings in the United States. Prior to the passage of the Base Closure and Realignment Act in 1988, base closings were considered one at a time. The president would include in his budget request authority to use funds to close specific bases, and the authorizing committees would consider each base closing proposal separately. Members from the state or district affected would strongly oppose the base closing. Other members would have little or no direct interest and would defer in the hopes of getting support when they needed it to prevent one of their bases from closing.

The rules established in the base closing act were carefully designed to avoid those pitfalls. Since members of Congress agreed in the abstract on the need to close some bases, they were willing to vote for a procedure that reduced their influence over any specific base closing. Congress now from time to time authorizes the president to appoint a base closing commission. The Defense Department submits to the commission a list of bases that it wants to close. The commission, after conducting hearings, sends the list to the president with any modifications that it proposes to make. The president then sends his proposed list of base closings to Congress. Under rules that Congress has imposed on itself, the president can close the bases unless both houses pass a resolution disapproving all the closings. Any member is entitled to a vote on the resolution, but motions to exempt specific bases are not in order. As a result, on five occasions, including in 2005, the Pentagon has received authority to close a number of domestic bases.

A less successful effort to alter the rules to reduce congressional influence over specifics and thereby to increase the chances for enacting legislation is in the field of trade. Reaching agreement on trade legislation had become very difficult because members would focus exclusively on the provisions of trade agreements that affected their own districts or states and would seek to limit free trade in their areas. To prevent that Congress has enacted from time to time what is called "fast track authority." Under such legislation, when the president submits a trade agreement to Congress, it can vote only to approve or disapprove the agreement; it cannot take out provisions or add restrictions. When actually seeking to use that authority, presidents have found that the trade agreements that they had negotiated did not command a majority in both houses, even though members could vote only yes or no. Both when President Clinton presented the NAFTA agreement and when President Bush presented CAFTA, both houses lacked sufficient votes for passage. Thus both presidents needed to delay sending up the legislation while they negotiated changes to the legislation that would secure additional votes.

Operating within the rules and seeing the face of an issue most salient to them, members of the House and Senate decide what issues are important and how to secure the outcomes that they seek. In most cases that results in the enactment of legislation binding on the executive branch. But it can also take the form of less binding action, such as "sense of the Congress" language inserted in legislation or committee and conference reports and floor colloquies, all designed to influence executive branch actions to advance members' interests and national security as members view it through the lens of their interests.

The foreign policy views of personnel in both the executive and legislative branches are affected by many similar interests. Nevertheless, the executive branch officials dealing with foreign policy often are dedicated solely to foreign policy issues. Members of Congress, on the other hand—even those whose expertise is foreign policy or who serve on one of the foreign policy–oriented committees—must focus on numerous other issues as well.

The congressional role in foreign policy decisionmaking also merits close scrutiny because, while Congress can function as another department exerting influence on presidential foreign policy decisions, it rarely speaks with one voice. The views of individual members and committees influence foreign policy decisions even when Congress as a whole does not act in concert. In this respect, Congress can be hydra-headed, influencing foreign policy through both legislation and pressure by individual members. And like that of the executive branch bureaucracy, Congress's role in foreign policy is fluid—it neither stops nor starts with a presidential decision.

At last we are done, and the framework for explaining national security decisions and actions is in place. What we have described here should not, however, be considered a causal theory by which one may determine which variant of this complex process will be operative under what conditions. The highly politicized policymaking process for national security (and probably most other areas of national interest) can take any one of a rather large number of variations. For any one case in national security decisionmaking, such as the ABM case that we revisit in the next chapter, the framework developed here really provides only a starting point and research orientation that serves to sensitize the analyst examining the available evidence to the features and intricacies of the decisionmaking process. We do not claim that this broad framework is a substitute for rigorous historical explanation. Nevertheless, we do feel that it aids the analyst to interpret more realistically the reasons for foreign policy decisions and actions.

PART IV

Conclusions

CHAPTER SEVENTEEN

Back to ABM: Some Tentative Answers

We are now ready to return to the puzzles posed in chapter 1 about the decision to deploy the ABM. Some tentative answers to those puzzles emerge when the framework presented in the intervening chapters is employed in the search for explanations.

BUREAUCRATIC TUG-OF-WAR

Our first question is why in January 1967 President Johnson asked Congress to appropriate the funds to deploy an ABM but stated that he would defer deployment pending an effort to get the Soviet Union to engage in talks on limiting the arms race.

Technological improvement is part of the answer. The technology of ballistic missile defense had in certain respects improved remarkably in the preceding few years. Those responsible for the program in the scientific community, in the Director of Defense Research and Engineering (DDR&E) and its operating arm, the Advanced Research Projects Agency (ARPA), as well as in the Army, were now arguing that an effective ABM system could be built and ultimately could be improved to handle even a large Russian attack. In past years the contradictory testimony of scientists had offset pressure from the Joint Chiefs of Staff (JCS) and enabled McNamara to persuade the president and Congress that ABM deployment was not technologically feasible. The scientists now thought otherwise.[1]

1. Jayne, "The ABM Debate," pp. 308–09.

Soviet ABM deployment became an accepted fact. There was growing evidence that the Soviet Union was beginning to deploy an ABM system around Moscow. In the past the intelligence community had been split as to whether another system, the so-called Tallinn system deployed across the northern part of the Soviet Union, was in fact an ABM system. Though some military intelligence agencies had pressed the view that Tallinn was an ABM system, a majority in the intelligence community concluded that it was an air defense system. However, there was no dispute at all that the new deployment around Moscow was an ABM system. That added to pressures to begin an American deployment in order to avoid an ABM gap.

JCS pressure increased. In part because of the changes in technology and the Russian ABM deployment, the Joint Chiefs of Staff were no longer willing to acquiesce in delaying ABM deployment. They were determined to go firmly on record before Congress in favor of a deployment *now* and, in particular, for a deployment that would eventually develop into a large anti-Russian system.

Senate pressure also increased. Pressure was mounting from senior senators on the Armed Services Committee, including Richard B. Russell, Henry "Scoop" Jackson, and Strom Thurmond, who had all spoken out in favor of an early ABM deployment. The general expectation in the executive branch was that Congress would put great pressure on the president to agree to deployment if he did not include it in his budget message.[2]

Republican pressure was feared. It was becoming evident that the Republican Party planned to make a campaign issue out of the alleged ABM gap. On a *Meet the Press* broadcast in November, Michigan governor George Romney, then believed to be the leading Republican candidate for the presidential nomination in 1968, had talked of an ABM gap and made it clear that that would be an issue in the campaign. Senator Thurmond spoke as a leading Republican expert on defense matters as well as a Senate leader in attacking the failure to deploy an ABM system.[3]

There was no doubt that JCS demands for immediate ABM deployment would be made known to leaders on the Hill, as would the growing evidence of Soviet ABM deployment around Moscow. Congress had in the previous year included funds for ABM deployment even though the president had not requested any, and the stage was set for a confrontation should Johnson again accept the advice of his secretary of defense and delay deployment.

---

2. See, for example, *Baltimore Sun*, November 21, 1966, and December 3, 1966; *Washington Post*, November 24, 1966.

3. Jayne, "The ABM Debate," p. 346.

The president's choices toward the end of 1966 seemed rather narrow. He could reject ballistic missile defense, embracing McNamara's arguments against deployment, and prepare to take his case to congressional leaders and the public. Alternatively, he could proceed with a ballistic missile defense deployment at the cost of overruling his secretary of defense. The odds were high that the president would proceed with the ballistic missile defense deployment being pressed on him by the Joint Chiefs and the Senate leaders. Only if he could find another option did McNamara stand any chance of again delaying presidential commitment to ballistic missile defense.

It appears that McNamara first discussed the subject with the president at meetings held at his Texas ranch on November 3 and November 10. Those discussions were reported to have focused on two matters: ABM and the question of bombing additional targets in North Vietnam.[4]

Following the November 10 meeting, McNamara reported at a press conference that the Russians were now believed to be deploying an ABM system around Moscow. McNamara's initiative in releasing this information made it possible for him to preempt an inevitable news leak and, at the same time, to air his view that the Russian ABM deployment required improvements in U.S. offensive capability rather than a matching deployment. McNamara noted that the United States was moving ahead with Minuteman III and Poseidon and therefore was fully confident of its ability to offset the Russian ABM. He declared that it was too early to begin deployment of an anti-Chinese system and that no decision had been made on other possible reasons for a deployment.[5]

The decisive meeting with the president appears to have been held on December 6. At that meeting—attended by the president, Secretary McNamara, Deputy Secretary of Defense Cyrus Vance, the Joint Chiefs of Staff, and presidential assistant Walt Rostow—the Joint Chiefs were given the opportunity to put forward their argument for what was then called Posture A, which provided full coverage of the United States with a system designed for defense against more than a Chinese attack. The Joint Chiefs made it clear that they saw Posture A evolving into Posture B, a larger anti-Russian system designed to reduce casualties in the United States in the event of a large attack, and that they would accept nothing less. McNamara countered by presenting the arguments against an anti-Russian system, emphasizing that the Soviet Union could be expected to increase offensive capability to the extent necessary to fully offset the value of a U.S. ABM. At that point he appears to have suggested

4. This and the subsequent meetings are described in Jayne, "The ABM Debate," p. 346.
5. *New York Times*, November 13, 1966.

to the president two possible compromises. The first, which he was ultimately able to persuade the president to accept, called for procurement orders for those ABM components that would take a long time to produce; postponement of a decision regarding what system, if any, would be deployed; and an effort to begin arms limitation talks with the Soviet Union. The second option was to begin deployment of a small anti-Chinese system. The meeting ended with Johnson agreeing that the State Department should begin to probe the Russians on the possibility of talks but apparently withholding any decision on ABM deployment.

The State Department thus proceeded to explore the possibilities of arms limitation talks with the Soviet Union. Meanwhile McNamara presented the president with a memorandum summarizing his arguments against an anti-Russian system but suggesting that an ABM defense against China might prove useful.

To demonstrate that he was not the only opponent of a large Soviet-oriented ABM system, McNamara arranged for the president and the Joint Chiefs of Staff to meet in early January 1967 with past and current special assistants to the president for science and technology and former directors of defense research and engineering. None of the scientists present dissented from the view (not shared by the then-current head of DDR&E) that an ABM to defend the American people against a Russian missile attack was not feasible and should not be built. There was some discussion of an anti-Chinese system and some divergence of views, but a majority was opposed to deployment.[6]

Following that meeting, McNamara was apparently able to persuade Johnson to delay any deployment, whether anti-Russian or anti-Chinese, and to pursue the option of initial procurement combined with a concentrated effort to open arms limitation talks with the Soviet Union.

The proposal for such talks seemed to be a vehicle for the pursuit of a number of presidential objectives. Johnson was haunted, as all of his postwar predecessors had been, by the specter of nuclear war. He was anxious to try to do something to bring nuclear weapons under control. Moreover, it was an issue through which the president could appeal to the general public desire for peace and specifically to the left wing of the Democratic Party, which was becoming increasingly disaffected on Vietnam. It was also an issue with which Johnson could make history as the president who had made the decisive move

6. The scientists present were science advisers James R. Killian Jr., George B. Kistiakowsky, Jerome B. Wiesner, and Donald F. Hornig and defense research directors Herbert York, Harold Brown, and John S. Foster Jr. This meeting is described in York, *Race to Oblivion*, pp. 194–95; Jayne, "The ABM Debate," pp. 347–48; and Cahn, "Eggheads and Warheads," pp. 37–38.

to end the nuclear arms race that threatened mankind's doom. Johnson was quick to sense those possibilities.

McNamara was able to argue that an American decision to proceed with ballistic missile defense would hamper arms limitation talks with the Russians, since one of the main purposes of such talks would be to seek an agreement by both sides to avoid ABM deployment. McNamara could also argue that a dramatic act of restraint by the United States would increase the probability that the Soviet Union would respond favorably and that the talks would begin. In any case a bold gesture by the president for peace would undercut much of the opposition to his decision not to proceed right away with a ballistic missile defense.

At the same time, by asking for funds for ABMs and implying that he would be prepared to spend them if talks did not get under way, the president was able to avoid making the argument that the United States should unilaterally forgo deployment of a ballistic missile defense. Johnson would be able to tell military commanders and congressional leaders that he had certainly not ruled out a ballistic missile defense, that in fact he had taken a major step toward such a deployment but was postponing actual deployment pending an effort to get an arms control agreement with the Soviet Union. Although military and congressional leaders might be somewhat uneasy about the further delay, they could not effectively mount a campaign against an effort to seek an agreement with the Soviet Union, given the widespread popularity of such efforts.

Thus the proposal to link the two issues enabled McNamara to gain a further delay, hoping that it might last indefinitely as the talks continued. The president could avoid paying any major price in his relations with McNamara, the Joint Chiefs, or Congress. He put off a hard choice and opened up the possibility of arms control negotiations, which would substantially enhance his domestic position and ensure a favorable spot in the history books.[7]

SOMETHING FOR EVERYONE

We wish to ask further why the decision to deploy an ABM was announced at the tail end of a speech whose whole structure and purpose was to explain that an ABM defense against the Soviet Union was impossible. Why did the secretary of defense describe the system as one directed against China, while the Joint Chiefs of Staff and their allies in Congress described it as a first step toward a full-scale defense against the Soviet Union? What has been said thus

---

7. On the tendency of chief executives to make the minimum commitment necessary, see Schilling, "The H–Bomb Decision," pp. 24–46.

far should make it clear that the answers lie in the bargaining between McNamara and Johnson, as affected by the positions of the Joint Chiefs and certain leaders in Congress.

The effort to get the Soviets to agree to set a date for arms limitation talks was unsuccessful. When President Johnson met with Premier Kosygin in a hastily arranged summit conference at Glassboro, New Jersey, on June 23 and 25, 1967, there was still no Soviet agreement to talk. Johnson brought McNamara along, and while the two leaders ate lunch the secretary of defense gave them a lecture on nuclear strategy, previewing his San Francisco speech and emphasizing the value of an agreement to both sides. The Russian leader was unyielding; he described ABMs as defensive and unobjectionable and was not prepared to agree to talks.[8]

Following the conference at Glassboro, there could be little doubt that talks would not be under way before the president's next budget message in January 1968. Almost immediately Johnson informed McNamara that some kind of ABM deployment would have to be announced by January at the latest. The president would then have to account for the disposition of ABM contingency funds that he had requested and state whether he was seeking additional sums for deployment of an ABM system. Given the stakes involved and the implicit commitment that the president had made in January 1967 to go forward in the absence of arms talks, his decision was not difficult to predict. January 1968 would be Johnson's last chance to announce the deployment in a budget message before the November presidential elections. To hedge again, stating that he was still seeking talks, would have seemed unconvincing. The intermediate options had run out. The president was determined to go ahead, even if it meant paying a price in his relations with the secretary of defense. Apparently, Johnson also felt that by beginning to deploy an ABM he might convince the Russians to enter into arms limitation talks.[9]

Having decided to proceed with an ABM deployment, Johnson was obviously concerned about minimizing the cost in terms of his relations with McNamara. He was willing to let the secretary announce the deployment in any way that he chose. For the sake of military and congressional acceptance, the president may have insisted that the deployment be described in such a way that others could describe it as the first step toward an anti-Russian system.[10]

8. Jayne, "The ABM Debate," pp. 366–69.
9. Ibid., pp. 372–73.
10. Johnson had apparently been told explicitly by General Earle Wheeler that the Army would support a limited deployment only if it could describe it as the first step toward a large system. See Cahn, "Eggheads and Warheads," p. 37.

From McNamara's point of view the primary goal remained that of preventing a large system directed at the Soviet Union. If the United States were to go forward with any ABM deployment, it was important to him to do what was possible to create in the public mind a clear difference between the system being deployed and a large system. Thus it was in McNamara's interest to be able to explain his view of the arms race, explain his opposition to a large anti-Russian system, and only then announce an ABM deployment. The apparent contradiction in the speech was deliberate. McNamara may have hoped that his speech would generate substantial public opposition to an ABM deployment.

McNamara had recognized several years before that he might lose the battle against deploying any kind of ABM system, and he had begun laying the groundwork for a fallback position in the form of a small ABM system directed against China. In February 1965 McNamara publicly raised the possibility of ABM protection against a small nuclear attack from China but argued that even then the decision was not needed because "the lead-time for additional nations to develop and deploy an effective ballistic missile system capable of reaching the United States is greater than we require to deploy the defense."[11]

Thus in September 1967 McNamara could announce that the lead time required for American deployment of an ABM system was now about the same as the lead time for a Chinese deployment of ICBMs in significant numbers. Therefore it was now prudent to proceed with the sort of ABM installation that he had been discussing for several years. And McNamara appears to have been convinced that in its own terms ABM defense against China was, as he described it in his speech, "marginal" but nevertheless "prudent." Thus in announcing the decision to deploy an ABM system against China, McNamara could put forward arguments which he believed.

Even more important was McNamara's desire to prevent a large deployment directed at the Soviet Union. Such a system, he felt, would force the Russians to respond and thereby set off another round in the arms race. An anti-Chinese system could be more easily limited than a small system directed against the Soviet Union. One alternative was to describe the system as one designed to protect the U.S. Minuteman missiles, although it would be difficult to justify on grounds of its cost-effectiveness. Moreover, a system deployed only around missile sites would have been resisted by the Joint Chiefs and Senate leaders, since it would not pave the way for a larger system against the Soviet Union and

11. Jayne, "The ABM Debate," p. 273.

could not be described as the beginning of a larger system. Whether McNamara himself or the president ruled out that alternative is not clear.[12]

PRESSURES FOR EXPANSION

There is a final question that we want to answer. Why was the system authorized for deployment designed as if its purpose was to protect American cities against a large Soviet attack?

Once a presidential decision is made on a policy issue, the details of implementation must be turned over to an individual or organization. In the case of the ABM system, there was no choice but to assign responsibility to the Army. Although McNamara could and did attempt to monitor how the Army would deploy the system, he was unable or unwilling to ensure that the system would be designed so as to minimize the possibility of growth. The Army's freedom may have been enhanced by the fact that McNamara's scientific and technical advisers themselves tended to favor keeping open the option to expand the system. Deputy Secretary of Defense Paul Nitze, to whom general responsibility for much of the day-to-day administration of the Pentagon fell as McNamara devoted more and more of his time to Vietnam, also tended to favor keeping the option open.

But there was a more fundamental problem. Once a decision was made to proceed with a ballistic missile defense system against China, there was strong pressure to move forward quickly. The president could not then admit that the government had no hardware for such a system and that three or four years of research and development would be necessary before deployment would begin. Thus deployment began with the components that were already developed, even though they were far from optimal for a missile network that would serve against China but not grow into a large ABM system turned toward the Soviet Union.

Geography also worked against a limited system. Both Russian and Chinese ICBMs are set up to approach the United States through the same corridor over the North Pole. Radars for an anti-Chinese system would be the same as

12. In his San Francisco speech McNamara stated, with regard to Minuteman defense, that "the Chinese–oriented ABM deployment would enable us to add—as a concurrent benefit—a further defense of our Minuteman sites against Soviet attack, which means that at modest cost we would in fact be adding even greater effectiveness to our offensive missile force and avoiding a much more costly expansion of that force." A short time later, in an interview, "Defense Fantasy Now Come True," pp. 28A–28C, elaborating on the speech, he stated unequivocally that ABMs would be emplaced to defend Minuteman missiles. However, following a trip to Europe for a meeting of the NATO Nuclear Planning Group, McNamara stated that no decision had been made as to whether the option to defend Minuteman would be exercised.

those for an anti-Russian system, and long-range missile launchers would be useful against both threats.

DDR&E, which favored a large Soviet-oriented system, had no motive to use its ingenuity to develop components that might be effective against China but have little potential for a large anti-Russian system. And in making precise decisions about where to locate radar and missile launching sites, the Army in fact chose sites close to cities, to permit the deployment of a large anti-Russian system should the decision to do so be made at a later date.

McNamara's control over the implementation of the decision simply was not great enough to prevent such developments. He was increasingly immersed in Vietnam and clearly on his way out of office. He did not have the support of the president in seeking to limit the system. His principal assistant did not share his desire to reduce the possibility that the system could grow, and the Army, charged with deployment, favored a large anti-Russian system. Thus, despite McNamara's efforts in his statements to distinguish sharply between an anti-Chinese and an anti-Russian system, the Army was able to tell Congress that actual deployment was not different in any significant way from projected first stages of an anti-Russian system and that the system being deployed was expected to grow.

DECISIONS AND CHANGE

The Johnson administration's decision to deploy an ABM system, the way in which it was announced, and the deployment preparations that followed illustrate the policy process described in this book and demonstrate how awareness of politics inside government can help in analyzing a particular decision or action. As is typical, no single actor's views of what should be done dominated, although the president's views played a major role in shaping the general direction of American actions.

Two independent decisions were involved, with different actors influencing the course of each. The first decision was simply whether to deploy defensive missiles at all. That was necessarily a presidential decision; there was no end run around him. As the ABM decision illustrates, the president is qualitatively different—not simply a very powerful participant among less powerful participants.

The second decision related to the timing, substance, and shape of deployment, given the previous decision calling for an ABM system of some kind. In the latter decision the president played a much less central role and other players were more influential. Johnson was both less interested and less in control.

The decision that some sort of deployment would be announced by January 1968 can thus best be explained by exploring the multiple constituencies and interests that the president had to balance. During the cold war period, the foreign policy interests of every president came to focus on relations with the Soviet Union as they affected the nuclear balance and the need to avoid nuclear war. During the first half of that period, those concerns led to support for greater military efforts. During the second half of the period, military efforts were increasingly accompanied by interest in negotiating arms control agreements. Each president thought about the image that might be painted of him in the history books and developed a desire to go down as a man of peace. All of them felt, as Johnson did, the responsibility to avoid a nuclear holocaust that would destroy civilization. That was exactly the dilemma that confronted President Ronald Reagan two decades later, when he decided to pursue an all-out effort to develop a viable ballistic missile defense system and, at the same time, press the Soviet Union for the most far-reaching nuclear arms control agreements that had ever been contemplated.[13]

On the other hand, no president can ignore the pressures on him from the bureaucracy, especially senior military and department officers, or the pressures from congressional leaders and the public when a presidential campaign is around the corner. All those pressures came to bear on Lyndon Johnson as he pondered the ABM question in 1967. Johnson appeared here in the characteristic presidential role of conciliator, someone who attempts to give as much as he or she can to each of a number of principal subordinates and the permanent bureaucracies while seeking a position that avoids any conflict between his or her own various interests and constituencies beyond the government. The limited ABM system that Johnson ultimately authorized could be described by Robert McNamara as anti-Chinese and hence not a danger to Soviet-American relations in general or future arms talks in particular. At the same time, the Joint Chiefs and Senate leaders had their own payoffs. Despite McNamara's statement, they still could describe deployment as a first step toward an anti-Russian system. Moreover, the "small" anti-Chinese system that Johnson approved was much larger than the system the Soviet Union was deploying around Moscow. Given the ambiguities and the simpli-

---

13. In *The Master of the Game*, Strobe Talbott describes President Reagan's SDI and arms control initiatives in much the way we have analyzed President Johnson's ABM decision. There are interesting historical parallels between the two periods for foreign policy decisionmaking.

fied view the public takes on such questions, the Republican Party could be denied a missile gap issue. That was the president's payoff.

Johnson also was able to reconcile his own desire to seek an end to the nuclear arms race with the need to maintain American military strength. In early 1967, he was prepared to go along with McNamara's proposal to seek arms talks with the Soviet Union before a firm final decision was made to proceed with ABM deployment. After talking with Kosygin he concluded that under the current circumstances the Soviet Union would not enter talks. He believed that perhaps the pressure that would be put on Russia's leaders by the beginning of American deployment would move them to agree to talks. In ordering the deployment Johnson was not abandoning his efforts to get arms talks and an arms agreement with the Soviet Union. He thought of himself as structuring the situation to make an American ABM deployment a way to get the very talks that both he and McNamara desired.

If the decision to order a deployment can be most clearly understood in terms of the conflicting pressures on the president, the precise nature of the deployment can be understood largely in terms of pressures within the bureaucracy below the president, constrained by the operating procedures of the Army and of the Pentagon as a whole. Although McNamara himself wanted no deployment or a limited deployment, the staffs on which he had to depend to monitor and implement the president's decision were unanimous in their belief that an ABM system should be built that could grow into a large anti-Russian system. His science adviser, John S. Foster, who would have the major role in monitoring both the research on the ABM system and its development and production, believed strongly that the option for a large system should be left open, as did Paul Nitze, McNamara's deputy secretary of defense (following the departure of Cyrus Vance, who more closely shared McNamara's views). The Army itself favored a big system. No imaginative thought had gone into the design of components for a specifically anti-Chinese system. In fact, the implementers were straining as hard as they could to design and later deploy a system that could be expanded. McNamara was stymied. He lacked a strong presidential directive to keep the system small; he lacked strong staff support in that direction. He was himself primarily preoccupied with Vietnam, and his days as secretary of defense were obviously numbered.

One of the truisms about bureaucracy is that it resists change. In that light, the ABM issue appears to be an anomaly, but it was not. Although McNamara was in one sense a defender of the status quo, he had to take the initiative to try to prevent ABM deployment, since the system seemed to be grinding inevitably toward that end. The system was heavily biased toward the deployment of new weapons under certain conditions; ABM deployment was not seen as change. The rules of the game, shared images, and organizational procedures of the American government produced a situation from the time of the Korean War through the end of the 1960s in which the procurement of new weapons was part of the routine.

As noted earlier, the budgetary process itself creates a unique set of pressures. The fact that ABM decisions had to be recorded in the budget meant to proponents that the issue would reach the president without any effort on their part. That was particularly true because of the rule giving the JCS the right to appeal any decision of the secretary of defense or the budget director to the president. No other career service enjoys that right. Moreover, the president had to make a decision and announce it publicly according to a deadline determined by the budget. To urge him to delay was to urge him to take a public stand against ABM deployment at that time.

The operating rules of the Joint Chiefs of Staff, as well as their access to powerful senators and representatives, also biased the system toward deployment of any weapons system favored strongly by one of the services. Given strong Army support for an ABM system and given the judgment of Pentagon scientists that it was technically feasible, unanimous JCS support for the system was forthcoming under the logrolling rules that the Joint Chiefs had begun to use in the McNamara period. The fact that they would report their views to Congress when asked meant that the president could not keep differences hidden and would have to publicly challenge the JCS in order to prevent deployment.

The timing of the private negotiations that the president and the secretary of defense conducted with the Joint Chiefs in itself biased decisions toward deployment. That is to say, the normal aversion of the budget bureau to expensive weapons, the skepticism of the members of the president's Science Advisory Committee, and the opposition of some parts of the State Department to deployment could not be brought into play early enough in the process to affect the outcome.

The shared images that officials believed dominated American society further pushed the system toward ABM deployment. There was a widely accepted view that the United States ought to maintain strategic superiority over the Soviet Union and therefore ought to more than match any system that the Soviets deployed. The general view was that the United States should deploy any strategic system that worked well and appeared to have the prospect of reducing damage should war occur. The existence of that shared view made it difficult to put forward arguments within the bureaucracy against ABM deployment and even more difficult to shape arguments that the president would judge to be effective with Congress and with the public. Given the situation, the president had to be concerned with the domestic political effects, particularly on his reelection prospects in 1968. He did not want to be accused of opening an ABM gap, failing to match the Soviet system, and giving up American nuclear superiority.

The organizational procedures of the Pentagon likewise moved the government in the direction of deployment. Research, both in the Army and in the Advanced Research Projects Agency, was dominated by scientists who believed that any feasible system should be deployed. Moreover, the focus tended to be on the greatest conceivable threat and hence on designing missiles to counter a large Russian attack. The desire to make an effective case for deployment led to underestimates of cost and overestimates of feasibility.

McNamara seemed to recognize that, because of the constraints within the government, he probably could not stop ABM deployment. Thus his effort had to be directed as much toward changing long-standing biases with respect to nuclear strategy as to devising delaying action against deployment. Although he lost the short-run battle to prevent deployment (or confine deployment to a missile type that could not grow into a large anti-Russian system), his effort to change the terms of the debate as carried on within the bureaucracy, in Congress, and among the public were considerably more successful.

Thus by 1969 President Nixon accepted nuclear sufficiency rather than superiority as the American goal. He also embraced as his own McNamara's arguments against an anti-Russian system. He announced that the United States had no intention of deploying such a system, not only because it was technically infeasible but also because such a system would threaten the Soviet Union's deterrent. He proceeded with a system designed to defend the country against China and to defend Minuteman, but he directed that the system be designed so that it could not be expanded—or appear to the Russians capable of being expanded—into a large system. In part as a result of the arguments McNamara had made, the attitude of the Senate changed dramatically on this issue.

Perhaps the most successful conversion came with the Russians. Kosygin was arguing at Glassboro that ABMs were purely defensive weapons and that the American effort to prevent their deployment was immoral. However, by 1971, at the strategic arms talks, the Russians were pressing for an agreement to limit ABMs. Even the fact that the talks were under way can be attributed to McNamara's efforts to prevent ABM deployment. The treaty limiting ABMs to very low levels, negotiated in Moscow in May 1972, was a final vindication of McNamara's position.

During subsequent decades of arms control negotiations, however, the proponents of an ABM system continued to fight against limits on U.S. efforts to develop a missile defense system. Although Ronald Reagan made the Strategic Defense Initiative (SDI) a hallmark of his administration, he kept the ABM treaty in place and promoted negotiations with the Soviet Union for substantial reductions in nuclear weapons. After the Soviet Union split up, attention in Washington turned increasingly to the task of preventing the dismantled Soviet weapons from falling into the hands of hostile actors. The desire for an effective missile defense against a variety of threats was reborn in earnest during the presidency of George W. Bush and the long-time opponents of the ABM treaty finally succeeded in convincing him to withdraw from the treaty.

CHAPTER EIGHTEEN

A Complicated
Reality

This book has tried to do two things. At the most general
level, it has presented a way of thinking about how governments function in the
area of national security. It also has provided a good deal of detail about the
nature of the American bureaucratic system in the period since World War II.

Having concentrated largely on the specifics of the American system in
this period, we wish to pull back briefly to view the broader perspective and
look at the implications of this approach for an understanding of international politics and of the impact of American actions on the behavior of other
nations.

In general, when someone thinks in the conventional way about international politics, he or she takes for granted the analogy of two individuals
talking clearly and purposefully to each other and reacting in terms of carefully calculated interests. Thus the United States and other nations are believed
each to possess unity of purpose and action in responding to the other's
moves.[1]

If, as we believe, other governments are similar to the U.S. government as we
have described it here, then the reality is quite different. Understanding of any
international event and especially understanding of how American behavior
influences the behavior of other countries would be greatly improved if the
usual model were replaced by a different, more complicated image of what

1. Graham Allison has presented persuasive evidence of the extent to which this is the
dominant way of thinking about international politics. He terms this approach "Model One:
The Rational Actor." See Allison, *Essence of Decision*, pp. 10–38.

international politics is all about. That image, derived from the discussion of the American government presented here, would reveal the following features.

Most governments are not, in fact, the equivalent of a single individual with a single purpose and the ability to control completely the government's actions. Rather, each government consists of numerous individuals, many of them working in large organizations. Constrained, to be sure, by the shared images of their society, those individuals nevertheless have very different interests and priorities, and they are concerned with very different questions. Many of them are preoccupied by events at home and deal with events abroad only as those events interact with and affect their ability to pursue their interests at home. Others are concerned directly with what happens abroad but do not agree on what should be done. At any one time a government is concerned with countless issues and problems at home and abroad.

An action by one government, which looks to an outside observer like a deliberate and calculated attempt to influence the behavior of another government, in fact is likely to have emerged from the process of pulling and hauling that we have described above for the American government. One participant's idea of what actions should be taken to influence another government has likely been compromised by other participants' point of view about what will influence that government and by still other participants' concern with organizational and domestic interests. Any decision that was taken might well have been adventitious, and what was then done was no doubt influenced by those who had to implement the decision. The implementers are likely not to have fully understood what was decided, and they are constrained by the standard operating procedures of their organization. They also might have the desire and the ability to resist orders and do something else. Thus actions that appear to be designed to influence another government actually have much more complicated origins.

Nor will the government toward which the action seems to be directed respond according to the common image of two individuals communicating accurately with each other. For one thing, officials in the second government do not know whether the act that they observe in fact resulted from high-level decisions, more or less faithfully implemented, or from other sources and purposes. In any case, they interpret the action according to the shared images of their own society. They view the action in light of their own interests within their own bureaucracy and society. Thus the impact of an action by one government on another depends on the nature of the internal debate in that government, on which participants are strengthened or disheartened by the action, and on the common interpretation that comes to be given to it in the second government. How that government responds is influenced by all of the pulling and hauling discussed above.

Efforts to explain the behavior of two nations in relation to each other are likely to seem less puzzling if such a framework is adopted for purposes of analysis. We would then ask, for example, not why the United States took a certain action and what calculations might have been in "its" mind, but what motives, interests, and sources of power of the various participants in the American government led to the decisions and then to the actions. In seeking to explain the response, we would apply the same analysis, taking account of the great difficulty in perceiving the sources of an action of another government.

This approach also has important implications for policy advice to the American government. Both inside and outside the government, proposals put forward to influence the behavior of other governments usually are based on the simple model of two individuals communicating accurately with each other. If the approach presented here is applied, then proposals that otherwise look sensible may appear unwise or even dangerous. What is ultimately decided after a proposal is put forward almost certainly will be a compromise drawn from suggestions by a number of individuals, and what is then done will be heavily influenced by the standard operating procedures and interests of the implementers. How the resulting action affects other governments will depend on their internal situations, their domestic conflicts, and their perceptions of U.S. interests and intentions. Only if we are able to make such an analysis of a policy proposal can we have reasonable confidence that what is being suggested is sensible.

References
and Bibliography

The first section of the references and bibliography lists the memoirs of individuals who were involved in the making of U.S. national security policy at one time or another during the post–World War II period. For the first edition of this book, an attempt was made to identify and examine every one of these sources, defined as books and articles in which an author describes his involvement in the policy process. Thus section A is a substantially complete listing of all such memoirs published through early 1973 and a much less compete list of books and articles published since that date. A number of interviews conducted and transcribed by the John F. Kennedy Library as part of its Oral History Program likewise contain reminiscences by participants in the policy process. The Oral History Interviews from which we quote are listed in section B. Section C lists all other sources that we consulted, a high proportion of which are quoted or cited in the text. Some are of special conceptual relevance in the study of bureaucratic politics.

A. MEMOIRS

Acheson, Dean. 1969. *Present at the Creation: My Years in the State Department.* New York: W. W. Norton.
———. *Sketches from Life of Men I Have Known.* 1959. New York: Harper & Brothers.
Adams, Sherman. 1961. *Firsthand Report: The Story of the Eisenhower Administration.* New York: Harper & Brothers.
Albright, Madeleine. 2003. *Madam Secretary: A Memoir.* New York: Miramax Books.
Anderson, Clinton P., with Milton Viorst. 1970. *Outsider in the Senate.* New York: World.

Attwood, William. 1967. *The Reds and the Blacks: A Personal Adventure.* New York: Harper & Row.

Ball, George W. 1968. *The Discipline of Power: Essentials of a Modern World Structure.* Boston: Little, Brown.

————. "Top Secret: The Prophecy the President Rejected." *Atlantic Monthly* (July 1972).

————. "Vietnam Hindsight." 1971. NBC News White Paper (December).

Bingham, Jonathan B. 1953. *Shirt-Sleeve Diplomacy.* New York: John Day.

Blachman, Morris J. 1970. "The Stupidity of Intelligence." In *Inside the System: A Washington Monthly Reader,* edited by Charles Peder and Timothy J. Adams (eds.). New York: Praeger.

Bohlen, Charles E. 1973. *Witness to History, 1929–1969.* New York: W. W. Norton.

Bonal, Philip W. 1971. *Cuba, Castro, and the United States.* University of Pittsburgh Press.

Bowles, Chester. 1971. *Promises to Keep: My Years in Public Life, 1941–1969.* New York: Harper & Row.

Bremer, L. Paul III. 2006. *My Year in Iraq: The Struggle to Build a Future of Hope.* New York: Simon and Schuster.

Briggs, Ellis. 1964. *Farewell to Foggy Bottom: The Recollections of a Career Diplomat.* New York: McKay.

Brzezinski, Zbigniew. 1983. *Power and Principle: Memoirs of the National Security Adviser, 1977–1981.* New York: Farrar, Straus & Giroux.

Bucher, Lloyd M., with Mark Rascovich. 1970. *Bucher: My Story.* New York: Doubleday.

Bush, George, and Brent Scowcroft. 1998. *A World Transformed.* New York: Alfred A. Knopf.

Bush, Vannevar. 1970. *Pieces of the Action.* New York: Morrow.

Byrnes, James F. 1958. *All in One Lifetime.* New York: Harper & Brothers.

————. 1947. *Speaking Frankly.* New York: Harper &Brothers.

Carter, Jimmy. 1995. *Keeping the Faith: Memoirs of a President.* University of Arkansas Press.

Christian, George. 1970. *The President Steps Down: A Personal Memoir of the Transfer of Power.* New York: Macmillan.

Clark, Mark W. 1954. *From the Danube to the Yalu.* New York: Harper & Brothers.

Clarke, Richard A. 2004. *Against All Enemies: Inside America's War on Terrorism.* New York: Free Press.

Clay, Lucius D. 1950. *Decision in Germany.* New York: Doubleday.

Cleveland, Harlan. 1970. *NATO: The Transatlantic Bargain.* New York: Harper & Row.

Clinton, Bill. 2002. *My Life.* New York: Knopf.

Collins, J. Lawton. 1969. *War in Peacetime.* Boston: Houghton Mifflin.

Conant, James B. 1970. *My Several Lives: Memoirs of a Social Inventor.* New York: Harper & Row.

Cooke, Charles. 1970. "Organizational Constraints in U.S. Performance in Vietnam." Paper presented at the 66th Annual Meeting of the American Political Science Association.

Corson, William R. 1968. *The Betrayal.* New York: W. W. Norton, 1968.

Cutler, Robert. 1965. *No Time for Rest.* Boston: Little, Brown.

Daniels, Jonathan. 1946. *Frontier on the Potomac.* New York: Macmillan.

Dobney, Frederick J., ed. 1971. *Selected Papers of Will Clayton.* Baltimore: Johns Hopkins Press.

Dulles, Allen. 1963. *The Craft of Intelligence*. New York: New American Library.

Dulles, Eleanor Lansing. 1968. *American Foreign Policy in the Making*. New York: Harper & Row.

Eccles, Marriner S. 1951. *Beckoning Frontiers*. New York: Knopf.

Eisenhower, Dwight D. 1963. *The White House Years*. Vol. 1, *Mandate for Change, 1953–1956*. New York: Doubleday.

———. 1965. *The White House Years*. Vol. 2, *Waging Peace, 1956–1961*. New York: Doubleday.

Eisenhower, Milton S. 1963. *The Wine Is Bitter: The United States and Latin America*. New York: Doubleday.

Enthoven, Alain C., and K. Wayne Smith. 1971. *How Much Is Enough? Shaping the Defense Program, 1961–1969*. New York: Harper & Row.

Fitzgerald, A. Ernest. 1972. *The High Priests of Waste*. New York: W. W. Norton.

Forrestal, James V. See Walter Millis.

Frankel, Charles. 1968. *High on Foggy Bottom: An Outsider's Inside View of the Government*. New York: Harper & Row.

Galbraith, John Kenneth. 1969. *Ambassador's Journal: A Personal Account of the Kennedy Years*. Boston: Houghton Mifflin.

Gavin, James M. 1958. *War and Peace in the Space Age*. New York: Harper & Brothers.

Goldman, Eric F. 1969. *The Tragedy of Lyndon Johnson*. New York: Knopf.

Goulding, Philip. 1970. *Confirm or Deny: Informing the People on National Security*. New York: Harper &Row.

Halle, Louis J. 1969. *The Society of Man*. New York: Dell.

Harriman, W. Averell. 1971. *America and Russia in a Changing World*. New York: Doubleday.

Hilsman, Roger. 1971. *The Politics of Policy-Making in Defense and Foreign Affairs*. New York: Harper & Row.

———. 1967. *To Move a Nation: The Politics of Foreign Policy in the Administration of John F. Kennedy*. New York: Doubleday.

Hoopes, Townsend. 1969. *The Limits of Intervention: An Inside Account of How the Johnson Policy of Escalation in Vietnam Was Reversed*. New York: McKay.

Hughes, Emmet John. 1963. *The Ordeal of Power: A Political Memoir of the Eisenhower Years*. New York: Atheneum.

Johnson, Lyndon Baines. 1971. *The Vantage Point: Perspectives of the Presidency, 1963-1969*. New York: Holt, Rinehart & Winston.

Jones, Joseph M. 1955. *The Fifteen Weeks: February 21–June 5, 1947*. New York: Viking.

Kennan, George F. 1967. *Memoirs, 1925-1950*. Boston: Little, Brown.

———. 1972. *Memoirs, 1950-1963*. Boston: Little, Brown.

Kennedy, Robert F. 1969. *Thirteen Days: A Memoir of the Cuban Missile Crisis*. New York: W.W. Norton.

Khrushchev, Nikita. 1970. *Khrushchev Remembers*. Boston: Little, Brown.

Kirkpatrick, Lyman B., Jr. 1968. *The Real CIA*. New York: Macmillan.

Kissinger, Henry. 1979. *The White House Years*. Boston: Little, Brown.

———. 1999. *Years of Renewal*. New York: Simon and Schuster.

Krock, Arthur. 1968. *Memoirs: Sixty Years on the Firing Line*. New York: Funk & Wagnalls.

Lansdale, Edward Gary. 1972. *In the Midst of Wars*. New York: Harper & Row.

Larson, Arthur. 1968. *Eisenhower: The President Nobody Knew*. New York: Scribner's.

LeMay, Curtis E., with MacKinlay Kantor. 1965. *Mission with LeMay: My Story.* New York: Doubleday.

Lilienthal, David E. 1964. *The Journals of David E. Lilienthal.* Vol. 2, *The Atomic Energy Years, 1945–1950.* New York: Harper & Row.

Lodge, Henry Cabot. 1973. *The Storm Has Many Eyes: A Personal Narrative.* New York: W. W. Norton.

MacArthur, Douglas. 1964. *Reminiscences.* New York: Fawcett.

McGarvey, Patrick J. 1972. *CIA: The Myth and the Madness.* New York: Saturday Review Press.

McNamara, Robert S. 1968. *The Essence of Security: Reflections in Office.* London: Hodder & Stoughton.

McPherson, Harry. 1972. *A Political Education.* Boston: Little, Brown.

Martin, John Bartlow. 1966. *Overtaken by Events: The Dominican Crisis from the Fall of Trujillo to the Civil War.* New York: Doubleday.

Mecklin, John. 1965. *Mission in Torment: An Intimate Account of the U.S. Role in Vietnam.* New York: Doubleday.

Medaris, John B. 1960. *Countdown for Decision.* New York: Putnam's.

Melby, John. 1972. *The Mandate of Heaven: Record of a Civil War, China 1945–49.* New York: Doubleday Anchor.

Merson, Martin. 1955. *The Private Diary of a Public Servant.* New York: Macmillan.

Millis, Walter, ed., with E. S. Duffield. 1951. *The Forrestal Diaries.* New York: Viking.

Moyers, Bill. 1969. "Bill Moyers Talks about the War and LBJ: An Interview." In *Who We Are,* edited by Robert Manning and Michael Janeway. Boston: Little, Brown.

Murphy, Robert. 1964. *Diplomat among Warriors.* New York: Doubleday.

Nitze, Paul H. 1989. *From Hiroshima to Glasnost: At the Center of Decision—A Memoir.* New York: Grove Weidenfeld.

Nixon, Richard M. 1978. *RN: The Memoirs of Richard Nixon.* New York: Grosset & Dunlap.

Nixon, Richard M. 1962. *Six Crises.* New York: Doubleday.

O'Donnell, Kenneth. 1970. "LBJ and the Kennedys." *Life* (August 7).

Powell, Colin. 1995. *My American Journey.* New York: Ballantine Books.

Powers, Francis Gary, with Curt Gentry. 1970. *Operation Overflight.* New York: Holt, Rinehart & Winston.

Rankin, Karl Lott. 1964. *China Assignment.* University of Washington Press.

Reagan, Ronald. 1990. *An American Life: The Autobiography.* New York: Simon and Schuster.

Reedy, George E. 1970. *The Twilight of the Presidency.* New York: World.

Ridgway, Matthew B. 1967. *The Korean War.* New York: Popular Library.

———. 1956. *Soldier: The Memoirs of Matthew B. Ridgway.* New York: Harper & Brothers.

Roberts, Chalmers M. 1973. *First Rough Draft.* New York: Praeger.

Ross, Dennis. 2004. *The Missing Peace: The Inside Story of the Fight for Middle East Peace.* New York: Farrar, Straus and Giroux.

Rostow, W. W. 1972. *The Diffusion of Power, 1957–1972.* New York: Macmillan.

Rubin, Robert E. 2003. *In an Uncertain World.* New York: Random House.

Rusk, Dean. 1969. "Mr. Secretary on the Eve of Emeritus." *Life* (January 17).

Salinger, Pierre. 1966. *With Kennedy.* New York: Doubleday.

Schlesinger, Arthur M., Jr. 1965. *A Thousand Days: John F. Kennedy in the White House*. Boston: Houghton Mifflin.

Sebald, William J., with Russell Brines. 1965. *With MacArthur in Japan*. New York: W. W. Norton.

Shultz, George. 1993. *Turmoil and Triumph: My Years as Secretary of State*. New York: Scribner's.

Smith, Earl E. T. 1962. *The Fourth Floor: An Account of the Castro Communist Revolution*. New York. Random House.

Smith, Walter Bedell. 1949. *My Three Years in Moscow*. Philadelphia: Lippincott.

Sorensen, Theodore C. 1963. *Decision-Making in the White House: The Olive Branch or the Arrows*. Columbia University Press.

———. 1965. *Kennedy*. New York: Harper & Row.

Sorensen, Thomas C. 1968. *The Word War: The Story of American Propaganda*. New York: Harper & Row.

Sparks, Will. 1971. *Who Talked to the President Last?* New York: W. W. Norton.

Strauss, Lewis L. 1962. *Men and Decisions*. New York: Doubleday.

Sulzberger, C. L. 1969. *A Long Row of Candles: Memoirs and Diaries, 1934–1954*. New York: Macmillan.

Taylor, Maxwell D. 1972. *Swords and Plowshares*. New York: W. W. Norton.

———. 1959. *The Uncertain Trumpet*. New York: Harper & Brothers.

Thayer, Charles W. 1959. *Diplomat*. New York: Harper & Brothers.

Trivers, Howard. 1972. *Three Crises in American Foreign Affairs and a Continuing Revolution*. Southern Illinois University Press.

Truman, Harry S. 1955. *Memoirs*. Vol. 1, *Year of Decisions*. New York: Doubleday.

———. 1956. *Memoirs*. Vol. 2, *Years of Trial and Hope*. New York: Doubleday, 1956.

Twining, Nathan. 1966. *Neither Liberty nor Safety*. New York: Holt, Rinehart & Winston.

Walt, Lewis W. 1970. *Strange War, Strange Strategy: A General's Report on Vietnam*. New York: Funk & Wagnalls.

Wedemeyer, Albert C. 1958. *Wedemeyer Reports!* New York: Holt.

York, Herbert F. 1970. *Race to Oblivion: A Participant's View of the Arms Race*. New York: Simon & Schuster.

Zelikow, Philip, and Condoleezza Rice. 1997. *Germany Unified and Europe Transformed: A Study in Statecraft*. Harvard University Press.

B. INTERVIEWS

The following Oral History Interviews—conducted, transcribed, and preserved by the John F. Kennedy Library, Cambridge, Massachusetts—have been consulted for the light they throw on the policy process. The interviewer's name follows in parentheses.

Acheson, Dean (Lucius Battle), April 27, 1964.
Clay, Lucius (Richard Scammon), July 1, 1964.
Douglas Hume, Alex (statement by Hume himself), March 17, 1965.
Farley, Phillip (Joseph O'Connor), November 1, 1966.

Fisher, Adrian (Frank Sieberts), May 13, 1964.
Horowitz, Solis (Joseph O'Connor), March 18, 1966.
Hunvitch, Robert (John Plank), April 24, 1964.
Johnson, U. Alexis (William Brubeck), September 13, 1965.
Kennan, George (Louis Fisher), March 23, 1966.
Reinhardt, Frederick G. (Joseph O'Connor), October 1, 1966.
Wilson, Donald (James Greenfield), September 2, 1964.
York, Herbert (Steven Rivkin), June 16, 1964.

C. OTHER SOURCES

Abel, Elie. 1966. *The Missile Crisis.* Philadelphia: Lippincott.
Acheson, Dean. 1960. "The President and the Secretary of State." In *The Secretary of State,* edited by Don K. Price. Englewood Cliffs, N.J.: Prentice-Hall.
Allison, Graham T. 1970–71. "Cool It: The Foreign Policy of Young America." *Foreign Policy 1* (Winter).
———. 1971. *Essence of Decision: Explaining the Cuban Missile Crisis.* Boston: Little, Brown.
Alperovitz, Gar. 1965. *Atomic Diplomacy.* New York: Vintage Books.
Alsop, Stewart. 1968. *The Center: People and Power in Political Washington.* New York: Harper & Row.
Anderson, Patrick. 1968. *The President's Men.* New York: Doubleday.
Argyris, Chris. 1967. *Some Causes of Organizational Ineffectiveness within the Department of State.* Occasional Papers 2, Center for International Systems Research, Department of State. Government Printing Office, 1967.
Armacost, Michael H. 1969. *The Politics of Weapons Innovation: The Thor-Jupiter Controversy.* Columbia University Press.
Aronson, James. 1970. "Views of the Press: The Sell-Out of the Pulitzer Prize." *Washington Monthly* (October).
Art, Robert J. 1968. *The TFX Decision: McNamara and the Military.* Boston: Little, Brown.
Aspin, Les. 1978. "The Power of Procedure." In *Congress and Arms Control,* edited by Alan Platt and Lawrence D. Weiler. Boulder, Colo.: Westview Press.
Baar, James, and William E. Howard. 1960. *Polaris.* New York: Harcourt, Brace.
Beal, John Robinson. 1970. *Marshall in China.* New York: Doubleday.
Beichman, Arnold. 1967. *The "Other" State Department.* New York: Basic Books.
Bernstein, Marver H. 1958. *The Job of the Federal Executive.* Brookings.
Beschloss, Michael, and Strobe Talbott. 1993. *At the Highest Levels: The Inside Story of the End of the Cold War.* Little, Brown and Company.
Blue Ribbon Defense Panel. 1970. *Report to the President and the Secretary of Defense on the Department of Defense by the Blue Ribbon Defense Panel.* Government Printing Office.
Bottome, Edgar M. 1971. *The Missile Gap: A Study of the Formulation of Military and Political Policy.* Fairleigh Dickinson University Press.
Bowie, Robert R. 1960. "The Secretary and the Development and Coordination of Policy." In *The Secretary of State,* edited by Don K. Price. Englewood Cliffs, N.J.: Prentice-Hall.

Brandon, Henry. 1969. *Anatomy of Error.* Boston: Gambit.

———. 1964. "Schlesinger at the White House: An Historian's Inside View of Kennedy at Work." *Harper's* (July).

Bundy, McGeorge. 1972. "Statement before the Senate Foreign Relations Committee." In *The Geneva Protocol of 1925: Hearing before the Senate Foreign Relations Committee.* 91 Cong. 2 sess., March 19, 1971. Government Printing Office.

Cahn, Anne Hessing. 1971. "Eggheads and Warheads: Scientists and the ABM." M.I.T. Center for International Studies.

Campbell, Angus, Gerald Gurin, and Warren Miller. 1954. *The Voter Decides.* Evanston, Ill.: Row, Peterson.

Campbell, John Franklin. 1971. *The Foreign Affairs Fudge Factory.* New York: Basic Books.

Caraley, Demetrios. 1966. *The Politics of Military Unification: A Study of Conflict and the Policy Process.* Columbia University Press.

Caridi, Ronald J. 1968. *The Korean War and American Politics: The Republican Party as a Case Study.* University of Pennsylvania Press.

Carter, Jimmy. Letter to the editor. *Foreign Affairs* 78, no. 6 (November-December 1999).

Cater, Douglass. 1959. *The Fourth Branch of Government.* Boston: Houghton Mifflin.

———. 1964. *Power in Washington.* New York: Vintage Books.

Chester, Lewis, Godfrey Hodgson, and Bruce Page. 1969. *An American Melodrama: The Presidential Campaign of 1968.* New York: Viking.

Clark, Blair. 1970. "Westmoreland Appraised: Questions and Answers." *Harper's* (November).

Clark, Keith C., and Laurence J. Legere, eds. *The President and the Management of National Security: A Report by the Institute for Defense Analyses.* New York: Praeger.

Cohen, Bernard C. 1957. *The Political Process and Foreign Policy: The Making of the Japanese Peace Settlement.* Princeton University Press.

———. 1963. *The Press and Foreign Policy.* Princeton University Press.

Cornford, F. M. 1922. *Microcosmographia Academica, Being a Guide for the Young Academic Politician.* Cambridge: Bowes & Bowes.

Crile, George. 2003. *Charlie Wilson's War: The Extraordinary Story of the Largest Covert Operation in History.* New York: Atlantic Monthly Press.

Crozier, Michel. 1964. *The Bureaucratic Phenomenon.* Chicago: Phoenix Books.

Cutler, Robert. 1965. "The National Security Council under President Eisenhower." In *The National Security Council: Jackson Subcommittee Papers on Policy-Making at the Presidential Level,* edited by Henry M. Jackson. New York: Praeger.

Cyert, Richard, and James March, with contributions by G. P. E. Clarkson and others. 1963. *A Behavioral Theory of the Firm.* Englewood Cliffs, N.J.: Prentice-Hall.

Davis, Arthur K. 1952. "Bureaucratic Patterns in the Navy Officer Corp." In *Reader in Bureaucracy,* edited by Robert K. Merton and others. Glencoe, Ill.: Free Press.

Davis, Nuel Pharr. 1968. *Lawrence and Oppenheimer.* New York: Simon & Schuster.

Deagle, Edwin Augustus, Jr. 1969. "The Agony of Restraint—Korea 1951–1953: A Study of Limited War and Civil-Military Policy Processes." Draft manuscript. Office of the Chief of Military History, Department of the Army.

De Rivera, Joseph. 1968. *The Psychological Dimension of Foreign Policy.* Columbus, Ohio: Merrill Publishing.

Destler, I. M. 1972. *Presidents, Bureaucrats, and Foreign Policy.* Princeton University Press.

Domnien, Arthur J. 1964. *Conflict in Laos: The Politics of Neutralization.* New York: Praeger.

Donovan, Robert J. 1956. *Eisenhower: The Inside Story.* New York: Harper & Brothers.

Downs, Anthony. 1967. *Inside Bureaucracy.* Boston: Little, Brown.

Draper, Theodore. 1966. "The Dominican Crisis: A Case Study in American Policy." *Commentary* 41 (April-May).

Drew, Elizabeth B. 1970. "Washington." *Atlantic Monthly* (June).

Dunn, Frederick S. 1963. *Peace-Making and the Settlement with Japan.* Princeton University Press.

Edgerton, Russell. 1970. *Sub-Cabinet Politics and Policy Commitment: The Birth of the Development Loan Fund.* Syracuse, N.Y.: Interuniversity Case Program.

Evans, Rowland, and Robert Novak. 1966. *Lyndon B. Johnson: The Exercise of Power.* New York: New American Library.

Fessenden, Helen. 2005. "The Limits of Intelligence Reform." *Foreign Affairs* 84, no. 6 (November-December 2005).

Flash, Edward S., Jr. 1965. *Economic Advice and Presidential Leadership.* Columbia University Press.

Frankel, Max. Letter to Daniel Patrick Moynihan, March 5, 1971. Privately circulated.

Galbraith, John Kenneth. 1970-71. "Plain Lessons of a Bad Decade." *Foreign Policy* (Winter).

Gates, Thomas S., Jr. 1965. "The Secretary of Defense." In *The National Security Council: Jackson Subcommittee Papers on Policy-Making at the Presidential Level,* edited by Henry M. Jackson. New York: Praeger.

Gawthrop, Louis C. 1969. *Bureaucratic Behavior in the Executive Branch.* New York: Free Press.

Gelb, Leslie H. 1971. "Vietnam: The System Worked." *Foreign Policy* (Summer).

George, Alexander L. 1955. "American Policy-Making and North Korean Aggression." *World Politics* (January).

———. 1972. "The Case for Multiple Advocacy in Making Foreign Policy." *American Political Science Review* (September).

Geyelin, Philip L. 1966. *Lyndon B. Johnson and the World.* New York: Praeger.

Gilpin, Robert, and Christopher Wright, eds. 1964. *Scientists and National Policy Making.* Columbia University Press.

Graff, Henry F. 1970. *The Tuesday Cabinet.* Englewood Cliffs, N.J.: Prentice-Hall.

Halberstam, David. 1972. *The Best and the Brightest.* New York: Random House.

———. 1969. "The Very Expensive Education of McGeorge Bundy." *Harper's* (July).

Halperin, Morton H. 1961. "The Gaither Committee and the Policy Process." *World Politics* (April).

———. 1972. "The President and the Military." *Foreign Affairs* (January).

Halperin, Morton H., and Arnold Kanter, eds. 1973. *Readings in American Foreign Policy: A Bureaucratic Perspective.* Boston: Little, Brown.

Hammond, Paul Y. 1962. "NSC-68: Prologue to Rearmament." In *Strategy, Politics, and Defense Budgets,* edited by Warner R. Schilling, Paul Y. Hammond, and Glenn H. Snyder. Columbia University Press.

———. *Organizing for Defense.* 1961. Princeton University Press.

———. 1963. "Super Carriers and B-36 Bombers: Appropriations, Strategy, and Politics." In *American Civil-Military Decisions,* edited by Harold Stein. University of Alabama Press.

Harr, John Ensor. 1969. *The Professional Diplomat.* Princeton University Press.

Henry, John B., II. 1971. "February 1968." *Foreign Policy* (Fall).

Herr, Michael. 1969. "Khe Sanh." *Esquire* (September).

Hersh, Seymour M. 1970. *My Lai 4: A Report on the Massacre and Its Aftermath.* New York: Random House.

Hilsman, Roger. 1967. *To Move a Nation: The Politics of Foreign Policy in the Administration of John F. Kennedy.* New York: Doubleday.

Holbrooke, Richard. 1970–71."The Machine That Fails." *Foreign Policy* (Winter).

Howley, Frank L. 1950. *Berlin Command.* New York: Putnam's.

Hoxie, R. Gordon, ed. 1971. *The White House: Organization and Operations.* New York: Center for the Study of the Presidency.

Huntington, Samuel P. 1961. *The Common Defense: Strategic Programs in National Defense.* Columbia University Press.

Ikle, Fred Charles. 1971. *Every War Must End.* Columbia University Press.

Jackson, Henry M., ed. 1965. *The National Security Council: Jackson Subcommittee Papers on Policy-Making at the Presidential Level.* New York: Praeger.

Jackson Subcommittee on National Security Staffing and Operations of the Senate Committee on Government Operations. 1962. *Administration of National Security: Selected Papers: Hearing.* 87 Cong. 2 sess. Government Printing Office.

Jayne, Edward Randolph, II. 1969. "The ABM Debate: Strategic Defense and National Security." Ph.D. dissertation, Massachusetts Institute of Technology.

Jervis, Robert. 1968. "Hypotheses on Misperception." *World Politics* (April).

Johnson, Haynes, with Manuel Artime and others. 1964. *The Bay of Pigs: The Leaders' Story of Brigade 2506.* New York: W. W. Norton.

Johnson, Lyndon B. 1968. *Public Papers of the Presidents of the United States, 1967.* Washington: Government Printing Office.

———. "LBJ: The Decision to Halt the Bombing." CBS News Special, February 6, 1970.

Johnson, Richard A. 1971. *The Administration of United States Foreign Policy.* University of Texas Press.

Johnson, Robert H. 1969. "The National Security Council: The Relevance of Its Past to Its Future." *Orbis* (Fall).

Kalb, Marvin, and Elie Abel. 1971. *Roots of Involvement: The U.S. in Asia, 1784–1971.* New York: W. W. Norton.

Kennan, George F. 1958. "America's Administrative Response to Its World Problems." *Daedalus* (Spring).

Khanasch, Robert N. 1973. *The Institutional Imperative.* New York: Charterhouse Books.

Kiker, Douglas. 1969. "Washington." In *Who We Are,* edited by Robert Manning and Michael Janeway. Boston: Little, Brown.

King, Edward L. 1972. *The Death of the Army: A Post-Mortem.* New York: Saturday Review Press.

Kissinger, Henry A. 1969. *American Foreign Policy: Three Essays.* New York: W. W. Norton.

———. 1971. Background briefing. 92 Cong. 1 sess. *Congressional Record* 117, pt. 35.

———. 1973. "Bureaucracy and Policy Making." In *Readings in American Foreign Policy: A Bureaucratic Perspective,* edited by Morton H. Halperin and Arnold Kanter. Boston: Little, Brown.

———. 1957. *Nuclear Weapons and Foreign Policy.* New York: Harper & Brothers.

Korb, Lawrence J. 1970. "Budget Strategies of the Joint Chiefs of Staff (Fiscal) 1965–1968: An Examination." Paper presented at the 66th Annual Meeting of the American Political Science Association.

———. 1969. "The Role of the Joint Chiefs of Staff in the Defense Budget Process from 1947 to 1967." Ph.D. dissertation. State University of New York at Albany.

Kraft, Joseph. 1966. *Profiles in Power: A Washington Insight.* New York: New American Library.

———. 1969. "After McNamara." In *Who We Are,* edited by Robert Manning and Michael Janeway. Boston: Little, Brown.

———. 1972. "Undermining Kissinger." *Washington Post,* January 11.

Kurzman, Dan. 1970. *Genesis 1948: The First Arab-Israeli War.* New York: World.

Lake, Anthony. 1990. *Somoza Falling: A Case Study of Washington at Work.* University of Massachusetts Press.

Lambright, W. Henry. 1967. *Shooting Down the Nuclear Plane.* Indianapolis: Bobbs-Merrill.

Leacacos, John P. 1968. *Fires in the In-Basket: The ABCs of the State Department.* New York: World.

Lichterman, Martin. 1963. "To the Yalu and Back." In *American Civil-Military Decisions,* edited by Harold Stein. University of Alabama Press.

Lindblom, Charles. 1965. *The Intelligence of Democracy.* New York: Free Press, 1965.

Locher, James R., III. 2002. *Victory on the Potomac: The Goldwater-Nichols Act Unifies the Pentagon.* Texas A&M University Press.

Lovett, Robert A. 1965. "Perspective on the Policy Process." In *The National Security Council: Jackson Subcommittee Papers on Policy-Making at the Presidential Level,* edited by Henry M. Jackson. New York: Praeger.

Lowenthal, Abraham F. 1972. *The Dominican Intervention.* Harvard University Press.

Lowi, Theodore J. 1963. "Bases in Spain." In *American Civil-Military Decisions,* edited by Harold Stein. University of Alabama Press.

McGarvey, Patrick J. 1970. "Army Aviation: After Vietnam, What?" *Government Executive* (March).

———. 1970. "The Culture of Bureaucracy: DIA Intelligence to Please." *Washington Monthly* (July).

McNamara, Robert S. 1967. "The Dynamics of Nuclear Strategy." *Department of State Bulletin* (October 9).

———. 1967. "Defense Fantasy Now Come True." *Life* (September 29).

———. 1965. "The Secretary of Defense." In *The National Security Council: Jackson Subcommittee Papers on Policy-Making at the Presidential Level,* edited by Henry M. Jackson. New York: Praeger.

Macomber, William B., Jr. 1970. *Diplomacy for the 70s: A Program of Management Reform for the Department of State.* Government Printing Office.

Manning, Robert, and Michael Janeway, eds. 1965. *Who We Are: Chronicle of the United States and Vietnam.* Boston: Little, Brown.

March, James G., and Herbert A. Simon. 1958. *Organizations.* New York: Wiley.

Martin, Laurence W. 1963. "The American Decision to Rearm Germany." In *American Civil-Military Decisions,* edited by Harold Stein. University of Alabama Press.

May, Ernest R. 1962. "The Nature of Foreign Policy: The Calculated versus the Axiomatic." *Daedalus* (Fall).

Merton, Robert K., and others, eds. 1952. *Reader in Bureaucracy.* Glencoe, Ill.: Free Press.

Millis, Walter, Harvey C. Mansfield, and Harold Stein. 1958. *Arms and the State.* New York: Twentieth Century Fund.

Mosher, Frederick C., and John E. Harr. 1970. *Programming Systems and Foreign Affairs Leadership.* Oxford University Press.

Nathan, James A., and James K. Oliver. 1994. *Foreign Policy Making and the American Political System.* Johns Hopkins University Press.

Neustadt, Richard E. 1970. *Alliance Politics.* Columbia University Press.

———. 1965. "Politics and Bureaucrats." In *The Congress and America's Future,* edited by David B. Truman. Englewood Cliffs, N.J.: Prentice-Hall.

———. 1960. *Presidential Power: The Politics of Leadership.* New York: Wiley.

Newhouse, John. 1973. *Cold Dawn: The Story of SALT.* New York: Holt, Rinehart &Winston.

———. 2003. *Imperial America: The Bush Assault on the World Order.* New York: Alfred A. Knopf.

9/11 Commission Report: Final Report of the National Commission on Terrorist Attacks upon the United States. New York: W.W. Norton & Company, 2004.

Nixon, Richard M. 1971. *U.S. Foreign Policy for the 1970s: Building for Peace.* Government Printing Office.

Oberdorfer, Don. 1971. *Tet!* New York: Doubleday.

Paige, Glenn D. 1968. *The Korean Decision: June 24-30, 1950.* New York: Free Press.

Parkinson, C. Northcote. 1957. *Parkinson's Law.* Boston: Houghton Mifflin.

Percy, Charles H. 1970. "Paying for NATO." *Washington Monthly* (July).

Peters, Ronald M., Jr., ed. 1994. *The Speaker: Leadership in the U.S. House of Representatives.* Washington: Congressional Quarterly, 1994.

Pett, Saul. 1970. "Henry A. Kissinger: Loyal Retainer or Nixon's Svengali?" *Washington Post,* August 23.

Phillips, Cabell. 1966. *The Truman Presidency.* Baltimore: Penguin Books.

Pillar, Paul R. 2006. "Intelligence, Policy, and the War in Iraq." *Foreign Affairs* 85, no. 2 (March-April).

Platt, Alan, and Lawrence D. Weiler, eds. 1978. *Congress and Arms Control.* Boulder, Colo.: Westview Press.

Price, Don K. 1960. "The Secretary and Our Unwritten Constitution." In *The Secretary of State,* edited by Don K. Price. Englewood Cliffs, N.J.: Prentice-Hall.

Pyle, Christopher H. 1970. "Conus Revisited: The Army Covers Up." *Washington Monthly* (July).

Ransom, Harry Howe. 1970. *The Intelligence Establishment.* Harvard University Press.

Reston, James. 1966. *The Artillery of the Press: Its Influence on American Foreign Policy.* New York: Harper & Row.

Roberts, Charles. 1965. *LBJ's Inner Circle.* New York: Delacorte.

Robinson, James A. 1965. *The Monroney Resolution: Congressional Initiative in American Foreign Policy Making.* New York: Macmillan.

Rockefeller, Nelson A. 1965. "The Executive Office of the President." In *The National Security Council: Jackson Subcommittee Papers on Policy-Making at the Presidential Level,* edited by Henry M. Jackson. New York: Praeger.

Rostow, W. W. 1973. "The American Agenda." In *Readings in American Foreign Policy: A Bureaucratic Perspective,* edited by Morton H. Halperin and Arnold Kanter. Boston: Little, Brown.

Rourke, Francis E. 1972. *Bureaucracy and Foreign Policy.* Johns Hopkins Press.

———. 1969. *Bureaucracy, Politics, and Public Policy.* Boston: Little, Brown.

Rusk, Dean. "The Secretary of State." 1965. In *The National Security Council: Jackson*

Subcommittee Papers on Policy-Making at the Presidential Level, edited by Henry M. Jackson. New York: Praeger.

Sapin, Burton M. 1966. *The Making of United States Foreign Policy.* Brookings.

Schilling, Warner R. 1961. "The H-Bomb Decision: How to Decide without Actually Choosing." *Political Science Quarterly* (March).

———. 1962. "The Politics of National Defense: Fiscal 1950." In *Strategy, Politics, and Defense Budgets,* edited by Warner R. Schilling, Paul Y. Hammond, and Glenn H. Snyder. Columbia University Press.

———. 1964. "Scientists, Foreign Policy, and Politics." In *Scientists and National Policy Making,* edited by Robert Gilpin and Christopher Wright. Columbia University Press.

Schilling, Warner R., Paul Y. Hammond, and Glenn H. Snyder, eds. 1962. *Strategy, Politics, and Defense Budgets.* Columbia University Press, 1962.

Schlesinger, Arthur M., Jr. 1967. *The Bitter Heritage: Vietnam and American Democracy, 1941–1966.* Boston: Houghton Mifflin.

Scott, Andrew M. 1969. "The Department of State: Formal Organization and Informal Culture." *International Studies Quarterly* 13 (March).

———. 1970. "Environmental Change and Organizational Adaptation: The Problem of the State Department." *International Studies Quarterly* 14 (March).

Scott, Andrew M., and Raymond H. Dawson, eds. 1965. *Readings in the Making of American Foreign Policy.* New York: Macmillan.

Seidman, Harold. 1970. *Politics, Position, and Power: The Dynamics of Federal Organization.* Oxford University Press.

Sidey, Hugh. 1970. "Nixon in a Crisis of Leadership." *Life* (May 15).

———. 1968. *A Very Personal Presidency: Lyndon Johnson in the White House.* New York: Atheneum.

Sigal, Leon V. 1971. "Bureaucratic Objectives and Tactical Use of the Press: Why Bureaucrats Leak." Paper presented at the Sixty-Seventh Annual Meeting of the American Political Science Association.

———. 1973. *Reporters and Offcials: The Organization and Politics of Newsmaking.* Lexington, Mass.: D. C. Heath.

Simpson, Smith. 1967. *Anatomy of the State Department.* Boston: Beacon Press.

Slater, Jerome. 1970. *Negotiation and Intervention: The United States and the Dominican Revolution.* New York: Harper & Row.

Smith, Beverly. 1951. "The White House Story: Why We Went to War in Korea." *Saturday Evening Post* (November 10).

Smith, Bruce L. R. 1966. *The Rand Corporation.* Harvard University Press.

Smith, Perry McCoy. 1970. *The Air Force Plans for Peace, 1943–1945.* Johns Hopkins Press.

Snyder, Glenn H. 1962. "The 'New Look' of 1953." In *Strategy, Politics, and Defense Budgets,* edited by Warner R. Schilling, Paul Y. Hammond, and Glenn H. Snyder. Columbia University Press.

———. 1966. *Stockpiling Strategic Materials: Politics and National Defense.* San Francisco: Chandler.

Souers, Sidney W. 1965. "The National Security Council under President Truman." In *The National Security Council: Jackson Subcommittee Papers on Policy-Making at the Presidential Level,* edited by Henry M. Jackson. New York: Praeger.

Spanier, John W. 1965. *The Truman-MacArthur Controversy and the Korean War.* New York: W. W. Norton.

Stein, Harold, ed. 1963. *American Civil-Military Decisions.* University of Alabama Press.

Steinberg, Alfred. 1962. *The Man from Missouri: The Life and Times of Harry S. Truman.* New York: Putnam's.

Steinbruner, John. 1974. *The Cybernetic Theory of Decision: New Dimensions of Political Analysis.* Princeton University Press.

Stevenson, Charles A. 1972. *The End of Nowhere: American Policy toward Laos since 1954.* Boston: Beacon Press.

Stone, Jeremy J. 1967. *Strategic Persuasion.* New York: Columbia University Press.

Stupak, Ronald J. 1969. *The Shaping of Foreign Policy: The Role of the Secretary of State as Seen by Dean Acheson.* New York: Odyssey Press.

Suskind, Ron. 2004. *The Price of Loyalty: George W. Bush, the White House, and the Education of Paul O'Neill.* New York: Simon and Schuster.

Szilard, Leo. 1968. "Reminiscences." In *Perspectives in American History.* Vol. 2, *The Intellectual Migration: Europe and America, 1930-1960*, edited by Bernard Bailyn and Donald Fleming. Belknap Press of Harvard University Press.

Tai-hsun, Tsuan. 1969. "An Explanation of the Change in U.S. Policy toward China in 1950." Ph.D. dissertation, University of Pennsylvania.

Talbott, Strobe. 1988. *The Master of the Game.* New York: Alfred A. Knopf.

Thomas, Hugh. 1966. *Suez.* New York: Harper & Row.

Thomson, James C., Jr. 1969. "How Could Vietnam Happen?" In *Who We Are,* edited by Robert Manning and Michael Janeway. Boston: Little, Brown.

Tullock, Gordon. 1965. *The Politics of Bureaucracy.* Washington: Public Affairs Press.

U.S. Congress. Senate. Committee on Foreign Relations. 1972. *The Geneva Protocol of 1925.* Hearing. 92 Cong. 1 sess. Government Printing Office.

U.S. Congress. Senate. Subcommittee on National Security and International Operations of the Committee on Government Operations. 1965. *Conduct of National Security Policy: Hearing.* 89 Cong. 1 sess., pt. 3 (June 29 and July 27, 1965). Government Printing Office.

U.S. Congress. Senate. Subcommittee on United States Security Agreements and Commitments Abroad of the Committee on Foreign Relations. 1970. *United States Security Agreements and Commitments Abroad: Japan and Okinawa: Hearing.* 91 Cong. 2 sess., pt. 5 (January 26–29, 1970). Government Printing Office.

Villard, Henry S. 1965. *Affairs of State.* New York: Thomas Y. Crowell.

———. 1964. "How to Save Money: An Open Letter to Congressman John J. Rooney." *Harper's* (January 1964).

Waltz, Kenneth N. 1967. *Foreign Policy and Democratic Politics: The American and British Experience.* Boston: Little, Brown.

Weintal, Edward, and Charles Bartlett. 1967. *Facing the Brink: An Intimate Study in Crisis Diplomacy.* New York: Scribner's.

Weissman, Stephen R. 1995. *A Culture of Deference: Congress's Failure of Leadership in Foreign Policy.* New York: Basic Books.

Wicker, Tom. 1968. *JFK and LBJ: The Influence of Personality upon Politics.* New York: Morrow.

Wilensky, Harold L. 1967. *Organizational Intelligence.* New York: Basic Books.

Wills, Garry. 1970. *Nixon Agonistes: The Crisis of the Self-Made Man.* Boston: Houghton Mifflin.

Wise, David, and Thomas B. Ross. 1962. *The U-2 Affair.* New York: Random House.

Wishnatsky, Martin. 1971. "Symbolic Politics and the Origins of the Cold War." Paper prepared for the Sixty-Seventh Annual Meeting of the American Political Science Association.

Withers, George. 2005. "Who's in Charge? Foreign Assistance Responsibilities Shift from State to Defense." Memorandum from the Washington Office on Latin America (November).

Wohlstetter, Roberta. 1965. *Cuba and Pearl Harbor: Hindsight and Foresight.* Santa Monica, Calif.: Rand Corporation.

Wolfers, Arnold. 1962. *Discord and Collaboration: Essays on International Politics.* Baltimore: Johns Hopkins Press.

Woodward, Bob. 2004. *Plan of Attack.* New York: Simon and Schuster.

Wriggins, W. Howard. 1969. *The Ruler's Imperative: Strategies for Political Survival in Asia and Africa.* Columbia University Press.

Yarmolinsky, Adam. 1969. "Bureaucratic Structures and Political Outcomes." *Journal of International Affairs* 23, no. 2.

———. 1971. *The Military Establishment: Its Impacts on American Society.* New York: Harper & Row.

———. 1970–71. "The Military Establishment." *Foreign Policy* (Winter).

Young, Hugo, Bryan Silcock, and Peter Dunn. 1970. "Why We Went to the Moon: From the Bay of Pigs to the Sea of Tranquility." *Washington Monthly* 2 (April).

Index

Abel, Elie, 158

ABM treaty. *See* Antiballistic missile treaty

ABMs. *See* Antiballistic missiles

ACDA. *See* Arms Control and Disarmament Agency

Acheson, Dean, 218, 265, 280; Cuban missile crisis and, 153, 157, 289; Eisenhower, Dwight D. and, 92; the Establishment and, 75; explanation of NSC-*68*, 161; German rearmament and, 217–18; Indochina and, 59; Johnson, Louis and, 186; Johnson, Lyndon B. and, 298; NSC *68* and, 221; presidential speeches and, 200; as secretary of state, 80, 116, 124, 173–74, 207–08, 228, 230, 231–32; Truman Doctrine and, 79; Truman, Harry S. and, 70–71, 112; views of government, 230

Adams, Sherman, 110, 168–69, 212, 213, 227, 267–68

Adenauer, Konrad, 189

Advanced Research Projects Agency (ARPA), 347, 359

AEC. *See* Atomic Energy Commission

Afghanistan, 33, 34, 48, 332

Airplanes: B-*36* bombers, 31; B-*52*, 28, 29; B-*70*/WS-*11*o, 29, 72; C-*5A*, 30; C-*17* Globemasters (Boeing), 335; convertiplane, 43; F-*4H*, 42; helicopters, 43, 45, 49; manned strategic bombers, 38, 41; Missileer, 42; nuclear airplanes (ANP; aircraft nuclear propulsion), 29, 42, 81; Predator unmanned aircraft, 48; TFX/F-*111*, 28, 42

Air power, 164–65

Allison, Graham, 50, 144

al Qaeda, 65, 80, 101, 166

Alsop, Joseph, 183

Ambassadors. *See* Foreign Service

Anderson, Clinton, 93–94

Anderson, George W., 300

Anderson, Jack, 183

Angola, 70

Antiballistic missiles (ABMs), 2, 14, 15, 159, 317, 347

Antiballistic missile systems: Army and, 26, 40, 100; budget issues of, 15, 25, 56, 223, 348, 352, 358, 359; Congress and, 19, 316–17, 348; discussions and decisionmaking, 1–2, 21, 215–16, 347–60; new technology and, 102; Postures A and B of, 349

Antiballistic missile systems—

379

CPSIA information can be obtained at www.ICGtesting.com
Printed in the USA
BVOW071954160812

298072BV00001B/63/P